How to Use This Book

What makes a good text about Computer Concepts? Sound instruction and hands-on skill-building and reinforcement. That is what you will find in *Computer Concepts BASICS*. Not only will you find a colorful and inviting layout, but also many features to enhance learning.

Objectives— Objectives are listed at the beginning of each lesson, along with a suggested time for completion of the lesson. This allows you to look ahead to what you will be learning and to pace your work.

Step-by-step Exercises— Preceded by a short topic discussion, these exercises are the "hands-on practice" part of the lesson. Simply follow the steps, either using a data file or creating a file from scratch. Each lesson contains a series of these step-by-step exercises.

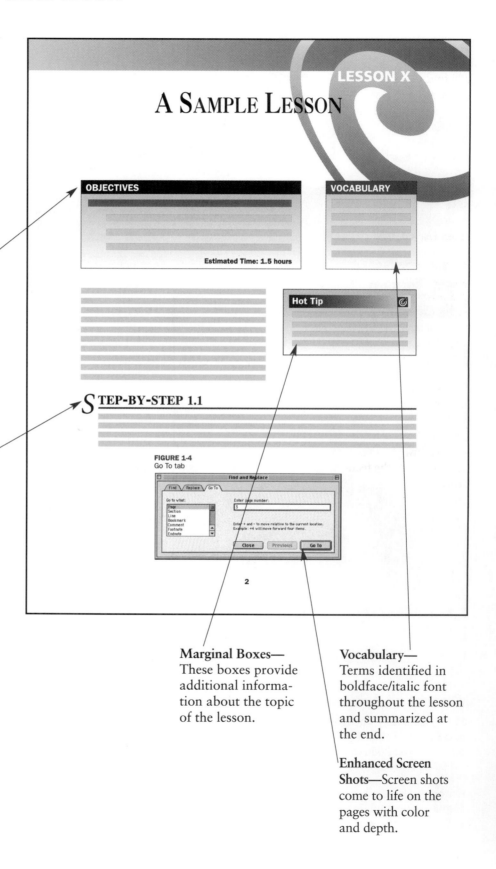

A SAMPLE LESSON

LESSON X

OBJECTIVES

Estimated Time: 1.5 hours

VOCABULARY

Hot Tip

S TEP-BY-STEP 1.1

FIGURE 1-4
Go To tab

2

Marginal Boxes— These boxes provide additional information about the topic of the lesson.

Vocabulary— Terms identified in boldface/italic font throughout the lesson and summarized at the end.

Enhanced Screen Shots— Screen shots come to life on the pages with color and depth.

How to Use This Book

Summary—At the end of each lesson, you will find a summary to prepare you to complete the end-of-lesson activities.

Vocabulary Review—Review of important terms defined in the lesson reinforce the concepts learned.

Review Questions—Review material at the end of each lesson and each unit enables you to prepare for assessment of the content presented.

Lesson Projects—End-of-lesson hands-on application of what has been learned in the lesson allows you to actually apply the techniques covered.

SUMMARY

VOCABULARY *Review*

REVIEW *Questions*

PROJECTS

CROSS-CURRICULAR—MATHEMATICS

CROSS-CURRICULAR—SCIENCE

CROSS-CURRICULAR—SOCIAL STUDIES

CROSS-CURRICULAR—LANGUAGE ARTS

WEB PROJECT

TEAMWORK PROJECT

PROJECTS

End-of-Unit Projects—End-of-unit hands-on application of the concepts learned in the unit provides opportunity for a comprehensive review.

PREFACE

Computer Concepts BASICS, Third Edition, is a brief introduction to computers. This text covers computer hardware, software, application skills, keyboarding skills, the Internet and Internet searching, Web page creation, networking, careers, and computer ethics. It can be used in any class on business applications, technology, or computer applications. This textbook, along with the Instructor's Resource CD-ROM and Activities Workbook, is all that is needed for a brief course on computer concepts and the Internet and can be used for 35 or more hours of instruction. After completing these materials, the student should have an understanding of the basics of computers, how technology is changing the world in which we live, and the importance of the Internet.

Partnered with a tutorial on a software application, such as Microsoft Office, Microsoft Works Lotus SmartSuites, or Star Office, this text provides a complete course on computer concepts—with hands-on applications. It is assumed in this course that students have no prior experience with computer concepts. Other possible applications include supplementing a mathematics, science, language arts, or social studies class through the integrated end-of-lesson and workbook activities and exercises.

About the Materials

The full materials for this course include the textbook, the Activities Workbook, and the Instructor's Resource CD-ROM. Although advanced students may complete the course successfully in a self-guided manner, it is recommended that the course be taken in an instructor-guided, hands-on environment, especially for beginning or intermediate students. Please visit www.doloreswells.com for more information, including a WebCT e-pack, an updated list of links, and other teaching suggestions.

Features of the Text

Seventeen lessons gradually introduce the skills necessary to learn computer fundamentals and software applications, including how to access and use the Internet and World Wide Web. Step-by-step exercises divide each lesson into conceptual blocks and reinforce the presented information. At the end of each lesson is a summary, review questions including multiple choice, true/false, and fill-in-the-blank, Web projects, team projects, and cross-curricular projects. Other features include margin notes on topics such as Did You Know?, Internet Tips, and Hot Tips.

Included within each lesson are objectives, vocabulary lists, estimated completion times, screen illustrations for visual reinforcement, and photos and illustrations to provide interest and clarity. Special sections on ethics and careers are included.

Activities Workbook

The student workbook contains additional projects and additional review questions. Definitions, short answer, fill in the blank, and true/false questions are provided in the activities workbook as a basis for study, lesson review, or test preparation.

Instructor's Resource and Review Pack CD-ROMs

All data files necessary for the step-by-step exercises, end-of-lesson projects, and end-of-unit projects and simulations are located on the *Review Pack* CD-ROM.

The *Instructor's Resource* CD-ROM contains a wealth of instructional material you can use to prepare for teaching this course. The CD-ROM stores the following information:

■ ExamView® tests for each lesson. ExamView is a powerful testing software package that allows instructors to create and administer printed, computer (LAN-based), and Internet exams. ExamView includes hundreds of questions that correspond to the topics covered in this text, enabling learners to generate detailed study guides that include page references for further review. The computer-based and Internet testing components allow learners to take exams at their computers, and also save the instructor time by grading each exam automatically.

■ An *Instructor's Manual* that includes lesson plans, answers to the lesson and unit review questions, and suggested/sample solutions for step-by-step exercises, end-of-lesson activities, and Unit Review projects.

■ Copies of the figures that appear in the learner text, which can be used to prepare transparencies.

■ PowerPoint presentations that illustrate objectives for each lesson in the text.

START-UP CHECKLIST

HARDWARE

✓ IBM or IBM-compatible PC

✓ 233-MHz or higher Pentium-compatible processor (600-MHz or faster is preferred)

✓ 64 MB of RAM (256 MB of RAM is preferred)

✓ One hard disk (2 GB) with at least 650 MB of free hard disk space

✓ CD-ROM drive

✓ SVGA-capable video adapter and monitor (SVGA resolution of a minimum of 800 x 600 pixels with 256 or more colors)

✓ Enhanced keyboard

✓ Mouse or pen pointer

✓ Internet connection (broadband or baseband)

✓ Printer

SOFTWARE

✓ Windows 2000 or later version

✓ Microsoft Office

✓ Web browser

Macintosh users can open Word, Excel, and PowerPoint files using Microsoft Office for the Macintosh.

Photo Credits

Lesson 5

Figure 5-1	Courtesy of DreamWare Computers
Figure 5-2a	Microsoft product screen shot reprinted with permission from Microsoft Corporation.
Figure 5-3a	Microsoft product screen shot reprinted with permission from Microsoft Corporation.
Figure 5-3b	Microsoft product screen shot reprinted with permission from Microsoft Corporation.
Figure 5-4	Microsoft product screen shot reprinted with permission from Microsoft Corporation.
Figure 5-5	Courtesy of Logitech
Figure 5-7	Courtesy of 3M Worldwide
Figure 5-16	Courtesy of Iomega
Figure 5-20b	Courtesy of US Modular

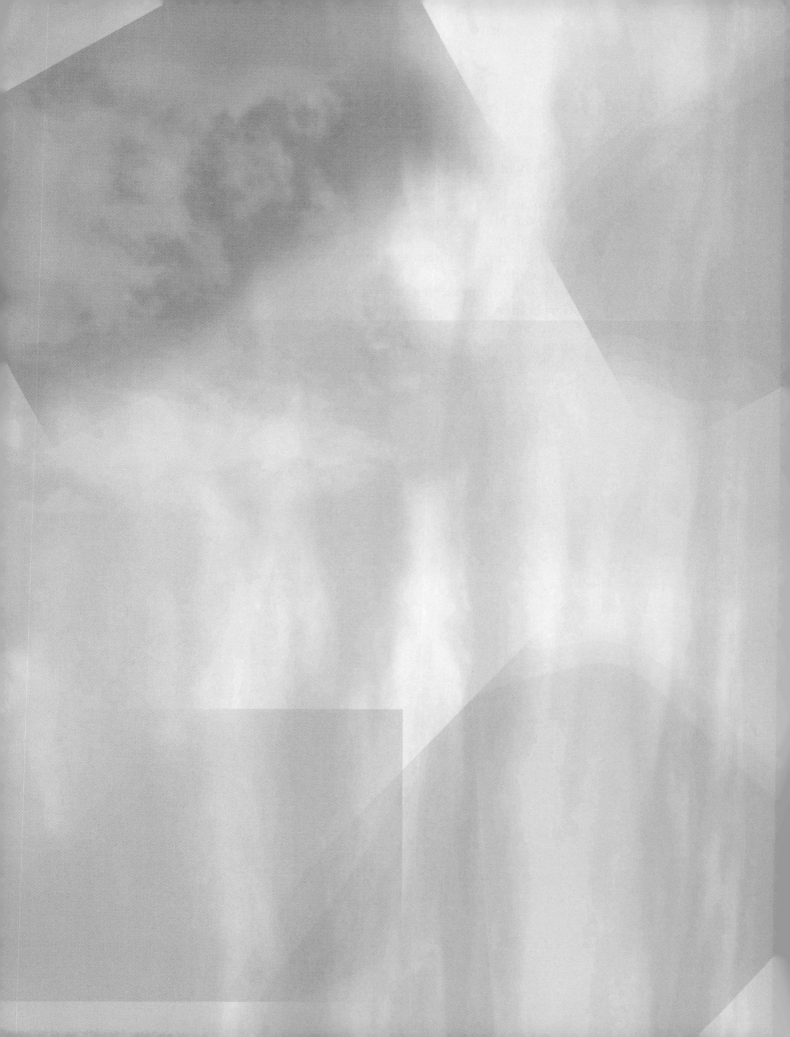

TABLE OF CONTENTS

UNIT 1 COMPUTER BASICS

UNIT 2 USING THE COMPUTER

UNIT 3 COMPUTERS AND SOCIETY

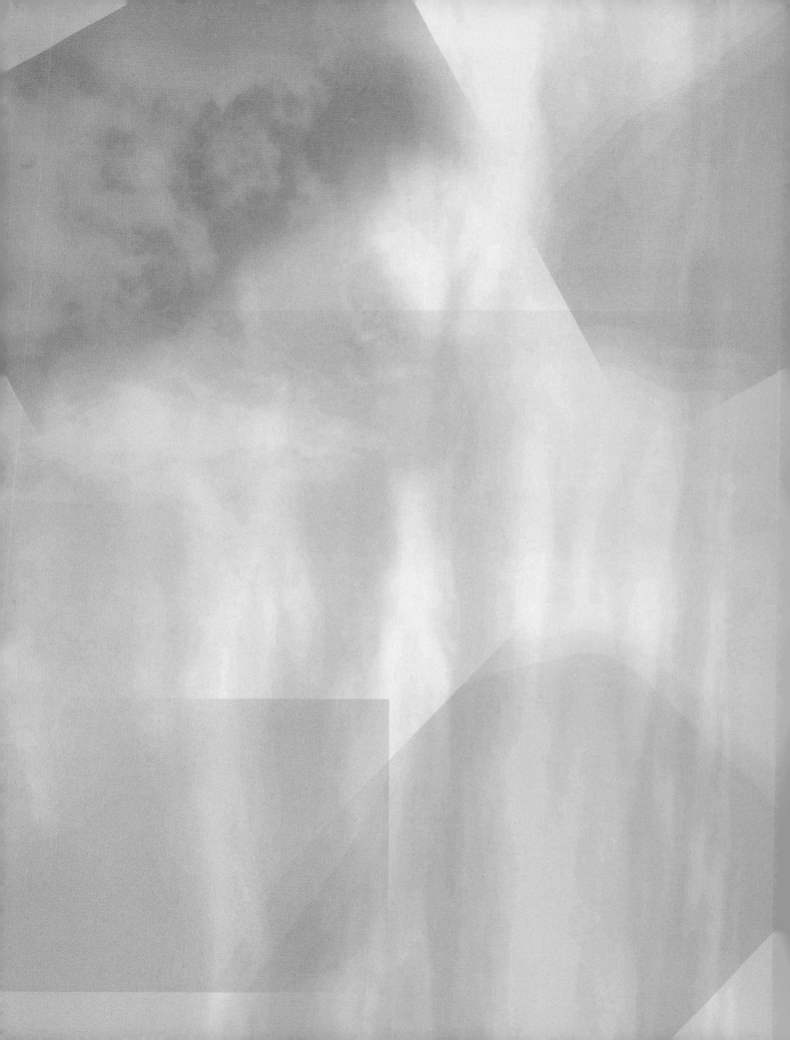

COMPUTER BASICS

Unit 1

⏱ **Estimated Time for Unit: 10.5 hours**

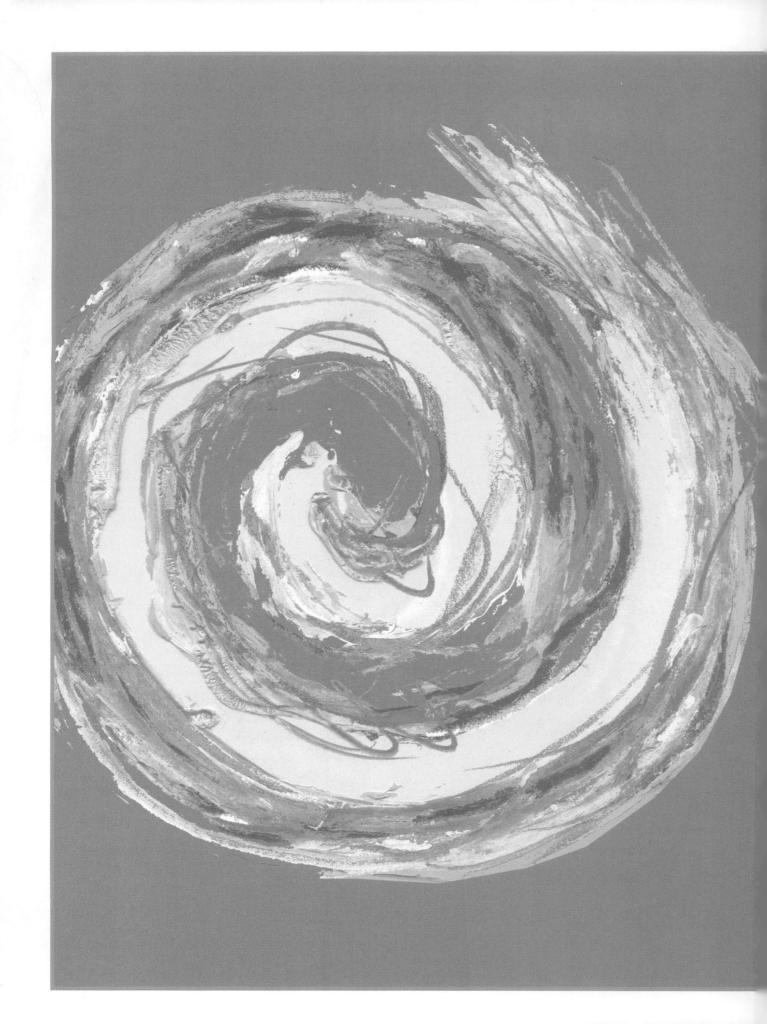

UNDERSTANDING COMPUTERS AND COMPUTER LITERACY

OBJECTIVES

Upon completion of this lesson, you should be able to:

- Discuss the history of computers.
- Define the term computer and describe a computer system.
- Describe the five computer classification categories.
- Describe the two types of computer software.
- Describe communications and networks.
- Identify how we use computers and technology in our daily lives.

Estimated Time: 1.5 hours

VOCABULARY

Clients
Computer
Data
Desktop computer
Electronic communication
Extranet
Hardware
Icon
Information
Internet
Intranet
Mainframe computer
Mid-range server
Mobile computers
Mobile devices
Network
Nodes
Personal computers
Servers
Software
Supercomputer
Users

Introducing Computers

The computer is one of the most important inventions of the past century. The widespread use of computers affects us individually and as a society. You can see computers in use almost everywhere! For instance, consider the following:

- Educational institutions use computers in all disciplines to enhance instruction.
- Video game systems transport you to an imaginary world.
- Using ATMs, you can withdraw money from your bank account from almost any location in the world.
- On television and at the movies, you can see instant replays in sports or amazing special effects that take you to outer space.
- Instant messaging, e-mail, and video conferencing allow you to communicate with people at almost any location.

As indicated by the examples on the previous page, computers and computer technology are pervasive throughout our society—from businesses and financial organizations, to home electronics and appliances, and even in electronic toys.

The importance of the computer is not surprising. Many individuals consider the computer to be the single most important invention of the twentieth century! This technology affects all aspects of our daily lives. Computers are no longer just the bulky machines that sit on our desktops. Computers come in every shape and size and are found everywhere. As more powerful and special-purpose computers become available, society will find more ways to use this technology to enhance our lives. See Figure 1-1.

Net Fun

Explore the geography of the Ecuadorian Amazon through online simulation games and activities. The Web site for this fun and adventure is *www. eduweb.com/amazon.html*.

FIGURE 1-1
A group of students playing an online video game

A Brief History of the Computer

Computers have been around for more than 60 years. The first computers were developed in the late 1940s and early 1950s. They were massive, special-purpose machines with names like *UNIVAC* and *ENIAC* and were designed initially for use by the military and government. These early computers had less processing power than today's pocket calculators, occupied small buildings or entire city blocks, and cost millions of dollars. Computers in the mid-1950s through early 1970s were somewhat smaller and more powerful, but still were limited in what they could do. They remained expensive, so only major companies and government organizations could afford these systems. See Figure 1-2 on the next page.

FIGURE 1-2
Early computers

In 1971, Dr. Ted Hoff developed the microprocessor It took visionaries like Steve Jobs and Steve Wozniak to see a future for the microprocessor and its application to personal computers. Jobs and Wozniak built the first Apple computer in 1976. Shortly thereafter, a second version, the Apple II, was released. It became an immediate success, especially in schools. In 1980, Bill Gates worked with IBM to develop the operating system for the IBM PC. This computer, introduced in 1981, quickly became the PC of choice in business. See Figure 1-3.

FIGURE 1-3
The Apple II and IBM PC

What Are a Computer and Computer System?

Throughout a normal workday, millions of people interact globally with computers, often without even knowing it. Doctors, lawyers, warehouse workers, store clerks, homemakers, musicians, and students, to name a few examples, constantly depend on computers to perform part of their daily duties.

So, what exactly is a computer? What does it really do? A *computer* is an electronic device that receives data (*input*), processes data, stores data, and produces a result (*output*).

A *computer system* includes hardware, software, data, and people. The actual machine, wires, transistors, and circuits are called *hardware*. Peripheral devices such as printers and monitors also are hardware. The instructions, or programs, for controlling the computer are called *software*. *Data* is text, numbers, sound, images, or video. The computer receives data through an input device, processes the data, stores the data on a storage device, and produces output or *information*. The *users*, the people who use computers, also are part of the system. See Figure 1-4.

FIGURE 1-4
Using a computer to process data into information

Compare the description of a computer system with examples of ways a store clerk might use a computer at a DVD movie rental store.

- *Receives data*: The store clerk enters the customer's name and scans the ISBN of a rented DVD into the computer through input devices, such as the keyboard and digital scanner.

- *Processes data*: The computer uses stored instructions to process the data into information.

- *Outputs information*: An output device, such as a monitor and/or a printer, displays the information.

■ *Stores data*: The data and information are stored in temporary memory and on a permanent storage device, such as a hard disk drive.

This series of steps often is referred to as the *information processing cycle*. See Figure 1-5.

FIGURE 1-5
The information processing cycle

This brief overview of a computer and the listing of some of the tasks you can accomplish with a computer might appear to imply that the computer is a very complicated device. A computer, however, performs only two operations:

■ Arithmetic computations such as addition, subtraction, multiplication, and division, and comparisons such as greater than, less than, or equal to

■ Logical operations using logical operators, such as AND, OR, and NOT

You will learn more about these operations, how a computer works, and how data is transformed into information in Lesson 4.

> **Did You Know?**
>
> A computer won a World Chess Championship playing against a human being.

Are Computers Intelligent?

Computers are not intelligent. They do only what we ask them to do. If this is so, then what are the advantages of using a computer?

■ *Speed*: Some computers can perform billions of calculations per second.

■ *Reliability*: The electronic components are dependable.

> **Net Tip**
>
> Visit the Journey Inside Intel Web site at *www.intel.com/ education/journey/* and discover how a microprocessor works.

■ *Accuracy*: If data is entered correctly, computers generate error-free results.

■ *Storage*: Computers can store and retrieve volumes of data and information.

■ *Communications*: Computers communicate and share resources with other computers.

Classifying Computers

Computers today come in all shapes and sizes, with specific types being especially suited for specific tasks. Computers are considered special purpose or general purpose. *Special-purpose computers* are used mostly to control something else. Tiny chips are embedded in devices, such as a dishwasher, bathroom scale, or airport radar system, and these chips control these particular devices.

General-purpose computers are divided into five categories, based on their physical size, function, cost, and performance.

- Desktop and notebook computers are today's most widely used *personal computers* (PCs). A *desktop computer* is designed so that all components fit on or under a desk. Two popular types of personal computers are the PC (based on the original IBM personal computer design) and the Apple.

- *Mobile computers* are personal computers such as *notebook computers* (also called a laptop) and *tablet PCs*. They are designed to be carried from one location to another. *Mobile devices* fit into the palm of your hand. Most mobile computers and many mobile devices can connect wirelessly to the Internet. Examples of mobile devices are PDAs, handheld computers, and smart phones.

- The *mid-range server* (also called a minicomputer) is used by small to medium-size companies and generally supports hundreds of users. A company would choose to use minicomputers rather than personal computers with many users and large amounts of data.

- The modern *mainframe computer* is a large, expensive computer, capable of supporting hundreds or even thousands of users. This type of computer is big compared to personal computers. Large companies use these to perform processing tasks for hundreds or thousands of users.

- A *supercomputer* is the fastest type of computer. Government agencies and large corporations use these computers for specialized applications to process enormous amounts of data. The cost of a supercomputer can be as much as several million dollars.

Today's small personal and handheld computers are more powerful than the mainframes and supercomputers of yesteryear. Figure 1-6 on the next page shows an example of each type of computer.

FIGURE 1-6
1. Desktop computer 2. Notebook computer 3. Pocket PC 4. Mainframe
5. Supercomputer

1.

2.

3.

4.

5.

Computer Software

Two basic types of software (also called programs) are *application software* and *system software*. Application software is a set of programs that performs specific tasks for users, such as word processing, spreadsheets, and databases. System software is a set of programs that controls the operations of the computer and its devices. Most microcomputers use either the Windows or the Mac system software.

> **Extra for Experts**
>
> Supercomputers often are used to test medical experiments.

Most software has a *graphical user interface* (GUI, pronounced "gooey"). If you are using a PC, almost everything you do within the GUI environment requires working with Windows and icons. An *icon* is a small image that represents a file, command, or another computer function. You execute the associated command by clicking or double-clicking the icon. For an overview of Windows, Step-by-step 1.1 illustrates how to start Windows, display the desktop, open and close an application (Notepad), and then shut down the system. In later lessons, you learn how to save and print your documents.

The step-by-step exercises in this book use Windows XP. The menus and screens for earlier versions of Windows are similar. Please make appropriate adjustments if you are using a different Windows version and/or you are working on a network. To start Windows is as simple as turning on your computer.

S TEP-BY-STEP 1.1

1. Turn on the computer. If your computer is on a network, you might be prompted to enter your user name and a password. Your instructor will provide you with this information.

2. Click the **Start** button. The Start menu opens. The Windows XP Start menu is shown in Figure 1-7. The Start menu in earlier versions of Windows will look similar.

FIGURE 1-7
Windows Start menu

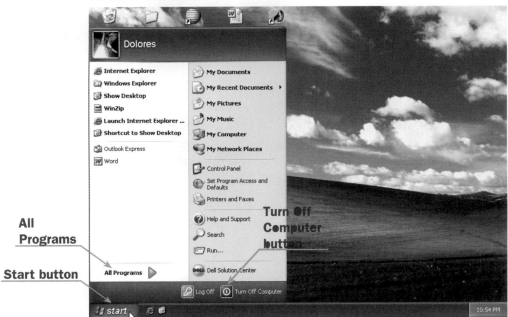

3. Point to **All Programs**, then **Accessories**, and then **Notepad**. See Figure 1-8.

FIGURE 1-8
Starting Notepad

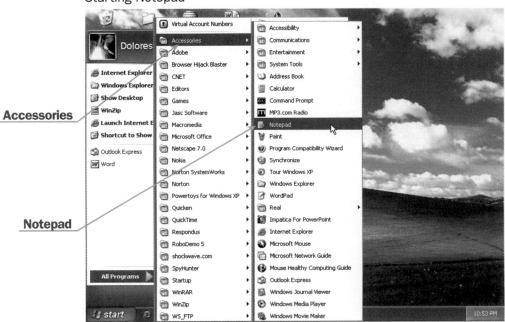

STEP-BY-STEP 1.1 Continued

4. Click **Notepad**. The Notepad window opens.

5. Type a sentence or two about your favorite movie. See Figure 1-9.

FIGURE 1-9
Working in Notepad

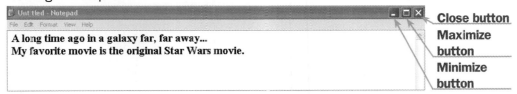

6. Click the **Close** button.

7. A dialog box displays, asking if you want to save the changes. See Figure 1-10.

FIGURE 1-10
Notepad dialog box

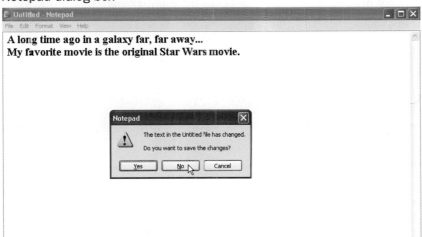

8. Click **No**. The Notepad window closes, and you are returned to the Windows desktop.

9. Click the **Start** button and then click **Turn Off Computer**. The Turn off computer dialog box displays. (*Note*: If your computer is on a network, click **Shut Down**. The Shut Down dialog box displays.)

10. Click the **Turn Off** button or the **Shut Down Windows** button.

Communications and Networks

E*lectronic communication* is the technology that enables computers to communicate with each other and other devices. It is the transmission of text, numbers, voice, and video from one computer or device to another. Communication has changed the way the world does business and the way we live our lives.

When computers were developed in the 1950s, they did not communicate with each other. This all changed in 1969. ARPANET was established and served as a testing ground for new networking technologies. ARPANET was a large wide-area network created by the United States Defense Advanced Research Project Agency (ARPA). On Labor Day in 1969, the first message was sent via telephone lines from a computer at UCLA to another computer at Stanford Research Institute. This was the beginning of the Internet and electronic communication as we know it today.

Electronic communication requires the following four components:

- *Sender*: The computer that is sending the message

- *Receiver*: The computer receiving the message

- *Channel*: The media that carries or transports the message; this could be telephone wire, coaxial cable, microwave signal, or fiber-optic cable

- *Protocol*: The rules that govern the transfer of data

> **Hot Tip** ⌖
>
> Original music can be created using computers. People do not need a lot of musical talent or even specific instruments to make music. They just need to press a button or key on a computerized keyboard.

This technology has made it possible to communicate around the globe using tools such as the Internet, electronic mail (e-mail), faxes, e-commerce, and electronic banking. See Figure 1-11.

FIGURE 1-11
Transmitting a message from sender to receiver

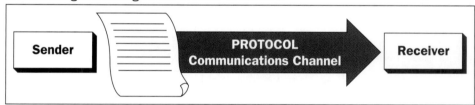

Networks

A *network* is a group of two or more computer systems linked together via communication devices. This connection enables the computers to share resources such as printers, data, information, and programs. A network can consist of two computers or millions of computers and other devices and can connect all categories of computers, including mobile devices, personal computers, mid-range servers, mainframes, and even supercomputers.

Computers on a network are called *nodes* or *clients*. *Servers* are computers that allocate resources on a network. Networks are covered in detail in Lesson 7. See Figure 1-12 on the next page for a networking representation.

FIGURE 1-12
A networking connecting users through various communication devices

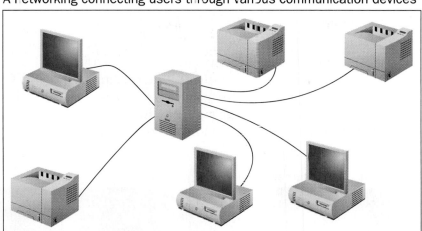

Intranets and Extranets

Many companies have implemented intranets within their organizations. An *intranet* is a network for the exclusive use of workers within an organization and contains company information. Company manuals, handbooks, and newsletters are just a few of the types of documents distributed via an intranet. Online forms also are a popular intranet feature. The major advantages of using an intranet are reliability and security—possible because the organization controls access.

Extranets are systems that allow outside organizations to access a company's internal information system. Access is controlled tightly and usually reserved for suppliers and customers.

The Internet

The **Internet**, the world's largest network, evolved from ARPANET. Following the first historic message between two computers in 1969, ARPANET quickly grew into a global network consisting of hundreds of military and university sites. In 1990, ARPANET was disbanded and the Internet was born. Today, millions of users surf the Internet and the World Wide Web, one of the more popular segments of the Internet. Other Internet services are e-mail, chat rooms, instant messaging, mailing lists, blogging, and newsgroups. The Internet and World Wide Web are covered in detail in Lesson 2. Figure 1-13 shows an illustration of the Internet.

FIGURE 1-13
A graphical representation of the Internet

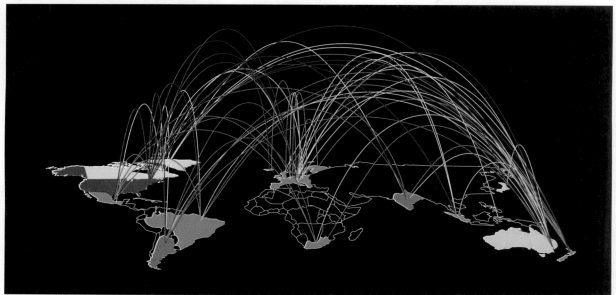

Technology for Everyday Life

Computers affect our lives every day and have changed dramatically the way in which we live. Without computers, the world as we know it today would come to a sudden halt. They have become necessary tools in almost every type of activity and in almost every type of business. Think of the many ways computers affect you every day. For example:

■ In school, instruction is enhanced and information is accessible from anywhere in the world.

■ Obtaining a high school or college degree via distance learning is possible.

■ Electronic security systems protect our homes and workplaces.

■ In game rooms, simulations transport you to an imaginary world.

■ In government research operations, computer systems guide satellites through space.

■ At home, our appliances are computerized.

■ On television, we can watch an instant replay of a tackle in a football game.

In most everyday activities in which you participate you benefit from the variety of applications and ways in which computers are used.

Computers in Our Future

It is a fair assumption that computers of the future will be more powerful and less expensive. It also is a fair assumption that almost every type of job will somehow involve a computer. With long-distance connectivity, more people will work full-time or part-time from home. See Figure 1-14.

FIGURE 1-14
Working from home

One of the major areas of change in the evolution of computers will be connectivity, or the ability to connect with other computers. Wireless and mobile devices will become the norm. Computer literacy, which is the knowledge and understanding of computers and their uses, will become even more important.

Net Fun

Visit NASA's Web site, *www.nasa.gov*, to learn how computers and computer-related technologies are used in space exploration.

SUMMARY

In this lesson, you learned:

- Computers have been around for more than 60 years.

- A computer is an electronic device that receives data, processes data, produces information, and stores the data and information.

- A computer derives its power from its speed, reliability, accuracy, storage, and communications capability.

- Computer classifications include personal computers (desktop and notebook), mobile devices, mid-range servers, mainframes, and supercomputers.

- The two basic types of software are application software and system software.

- Electronic communications enable computers to communicate with each other and other devices.

- A network is a group of two or more connected computers; an intranet is a closed network within an organization, and an extranet is a closed network for an organization and its customers and suppliers.

- The Internet is the world's largest network.

- Computers and technology affect almost every facet of our daily lives.

- Computers in our future will be more powerful and less expensive.

- Computer literacy is the ability to use a computer and its software to accomplish practical tasks.

VOCABULARY *Review*

Define the following terms:

Clients	Information	Network
Computer	Internet	Nodes
Data	Intranet	Personal computers
Desktop computer	Mainframe computer	Servers
Electronic communication	Mid-range server	Software
Extranet	Mobile computers	Supercomputer
Hardware	Mobile devices	Users
Icon		

REVIEW *Questions*

MULTIPLE CHOICE

Select the best response for the following statements.

1. _____ is text, numbers, sound, images, or video.
   A. Software
   B. Icon
   C. Hardware
   D. Data

2. A(n) _____ consists of hardware, software, data, and users.
   A. icon
   B. computer system
   C. mobile device
   D. node

3. A _____ is the fastest type of computer.
   A. mainframe computer
   B. handheld computer
   C. notebook computer
   D. supercomputer

4. The world's largest network is _____.
   A. an extranet
   B. an intranet
   C. the Internet
   D. the World Wide Web

5. _____ fit in the palm of your hand.
   A. Mobile devices
   B. Desktop computers
   C. Supercomputers
   D. Mid-range servers

TRUE / FALSE

Circle T if the statement is true or F if the statement is false.

T   F   1. Information is processed data.

T   F   2. Most computers are very reliable.

T   F   3. Data is stored in temporary memory and on a permanent storage device.

T   F   4. A notebook computer can fit in the palm of your hand.

T   F   5. Computers are necessary tools in almost every type of business.

MATCHING

Match the correct term in Column 1 to its description in Column 2.

Column 1	Column 2
___ 1. Information	A. text, numbers, sound, images, or video
___ 2. Data	B. processed data
___ 3. Network	C. a group of two or more connected computers
___ 4. Notebook computer	D. a computer that will fit in a briefcase
___ 5. Software	E. another term for program

PROJECTS

CROSS-CURRICULAR—MATHEMATICS

Select a career in the field of mathematics, such as a teacher or statistician. Use the Internet or other resources to search for information explaining how computers are used in a specific mathematics career. Use the keywords *mathematics careers* with one or two search engines, such as *www.google.com, www.yahoo.com,* or *www.ask.com*. Prepare a two-page report on what you discover.

CROSS-CURRICULAR—SCIENCE

Use the Internet and other resources to find information about wireless technology and computers of the future. Prepare a two-page report describing what you found. Use *www.ask.com* to locate resources for this report.

CROSS-CURRICULAR—SOCIAL STUDIES

Use the Internet or other resources to locate information on computer history. Prepare a one- or two-page report on computers developed in the 1950s and 1960s. Include the specific uses of these early computers. You might visit *www.looksmart.com* to find information about early computers. Try *computer history* for your keyword search.

CROSS-CURRICULAR—LANGUAGE ARTS

The computer has influenced the way in which we communicate. Use the Internet and other resources to find information on different methods of communication. Prepare a two-page report on your findings.

WEB PROJECT

You are a member of a special group exploring the history of computers. Your instructor has asked you to investigate the history of computing and report your findings to the class. You are to research and report on significant contributors/contributions to the evolution of computing, using the Internet and other resources. The Web site located at *www.computerhistory.org/* is a good starting point.

 TEAMWORK PROJECT

Your part-time job at a movie rental store consists of setting up and connecting new computers. Your supervisor is considering putting a computer in her office and one in the office used by the part-time supervisor and other employees. She asks that you research the possibilities of networking these two computers with the existing computer located in the store.

She would like answers to the following questions: Is there a minimum number of computers required for a network? What information and resources can be shared? What special hardware is required? Prepare a report on your findings. Include any other information about networks you think will be helpful. Use *www.about.com* or *http://en.wikipedia.org* and search for *computer networks.*

CRITICAL*Thinking*

The computer has influenced the way in which we communicate. Use the Internet and other resources to locate information on how the computer has affected our methods of communications. What other communication changes do you think could occur in the future? Write a two-page report on your findings.

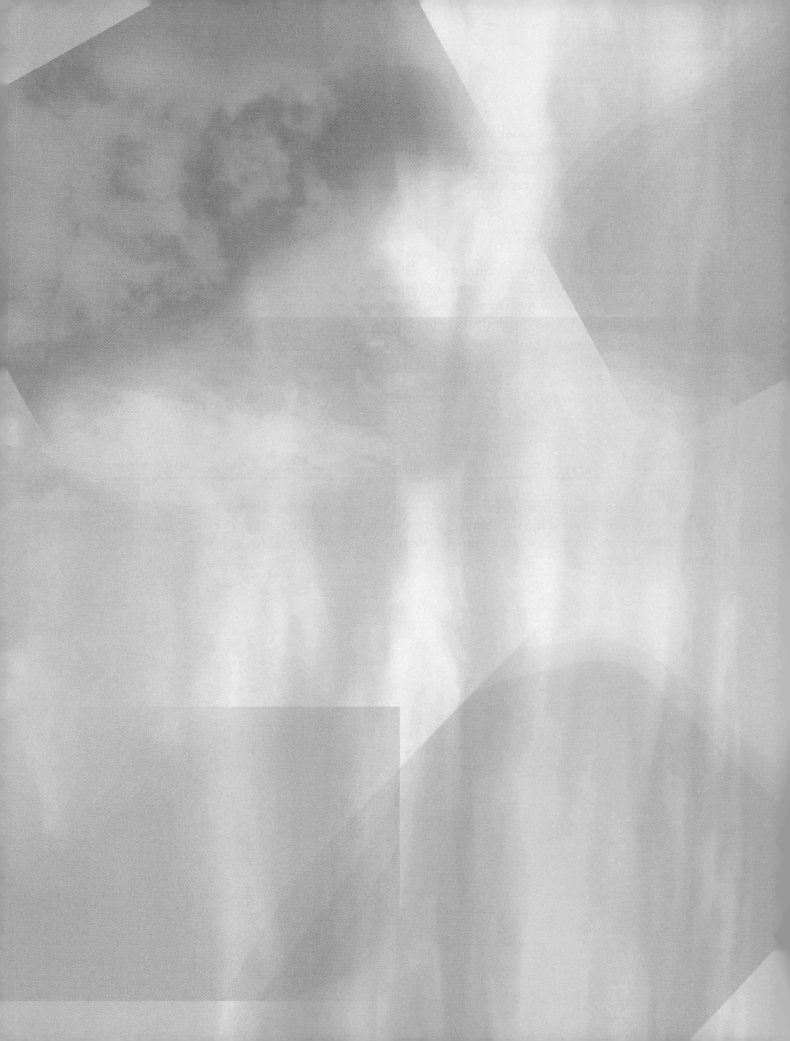

THE INTERNET AND THE WORLD WIDE WEB

OBJECTIVES

Upon completion of this lesson, you should be able to:

- Explain the origin of the Internet and describe how the Internet works.
- Explain the difference between the World Wide Web and the Internet.
- Describe the major features of the Internet.
- Explain how to connect to the Internet.
- Describe a browser.
- Identify browser features.
- Apply and use browser features.
- Describe other Internet features.

Estimated Time: 2 hours

VOCABULARY

Address bar

Browser

Domain name

Home page

Host computer

Host node

Hyperlink

Hypertext markup language (HTML)

Hypertext transfer protocol (HTTP)

Internet service provider (ISP)

Online service provider (OSP)

Protocol

Transmission Control Protocol and Internet Protocol (TCP/IP)

Uniform Resource Locator (URL)

Web page

World Wide Web

Each day millions of people "surf," or explore, the information superhighway. The "information superhighway" refers to the Internet. It is compared to a highway system because it functions much like a network of interstate highways. People use the Internet to research information, to shop, to go to school, to communicate with family and friends, to read the daily newspaper, to make airplane and hotel reservations, and so on. They use the Internet at work, at home, and while traveling. Anyone with access to the Internet can connect with and communicate with anyone else in the world who also has Internet access.

Evolution of the Internet

Even though no one person or organization can claim credit for creating the Internet, its origins can be traced to the 1960s and the United States Department of Defense. The birth of the Internet is tied closely to a computer-networking project started by a governmental division called the Advanced Research Projects Agency (ARPA). The goal was to create a network that would allow scientists to share information on military and scientific research.

The original name for the Internet was ARPANET. In 1969, ARPANET was a wide area network with four main host node computers. A *host node* is any computer directly connected to the network. These computers were located at the University of California at Santa Barbara, the University of California at Los Angeles, the Stanford Research Institute, and the University of Utah.

Over the next several years, the Internet grew steadily but quietly. Some interesting details are as follows:

- The addition of e-mail in 1972 spurred some growth.

- By 1989, more than 100,000 host computers were linked to ARPANET.

- In 1990, ARPANET ceased to exist, but few noticed because its functions continued.

- The real growth began when the World Wide Web came into being in 1992.

- The thousands of interconnected networks were called an Inter-Net-Network and became known as the Internet, or a network of networks.

- In 1993, the world's first browser, Mosaic, was released. A *browser* is a software program that provides a graphical interface for the Internet. Mosaic made it so easy to access the Internet that there was a 340 percent growth in the number of Internet users in this one year.

- The Internet is still growing at an unprecedented rate. See Figure 2-1.

FIGURE 2-1
Global Internet map

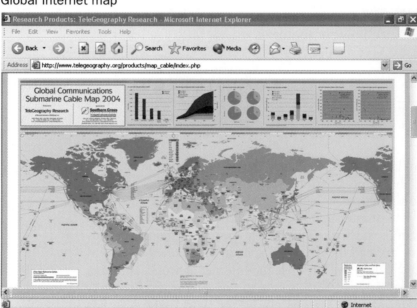

The Internet's Impact on Society

The use of the Internet in American homes has spread quickly among all demographic groups and across geographic regions. This increase is fueled by expanding computer use in schools and workplaces. In mid-2005, over two-thirds of all Americans, nearly 210 million people, used the Internet at home, work, or school.

The benefits of the Internet are so numerous and widespread that its value is almost incalculable. Businesses have automated record-keeping tasks that previously required countless hours, freeing workers for more productive activities. Marketers instantaneously send information via the Internet to prospective customers anywhere in the world. Shoppers can compare products, prices, and services offered by dozens or even hundreds of possible sellers, all without making a single phone call.

People who have difficulty moving around physically now can conduct many activities through the Internet that previously would not have been possible. The Internet is creating new opportunities every day—to learn and research, to keep in touch with distant friends and family members, to stay informed about political developments and make views known to government officials, and to nurture relationships that bridge and break down national, ethnic, and cultural barriers in an increasingly interconnected world.

Internet Basics

Recall from Lesson 1 that a network is a group of two or more computers linked together. The Internet is a loose association of thousands of networks and millions of computers across the world that all work together to share information. It is transitory and is constantly changing, reshaping, and remolding itself. The beauty of this network of networks is that all brands, models, and makes of computers can communicate with each other. This is called *interoperability*.

So how do we communicate across the Internet? Consider our postal service. If you want to send someone a letter anywhere in the world, you can do that—as long as you know the address. The Internet works in a similar fashion. From your computer, you can connect with any other networked computer anywhere in the world—as long as you know the address or know how to find the address.

Computers on the Internet communicate with each other using a set of protocols known as *TCP/IP* or *Transmission Control Protocol and Internet Protocol*. A *protocol* is a standard format for transferring data between two devices. TCP/IP is the agreed upon international standard for transmitting data. It is considered the language of the Internet and supports nearly all Internet applications. The TCP protocol enables two host computers to establish a connection and exchange data. A *host computer* is a computer that you access remotely from your computer. The *IP protocol* works with the addressing scheme. It allows you to enter an address and send it to another computer; from there the TCP protocol takes over and establishes a connection between the two computers. Returning to the postal service analogy, this is similar to what happens when you take a letter to the post office. You deliver the letter to the post office and then the post office takes over and delivers the letter to the recipient. See Figure 2-2 on the next page.

FIGURE 2-2
Data travels the Internet using TCP/IP

Postal addresses usually contain numbers and street names. Likewise, when we access another computer on the Internet, we are accessing it via a number. We do not need to remember or type the number. Instead, we can type in the domain name. The *domain name* identifies a site on the Internet. For example, the domain name in the Web address *www.microsoft.com* is microsoft.com. If you want to access the Microsoft Corporation's computers that are connected to the Internet, you open your Web browser and type the domain name into the browser's Address box. Browsers are discussed later in this lesson.

The World Wide Web

The Internet is made up of many services. Some of the more popular of these services include blogs, chat rooms, e-mail, FTP (file transfer protocol), instant messaging, mailing lists, and newsgroups. These services are discussed later in this lesson. One of the more popular Internet services is the World Wide Web.

Many people use the terms *World Wide Web*, or *Web* for short, and *Internet* interchangeably. In reality, they are two different things. The Web is a subset or an application that makes use of the Internet. The Internet can exist without the Web, but the Web cannot exist without the Internet. The Web actually began in 1990, when Dr. Tim Berners-Lee, who currently is the director of the World Wide Web Consortium, wrote a small computer program for his own personal use. This program, referred to as the *Hypertext Transfer Protocol (HTTP)*, became the language computers would use to communicate hypertext documents over the Internet. Dr. Berners-Lee next designed a scheme to give documents addresses on the Internet, and then created a text-based program that permitted pages to be linked through a formatting process known as *hypertext markup language (HTML)*. Clicking a linked word or image transfers you from one Web page to another or to another part of the same Web page. Dr. Berners-Lee's contributions were a step forward, but they were not the catalyst that made the Web what it is today.

In 1993, the number of people using the Web greatly increased. This increase occurred when Marc Andreessen, working for the National Center for Supercomputing Applications at the University of Illinois, released Mosaic. Mosaic was the first graphical browser. See Figure 2-3.

FIGURE 2-3
Mosaic Web page

In 1994, Andreessen co-founded Netscape Communications. With the introduction of Mosaic and the Web browsers that followed, the Web became a communications tool for a much wider audience. Currently, the most popular Web browser is Internet Explorer. Some other popular browsers include Netscape, Firefox, Mozilla, AOL, MSN, and Opera. Because of these enhancements, the Web is one of the more widely used services on the Internet.

Did You Know?

Many people create a personal home page. Some Web sites, such as *tripod.com*, provide free hosting.

Web Protocols—HTTP

The Web has several underlying protocols. One of these protocols, mentioned earlier, is HTTP, or hypertext transfer protocol. This protocol or standard defines how pages are transmitted. On the Web, you can send and receive Web pages over the Internet because Web servers and Web browsers both understand HTTP. When you enter a Web site address in your browser, for instance, this sends an HTTP command to the Web server to tell it to locate and transmit the requested Web page. A *Web server* is a computer that delivers, or serves up, Web pages. By installing special software, any computer can become a Web server. Every Web server has its own IP address and most have a domain name.

The Web page address often is referred to as the *URL*, or *Uniform Resource Locator*. Every Web page on the Internet has its own unique address. The first part of the address indicates what protocol to use, and the second part specifies the IP address or the domain name where the resource is located. For example, in the URL *http://www.si.edu/*, the *http* protocol indicates that this is a Web page and that the domain name is *si*. See Figure 2-4. The *.edu* at the end of the name indicates that this is an educational site. Table 2-1 contains a list of top-level domain abbreviations; however, many other infrequently used domain abbreviations also exist.

FIGURE 2-4
Smithsonian Institute Web page

URL (Web
site address)

TABLE 2-1
Top-level domain name abbreviations

TOP-LEVEL DOMAIN ABBREVIATIONS	TYPE OF ORGANIZATION
edu	Educational institutions
com	Commercial businesses, companies, and organizations
gov	Government institutions, such as the IRS
mil	Military organizations, such as the U.S. Army
net	Network provider
org	Associations and organizations

Web Protocols—HTML

A second protocol or standard that controls how the World Wide Web works is HTML, or hypertext markup language. This computer language determines how Web pages are formatted and displayed and allows the users to exchange text, images, sound, video, and multimedia files. *Hypertext* is a link to another location, often referred to as a *hyperlink*. The location can be within the same document, in another document on the same Web server, or on a Web server on the other side of the world. You click the link and are transported to the Web page.

A *Web page* is nothing more than an ordinary text page that is coded with HTML markup tags and then displayed within a browser. Markup tags consist of a set of text commands that are interpreted by the browser. Different browsers might interpret HTML tags differently or might not support all HTML tags. Thus, the same Web page can display differently when viewed in different browsers. Altogether, three items determine how a Web page displays:

- The type and version of the browser displaying the Web page

- The HTML markup tags used to code the page

- The user's monitor and monitor resolution

Hundreds of markup tags exist that can be used within a document. All Web pages, however, have a minimum basic requirement. Lesson 16 contains instructions on how to create a Web page.

> **Net Tip**
>
> When surfing the Web, at one time or another you are going to receive a "401 – Unauthorized" message. This means that you are trying to access a Web site that is protected.

Accessing the Internet

Before you can begin to access the Internet, you have to be connected and become part of the network. If you connect to the Internet through an organization such as a school or business, you probably are connecting through a local area network. A *local area network (LAN)* connects computers and devices within a limited geographical area. You connect to the Internet using a *network interface card (NIC)*. This is a special card inside your computer that allows the computer to be networked. A direct connection is made from the local area network to a high-speed connection line, most likely leased from the local telephone company.

Home users generally connect to the Internet using one of the following methods: a modem and a telephone line, a cable modem, a digital subscriber line (high-speed digital telephone line), fiber optics, or wireless.

> **Did You Know?**
>
> Data transmission is measured in *Kbps* (thousands of bits per second) and *Mbps* (millions of bits per second).

Getting Connected

Connecting to the Internet is a simple process, but you must first complete a few steps:

- **Step 1:** The first step is to locate an *Internet service provider (ISP)* or an *online service provider (OSP)*. There are thousands of ISPs. Many are small local companies. Their service is primarily an Internet connection. OSPs are large national and international companies. Two of the largest online service providers are America Online and MSN. Generally, the local ISP is less expensive than the OSP, but many people use an OSP because of the additional information and services offered.

■ **Step 2:** Once you decide which service provider to use, you must install some type of communication software. This software enables your computer to connect to another computer. Most likely, your ISP or OSP will provide this software.

■ **Step 3:** You will need to install a Web browser in order to use the Web. The most popular browser is Microsoft's Internet Explorer. Some OSPs, such as AOL, provide their own browser versions.

Once you have contracted with your ISP and installed your software, you are ready to connect to the Internet. This is the easy part. You may have to give instructions to your computer to dial a local telephone number if you are using a dial-up modem. This connects you to your ISP's computer, which in turn connects you to the Internet. If you are using a cable connection, DSL, fiber optics, or a wireless service, you are connected when you turn on your computer.

The next step is learning how to use the Web browser.

> ### Extra for Experts
>
> A common error message you might receive when surfing the Internet is "404 - Not found." This indicates that the server that hosts the site cannot find the HTML document. This could mean several things: You might have mistyped the URL; the Web page no longer exists; or the Web page has moved. When this happens, try going up one level by deleting the last part of the URL to the nearest slash. This will give you an indication if the Web site still exists. If this does not work, you can try one more procedure. Delete the last slash and type .html or .htm.

Browser Basics

Recall that a browser is the software program you use to retrieve documents from the Web and to display them in a readable format. The Web is the graphical portion of the Internet. The browser functions as an interface between you and the Web. Using a browser, you can display both text and images. Newer versions of most browsers also support multimedia information, including sound, animation, and video. Companies constantly update browsers to support the latest information the Web has to offer. It is important to keep your browser software updated to the most recent version your computer can handle.

The browser sends a message to the Web server to retrieve your requested Web page. Then the browser renders the HTML code to display the page. Recall that HTML is the language used to create documents for the Web. You navigate the Web by using your mouse to point to and click hyperlinks displayed in the browser window. A *hyperlink* is a highlighted word or image within a hypertext document which, when clicked, takes you to another place within that document or to another Web page.

Browser Terminology and Browser Basics

Understanding browser terminology is the key to using a browser effectively. Although most browsers have similar features, the menu options to select these features might be somewhat different. The major differences are special built-in tools. These tools include programs for mail, chat, viewing and listening to multimedia, and so on. This book uses Internet Explorer. See Figure 2-5 on the next page. Table 2-2 on the next page describes the major parts of the Internet Explorer window. If you are using another browser, use your browser's Help feature to find more information about its specific tools.

FIGURE 2-5
Internet Explorer browser window

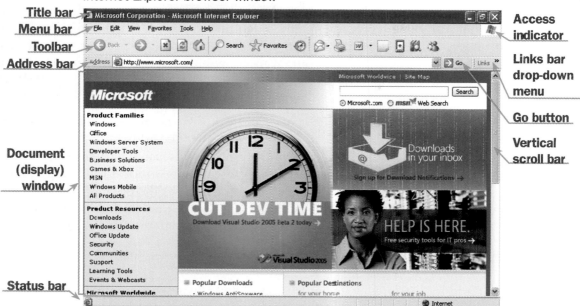

TABLE 2-2
Parts of the Internet Explorer window

COMPONENT	DEFINITIONS
Title bar	The bar on top of the window that contains the name of the document
Menu bar	A horizontal menu that appears at top of the program window; provides a selection of options related to the Web page
Standard buttons toolbar	Icons for single-click access to most often used menu commands
Address bar	Contains the URL or address of the active Web page; also, where you type the location for the Web page you want to visit
Go button	Connects you to the address displayed in the Address bar
Document window	Displays the active Web page
Status bar	Located at the bottom of the browser; shows the progress of Web page transactions
Access indicator	A small picture in the upper-right corner of the browser; when animated, it means that your browser is accessing data from a remote computer
Links bar	A drop-down menu containing a list of linked Web sites; click the Go button to display the menu.
Scroll bars	Vertical and horizontal scroll bars let you scroll vertically and horizontally if the Web page is too long or too wide to fit within one screen

Launching the Browser

In this lesson, it is assumed that you have an Internet connection—either a dial-up or direct connection. To connect to the Internet if you have a dial-up modem, you first might have to start a program that dials the Internet connection. If you have a direct high-speed or a wireless connection, however, you will simply start your Web browser to access the Internet. In most instances, you can double-click the browser icon located on your computer's desktop. If the icon is not available, open the browser from the Start menu.

If you want to visit a specific Web site, you need to know the address. The *Address bar*, located near the top of the browser window, is where you enter the address or URL of the Web site you want to visit (see Figure 2-5 on the previous page). As discussed earlier in this lesson, a unique URL identifies each Web page and tells the browser where to locate the page. The first part of the URL indicates the protocol and the second part specifies the domain name. To visit a specific Web site, type the address of the Web site you want to visit in the Address bar. Press Enter or click the Go button after typing the address to link to and display the Web page.

Toolbar and Menu Bar

The menu bar and toolbar are located at the top of your browser window. See Figure 2-6 on the next page. The following is an overview of the toolbar buttons. (The buttons on your toolbar might differ slightly from those described here.)

- *Back:* Returns you to the previous page.

- *Forward:* Takes you to the page you viewed before clicking the Back button.

- *Stop:* Stops the current page from loading.

- *Refresh:* Refreshes or reloads the current Web page.

- *Home:* Takes you to your home page.

- *Search:* Connects you to the Microsoft Internet search sites.

- *Favorites:* Opens the Favorites pane where you can store and access shortcuts to your most frequently visited Web sites.

- *History:* Opens the History pane, displaying a record of all the sites you recently have visited.

- *Mail:* Clicking the icon displays a drop-down menu with options to read your mail, create a new message, send a link, send a page, or read news.

- *Print:* Prints the current document.

- *Edit:* Displays a drop-down menu with options to edit the Web page shown in the display area.

- *Discuss:* Initiates discussions with other online users.

- *Create Mobile Favorites:* Used with a Pocket PC to save favorite links.

- *Research:* Displays a Search panel, providing a list of reference books and research sites.

- *Messenger:* Starts Windows Messenger, which allows real-time communication with other people who are signed in to the .NET Messenger service.

FIGURE 2-6
Internet Explorer menu and toolbar

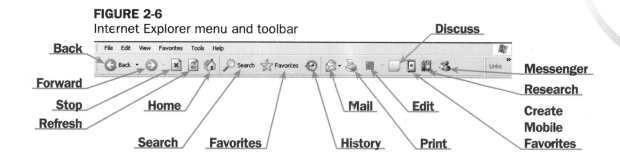

Some other browser features are as follows:

- *AutoComplete*: Keeps track of and saves previous entries you have made for Web addresses, forms, and passwords.

- *Address List*: Displays previously visited Web pages; click the Address bar list arrow to view these. See Figure 2-7.

FIGURE 2-7
Internet Explorer browser address list

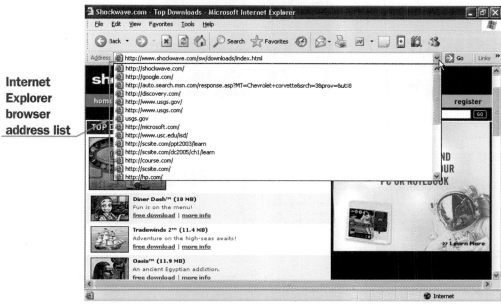

To explore various methods of navigating through a Web site, complete the following exercise.

S TEP-BY-STEP 2.1

1. Start your Internet browser. The first page you see is your home page.

2. Type **www.usgs.gov** in the Address bar. Click the **Go** button to the right of the Address bar or press **Enter**. This takes you to the U.S. Geological Survey home page.

STEP-BY-STEP 2.1 Continued

3. You can navigate through the pages of this site using several navigation tools:

   a. Notice the list of links on the left side of the home page below the topic heading *In the Spotlight*. Click a link of your choice and review the information on the page to which you linked. Click the browser's **Back** button to return to the USGS home page.

   b. Click a link below the *Science Features* topic heading. Review the information on the page to which you linked. Click the browser's **Back** button to return to the USGS home page.

   c. Below the topic heading *Science In Your State*, click your state on the displayed map. You link to a page for your state. The page contains links to real-time information for the state you chose. Figure 2-8 shows the page for the state of Florida.

   d. Click one of the real-time information links. Review the information you find.

FIGURE 2-8
Real-time information for Florida

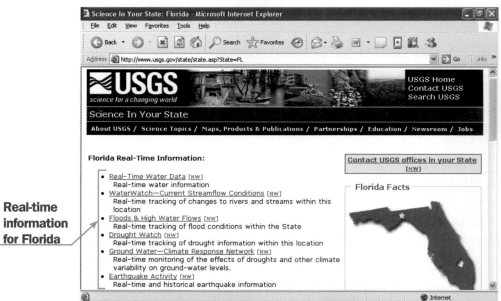

4. Click the **Back** button several times to return to the USGS.gov home page.

5. Click the **Home** button on the toolbar to return to your browser's home page. Leave your browser open for the next step-by-step.

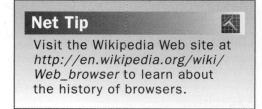

Net Tip

Visit the Wikipedia Web site at *http://en.wikipedia.org/wiki/ Web_browser* to learn about the history of browsers.

Your Home Page

When your browser is installed, a default home page is selected. The *home page* is the first page that is displayed when you start your browser. The Address bar located near the top of the browser window contains the address of the current page. In Step-by-step 2.2, you change the default home page to *discovery.com* and then return it to its original default.

STEP-BY-STEP 2.2

1. In the Internet Explorer Address bar, type **discovery.com**.

2. Click the **Go** button to the right of the Address bar or press **Enter**.

3. Click **Tools** on the menu bar, and then click **Internet Options**. The Internet Options dialog box is displayed. Click the **General** tab, if necessary. See Figure 2-9.

FIGURE 2-9
Internet Explorer Internet Options dialog box with the General tab selected

4. In the Home page section, click **Use Current** and click **OK**. Close your browser.

5. Start your browser. Note that it now opens to discovery.com. Click **Tools** on the menu bar, click **Internet Options**, and, if necessary, click the **General** tab. Return the home page to its original settings by clicking **Use Default**. (This is the original default page that was selected when your system was purchased. Verify with your instructor if another home page should be selected.)

6. Click the **OK** button to close the Internet Options dialog box. Leave your browser open for the next step-by-step.

Searching

Internet Explorer has a special feature called *AutoSearch* that makes it easy for you to locate your desired information quickly. Type a common term in the Address bar and press Enter. For example, imagine that you are saving your money for a new car, and you would like to have additional information about a Chevrolet Corvette. Launch your browser, type *Chevrolet Corvette*, and press Enter. Internet Explorer displays the MSN Search page with links to over five million Chevrolet Corvette Web pages, as shown in Figure 2-10 on next page.

FIGURE 2-10
AutoSearch results

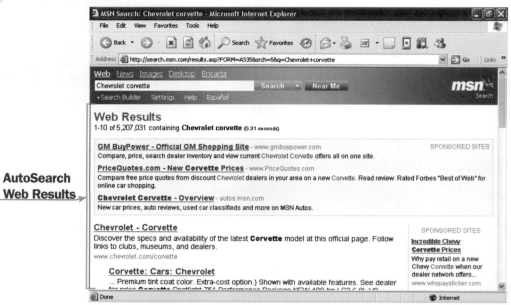

If the AutoSearch feature does not provide the information needed or these settings are turned off within the browser you are using, click the Search button. Clicking the Search button opens the Search pane. This is a separate pane on the left side of the window. Type the words for which you are searching and then click Search. The MSN Search page is displayed with a list of selected Web sites. Additional searching techniques are discussed in Lesson 3.

History

The Back and Forward buttons take you to sites you have visited in your current session. However, what if you want to return to that Web page you found last week and you cannot remember the URL? Then the History button is for you.

In Internet Explorer, click the History button on the toolbar. The History pane opens on the left side of the window and displays a record of all the sites you have visited in the last 20 days. The number of days (20) is the default. You can change the number of days through options on the Tools menu. To make it easier to find the site for which you are searching, you can sort the list by date, by site, by most visited, and by order visited today. You also can search the list for a keyword in a site name. See Figure 2-11.

FIGURE 2-11
History list

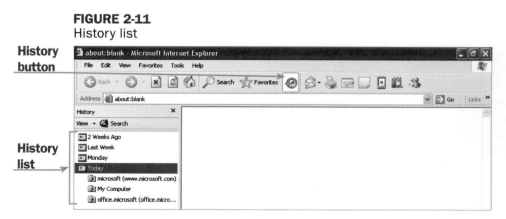

To clear the History list, click Tools on the menu bar, and then click Internet Options to display the Internet Options dialog box. Click the General tab and then click the Clear History button.

Favorites

The Web has so much to offer that it is very likely you are going to find some Web sites you really like and want to return to often. It is easy to keep these sites just a mouse click away by adding them to your *Favorites* list.

To add a site to your list of favorite sites:

■ Go to the site you want to add.

■ Click Favorites on the menu bar, and then click Add to Favorites.

■ To revisit any of the Favorites, just click the Favorites button, and then select the shortcut to the site.

As your list begins to grow, you can organize it by creating folders. You can organize by topics in much the same way you would organize files in a file drawer. In Step-by-step 2.3, you create a folder within the Favorites list.

STEP-BY-STEP 2.3

1. Click **Favorites** on the menu bar, and then click **Organize Favorites**. The Organize Favorites dialog box opens, as shown in Figure 2-12.

FIGURE 2-12
Organize Favorites dialog box

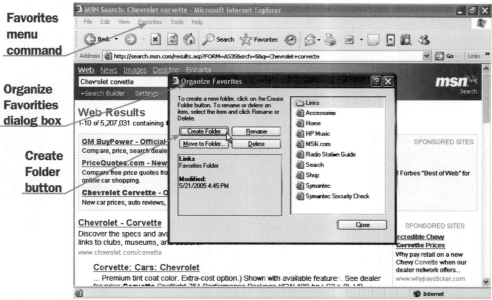

Favorites
menu
command

Organize
Favorites
dialog box

Create
Folder
button

2. Click the **Create Folder** button, type a name of your choice for the folder, and then press **Enter**.

STEP-BY-STEP 2.3 Continued

3. Now, delete the folder. Click the folder name, and then click the **Delete** button. When the Confirm Folder Delete dialog box displays, click the **Yes** button.

4. Click the **Close** button. Leave your browser open for the next step-by-step.

Controlling Access

The *Content Advisor* in Internet Explorer provides some control over what content can be viewed on the Internet. It enables you to:

■ Control access to settings through a password.

■ View and adjust the ratings settings to reflect what you think is appropriate content.

■ Adjust what types of content other people can view with or without your permission.

■ Set up a list of Web sites that other people can never view and a list of Web sites other people can always view.

■ Set up a list of Web sites that other people can always view, regardless of how the sites' contents are rated.

Web site publishers voluntarily rate their pages. The Internet rating standard is known as PICS: Platform for Internet Content Selection. The Content Advisor uses two independent PICS-compliant ratings systems—RSACi and SafeSurf. Each system uses a different method to describe in as much detail as possible the levels of offensive content on Web pages.

 Ethics in Technology

INTERNET SECURITY

If you have accessed the Internet recently, you know that you can purchase just about any item you want, from a Mercedes Benz to Uncle Bill's Jam and Jellies. You can have your purchase shipped to you and pay for it when it arrives, or you can use a credit card. The question is, how safe do you feel about transmitting credit card and other financial information over the Internet?

When you provide your credit card number, it travels through several computers before it reaches its final destination. To ensure that your credit card number is not stolen easily, companies use a technology called *encryption*. Encryption software acts somewhat similarly to the cable converter box on your television. The data is scrambled with a secret code so that no one can interpret it while it is being transmitted. When the data reaches its destination, the same software unscrambles the information.

Not all Web sites use security measures. One way to identify a secure site is to check the status bar at the bottom of your Web browser. There you will see a small icon— usually a lock. When the lock is closed, it indicates that the site is using security technology.

Cleanup Time

When you explore the Web, your browser keeps a record of the sites you visit. The pages are stored in temporary folders on your hard drive in your *disk cache* (pronounced *cash*). This process enables you to view the saved pages offline or without being connected to the Internet.

If you return to a cached Web page, that page will load faster because it is loading from cache. This can sometimes be a problem because the page might have changed since you were last at the site. The Refresh button was discussed earlier in this lesson. Clicking the Refresh button will load the current page from the server. Another option is to change the *Checking for newer versions of stored pages* setting. You will explore this setting in Step-by-step 2.4.

STEP-BY-STEP 2.4

1. Click **Tools** on the menu bar, and then click **Internet Options**. The Internet Options dialog box is displayed.

2. Click the **General** tab, if necessary. In the Temporary Internet files section, click the **Settings** button to display the Settings dialog box. (See Figure 2-13.) You have four options:
   - Every visit to the page
   - Every time you start Internet Explorer
   - Automatically
   - Never

FIGURE 2-13
Internet Explorer Settings dialog box

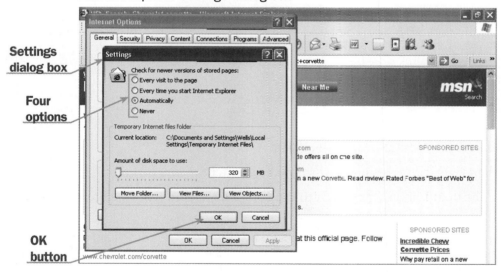

3. Select the option that is best for you and your individual requirements. The first option, *Every visit to the page,* can considerably slow down browsing time between pages. The *Never* option provides the fastest browsing time.

4. Click **OK** and then click **OK** again to return to Internet Explorer. Leave your browser open for the next step-by-step.

Net Ethics

HACKERS

Computer security violation is one of the biggest problems experienced on computer networks. People who break into computer systems are called hackers. The reasons they do this are many and varied. Some of more common reasons are as follows:

■ *Theft of services*: AOL, Prodigy, and other password-protected services charge a fee for usage. A hacker finds a way to bypass the password and uses the service without paying for it.

■ *Theft of information*: A hacker may break into a system to steal credit card numbers, test data, or even national security data.

■ *Hatred and vengeance*: Many people have groups or companies that they do not like. They may hack into the system to destroy files or to steal information to sell to opposing groups.

■ *For the thrill of it*: Some hackers break into sites just to see if they can do it. The thrill for them is in breaking the code.

Copy and Save Text, Web Pages, and Images

As you view pages on the Web, you will find things you would like to save so that you can refer to them later. You can save a complete Web page or any part of a Web page. This includes text, images, or hyperlinks.

To copy and save text:

■ Click Edit on the menu bar, and then click Select All or use your mouse to select a specific part of the page.

■ Click Edit on the menu bar, and then click Copy.

■ Paste the text into a Word document or other program.

■ Click the Save button.

To copy and save a hyperlink from a Web page:

■ Select and then right-click the link to display the shortcut menu.

■ Select Copy Shortcut to copy the link into the computer's memory. See Figure 2-14 on the next page.

■ Paste the link into another document.

■ Click the Save button.

FIGURE 2-14
Copying a hyperlink

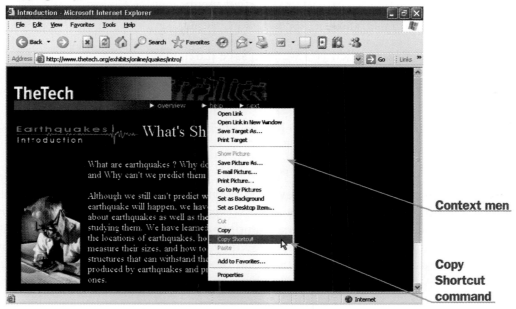

Context menu

Copy
Shortcut
command

To save an entire Web page:

- Click File on the menu bar, and then click Save As.

- Select the folder into which you want to save the page.

- In the File name box, type a name for the page.

- In Internet Explorer, in the Save as type box, select the *Web Page, complete* option. This option saves all of the files needed to display this page in its original format. This includes images and any other Web page elements. See Figure 2-15.

FIGURE 2-15
Save Web Page dialog box

Save Web
Page dialog
box

File name
text box

Save
button

Save as type
text box

To save an image:

■ Right-click the image to display the shortcut menu.

■ In Internet Explorer, select Save Picture As to display the Save Picture dialog box.

■ Select the folder into which you want to save the image.

■ Type the name for the image.

■ Click the Save button.

If you need a printed copy of a Web page, click the Print button in Internet Explorer.

Download and Install a Program

As you browse the Internet, you eventually will find a program you want to download. To *download* means to transfer from the Web server to your computer. The program could be a plug-in or enhancement for your browser, a utility program to help you better manage your computer system, a shareware game, and so on. Many companies that sell software allow you to pay for a new program online and then download the program directly from their site. Before completing Step-by-step 2.5 and downloading a program, obtain permission from your instructor.

S TEP-BY-STEP 2.5

1. Create a separate folder on your hard drive for your downloaded programs.

2. Go to the Web site where the program is located.

3. Follow the Web site's download instructions. These will vary from site to site, but most sites have some type of Download Now button. Click that button. The File Download dialog box appears.

4. Select the folder on your computer where you want to store the downloaded program. See Figure 2-16.

FIGURE 2-16
Save As dialog box

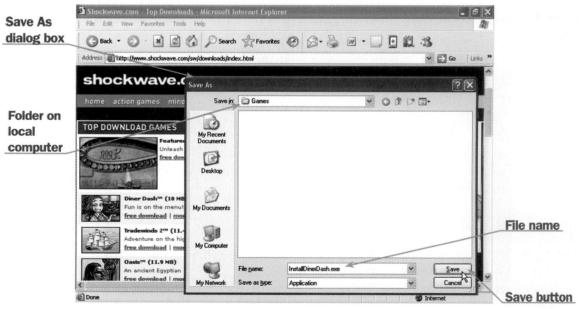

STEP-BY-STEP 2.5 Continued

5. Click the **Save** button to start the downloading process.

6. A downloading box displays, indicating the estimated download time and transfer rate.

7. Wait while the download takes place. When the download is completed, click the **Close** button.

8. Next, you need to install the program. Using Windows Explorer, locate the file you downloaded and double-click the filename. Follow the installation instructions as provided by the program.

9. Close your browser and turn off your computer if instructed to do so.

Other Internet Services

BLOG or WEB LOG

A *blog* (short for Web log) is a Web page that serves as a publicly accessible journal or log. Blogs cover many topics. A blog may consist of the recorded ideas of one person, or it could be a complex collaboration open to anyone. For example, it could focus on the daily activities of an individual (a sort of diary) or it could be an alliance open to the general public. The theme could be on a mixture of subjects or center on one topic. Generally, the blog is updated periodically, normally in reverse order, showing the oldest postings first.

Chat Rooms

You can call someone through the Internet and "talk" to them the way you do on the phone, only you are writing and reading on your computer rather than talking and listening with a phone in your hand. You are using the computer to create real-time communication between yourself and another user or a group of users. This is referred to as a *chat room*. To participate in a chat, you enter a virtual chat room. Once a chat is initiated, users enter text by typing on the keyboard, and the message appears on the monitor of the other participants. Chat rooms provide an opportunity for people with a common interest to talk together about the subject, although many chat rooms are more general in nature and provide a place for people to meet and talk. You should always be cautious in chat rooms and not give away information of a personal nature.

Instant Messaging

Instant messaging allows you to maintain a list of people with whom you wish to interact in real-time. You can send messages to any person on your list, often called a buddy list or contact list, as long as that person is online. Sending a message opens up a small window where you and your friend can type messages that both of you can see.

Mailing Lists

A *mailing list* is a group of people with a shared interest. Their e-mail addresses are collected into a group, and this group is identified by a single name. Whenever you send a message, everyone on the list receives a copy. Some mailing lists are called *LISTSERVs*, named after a mailing list software program. There are mailing lists for every imaginable topic. Many professional groups and associations utilize mailing lists as an effective way of communicating with members and potential members. You can subscribe to a mailing list just as you would subscribe to a magazine. A list owner is the person who manages the list.

Newsgroups and Bulletin Boards

A *newsgroup* is a discussion forum or a type of bulletin board. Each board is dedicated to a discussion on a particular topic. The difference between a newsgroup and a mailing list is that with a newsgroup you can select the topics you want to read. These messages are stored on a news server, which is a computer that contains the necessary newsgroup. Software messages or information sent to the group generally are read and reviewed by a moderator. The moderator determines whether the information is appropriate and relevant and, in some cases, might edit the material before posting to the group.

Online Conferencing

Technology now provides businesspeople, students taking online classes, members of a national organization, and even far-flung family members with the hardware and software needed to connect online to discuss issues, earn degrees, or just have a reunion. Freeware and commercial versions of software such as CuSeeMe are available that provide a chat setting with audio and video. Hardware requirements for *online conferencing* include a microphone and speakers for audio and a digitizing camera for video. Video and audio on the Internet require high-speed connections.

File Transfer Protocol

At one time or another, you might have been on the Internet, tried to access a special feature such as an audio file, and received a message that a plug-in was required. A plug-in is an add-on software application that adds a specific feature to your Web browser or other programs. You click a link, and the plug-in is downloaded or transmitted to your computer. You most likely used *file transfer protocol (FTP)*. This is an Internet standard that allows users to download and upload files from and to other computers on the Internet.

Many FTP servers are connected to the Internet. Some of these require user IDs and passwords. Others permit anonymous FTP access. This means that anyone can upload and download files from the server. The files on the server can be any type of file. Some examples are software updates for your printer, a revised instruction manual, or a new program that is being tested.

SUMMARY

In this lesson, you learned:

- No one person or organization can claim credit for creating the Internet.
- Origins of the Internet can be traced to the United States Department of Defense.
- The original name for the Internet was ARPANET.
- Mosaic was the Internet's first graphical interface.

- To connect to the Internet from a business, school, or other organization, you probably have a direct connection via a local area network and a network interface card.

- Types of Internet connections include modem and telephone line, DSL, cable modem, wireless, and fiber optics.

- To connect to the Internet, you need an Internet connection, telecommunications software, and a browser for the Web.

- Interoperability means that all brands, models, and makes of computers can communicate with each other.

- A protocol is a standard format for transferring data between two devices.

- TCP/IP is the agreed upon international standard for transmitting data.

- The domain name identifies a site on the Internet.

- The Internet is made up of many services.

- The Web is an application that makes use of the Internet.

- Web pages can be linked through hyperlinks.

- Microsoft Internet Explorer is a popular Web browser.

- The HTTP protocol defines how Web messages are formatted and transmitted.

- A Web site address is referred to as the URL or Universal Resource Locator.

- Every Web page on the Internet has its own unique address.

- HTML is a protocol that controls how Web pages are formatted and displayed.

- A Web page is coded with HTML markup tags.

- Other Internet services include blogs, chat rooms, instant messaging, mailing lists, newsgroups, bulletin boards, online conferencing, and FTP.

VOCABULARY *Review*

Define the following terms:

Address bar	Hypertext transfer protocol	Transmission Control
Browser	(HTTP)	Protocol and Internet
Domain name	Internet service provider	Protocol (TCP/IP)
Home page	(ISP)	Uniform Resource Locator
Host computer	Online service provider	(URL)
Host node	(OSP)	Web page
Hyperlink	Protocol	World Wide Web
Hypertext markup language		
(HTML)		

REVIEW *Questions*

MULTIPLE CHOICE

Select the best response for the following statements.

1. A URL is the same as the _____.
   A. Web site address
   B. Location bar
   C. Address bar
   D. toolbar

2. The _____ identifies the IP address.
   A. domain name
   B. history window
   C. content advisor
   D. disk cache

3. The first graphical browser was named _____.
   A. Internet Explorer
   B. Navigator
   C. Microsoft
   D. Mosaic

4. A(n) _____ serves as a publicly accessible journal or log.
   A. instant message
   B. blog
   C. newsgroup
   D. protocol

5. A _____ displays a record of all the sites you have visited recently.
   A. packet
   B. history list
   C. favorites list
   D. blog

TRUE/FALSE

Circle T if the statement is true or F if the statement is false.

T   F   1. Fiber optics is a type of Internet connection.

T   F   2. You must use a modem to communicate over a regular telephone line.

T   F   3. The home page is the first page that is displayed when you start your browser.

T   F   4. You can use AutoSearch to locate Web pages on the Internet.

T   F   5. You can view saved pages offline.

FILL IN THE BLANK

Complete the following sentences by writing the correct word or words in the blanks provided.

1. The original name for the Internet was _arpenet_

2. _Telecommunication_ software enables your computer to connect to another computer.

3. To _download_ means to transfer from the Web server to your computer.

4. To connect to the Internet, the first step is to locate a(n) _ISD/OSP_ or a(n) _____.

5. A(n) _dial up_ modem uses a telephone line.

PROJECTS

CROSS-CURRICULAR—MATHEMATICS

Access the Math Goodies Web site at *www.mathgoodies.com/* and complete one of the online interactive puzzles. Prepare a report on the puzzle you completed. Describe how it was interactive and what Internet features were used to create the puzzle.

CROSS-CURRICULAR—SCIENCE

The World Weather Watch is an interactive cross-curricular Internet project. To participate in the project, you collect weather data once a week for a specified time period. Your group can register to participate in the project, or you can post your data and use it for comparison discussions. The Web site is located at *http://www.cyberbee.com/weatherwatch/*.

CROSS-CURRICULAR—SOCIAL STUDIES

Who is who in the Internet world? Visit the Web site *http://wiwiw.org/* and learn about the pioneers who made the Internet what it is today. Select one or two of the pioneers and prepare a report. Include a picture if possible.

CROSS-CURRICULAR—LANGUAGE ARTS

Complete a research project on newsgroups. Include at least three newsgroups in which you would be interested. Explain in your project what software you would use and how you would connect to these newsgroups.

 WEB PROJECT

Internet etiquette is an important topic for someone who uses the Internet for e-mail, newsgroups, and other Internet features. Do an Internet search and locate information on Internet etiquette. Prepare a report on your findings. The following are some URLs to get you started:

http://www.albury.net.au/new-users/netiquet.htm

http://www.fau.edu/netiquette/net/

http://archive.ncsa.uiuc.edu/Edu/ICG/pt1.ch2.Etiquette.html

TEAMWORK PROJECT

Your instructor is impressed with your knowledge of the Internet. She has asked you to coordinate a project with two other students. There is no Internet connection at your school. Your instructor wants to convince the principal that an Internet connection would be a vital enhancement for your class and for the entire school. Your goal is to create a persuasive presentation for your instructor that she can present to the principal.

CRITICAL *Thinking*

Do you think the government will ever be able to regulate the Internet? That is, will any agency ever be able to control and limit what someone uploads online? Use your word-processing program and write a page on your thoughts about this issue.

THE INTERNET AND RESEARCH

VOCABULARY

Boolean logic

Concept searching

Database

Hits (Results)

Index (Indexer)

Invisible Web (Deep Web)

Keyword

Math symbols

MP3

Related search

Search engine

Search engine math

Spider

Stemming

Subject directories

Truncation

Usenet

Wildcard character

The Internet contains a wealth of information. In fact, you can find information on just about any topic you can imagine. The problem is that the Internet contains so much information it can be difficult to locate just what you need. In this lesson, you learn Internet search techniques to help you locate the specific information you seek.

Why Search the Internet?

You might ask yourself, "Why would I want to search the Internet? What information does it contain that can help me?" The reasons people search the Internet are varied and many. The following are just a few examples:

- You need to do research for the term paper due in your English class next week.
- Your grandmother is losing her hearing and has asked you to help her find some information on hearing aids.
- You lost the manual for your DVD player and need a replacement.
- You plan to take a trip to Australia this summer and would like information on some of the hotels.

As you can see from these examples, hundreds of reasons exist as to why you might want to conduct an Internet search. See Figure 3-1.

FIGURE 3-1
Searching the Internet

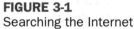

The Key to a Successful Search

We live in the information age, and information continues to grow at an ever-spiraling rate. To conduct an effective online search on a particular topic can be a challenge. You easily can be overwhelmed by the abundance of raw data. With the right tools, however, the task becomes easier. One key to a successful Internet search is an understanding of the many search tools that are available. Learning to use and apply the different tools will help you devise a better search strategy.

Two of the more popular tools available for online searches are search engines and subject directories. You use a search engine to search for keywords. You use a directory to find specialized topics. The primary difference between these two search tools is that people assemble directories and organize Web sites into categories, while search engines are automated. Some search sites, such as Yahoo.com, are hybrids and offer both types of searches. Search engines are discussed in the first part of this lesson, and an overview of directories is contained in the second part.

Did You Know?

No single Web tool indexes or organizes the whole Web. When using an online search tool, you are searching and viewing data extracted from the Web. This data has been placed into the search engine's database. It is the database that is searched—not the Web itself. This is one of the reasons you get different results when you use different search engines.

Note

When typing the Web site address in the browser text box, do not include the period that marks the end of the sentence in this lesson.

Search Engines

A *search engine* is a software program that enables the user to search the Internet using keywords. A *keyword* (also called a search term) is a descriptive word within the Web document. The Internet contains hundreds of search engines. Each search engine might work a little differently, but most of them have some common search features. For example, all search engines support keyword searches. Although keyword searches might not be the most effective way to search, this is the search method used by most individuals.

Some search engines support an additional enhancement called *concept searching*. The search engine tries to determine what you mean and displays links to Web sites that relate to the keywords. If you search for "video games," for example, the search engine also might return results on sites that contain Nintendo and Playstation.

Another feature supported by some search engines is *stemming* or *truncation*. When you search for a word, the search engine also includes the "stem" of the word. For example, you enter the search word "player," and you might receive results for play, plays, and playing.

How Does a Search Engine Work?

As indicated previously, a search engine is a software program. In addition to the software component, the search engine contains two other programmed elements: spiders and the index.

The *spider* (or crawler) is a search engine robot that searches the Internet for the keywords. It is called a spider because it "crawls" the Web continually, examining Web sites and finding and looking for links. Every month or so, it might return to a previous Web site to look for changes.

The third part of the search engine is the *index* or *indexer*. When the spider finds a page, it feeds the data to the index. After a Web page is indexed, it becomes part of the search engine's database and is available to anyone using that search engine. A *database* is a collection of organized information.

Some search engines index just Web page titles, while some search engines claim to index all words, even the articles, "a," "an," and "the." Other search engines index all words, except articles and stop words such as "www," "but," "or," "nor," "for," "so," or "yet." Some search engines index all words without reference to capitalization. Other engines differentiate uppercase from lowercase.

> ### Net Tip
> If you are using Web sources for your research paper, you need to give credit for the sources. You can find information on citing Internet sources at *www.lib.berkeley.edu/ TeachingLib/Guides/Internet/ Style.html*.

When you type a keyword or keywords into a search engine's Search text box, your input is checked against the index of all the Web pages in the engine's database. The relevant sites are returned to you as hits, ranked in order with the best results at the top. *Hits*, or *results*, are the number of returns or hyperlinked Web site addresses displayed based on your keyword(s). Recall from Lesson 2 that a hyperlink is a highlighted word or image within a hypertext document, which, when clicked, takes you to another location within the same Web page or to a different document.

To search using keywords, the process is as follows:

- Start your Web browser and display a search engine Web site.

- Type your keyword or keywords into the Search text box. These keywords describe the information you are trying to locate.

■ Click the Search button.

■ The search engine matches as many keywords as possible by searching its own database.

■ The search engine returns a hyperlinked list of Web site addresses where the keywords are found. You click the hyperlinks to display and view the Web sites.

■ If you are unable to find the information for which you are searching within these hyperlinked sites, you can revise your keywords and submit a new request.

Did You Know?

Many search engines have banner ads, which are advertisements using text or graphics. Most major search engines carry paid placement listings. Companies and organizations pay to guarantee their site a high ranking, usually in relation to desired words. The exact position of these listings can vary.

One of the more popular search engines is Google. In Step-by-step 3.1, you use Google to find out more about keywords and how they are used in Web searches.

S TEP-BY-STEP 3.1

1. Start your browser. Type **google.com** in the Address bar and press **Enter**.

2. Type **keywords definition** in the Google Search text box. See Figure 3-2.

FIGURE 3-2
Google search engine Web page

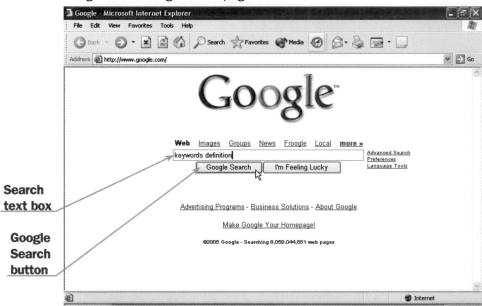

STEP-BY-STEP 3.1 Continued

3. Click the **Google Search** button. Within a few seconds, Google displays the results of your search. Your search results might be different from those shown in Figure 3-3.

FIGURE 3-3
Google's search results

Number of results

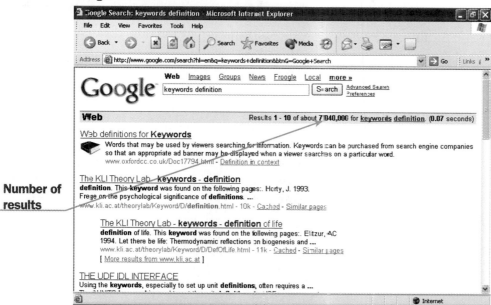

4. Click one of the links and see if you can find a definition for keywords (see Figure 3-4). If the first link does not provide the information, click the browser's **Back** button and then try another link.

FIGURE 3-4
Keywords defined

Back button

Print button

Keywords definitions

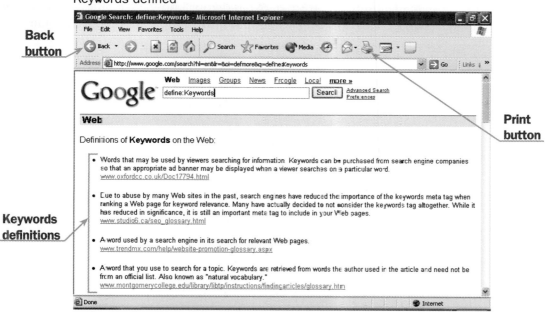

STEP-BY-STEP 3.1 Continued

5. If instructed to do so, click the **Print** button and submit a copy of your search results to your instructor. Leave your browser open for the next step-by-step.

As you see from this example and from Figure 3-3 on the previous page, the number of results (over seven million) is a bit overwhelming. At this point, you have several options:

■ You can click any of the links and review the information at the linked site.

■ You can redefine your keywords.

■ You can use another search engine.

If you do not locate the information for which you are searching in the first 20 or so hits, the third option could be your next best choice. It is impossible for any one search engine to index every page on the Web. Each search engine has its own technique it uses to index Web sites. Using a different engine, therefore, might provide a different list of hits. Many popular search engine sites exist, and you might need to try several before you find the information you are seeking. Some of the more well-known search engines are the following:

■ Yahoo at *yahoo.com*

■ Microsoft at *msn.com*

■ America Online at *aol.com*

■ Ask Jeeves at *ask.com*

■ Netscape at *netscape.com*

Note in Figure 3-4 on the previous page that Google changed the search term from *keywords definition* to *define:Keywords*. The Definitions option is one of several special features provided by Google. Other special features are discussed later in this lesson.

You also can use Google's Definition feature to expand your knowledge of how search engines work. Complete the following exercise to find additional information about search engines.

STEP-BY-STEP 3.2

1. Click the browser's **Back** button to return to the Google home page. Type **define:search engines** in the Google Search text box. See Figure 3-5.

FIGURE 3-5
Google search engine Web page

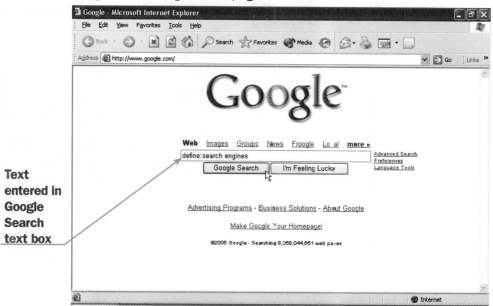

Text entered in Google Search text box

2. Click the **Google Search** button. Within a few seconds, Google displays the results. Scroll the page and read the various search engine definitions. Your search results might be different from those shown in Figure 3-6.

FIGURE 3-6
Google search engine definitions Web page

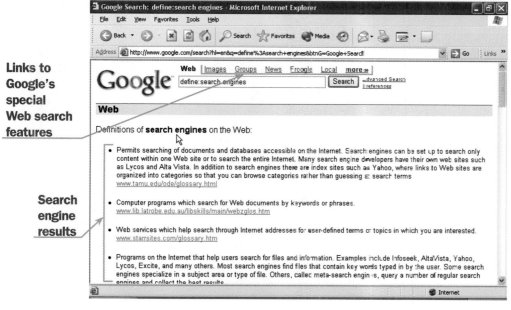

Links to Google's special Web search features

Search engine results

STEP-BY-STEP 3.2 Continued

3. If instructed to do so, click the **Print** button and submit a copy of your search results to your instructor. Click the browser's **Back** button to return to Google's home page. Leave your browser open for the next step-by-step.

In Figure 3-6 on the previous page, note the links above the Google Search text box. These are some of Google's special Web search features:

- *Images*: Displays a group of images in thumbnail format

- *Groups*: A free online community and discussion group service that offers the Web's most comprehensive archive of Usenet postings; *Usenet* is a collection of news or discussion groups

- *News*: Current news headlines

- *Froogle*: Google's product search service

- *Local*: Finds local businesses and services

Hot Tip

Have you been given a research assignment, but are having trouble coming up with a topic? Then check out *www.researchpaper.com* for a list of hot paper topics.

Try another search. Suppose you are going to use the Internet to purchase some video games. In Step-by-step 3.3, you use Google's Froogle search feature to execute a search on video games.

STEP-BY-STEP 3.3

1. Click the **Froogle** link. Delete any content in the search text box and then type **video games for sale** in the Froogle search box (see Figure 3-7).

FIGURE 3-7
Using Froogle to search for "video games for sale"

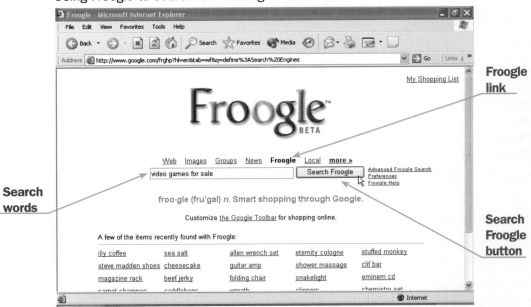

STEP-BY-STEP 3.3 Continued

    2. Click the **Search Froogle** button. See Figure 3-8.

        FIGURE 3-8
        Froogle search results

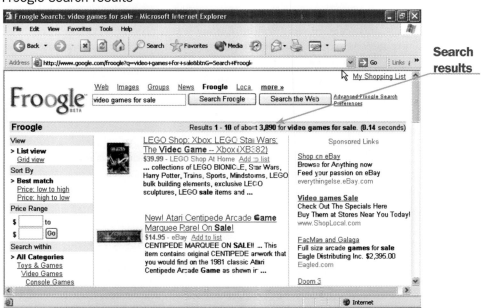

    3. Scroll down and review the results. Your results most likely will be different from those displayed in Figure 3-8.

    4. Click the browser's **Back** button to return to Google's home page. Leave your browser open for the next step-by-step.

Specialty Search Engines

So far in this lesson, we have discussed general search engines. There are, however, many specialized search engines on the Internet. These search engines sometimes are called *category-oriented search* tools. They generally focus on a particular topic. If you are looking for information in a particular format, your best bet is to search a site that specializes in indexing and retrieving that particular information. Some examples of uses for specialty search engines are as follows:

■ You are looking up a former classmate or a long-lost cousin—try the Switchboard Web site at *www.switchboard.com* or Yahoo's people search at *people.yahoo.com*.

■ You want to download a shareware game called AdventureMaker—try the Shareware Web site at *shareware.com*.

■ You want to do online jewelry shopping or item comparison—try Catalog City at *www.catalogcity.com* or Bottom Dollar at *www.bottomdollar.com*.

■ You are thinking about your future and what career options you might have—try CareerBuilder at *www.careerbuilder.com*.

The preceding are just a few examples of the many hundreds of specialty Web sites. If you are looking for a particular information source, but you are not sure where to look, try the State University of New York at Albany search engine collection site at *http://library.albany.edu/internet/engines.html*. This site contains links to hundreds of specialty search engines, including specialty, meta, deep Web, domain names, and other search engine types. See Figure 3-9.

FIGURE 3-9
State University of New York at Albany's search engine collection

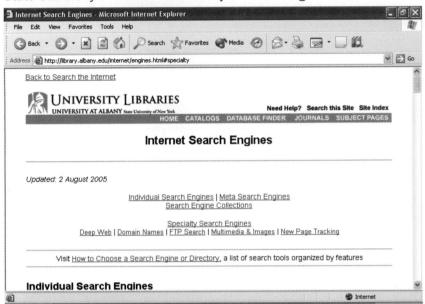

 Net Business

SEARCH ENGINE OPTIMIZATION

When Web site developers register their sites with search engines, they normally provide a list of keywords that will help get their site on a user's search results list. Web site owners often can improve their site rankings (or where they appear in the list) by employing cutting-edge Web marketing technology. For example, several organizations offer search engine optimization services to Web site entrepreneurs. These services can include an in-depth analysis of keywords that people will use while searching, design of banner ads and buttons to be placed on the search engine Web site, and so on.

In addition, you can use a service such as Wordtracker to find out what keywords are used most often to find products or services similar to yours. Also available are several "pay-per-click" search engines. With this type of search engine, Web site owners bid on keywords. When a person uses the keywords in a search, the links in the search results list appear in order from highest to lowest bid on the keywords. The owner of the Web site pays the search engine the per-click fee when someone clicks the link to the site.

Another Web site that lists search engines is the CNet site, located at *www.cnet.com*. This site has one of the Internet's best specialty search engines, which includes databases, indexes, and directories in a single site. Table 3-1 lists some other popular specialty search engines.

TABLE 3-1
Some popular specialty search engines

MAPS & TRAVEL	PEOPLE & INFORMATION	COMPANIES & CAREERS	WORLD DATA
Microsoft's *www.expedia.com*	People finder at *www.peoplesite.com*	*Occupational Outlook Handbook* at *www.bls.gov/oco*	World Health Organization at *www.who.int*
MapQuest at *www.mapquest.com*	Yellow Pages Search Power at *www.yellow.com*	America's Job Bank at *www.ajb.dni.us*	*CIA World Factbook* at *www.cia.gov/cia/ publications/factbook*
Worldwide Online *Reservations* at *www.orbitz.com*	Toll-free numbers at *www.inter800.com*	Monster job bank at *www.monster.com*	World Bank at *www.worldbank.org*
Great Outdoors at *www.gorp.com*	Canada Yellow Pages at *www.yellowpages.ca*	Career Resource Center at *www.careers.org*	World Data Center at *www.ngdc.noaa.gov/ wdc/wdcmain.html*

Multimedia Search Engines

Are you interested in finding graphics, video clips, animation, and even MP3 music files? If so, then a multimedia search engine is an option to consider. For music and MP3, you might want to try the Lycos search engine at *http://music.lycos.com/* or *www.musicsearch.com*. MP3 is a file format that allows audio compression at near-CD quality.

Other multimedia search engines include the following: Corbis at *www.corbis.com* boasts of "the world's largest collection of fine art and photography." AltaVista at *www.altavista.com* has a special tab for images, audio, and video. Or, try Ditto, the visual search engine, at *www.ditto.com*, to search for pictures, photographs, and artwork.

Meta-Search Engines

Have you searched and searched for the right information—going from search engine to search engine—and still not found what you need? If so, then you might want to try a meta-search engine. This type of search engine searches several major engines at one time. These search engines do not have their own databases. Instead, they act as a middle "person." They send the query to major search engines and then return the results or hits. Meta-search engines

> **Hot Tip**
>
> Some search engines automatically include plurals; others do not. To be on the safe side, include the plural. For example, if you are searching for *squirrels*, use keywords such as *"squirrel"* or *"squirrels."*

> **Internet**
>
> Meta-search engines send your search simultaneously to several individual search engines and their databases of Web pages. Find out about meta-search engines, how they work, and their limitations at *www.lib.berkeley.edu/ TeachingLib/Guides/Internet/ MetaSearch.html.*

generally work best with simple searches. Two popular meta-search engines are Dogpile at *www.dogpile.com* and MetaCrawler at *www.metacrawler.com*.

Search Engine Tools and Techniques

> **Internet**
>
> A meta tag is a special HTML tag that provides information about a Web page. Meta tags do not affect how the page is displayed. They provide information such as the title, description, and keywords. Many search engines use this information when creating their index.

In the previous step-by-step exercises, you used a keyword approach to search for your topic. As the Internet continues to expand, however, and more and more pages are added, effective searching requires new approaches and strategies. Remember that the more specific your search, the more likely you will find what you want. To find relevant information, you must use a variety of tools and techniques.

Phrase Searching

If you want to search for words that must appear next to each other, then phrase searching is your best choice. Enter a phrase using double quotation marks, and phrase searching matches only those words that appear adjacent to each other and in the order in which you specify. For example, if you are searching for baseball cards, enter the phrase *"baseball cards"* in double quotation marks. The results will contain Web sites with the words *baseball cards* adjacent to each other. Without the quotation marks, the search engine would find Web pages that contain the words *baseball* and *cards* anywhere within each page.

If you are searching for more than one phrase, you can separate multiple phrases or proper names with a comma. For example, to find Mickey Mantle baseball cards, you would enter *"baseball cards", "Mickey Mantle"*. It is always a good idea to capitalize proper nouns because some search engines distinguish between uppercase and lowercase letters. On the other hand, if you capitalize a common noun such as *Bread*, you will get fewer returns than if you typed *bread*.

Search Engine Math

Practically all the major search engines and directories support **search engine math**. You use **math symbols** to enter a formula to filter out unwanted listings. For example:

- Put a plus sign (+) before words that must display (also called an *inclusion operator*).

- Put a minus sign (-) before words that you do not want to display (also called an *exclusion operator*).

- Words without qualifiers need not display, but still are involved in sorting your search.

Suppose you are making cookies and would like to try some new recipes. Your search words are *+cookie+recipes*. Only pages that contain both words would appear in your results. Now suppose you want recipes for chocolate cookies. Your search words are *+cookie+recipe+chocolate*. This would display pages with all three words.

To take this a step further, you do not like coconut. You therefore do not want any recipes that contain the word *coconut*. The minus (-) symbol is helpful for reducing the number of unrelated results. You would type your search phrase as *+cookie+recipe+chocolate-coconut*. This tells the search engine to find pages that contain *cookie*, *recipe*, and *chocolate*, and then to remove any pages that contain the word *coconut*. To extend this idea and to get chocolate cookie recipes without coconut and honey,

your search phrase would be *+cookie+recipe+chocolate-coconut-honey*. Simply begin subtracting terms you know are not of interest, and you will get better results. You also can use math symbols with most directories. Directories are discussed later in this lesson.

Boolean Searching

When you search for a topic on the Internet, you are not going from server to server and viewing documents on that server. Instead, you are searching databases. Recall that a database is a collection of organized information. *Boolean logic* is another way that you can search databases. This works on a principle similar to search engine math, but has a little more power. Boolean logic consists of three logical operators:

- AND

- NOT

- OR

Returning to our cookie example, you are interested in a relationship between cookies and recipes. So you might search for *"cookies AND recipes"*. The more terms you combine with AND, the fewer returns you will receive. Or, you want chocolate cookie recipes without coconut. You would search for *"cookies AND recipes AND chocolate NOT coconut"*.

OR logic is more commonly used to search for similar terms or concepts. For example, you search for *"cookies AND recipes OR chocolate"* to retrieve results containing one term or the other, or both. The more terms you combine in a search with OR logic, the more results you will receive from your search.

The power of the Boolean search is the use of multiple parameters, which is not possible with the math symbols. For instance, you can create a search on *"cookies AND recipes NOT (coconut OR honey OR spinach)"*.

Some search engines assist you with search engine math and logical searching with forms. For example, if you access the AltaVista search engine, clicking the Advanced Search link brings up a form. Using this form, you can specify the language, words, and phrases to include and to omit, and even specify a time period. In addition, AltaVista provides a Boolean expression text box option. Keep in mind that some search engines do not support Boolean logic. Check the search engine Help feature to determine if Boolean logic is supported.

Complete Step-by-step 3.4 to build a query using AltaVista's Advanced Web Search form.

STEP-BY-STEP 3.4

1. Type **altavista.com** in the browser Address bar and then press **Enter** (see Figure 3-10). Your screen might look somewhat different.

FIGURE 3-10
AltaVista search engine Web page

2. Click the **Advanced Search** link. AltaVista's Advanced Web Search page appears.

3. In the *all of these words* text box, type **cookie recipes chocolate**.

4. In the *and none of these words* text box, type **coconut honey** (see Figure 3-11).

FIGURE 3-11
AltaVista Advanced Web Search page

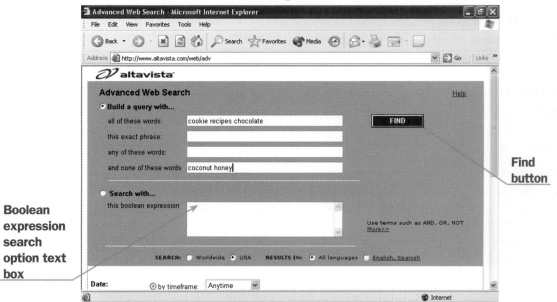

STEP-BY-STEP 3.4 Continued

5. Click the **Find** button to display the results of your query (see Figure 3-12). Leave your browser open for the next step-by-step.

FIGURE 3-12
AltaVista query results

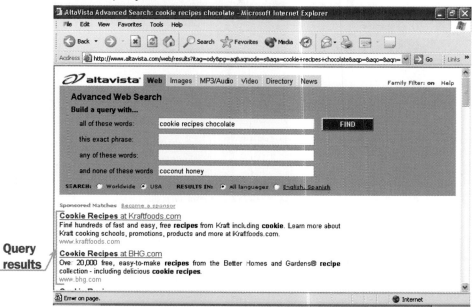

Wildcard Searching

The * symbol, or asterisk, is considered a **_wildcard character_**. If you do not know the spelling of a word or you want to search plurals or variations of a word, use the wildcard character. For example, you want to search for *"baseball cards and Nolan Ryan"* but you are not sure how to spell *Nolan*. You can construct your search using a wildcard—*"baseball cards"* and *"N* Ryan"*. Some search engines permit the * only at the end of the word; with others you can put the * at the end or beginning. Some search engines do not support wildcard searches. Check the search engine Help feature to determine if wildcard searches are supported.

Other Search Features

Another feature provided by several search engines is a **_related search_**. These are preprogrammed queries or questions suggested by the search engine. A related search can dramatically improve your odds of finding the information you are seeking. Several search engines offer this feature, although they might use different terminology. You might see terms such as "similar pages," "related pages," or "more pages like this." WebCrawler and Google use "Similar pages." All of these terms mean the same thing. See Figure 3-13.

FIGURE 3-13
Google uses the term "Similar pages"

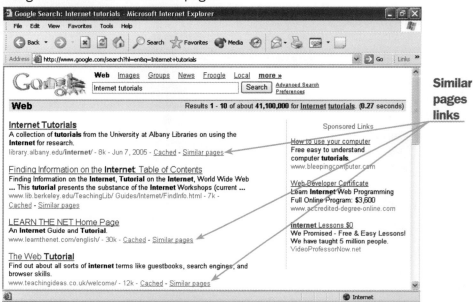

Subject Directory Searching

Recall that earlier in this lesson we discussed the primary difference between a search engine and a directory. Search engines use software programs to index sites; people assemble directories. Subject experts carefully check a Web site to make sure it meets a particular set of standards before the site is included in a directory. Then they add the URL for the Web site to the database.

Most *subject directories* are organized by subject categories, with a collection of links to Internet resources. These resources are arranged by subject and then displayed in a series of menus. To access a particular topic, you start from the top and "drill down" through the different levels—going from the general to the specific. This is similar to a traditional card catalog or the telephone yellow pages.

Suppose you want to visit the Great Smoky Mountains National Park. You can use a search engine and keywords to try to locate information, or you can use a subject directory search tool. The Yahoo! Directory provides a list and links to approximately 14 subject directories. See Figure 3-14 on the next page.

Internet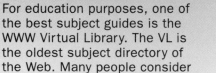

For education purposes, one of the best subject guides is the WWW Virtual Library. The VL is the oldest subject directory of the Web. Many people consider this site to have the highest quality guides to particular sections of the Internet. You can find the Virtual Library at *http://vlib.org/*.

FIGURE 3-14
A list of Yahoo subject directories

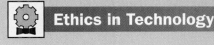

Yahoo's
Directory
categories

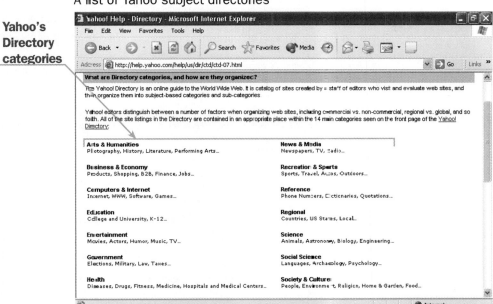

Complete Step-by-step 3.5 to learn how to use a directory and search for information on the Great Smoky Mountains National Park.

⚙️ **Ethics in Technology**

SPAMMING

You probably have heard of spam. No, it is not the luncheon meat that comes in a can. We are talking about Internet spam. Internet spam has several definitions. It is defined as electronic junk mail or junk newsgroup postings, or even unsolicited e-mail. The unsolicited e-mail most likely is some type of advertising or get-rich scheme, similar to the junk mail you receive almost every day. With traditional junk mail, however, the people who send the mail pay a fee to distribute their materials.

Spam, in contrast, is similar to receiving a postage-due letter. Even though you do not pay the postage as it arrives in your electronic mailbox, you still pay for it indirectly. The charges are in the form of disk space, connect time, and sometimes long-distance Internet connections.

Spam is not illegal, but several groups are trying to stop it. Numerous services exist to which you can submit a complaint or report a spam provider. Also available are spam-blocking and filtering services, as well as services and programs that hide your e-mail address from potential spammers. Visit *spam.abuse.net* to learn more about spam.

S TEP-BY-STEP 3.5

1. Type **dir.yahoo.com** in the browser Address bar, and then click the **Go** button. This takes you to the Yahoo! Directory Web site shown in Figure 3-15. (The content you see on this site most likely will differ from that shown in Figure 3-15.)

FIGURE 3-15
Yahoo! Directory Web page

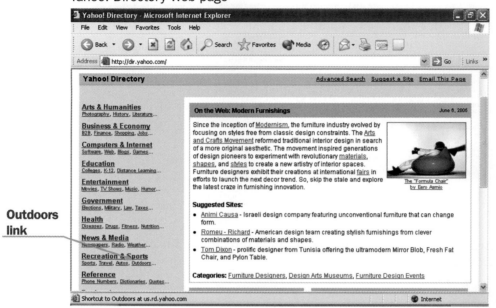

2. Click the **Outdoors** link below the Recreation & Sports category. This drills down one level and takes you to the Outdoors page, as shown in Figure 3-16. Now a list of Activities categories is displayed. Within this list is a link to Parks and Public Lands. Notice the number in parentheses to the right of each link. This is the number of links in that category.

FIGURE 3-16
Yahoo! Directory—Outdoors Web page

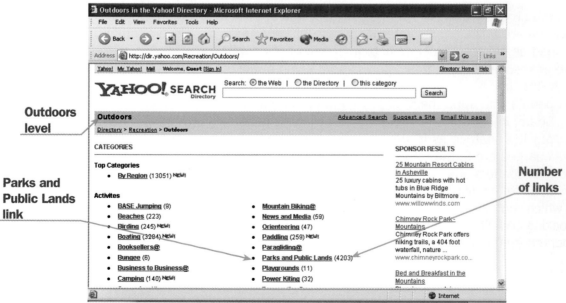

STEP-BY-STEP 3.5 Continued

3. Remember that you are looking for the Smoky Mountains National Park, so click **Parks and Public Lands** to move to the next level—the Parks and Public Lands page. You have moved down one level where all of the categories relate to parks and public lands. The United States is one of the top categories. Click **United States** to move down to the next level—Parks and Public Lands>United States. See Figure 3-17.

FIGURE 3-17
Yahoo! Directory—Parks and Public Lands>United States

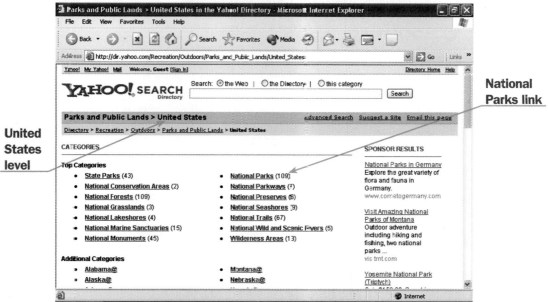

4. At the next level, you find that National Parks is one of your category selections. Click **National Parks** to move to the next level.

STEP-BY-STEP 3.5 Continued

5. You are getting closer to your goal—the National Parks Web page contains a link to the Great Smoky Mountains National Park. See Figure 3-18.

FIGURE 3-18
Yahoo! Directory—National Parks

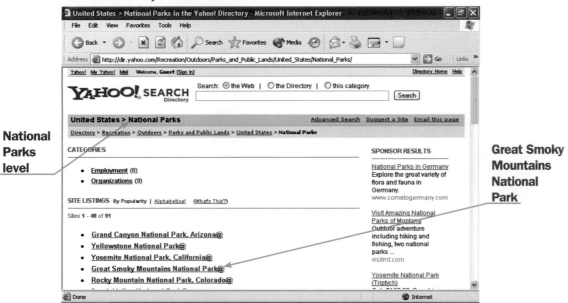

6. Click the **Great Smoky Mountains National Park** link to display the Web page and links to several related sites. Note that the Web page contains an option to sort the sites by popularity or alphabetically. See Figure 3-19. Click one or two of the links and review the content. When you are done, close your browser.

FIGURE 3-19
Yahoo! Directory—links to the Great Smoky Mountains National Park

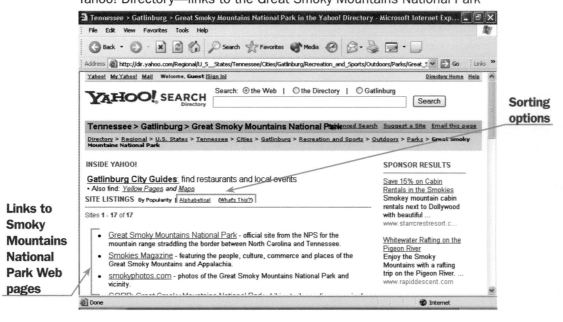

As you can see from this exercise, drilling down through a subject directory is a more guided approach than entering keywords into a search engine. Additional benefits of directories are as follows:

- They are easy to use.

- You are not searching the entire Web.

- The Web sites have been handpicked and evaluated.

- Most links include some type of description.

- They produce better quality hits on searches for common items.

See Table 3-2 for a list of some other popular subject directories.

TABLE 3-2
Some popular subject directories

DIRECTORY NAME	DESCRIPTION	PHRASE SEARCHING*
The Librarian's Index at *www.lii.org*	High quality; compiled by public librarians	Yes
About at *about.com*	Annotations created by guides and experts	Yes
Galaxy at *www.galaxy.com*	Good annotations; good quality	No
Infomine at *http://infomine.ucr.edu/*	Scholarly Internet resources	Yes
*Requires that the phrase be enclosed in double quotation marks		

The Invisible Web

Searching for information online can be deceptive. Search engines like Google and MSN make it appear easy. And, sometimes it is easy. You type your keywords, click the Search button, and hundreds or even thousands of links are displayed—links to Web sites that are part of the *visible* Web. The visible Web, however, is only one part of the Internet. A great deal more information is available freely in databases and waiting to be found. The problem, however, is that the spidering technology of the general search engines does not search every single database. These additional searchable databases are part of the *invisible* Web (also called the *Deep Web*). The content quality of the invisible Web is purported to be superior. One of the better invisible Web resources is *www.completeplanet.com*. This Web site contains links to over 70,000 searchable databases and specialty search engines. The ProFusion Web site at *www.profusion.com* also contains tools you can use to search the invisible Web.

As you learn more about Internet searching, keep in mind that no single organization indexes the Internet the way the Library of Congress catalogs books. So how many ways can you search? There are dozens of primary search engines and hundreds of specialty search engines. New ones are added on a continual basis. In many

Did You Know?

Some search engines, such as AltaVista, will translate your search results into another language.

instances, it is almost like looking for the needle in the haystack. With a little effort, however, you probably will find that special Web page that contains the information for which you are searching.

SUMMARY

In this lesson, you learned:

- Search engines and directories are two basic tools that you can use to find information on the Web.

- People assemble directories; search engines are automated.

- A search engine is a software program.

- Most search engines support keyword searches.

- Concept-based searching occurs when the search engine returns hits that relate to keywords.

- Stemming relates to the search engine's capability to find variations of a word.

- Meta tags are special tags embedded in a Web page; many search engines use the tags to create their indexes.

- Keywords describe the information you are trying to locate.

- Search engines contain a database of organized information.

- Some search engines use natural language.

- A search engine has three main parts: the search engine software, a spider that searches for keywords, and an index.

- Stop words, such as *www*, *but*, *or*, and so forth, are not indexed by many search engines.

- A search engine uses an algorithm to index Web sites.

- Specialized search engines focus on a particular topic.

- Multimedia search engines focus on video, animation, graphics, and music.

- Subject directories are organized by subject categories.

- Subject experts check the Web sites that are part of a subject directory's database.

- Use double quotation marks around a set of words for phrase searching.

- Use the plus and minus signs for inclusion and exclusion of words within a search.

- Boolean searching uses the three logical operators OR, AND, and NOT.

- The * symbol is used for wildcard searching.

- No single organization indexes the entire Internet.

VOCABULARY *Review*

Define the following terms:

Boolean logic	Keyword	Spider
Concept searching	Math symbols	Stemming
Database	MP3	Subject directories
Hits (Results)	Related search	Truncation
Index (Indexer)	Search engine	Usenet
Invisible Web (Deep Web)	Search engine math	Wildcard character

REVIEW *Questions*

MULTIPLE CHOICE

Select the best response for the following statements.

1. _____ occurs when the search engine includes other variations of the keyword.
   A. Concepts
   B. Stemming
   C. Truncation
   D. Natural language

2. The _____ is a search engine robot that roams the Internet looking for keywords.
   A. index
   B. searcher
   C. spider
   D. warthog

3. A(n) _____ is a collection of organized information.
   A. database
   B. stem
   C. indexer
   D. URL

4. If you were looking for video and music resources, you might use a _____ search engine.
   A. multimedia
   B. sports
   C. phrase
   D. spider

5. Searchable databases are part of the _____.
   A. index
   B. invisible Web
   C. subject directories
   D. stop words

TRUE/FALSE

Circle T if the statement is true or F if the statement is false.

T (F) 1. All search engines index all words in a Web page.

(T) F 2. Keywords describe the information you are trying to locate.

(T) F 3. Subject directories are organized by categories.

T (F) 4. The # symbol is the symbol used for a wildcard search.

T (F) 5. Boolean searches and math symbol searches are identical.

FILL IN THE BLANK

Complete the following sentences by writing the correct word or words in the blanks provided.

1. The ___*___ is a symbol for a wildcard character.

2. The Beaucomp Web site is a type of _searching in_ Web site.

3. Web pages for _local_ directories are reviewed by people.

4. _____ are the number of returns or hyperlinked Web site addresses displayed based on your keywords.

5. Google's special feature that finds local businesses and services is called _____.

PROJECTS

CROSS-CURRICULAR—MATHEMATICS

1. Use Google or another search engine of your choice. Use search engine math and math symbols to create searches for the following:
   A. Carnivals and circuses in Canada, but not in Vancouver
   B. Skateboard and roller skating parks in Florida

2. Use Boolean logic and the same search engine to search for the same topics as in 1A and 1B above.

3. Compare your findings and then prepare a report listing the similarities and differences between the two methods of searching.

CROSS-CURRICULAR—SCIENCE

Your instructor has assigned a research project. You are to select a type of insect and provide information about the life and habits of the insect. Create a "Search Strategy" form that your fellow classmates can use to search the Internet. Within the form, list possible search tools and ways in which to search. Include the Web site address for any suggested search engines or directory Web sites.

CROSS-CURRICULAR—SOCIAL STUDIES

One infamous question that most of us have heard throughout our lives is "Why did the chicken cross the road?" Use the search engine AskJeeves located at *www.aj.com* to find the answer to this question. How many links did you find? Prepare a report on your findings and present it to your class.

CROSS-CURRICULAR—LANGUAGE ARTS

Create a Boolean search on your favorite search engine to locate information about your two favorite bands or music groups. Prepare a one-page report on your findings. Include within the report: which search engine you used and why; how many sites you found; and how you were able to narrow the search.

 ## WEB PROJECT

You want to learn more about how the invisible Web works. Your instructor thinks this is a great idea and has asked you to prepare a report and share your findings with the class. Your report should include Web searching methodologies and Web-based resources.

 ## TEAMWORK PROJECT

Your teamwork project is to provide a detailed description of how MP3 technology works, how to download this music, what the copyright issues are for downloading music, what kind of MP3 hardware is available, and what type of player and encoder you would use. You and your team are to put together a two-page report containing this information and any other relevant information you might find. Include a list of all links you used as a reference source. A good place to start searching is *www.music.lycos.com/downloads*.

CRITICAL*Thinking*

Select a topic of your choice to research on the Web. Consider something original such as "What is utopia?" or "Who wrote the first opera?" Search for information using three different search engines. Use the same search techniques (keywords, Boolean operators, or related searches) for all three search engines. Create a table with a separate column for each search engine. Under the column headings, list the top 10 sites that the search engine locates. Determine which engine provided you with the highest-quality results.

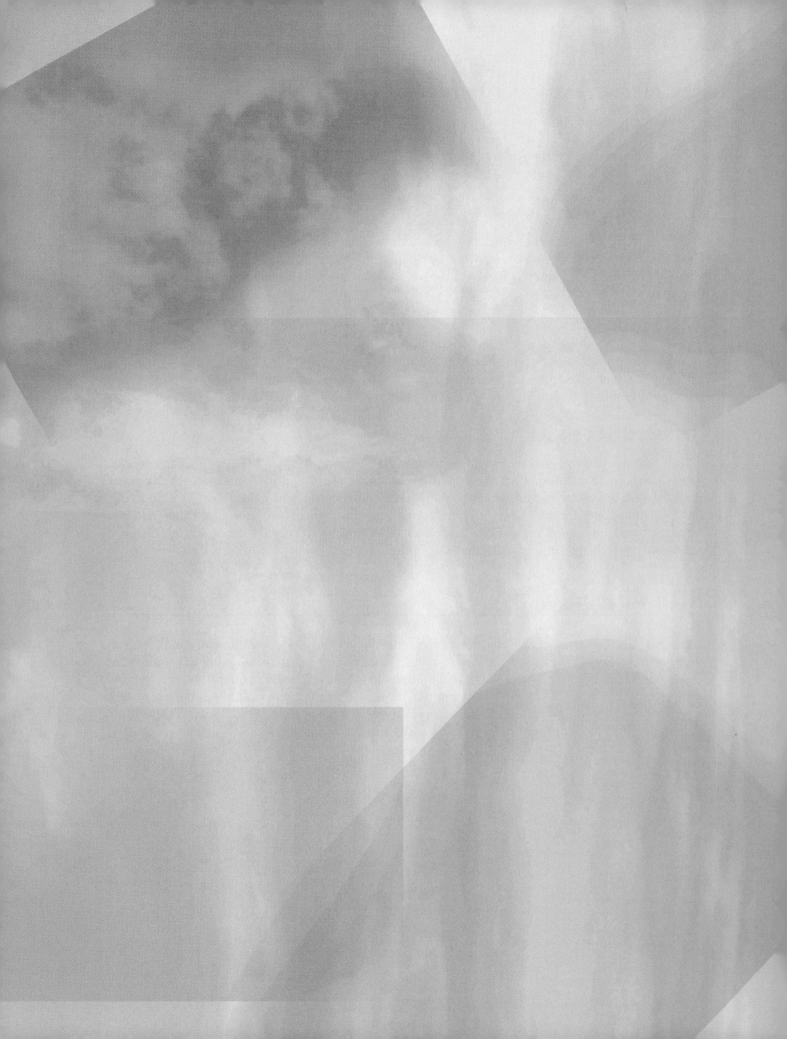

How a Computer Processes Data

With today's technology, a little knowledge about what is inside a computer can make you a more effective user and help you select the right computer for the job you need it to do. In this lesson, you learn how the CPU processes data and turns it into information. You also learn about some of the basic components contained on the computer's motherboard.

Computer Systems

We use computers for all kinds of tasks—to predict weather, to fly airplanes, to control traffic lights, to play games, to access the Internet, to send e-mail, and so on. You might wonder how a machine can do so many things.

To appreciate how a computer really operates requires knowledge of calculus, probability, and statistics—all of which are needed to understand physics and circuit analysis. Most of us, however, do not need this level of comprehension. Instead, we need a fundamental understanding. This lesson presents the fundamentals on how a computer operates.

Just about all computers, regardless of size, take raw data and change it into information. The procedure involves input, processing, output, and storage (IPOS). For example:

- You input data with some type of input device.

- The computer processes it to turn it into information.

- You output the information to some type of output device.

- You store it for later retrieval.

Input, output, and processing devices grouped together represent a *computer system*. In this lesson, we look at the components that the computer uses to process data. These components are contained within the system case. See Figure 4-1.

FIGURE 4-1
Computer system components

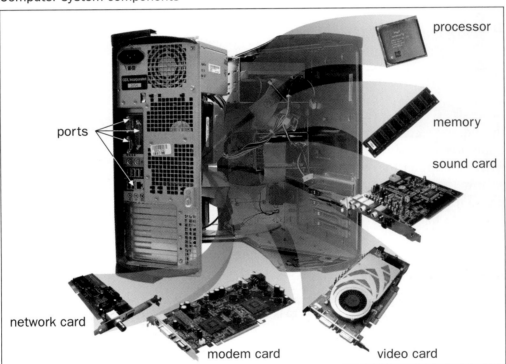

processor

ports

memory

sound card

network card

modem card

video card

System Components

The PC system case is the metal and plastic case that houses the main system components of the computer. Central to all of this is the *motherboard* or system board that mounts into the case. The motherboard is a circuit board that contains many integral components. A *circuit board* is simply a thin plate or board

Internet

The Computer History Museum has a wealth of information on computer history and development. You can find this Web site and a history timeline at *http://www.computerhistory. org/timeline/*.

that contains electronic components. See Figure 4-2. Some of the most important of these components are as follows:

■ The central processing unit

■ Memory

■ Basic controllers

■ Expansion ports and expansion slots

FIGURE 4-2
Motherboard

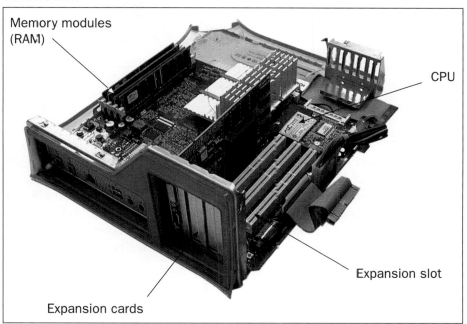

The Central Processing Unit

The *central processing unit (CPU)*, also called the microprocessor, the processor, or central processor, is the brains of the computer. The CPU is housed on a tiny silicon chip similar to that shown in Figure 4-3 on the next page. This chip contains millions of switches and pathways that help your computer make important decisions. The switches control the flow of the electricity as it travels across the miles of pathways. The CPU knows which switches to turn on and which to turn off because it receives its instructions from computer programs. Recall from Lesson 1 that programs are a set of special instructions, written by programmers, which control the activities of the computer. Programs also are known as software.

FIGURE 4-3
A microprocessor

The CPU has two primary sections: the arithmetic/logic unit and the control unit.

The Arithmetic/Logic Unit

The *arithmetic/logic unit (ALU)* performs arithmetic computations and logical operations. The arithmetic computations include addition, subtraction, multiplication, and division. The logical operations involve comparisons—asking the computer to determine if two numbers are equal or if one number is greater than or less than another number. These might seem like simple operations. However, by combining these operations, the ALU can execute complex tasks. For example, a video game uses arithmetic operations and comparisons to determine what appears on your screen.

The Control Unit

The *control unit* is the boss, so to speak, and coordinates all of the CPU's activities. Using programming instructions, it controls the flow of information through the processor by controlling what happens inside the processor.

We communicate with the computer through programming languages. You might have heard of programming languages called Java, COBOL, C++, or Visual Basic. These are just a few of the many languages we can use to give a computer instructions. For example, we might have a programming statement such as *Let X = 2 + 8*. With this statement, we are using a programming language to ask the computer to add 2 and 8 and assign the calculated value to X. However, when we input this instruction, something else has to happen. The computer does not understand our language. It understands only machine language, or *binary*, which is ones and zeros. This is where the control unit takes over.

The control unit reads and interprets the program instruction and changes the instruction into machine language. Recall that earlier we discussed the CPU and pathways and switches. It is through these pathways and the turning on and off of switches that the CPU represents the ones and zeros. When electricity is present, it represents a one. The absence of electricity represents a zero. After changing the instructions into machine language (binary), the control unit then sends out the necessary messages to execute the instructions.

To view an example of a binary number, complete Step-by-step 4.1.

S TEP-BY-STEP 4.1

1. Click the **Start** button on the taskbar, point to **All Programs** (or **Programs** in Windows 2000), point to **Accessories**, and then click **Calculator**. The Standard calculator is displayed (see Figure 4-4).

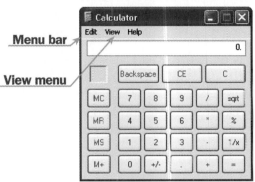

FIGURE 4-4
Windows Standard calculator

Menu bar

View menu

2. Click **View** on the menu bar and then choose **Scientific**. The Scientific calculator is displayed (see Figure 4-5).

FIGURE 4-5
Windows Scientific calculator

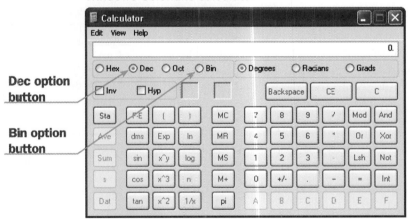

Dec option
button

Bin option
button

3. If necessary, click the **Dec** (decimal) option button. Enter **30** by clicking the calculator numeric buttons. Click the **Bin** (binary) option button. The number 11110 is displayed.

4. Click the **Dec** option button and convert the following decimal number to binary: **4545**. The number 10001110000010 is displayed. Convert **1112** to binary. The number 10001011000 is displayed.

5. What decimal number is equal to 101101 in the binary system? What decimal number is equal to 1111011? When you are finished, close the calculator by clicking the **Close** button in the upper-right corner.

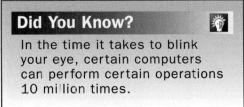

Did You Know?

In the time it takes to blink your eye, certain computers can perform certain operations 10 million times.

Memory

Memory also is found on the motherboard. Sometimes understanding memory can be confusing because it can mean different things to different people. The easiest way to understand memory is to think of it as either "short term" or "long term." When you want to store a file or information permanently, you use secondary storage devices such as the computer's hard disk drive or a floppy disk. You might think of this as long term.

Random Access Memory

You can think about the memory on the motherboard as short term. This type of memory is called *random access memory*, or *RAM*. RAM also is referred to as *main memory* and *primary memory*. You might have heard someone ask, "How much memory is in your computer?" Most likely, they are asking how much RAM is in your computer. The computer can read from and write to this type of memory. Data, information, and program instructions are stored temporarily within the CPU on a RAM chip or a set of RAM chips such as those shown in Figure 4-6.

FIGURE 4-6
RAM chips

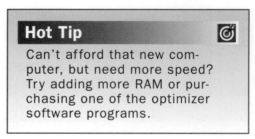

When the computer is turned off or if there is a loss of power, whatever is stored in the RAM memory chips disappears. Therefore, it is considered volatile. To understand how RAM works and how the computer processes data, think about how you would use a word-processing program to create an address list of your family and friends.

Hot Tip

Can't afford that new computer, but need more speed? Try adding more RAM or purchasing one of the optimizer software programs.

1. First, you start your word-processing program.
   The computer then loads your word-processing program instructions into RAM.

2. You input the names, addresses, and telephone numbers (your data). Your data also is stored in RAM.

3. Next, you give your word-processing program a command to process your data by arranging it in a special format. This command and your processed data, or information, are also now stored in RAM.

4. You then click the Print button. Instructions to print are transmitted to RAM and your document is sent to your printer.

5. Then, you click the Save button. Instructions to provide you with an opportunity to name and save your file are loaded into RAM. Once you save your file, you exit your word-processing program and turn off the computer.

6. All instructions, data, and information that you used to create your address are erased from RAM.

This process is known as the *instruction cycle* or *I-cycle* and the *execution cycle* or *E-cycle*. When the CPU receives an instruction to perform a specified task, the instruction cycle is the amount of time it takes to retrieve the instruction and complete the command. The execution cycle refers to the amount of time it takes the CPU to execute the instruction and store the results in RAM. Together, the instruction cycle and one or more execution cycles create a *machine cycle*.

For every instruction, a processor repeats a set of four basic operations, which comprise a machine cycle: (1) fetching, (2) decoding, (3) executing, and, if necessary, (4) storing (see Figure 4-7). *Fetching* is the process of obtaining a program instruction or data item from RAM. The term *decoding* refers to the process of translating the instruction into signals the computer can execute. *Executing* is the process of carrying out the commands. *Storing*, in this context, means writing the result to memory (not to a storage medium).

FIGURE 4-7
Processing cycle

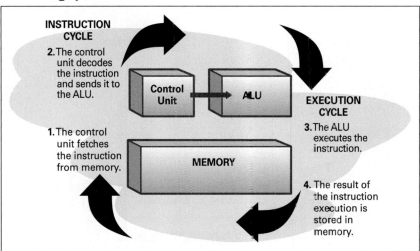

Machine cycles are measured in microseconds (millionths of a second), nanoseconds (billionths of a second), and even pico seconds (trillionths of a second) in some of the larger computers. The faster the machine cycle, the faster your computer processes data. The speed of the processor has a lot to do with the speed of the machine cycle. However, the amount of RAM in your computer also can help increase the speed with which the computer processes data. The more RAM you have, the faster the computer processes data. See Figure 4-8.

Did You Know?

If you have read computer ads lately, you most likely saw the abbreviations MHz (megahertz) and GHz (gigahertz). These speed specifications indicate the speed of the microprocessor clock—a timing device that specifies the speed for executing instructions.

FIGURE 4-8
Machine cycle

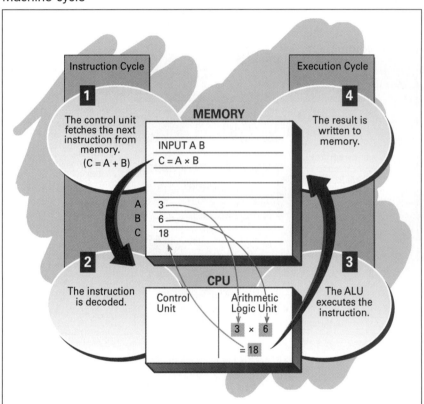

Read-Only Memory

Another type of memory you will find on the motherboard is *read-only memory*, or *ROM*. ROM chips are found throughout a computer system. The computer manufacturer uses this type of chip to store specific instructions that are needed for the computer operations. This type of memory is nonvolatile. These instructions remain on the chip even when the power is turned off. The more common of these is the *BIOS ROM*. The computer uses instructions contained on this chip to boot or start the system when you turn on your computer. A computer can read from a ROM chip, but cannot write or store data on the chip.

Did You Know?

Cache memory is another type of memory. This high-speed RAM is used to increase the speed of the processing cycle.

Basic Controllers

The motherboard also contains several controllers. A *controller* is a device that controls the transfer of data from the computer to a peripheral device and vice-versa. Examples of common *peripheral devices* are keyboards, monitors, printers, and the mouse. Controllers generally are stored on a single chip. When you purchase a computer, all the necessary controllers for the standard devices are contained on the motherboard. See Figure 4-2 shown on page 73 of this lesson.

Expansion Slots and Ports

Expansion slots are openings on the motherboard where an *expansion board*, also called an *adapter card*, can be inserted. Expansion boards enhance functions of a component of the system unit and/or provide connections through a port to peripheral devices. Expansion boards also are called expansion cards, add-ins, and add-ons. See Figure 4-9.

FIGURE 4-9
Expansion card

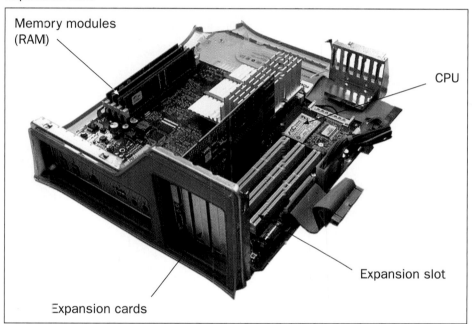

A *port* is the point at which a peripheral device attaches to a system unit so it can send data or receive information from the computer. We use devices such as *serial* and *parallel ports* to connect our peripheral devices to the computer. Serial devices transmit data one bit at a time. Parallel devices transfer eight bits at a time. A *bit* is represented by a zero or one. Typically, eight bits make one *byte*. Most computers traditionally have at least one parallel port and one serial port. In older computers, you likely will find a printer connected to a parallel port and perhaps a modem connected to a serial port. A *modem* is a device that allows one computer to talk to another.

The *Universal Serial Bus (USB)* is a newer device that supports data transfer rates of up to 480 million bits per second (Mbps). USB is replacing the standard serial and parallel ports on newer computers. Today's personal computers typically have four to eight USB ports either on the front or back of the system unit. Using a daisy-chain arrangement or a USB hub, you can use a single USB port to connect up to 127 peripheral devices. A *USB hub* is a device that plugs into a USB port and contains multiple USB ports into which cables from USB devices can be plugged.

USB also supports plug-and-play and hot plugging. *Plug-and-play* refers to the ability of a computer system to configure expansion boards and other devices automatically. *Hot plugging* is the ability to add and remove devices to a computer while the computer is running and have the operating system automatically recognize the change.

Another type of external bus is *FireWire*, also known as *IEEE 1394* and *IEEE 1394b*. The IEEE 1394 bus standard supports data transfer rates of up to 400 Mbps and can connect up to 63 external devices; IEEE 1394b provides speeds up to 3200 Mbps. Figure 4-10 shows an example of some of the more popular traditional ports and examples of FireWire and USB ports.

FIGURE 4-10
Computer ports

Technology Careers

PC SUPPORT SPECIALIST

The PC support specialist provides support for application software and related hardware via telephone and/or site visits to all workstation users.

As a PC support specialist, you need to be knowledgeable about current software and have good oral communication and organizational skills. You will be required to interact with all departments within the company and with users who have various skill levels ranging from novice to expert. You must be willing to learn other areas of Management Information Systems (MIS) such as networking, printer maintenance, and e-mail.

A bachelor's degree is preferred for most of these jobs; however, impressive experience also is accepted. Experience performing actual hands-on hardware and software upgrades is important.

In addition to the above described ports, you might find three additional special-purpose ports on various computing devices. These special-purpose ports are as follows:

SCSI—An abbreviation for *Small Computer System Interface*, SCSI (pronounced *skuzzy*) is a standard interface for connecting peripherals such as disk drives and printers.

IrDA—A wireless standard that allows data to be transferred between devices using infrared light instead of cables is called *IrDA*. Both the computer and the device must have an IrDA port, and the IrDA port on the device must align with the IrDA port on the computer (Figure 4-11).

Bluetooth—*Bluetooth* uses radio waves and provides wireless short-range communications of data and voice between both mobile and stationary devices. This technology does not require alignment; it is an alternative to IrDA.

IrDA and Bluetooth are discussed in more detail in Lesson 7.

FIGURE 4-11
Device showing IrDA port

IrDA port

Traditionally, ports have been located on the back of the system unit. With the introduction of portable devices, such as digital cameras and pocket PCs, many newer computers also include ports on the front of the system unit. This provides for easier access.

Windows provides several options to determine what hardware you have in your computer system. In Step-by-step 4.2, you learn how to view this information. When you view this information, most likely you will see abbreviations such as MB or GB. Table 4-1 defines these measurement terms.

TABLE 4-1
Measurement terms

TERM	ABBREVIATION	NUMBER OF BYTES
Kilobyte	K or K3	1,024 (approximately 1,000)
Megabyte	MB	1,048,576 (approximately 1 million)
Gigabyte	GB	1,073,741,824 (approximately 1 billion)
Terabyte	TB	1,099,511,627,776 (approximately 1 trillion)

Complete Step-by-step 4.2 to display information about your computer.

STEP-BY-STEP 4.2

1. Click **Start** on the taskbar, and then click **My Computer** (Windows XP). Or, right-click **My Computer** on the desktop and select **Properties** (Windows 2000). Windows 2000 users skip to Figure 4-13. The My Computer window appears, as shown in Figure 4-12.

FIGURE 4-12
My Computer window

2. Click **View system information** in the System Tasks pane. The System Properties dialog box appears. If necessary, click the **General** tab (see Figure (4-13). Most likely, your System Properties dialog box will display different system information than that in Figure 4-13.

FIGURE 4-13
System Properties dialog box

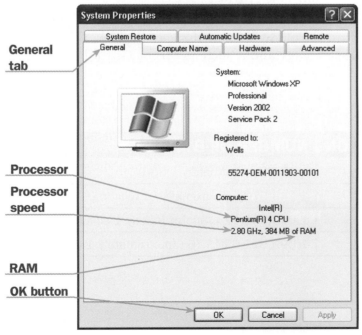

STEP-BY-STEP 4.2 Continued

3. What Microsoft Windows Version and Service Pack is listed for your computer? What processor does your computer contain? How much memory (RAM) is in your computer?

4. Click the **Computer Name** tab (Windows XP) or the **Network Identification** tab (Windows 2000). What description and name are assigned to your computer?

5. Click each of the other tabs and read the information contained on each tab. If directed by your instructor, use NotePad or your word-processing program and write an overview of the features contained within the System Properties dialog box.

6. Click the **OK** button to close the System Properties dialog box, and then close the My Computer window, if necessary.

Data Representation

Earlier in this lesson, you read about binary, and learned that a bit is either a zero or a one. You might wonder, though, exactly how the computer determines what combination of zeros and ones represent the letter *A* or the number *1*. It is really very simple. This is accomplished through standardized coding systems. The most popular system is called *ASCII* (pronounced AS-kee) and stands for *American Standard Code for Information Interchange*. There are other standard codes, but ASCII is the most widely used. It is used by nearly every type and brand of microcomputer and by many large computers.

As noted earlier in this lesson, eight bits or combinations of ones and zeros represent a letter such as *A*. Eight bits are called a *byte* or character, which is the basic unit of information. Each capital letter, lowercase letter, number, punctuation mark, and symbol has its own unique combination of ones and zeros.

Another type of standard code is called *Extended Binary Coded Decimal Interchange Code*, or *EBCDIC* (pronounced EB-si-dik). This code mostly is used in very large computers.

> **Net Tip**
>
> Find out more about the ASCII standard by visiting the Webopedia Web site located at *webopedia.internet.com/TERM/A/ASCII.html*. Type the URL exactly as shown here.

> **Did You Know?**
>
> Music and pictures are different from letters and numbers. For the computer to recognize and work with music and pictures, these objects must be digitized— converted to a digital format represented by 0s and 1s.

SUMMARY

In this lesson, you learned:

■ Just about all computers perform the same general functions: input, processing, output, and storage.

■ Input, output, and processing devices grouped together represent a computer system.

- The motherboard is the center of all processing.

- The motherboard contains the CPU, memory, and basic controllers for the system. It also contains ports and expansion slots.

- The central processing unit is the brains of the computer.

- The computer is given instructions through computer programs.

- The CPU has two main sections—the arithmetic/logic unit (ALU) and the control unit. All calculations and comparisons take place in the ALU. The control unit coordinates the CPU activities.

- The motherboard contains different types of memory.

- The machine cycle is made up of the instruction cycle and the execution cycle.

- Random access memory is volatile and is used to store instructions, data, and information temporarily.

- Read-only memory is nonvolatile and is used to store permanent instructions needed for computer operations.

- A controller is used to control the transfer of data between the computer and peripheral devices.

- Expansion slots contain expansion boards. Expansion boards are used to connect specialized peripheral devices or to add more memory to the computer.

- Peripheral devices are connected to the computer through serial and parallel ports.

- The Universal Serial Bus is a newer standard expected to replace serial and parallel ports.

- FireWire is a type of external bus that can connect up to 63 external devices.

- SCSI, IrDA, and Bluetooth are special-purpose ports.

- The ASCII and EBCDIC codes are standard codes used to represent the alphabet, numbers, symbols, and punctuation marks.

VOCABULARY *Review*

Define the following terms:

Arithmetic/logic unit (ALU)	Controller	Modem
Bit	Execution cycle (E-cycle)	Motherboard
Byte	Expansion slot	Port
Cache memory	FireWire	Random access
Central processing unit (CPU)	Instruction cycle (I-cycle)	memory (RAM)
Computer system	Machine cycle	Read-only memory (ROM)
Control unit	Memory	Universal Serial Bus (USB)

REVIEW *Questions*

MULTIPLE CHOICE

Select the best response for the following statements.

1. Eight _____ make one character.
   - A. characters
   - B. bits
   - C. bytes
   - D. codes

2. _____ is a special port that uses radio waves.
   - A. SCSI
   - B. IrDA
   - C. FireWire
   - D. Bluetooth

3. The _____ is considered the brains of the computer.
   - A. program
   - B. ALU
   - C. CPU
   - D. control unit

4. Random access memory is _____.
   - A. permanent
   - B. volatile
   - C. nonvolatile
   - D. the same as ROM

5. A printer would be considered a(n) _____.
   - A. controller
   - B. peripheral device
   - C. input device
   - D. USB

TRUE/FALSE

Circle T if the statement is true or F if the statement is false.

T   F   1. You would most likely use a serial port to connect a modem to your computer.

T   F   2. The EBCDIC code is the most widely used standardized coding system.

T   F   3. A bit has eight bytes.

T   F   4. The two primary sections of the CPU are the ALU and the control unit.

T   F   5. A computer understands only machine language.

FILL IN THE BLANK

Complete the following sentences by writing the correct word or words in the blanks provided.

1. You can think of RAM as _____ -term memory.

2. The instruction cycle and the execution cycle create a(n) _____ cycle.

3. The _____ the machine cycle, the faster your computer.

4. A(n) _____ is a board that contains electronic components.

5. You would add memory to a computer by inserting it into a(n) _____ slot.

PROJECTS

CROSS-CURRICULAR—MATHEMATICS

Collect three or four computer ads from your local Sunday paper. Using either a spreadsheet program or paper and pencil, create a comparison table. Include the following elements in your table: processor speed, amount of memory, number of expansion slots, and price. Based on your comparisons, write a short paragraph explaining which computer you would purchase and why.

CROSS-CURRICULAR—SCIENCE

If possible, find a computer system with the case removed. Examine the motherboard and the components connected to the motherboard. Locate and count the number of available expansion slots. Locate the RAM chips. See if you can find the CPU. Can you see the chip itself? Create a drawing of the system and label as many of the components as you can.

CROSS-CURRICULAR—SOCIAL STUDIES

The "digital divide theory" has been described as the gap between those people and communities who can access and make effective use of information technology and those who cannot. Research the digital divide theory and create a report expressing your opinion about this topic. Do you feel there is a digital divide? Explain why or why not.

CROSS-CURRICULAR—LANGUAGE ARTS

Using the Internet or other resources, see what you can find about the history of computers. See if you can find the answers to the following questions: (1) What was the name of the first commercially available electronic digital computer? (2) In what year was the IBM PC first introduced? (3) What software sent Bill Gates on his way to becoming one of the richest men in the world? (4) In what year did Apple introduce the Macintosh computer? Use your word-processing program to answer each of these questions and/or to provide some additional historical facts.

 WEB PROJECT

Launch your Web browser and type the following URL: *www.ask.com.*

When the Web site is displayed, ask Jeeves "Who invented the microprocessor?" and click **Search**. Jeeves will provide several answers for you. Choose the most appropriate answer, and click the link. This takes you to the Web site where you can find the answer to your question. Use a presentation program (such as Microsoft PowerPoint) to create a presentation on what you found at this Web site. Include the name of and an overview of the person who developed the first transistor. Add two or three more slides to your presentation with information you found at this Web site. Share your presentation with your friends or other students.

 TEAMWORK PROJECT

Some people say you should leave your computer on at all times—that turning the computer on and off creates stress on the components. Others argue that computers use a lot of energy, and that computers should be turned off when not in use. Your computer operating system, however, includes power-management settings. Your instructor has requested that you and your team investigate these options. Use Windows Help and Support and prepare a report describing these power-management options. Describe the differences between standby mode and hibernation and how to activate and deactivate these settings.

CRITICAL *Thinking*

Think about what you have read in this lesson. Your goal is to purchase a computer. Where would you shop—online, local computer dealer, retail store, or other? What type of processor would you purchase? How much memory would you need? Would you purchase a desktop, notebook, or other type of computer? Write a one-page report answering the above questions and outlining your thoughts about what other technologies you would include. Explain why you made these selections.

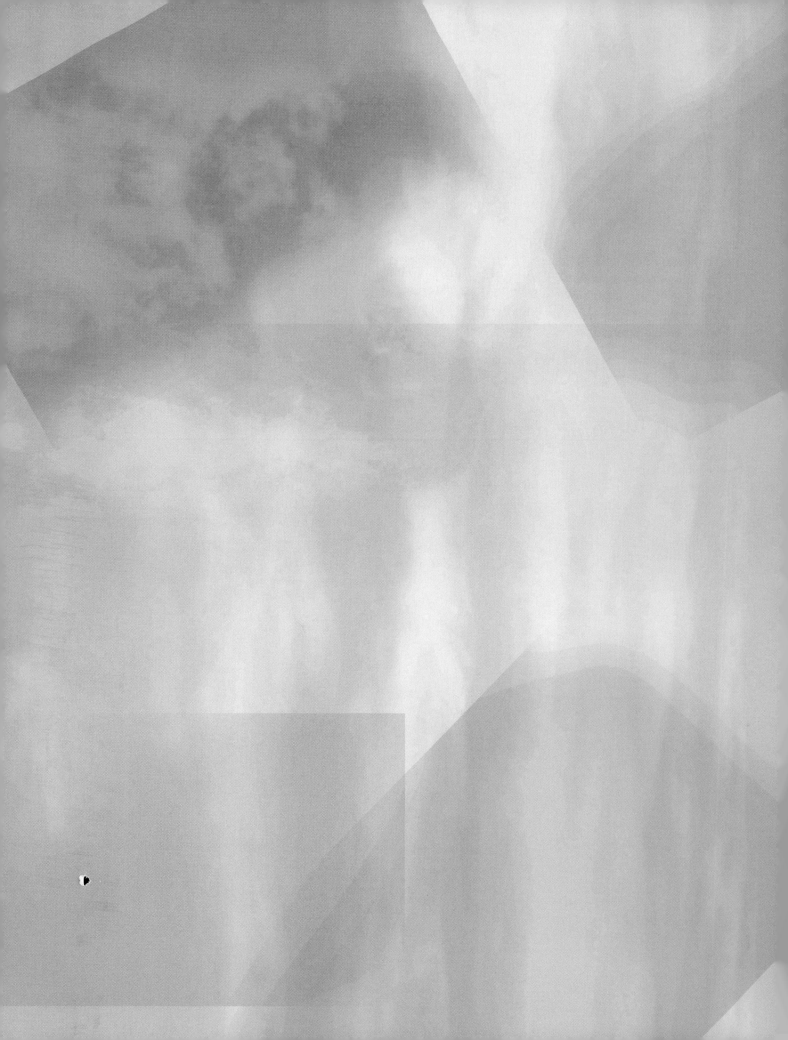

INPUT, OUTPUT, AND STORAGE

OBJECTIVES

Upon completion of this lesson, you should be able to:

- Identify and describe the most common input devices.

- Identify and describe the most common output devices.

- Identify and describe storage devices.

- Identify and describe how input and output devices are connected to the computer.

Estimated Time: 3 hours

VOCABULARY

Audio input

Biometrics

Floppy disk

Hard disk

Inkjet printer

Input

Input devices

Keyboard

Laser printer

Monitor

Mouse

Optical storage

Output

Output devices

Pointing device

Solid-state storage

Video input

We can agree that when it comes to processing data, it is the computer that does all of the work! However, it needs help. *Input*, which is data or instructions, must be entered into the computer. After the data is entered and processed, it has to be "presented" to the user. We use special devices for these tasks and refer to them as input and output devices.

Input devices enable you to input data and commands into the computer, and *output devices* enable the computer to give you the results of the processed data. Some devices perform both input and output functions. The modem is an example. It is used to send (output) and receive (input) messages over a telephone line.

Input Devices

The type of input device used is determined by the task to be completed. An input device can be as simple as the keyboard or as sophisticated as those used for specialized applications such as voice or retinal recognition.

Keyboard

The *keyboard* is the most commonly used input device for entering numeric and alphabetic data into a computer. If you are going to use the computer efficiently, it is important that you learn to type. Most of the keyboards used with desktop computers are enhanced. An enhanced keyboard has 12 function keys along the top, two ALT keys, two CTRL keys, and a set of directional/arrow keys between the typing area and the numeric keypad.

Some keyboards, such as the one shown in Figure 5-1, have multimedia hot keys that enable you to access e-mail

> ### Internet
>
> Many companies specialize in developing ergonomic keyboards that minimize the stress caused by keying data for long periods of time. Use a search engine such as *www.Ask.com* or *www.Dogpile.com* to locate several of these companies and see the types of products they produce.

and the Internet, adjust speaker volume, and have other features such as a *Zoom Slider.* This device makes it easy to zoom in for a closer look at documents, spreadsheets, pictures, maps, and Web pages.

FIGURE 5-1
Enhanced keyboard with Zoom Slider

Zoom slider

Multimedia hot keys

Not all keyboards, however, are traditional. Some other popular types of keyboards are as follows:

- *Ergonomic:* a keyboard designed to provide users with more natural, comfortable hand, wrist, and arm positions

- *Cordless:* a battery-powered keyboard that transmits data using wireless technology

- *Specialized:* a keyboard with specialized keys that represent items such as those used in fast-food restaurants

> ### Hot Tip
>
> Need more space on your desk? Then consider the Nearly Indestructible Keyboard (NIK)—it is flexible, can be rolled up and put into a briefcase, and even washed with soap and water or a spray cleaner (*http://www. dovecoteglobal.com/nik.html*).

■ *Security:* a keyboard that provides security features such as a biometric fingerprint reader and magnetic stripe and smartcard readers (see Figure 5-2A)

■ *Foldable:* an easily transported keyboard primarily used with PDA and pocket PC-type devices; it has a soft touch and is water resistant (see Figure 5-2B)

FIGURE 5-2
(A) Keyboard with fingerprint reader (B) Foldable keyboard

A.
B.

Pointing Devices

A *pointing device* is an input device that allows a user to position the *pointer* on the screen. The pointer can have several shapes, but the most common is an arrow. You use a pointing device to move the pointer, and to select objects, such as text or graphics, and click buttons, icons, menu items, and links. The following sections discuss several different pointing devices.

Mouse

The *mouse* is the most commonly used pointing device for personal computers. It moves around on a flat surface and controls the pointer on the screen. The mouse fits conveniently in the palm of your hand. A description of four types of mice follows:

■ *Mechanical:* This type of mouse has a ball located on the bottom that rolls around on a flat surface as the mouse is moved. Sensors inside the mouse determine the direction and distance of the movement. A mouse pad generally is used with a mechanical mouse.

■ *Optomechanical:* This mouse is the same as a mechanical mouse, but uses optical sensors to detect motion of the ball.

■ *Optical:* An optical mouse (see Figure 5-3A) uses a laser to detect the mouse's movement. Optical mice have no mechanical moving parts. They respond more quickly and precisely than mechanical and optomechanical mice.

■ *Cordless:* A cordless mouse (see Figure 5-3B) is a battery-powered device that relies on infrared or radio waves to communicate with the computer.

FIGURE 5-3
(A) Optical mouse (B) Cordless mouse and receiver

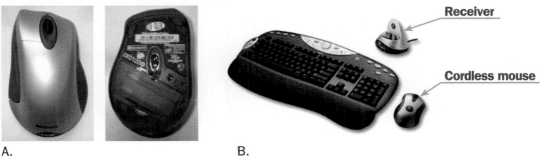

A.
B.

Most of these devices have two or three buttons; some have a wheel. You use the left button for most mouse operations. Generally, clicking the right button displays a context menu. After you place the on-screen pointer where you want it, press a button on the mouse. This will cause some type of action to take place in the computer; the type of action depends on the program. Use the wheel to scroll or zoom a page.

You use the mouse to accomplish the following techniques:

■ *Pointing:* placing the on-screen pointer at a designated location

■ *Clicking:* pressing and releasing the mouse button

■ *Dragging:* pressing down the mouse button and moving the mouse while continuing to hold down the button

■ *Double-clicking:* pressing and releasing the mouse button two times in rapid succession

■ *Right-clicking:* pressing the right mouse button

Except for the cordless mouse, mice connect to personal computers through a port. A cordless mouse communicates through a receiver connected to a port. Ports were discussed in Lesson 4.

Trackball

The *trackball* (see Figure 5-4) is a pointing device that works like a mechanical mouse turned upside down; the ball is on top of the device. You use your thumb and fingers to operate the ball, thus controlling the pointer on the screen. A trackball is a stationary device and is a good alternative to the mouse when the user has limited desktop space.

FIGURE 5-4
Trackball

Joystick and Wheel

The joystick and wheel also are pointing devices. Joysticks and wheels, such as the ones shown in Figure 5-5 on the next page, most often are used for games. The *joystick* consists of a plastic or metal rod mounted on a base. You can move the rod in any direction. Some joysticks have switches or buttons that can input data in an on/off response. A *wheel* is a steering-wheel type of device used to simulate driving a vehicle. Most wheels also include foot pedals, used for braking and acceleration actions.

FIGURE 5-5
Joystick and wheel

Pointing Stick

Many notebook computers contain a *pointing stick*—a pressure-sensitive device that looks like a pencil eraser. It is located on the keyboard, generally between the G, H, and B keys (see Figure 5-6). It is moved with the forefinger, while the thumb is used to press related keys. In a confined space, a lot of people find a pointing stick more convenient than a mouse. IBM popularized this device by introducing the TrackPoint on its ThinkPad notebooks.

FIGURE 5-6
Pointing stick

Other Input Devices

A variety of other input devices also are available, most of which are used for special applications. The following section describes these input devices.

Graphics Tablet

A *graphics tablet*, also called a digitizing table, is a flat drawing surface on which the user can draw figures or write something freehand. Architects, engineers, artists, mapmakers, and designers use these tablets to create precise drawings. After the drawing is created and saved, it can be manipulated like a regular graphic.

Touch Display Screen

The *touch display screen*, as shown in Figure 5-7, is a special screen with pictures or shapes. You use your fingers to "point" to the desired object to make a selection. You can find these screens in many public establishments such as airports, hotels, banks, libraries, delivery services, and fast-food restaurants. Many mobile devices (discussed in Lesson 1) have touch screens.

FIGURE 5-7
Retail stores often use touch screens

Stylus

A *stylus* and *digital pen* (see Figure 5-8) are pen-like writing instruments. These devices allow the user to input information by writing on a PDA or other mobile devices or to use the pen as a pointer.

FIGURE 5-8
Stylus for PDA

Audio Input

Audio input is the process of inputting sound into the computer. This could include speech, sound effects, and music. Audio input devices include microphones, CD/DVD players, radios, and other devices such as electronic keyboards.

Voice input is a category of audio input. *Voice recognition* devices are used to "speak"–commands into the computer and to enter text. These devices usually are microphones. The computer must have some type of voice recognition software installed before you can use a voice recognition device. Directory assistance is a type of voice recognition technology. Voice recognition technology also has made it possible for disabled persons to command wheelchairs and other objects that make them more mobile.

Touchpad

A *touchpad* is an input device commonly used in laptop computers. To move the pointer, slide your fingertip across the surface of the pad. To imitate mouse operations, such as clicking, tap or double-tap the surface of the touchpad.

Scanners

Scanners are devices that can change images into codes for input to the computer. Various sizes and types of scanners exist, including the following:

■ *Image scanners:* These devices convert images into an electronic form that can be stored in a computer's memory. The image then can be manipulated.

■ *Bar code scanners:* This type of scanner reads bar lines that are printed on products (for example, in a grocery store or department store). See Figure 5-9.

■ *Magnetic scanners:* These devices read encoded information on the back of credit cards. The magnetic strip on the back of the cards contains the encoded user's account number.

■ *Optical character recognition (OCR)* and *Optical Mark Recognition (OMR):* These devices use a light source to read characters, marks, and codes; the data then is converted into digital data. Banks use OCR technology to scan checks. Commonly known as Scantrons, schools and other organizations use OMR for testing purposes.

FIGURE 5-9
Bar code scanners are used to read prices

Digital Cameras

The pictures taken with a *digital camera* are stored digitally and then transferred to the computer's memory. Digital cameras use a variety of mobile storage media to store the images, including floppy disk, flash memory card, memory stick, USB, and mini-disc. The *Solid-State Storage Media* section later in this lesson discusses digital cameras and other solid-state storage devices. After the pictures are transferred to the computer, they can be viewed quickly and any imperfections can be edited with photo-editing software.

Video Input

Video input is the process of capturing full-motion images with a type of video camera and then saving the video on a storage medium such as a hard drive, CD, or DVD. After the video is saved, you can view and edit it. Some example video input devices are as follows:

- A digital video (DV) camera records video as digital signals; some cameras also capture still images. Some are just a little larger than a credit card (see Figure 5-10). A PC video camera is a type of digital video camera that allows the user to send live images over the Internet, make video telephone calls, and send e-mail messages with video attachments.

- A Web camera (or Webcam) is a real-time camera that displays images through the World Wide Web.

FIGURE 5-10
Miniaturized digital video camera

Biometric Input

Consider the following scenario: You are going on a two-week vacation to Tahiti and Bora Bora—you are packed and ready to go, but you do not need a wallet or credit cards. You use your fingerprint as an input device to pay for all of your expenses.

In information technology, *biometrics* is an authentication technique using automated methods of recognizing a person based on a physiological or behavioral characteristic. Biometric devices consist of a reader or scanning device, and software that converts the scanned information into a digital format. The scanned information then is compared to a database of stored biometric data.

Several types of biometric identification techniques exist. Some of the more common are the fingerprint, face, handwriting, and voice. Other less common techniques are retina (analysis of the capillary vessels located at the back of the eye), iris (analysis of the colored ring surrounding the eye's pupil), hand geometry (analysis of the shape of the hand and length of the fingers), and vein (analysis of pattern of veins on the back of the hand and the wrist).

The process or the way in which biometric technology works, however, basically is the same for all identification techniques:

■ *Enrollment:* The user enrolls in the system by establishing a baseline measurement for comparison.

■ *Submission:* The user presents biological proof of his or her identify to the capture system.

■ *Verification:* The system compares the submitted sample with the stored sample.

Privacy and civil liberties advocates, however, are concerned about the widespread adoption of biometric systems. They argue that using biometric data, third parties can access the data of an individual without their consent, and link it to other information, resulting in secondary uses of the information. This erodes the individual's personal control over the uses of his or her information. On the other hand, biometrics also can be applied to private security. For example, several companies now offer biometric computer keyboards and USB Flash drives with fingerprint authentication that can be used for personal applications (see Figure 5-11). Flash drives are discussed later in this lesson.

FIGURE 5-11
A biometric USB Flash drive

Fingerprint reader

S TEP-BY-STEP 5.1

1. Click the **Start** button on the taskbar, and then click **Control Panel** (Figure 5-12). (If you are using Windows 2000, point to **Settings** and then click **Control Panel**.) If the Control Panel appears in a view different from that shown in Figure 5-12, click **View** on the menu bar, and then click **Icons**. (If you are using Windows 2000, click **Large Icons**.) Most likely the Control Panel on your computer will display different devices.

FIGURE 5-12
Windows XP Control Panel

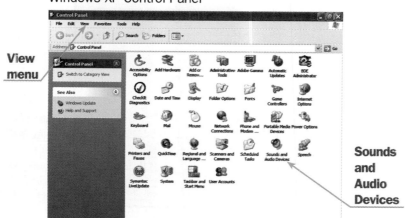

STEP-BY-STEP 5.1 Continued

2. Double-click **Sounds and Audio Devices**. (In Windows 2000, double-click **Sounds and Multimedia**.) The Sounds and Audio Devices Properties dialog box appears. Click the **Sounds** tab. Sounds for Program events (Sound Events in Windows 2000) are listed, as shown in Figure 5-13.

FIGURE 5-13
Sounds tab

3. Click **Asterisk** in the Program events list. Next, click the arrow to the right of the Windows XP Error textbox (see Figure 5-14) to listen to the sound. (In Windows 2000, click the arrow next to **chord.wav**.)

FIGURE 5-14
Listening to the Asterisk sound

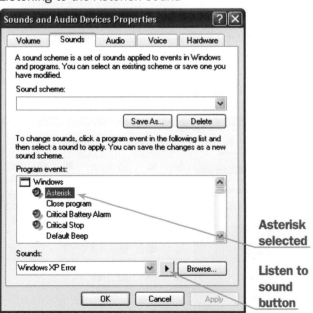

STEP-BY-STEP 5.1 Continued

4. Scroll through the list of Program events (Sound Events in Windows 2000) and listen to various sounds. When you are finished, click the **OK** button to close the Sounds and Audio Devices Properties dialog box, and then close the Control Panel. If instructed to do so, write a paragraph on what you learned about the sound options on your computer.

Storage Devices

As data is entered in the computer and processed, it is stored in RAM (temporary memory). If you want to keep a permanent copy of the data, you must store it on some type of storage medium. The more popular types of storage medium technology are USB drives, hard disk, CD and DVD, solid-state storage, and tape. Storage devices are categorized by the method they use to store data. The categories include magnetic technology, optical technology, and solid-state storage media.

Magnetic Storage Devices

Magnetic storage devices use oxide-coated plastic storage media called Mylar. As the disk rotates in the computer, an electromagnetic read/write head stores or retrieves data in circles called *tracks*. The number of tracks on a disk varies with the type of disk. The tracks are numbered from the outside to the inside. As data is stored on the disk, it is stored on a numbered track. Each track is labeled and the location is kept in a special log on the disk called a *file allocation table* (*FAT*).

The most common types of magnetic storage medium are floppy disk, Zip disk, hard drives, and magnetic tape.

Floppy Disk

A *floppy disk,* usually just called a disk, is a flat circle of iron oxide-coated plastic enclosed in a hard plastic case. Most floppy disks are 3½ inches, although you might see other sizes. They have a capacity to hold 1.44 MB or more of data (see Figure 5-15). To protect unwanted data from being added to or removed from a disk, write protection is provided. To write-protect a disk, open the write protect window on the disk. Since the introduction of USB drives and solid-state storage media, floppy disks are not as widely used.

FIGURE 5-15
The parts of a floppy disk

Zip Disk

A Zip disk is capable of holding a large amount of data. Even though they are the size of a 3½-inch floppy disk, they can hold as much as 1 GB of data—as much as can be stored on 700 floppy disks! See Figure 5-16.

FIGURE 5-16
Zip disk

Hard Disk

Most *hard disks* (also called hard disk drives) are used to store data inside the computer, although removable hard disks also are available. They provide two advantages: speed and capacity. Accessing data is faster and the amount of data that can be stored is much larger than what can be stored on a floppy disk. The size of the hard drive is measured in megabytes or giga-bytes and can have several disks. See Figure 5-17.

FIGURE 5-17
A hard drive

Magnetic Tape

Companies and other organizations use *magnetic tape* mostly for making backup copies of large volumes of data. This is a very slow process and therefore is not used for regularly saving data. The tape can be used to replace data that might have been lost from the hard drive.

Optical Storage Devices

Optical storage devices use laser technology to read and write data on silver platters (see Figure 5-18). The term *disc* is used for optical media. CDs and DVDs are a type of optical storage media. Most computers today come equipped with some type of optical storage—a CD drive or a DVD drive. The technology for CDs and DVDs is similar, but storage capacities are quite different and several variations exist. These storage devices come in several formats, as follows:

FIGURE 5-18
A laser reads data on a CD or DVD

- *CD-DA:* The Compact Disc Digital Audio format also is known as an audio CD; it is the industry-wide standard for music publishing and distribution.

- *CD-R:* The Compact Disc Recordable format makes it possible for you to create your own compact discs that can be read by any CD-ROM drive. After information is written to this type of disc, it cannot be changed.

- *CD-ROM:* The Compact Disc Read-Only Memory format can store up to 680 MB. This is the equivalent of about 450 floppy disks! You can read data from the CD; you cannot store data on a CD unless you are using a writable CD.

- *CD-RW:* The Compact Disc Read Writable is a type of compact disc that enables you to write onto it multiple times. Not all CD players can read CD-RWs.

- *DVD-ROM:* The Digital Versatile Disc Read Only Memory is a read-only DVD format commonly used for distribution of movies and computer games; its capacity ranges from 4.7GB to 17GB.

- *DVD-R:* The Digital Versatile Disc Recordable is similar to the CD-R except it has a much larger capacity; after information is written to this type of disc, it cannot be changed.

> **Did You Know?**
>
> DVD also is called Digital Video Disc and is backward-compatible with CD-ROMs.

- *DVD-RW:* The Digital Versatile Disc Read Writable stores data using technology similar to that of a CD-RW, but with a much larger capacity.

- *PhotoCD:* The PhotoCD is used to store digitized photographic images on a CD. The photos stored on these discs can be uploaded into the computer and used in other documents.

Solid-State Storage Media

Solid-state storage is a nonvolatile, removable medium that uses integrated circuits. The main advantage of this type of storage medium is that everything is processed electronically, and it contains no mechanical parts. Several types of solid-state storage are available. Miniature mobile media, for example, are popular solid-state storage devices for cameras, PDAs, music players, and other such electronics. Figure 5-19 contains an assortment of miniature mobile media, most of which are no larger than a postage stamp.

FIGURE 5-19
Miniature mobile storage media

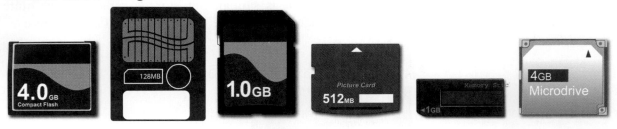

Another popular solid-state storage medium is the *USB Flash drive*. This small removable data storage device comes in a variety of configurations, such as those shown in Figure 5-20. It uses a USB connector to connect to your computer's USB port or other electronic device. Flash drives also are known by other names such as a keydrive, thumb drive, jump drive, USB flash memory drive, and USB stick.

FIGURE 5-20
Examples of a USB Flash drive

Caring for Storage Media

Removable storage media require special care if the data stored is to remain undamaged. Here are some safeguards that should be taken:

- Keep away from magnetic fields such as those contained in televisions and computer monitors (magnetic media).

- Avoid extreme temperatures.

- Remove media from drives and store them properly when not in use.

- When handling CD-ROMs and other optical discs, hold them at the edges.

- Never try to remove the media from a drive when the drive indicator light is on.

- Keep disks in a sturdy case when transporting.

Output Devices

Output is data that has been processed into a useful format. Examples of output are printed text, spoken words, music, pictures, video, or graphics. The most common output devices are monitors and printers. Output devices display information.

 Ethics in Technology

COMPUTER VIRUSES

The word "virus" can put fear into anyone who uses the Internet or exchanges disks. How can such a small word cause such fear? It is because a virus can cause tremendous damage to your computer files!

A virus is a computer program that is written intentionally to attach itself to other programs or disk boot sectors and duplicates itself whenever those programs are executed or the infected disks are accessed. A virus can wipe out all of the files that are on your computer.

Viruses can sit on your computer for weeks or months and not cause any damage until a predetermined date or time code is activated. Not all viruses cause damage. Some are just pranks; maybe your desktop will display some silly message. Viruses are created by persons who are impressed with the power they possess because of their expertise in the area of computers; sometimes they create them just for fun.

To protect your computer from virus damage, install an antivirus software program on your computer and keep it running at all times so that it can continuously scan for viruses.

Monitors

Desktop computers typically use a *monitor* as their display device. The screen is part of the monitor, which also includes the housing for its electrical components. Screen output is called *soft copy* because it is temporary.

Computer monitors come in many varieties. The *cathode ray tube* (**CRT**) was one of the earliest types of monitors. This type of monitor is similar to a standard television and can be either monochrome or color. A monochrome monitor screen has a one-color display. It could be white, green, or amber. Color monitors display thousands of colors. Most of today's monitors are color. CRT monitors are available in various sizes, with the more common being 17-, 19-, and 21-inch (see Figure 5-21A).

Flat-panel monitors come in two varieties: liquid crystal display (LCD) and gas plasma. Both types of monitors are more expensive than CRT monitors. They take up less space, however, and are much lighter in weight.

LCD panels (see Figure 5-21B) produce an image by manipulating light within a layer of liquid crystal cells. Until recently, LCD panels were used primarily on notebook computers and other mobile devices such as cell phones and PDAs. In 1997, several manufacturers started producing full-size LCD panels as alternatives to CRT monitors.

Gas plasma (see Figure 5-21C) technology consists of a tiny amount of gas that is activated by an electrical charge. The gas illuminates miniature colored fluorescent lights arranged in a panel-like screen. These monitors have a brilliant color display and are available in sizes up to 60 inches or more.

FIGURE 5-21
(A) CRT (B) LCD display (C) Gas plasma display

A.   B.   C.

Printers

Printers are used to produce a paper or hard copy of the processing results. Several types of printers are available, with tremendous differences in speed, print quality, price, and special features.

When selecting a printer, consider the following features:

■ *Speed:* Printer speed is measured in pages per minute (ppm). The number of pages a printer can print per minute varies for text and for graphics. Graphics print more slowly than regular text.

■ *Print quality:* Print quality is measured in dots per inch (dpi). The more dpi, the higher the resolution or print quality.

■ *Price:* The price includes the original cost of the printer as well as what it costs to maintain the printer. A good-quality printer can be purchased very inexpensively; a high-output system can cost thousands of dollars. The ink cartridges and toners need to be replaced periodically.

The three more popular types of printers are laser, ink jet, and dot matrix. Printers are classified as either impact or nonimpact. *Impact printers* use a mechanism that actually strikes the paper to form letters and images. Dot matrix printers are impact printers. *Nonimpact printers* form characters without striking the paper. Laser printers and ink jet printers are examples of nonimpact printers.

Laser Printers

A *laser printer* produces images using the same technology as copier machines. The image is made with a powder substance called toner. A laser printer produces high-quality output. The cost of a laser printer has come down substantially in the last two years or so. Color laser printers, however, are quite expensive, some costing thousands of dollars. See Figure 5-22.

FIGURE 5-22
How a laser printer works

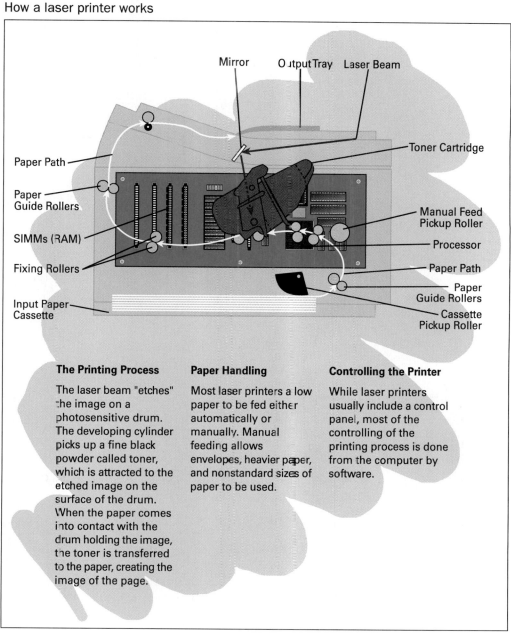

The Printing Process	Paper Handling	Controlling the Printer
The laser beam "etches" the image on a photosensitive drum. The developing cylinder picks up a fine black powder called toner, which is attracted to the etched image on the surface of the drum. When the paper comes into contact with the drum holding the image, the toner is transferred to the paper, creating the image of the page.	Most laser printers a low paper to be fed either automatically or manually. Manual feeding allows envelopes, heavier paper, and nonstandard sizes of paper to be used.	While laser printers usually include a control panel, most of the controlling of the printing process is done from the computer by software.

Labels in figure:
- Mirror
- Output Tray
- Laser Beam
- Paper Path
- Paper Guide Rollers
- SIMMs (RAM)
- Fixing Rollers
- Input Paper Cassette
- Toner Cartridge
- Manual Feed Pickup Roller
- Processor
- Paper Path
- Paper Guide Rollers
- Cassette Pickup Roller

Ink Jet Printers

An *ink jet printer* (see Figure 5-23) provides for less expensive color printing. The color is sprayed onto the paper. The same process used in laser printers is used in ink jet printers; it just works more slowly. Unlike earlier versions of the ink jet printer, newer versions can use regular photocopy paper.

FIGURE 5-23
How an ink jet printer works

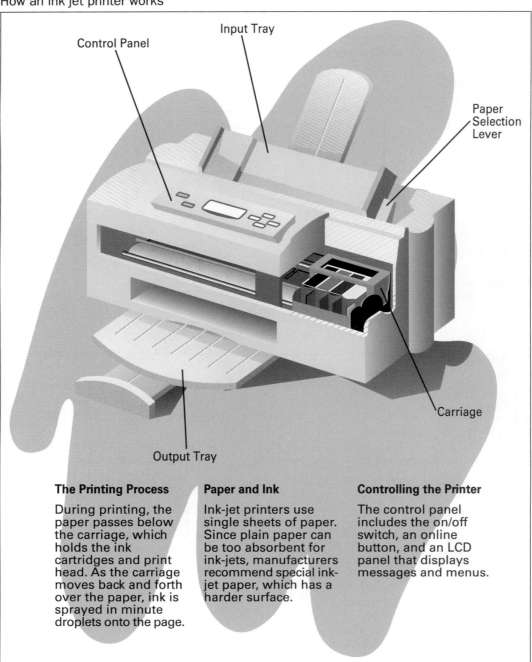

Control Panel

Input Tray

Paper Selection Lever

Carriage

Output Tray

The Printing Process

During printing, the paper passes below the carriage, which holds the ink cartridges and print head. As the carriage moves back and forth over the paper, ink is sprayed in minute droplets onto the page.

Paper and Ink

Ink-jet printers use single sheets of paper. Since plain paper can be too absorbent for ink-jets, manufacturers recommend special ink-jet paper, which has a harder surface.

Controlling the Printer

The control panel includes the on/off switch, an online button, and an LCD panel that displays messages and menus.

Dot Matrix Printers

Impact printers, such as the dot matrix and line printer, have been around for a long time. *Dot matrix* printers print by transferring ink to the paper by striking a ribbon with pins. The higher the number of pins (dpi), the better the resolution or output. The mechanism that actually does the printing is called a *printhead*. The speed of the dot matrix printer is measured in characters per second (cps). With the reduction in cost of laser and ink jet printers, dot matrix printers are used less often today. A variation of the dot matrix printer is the *line printer*. This type of high-speed printer is attached primarily to large computers such as mainframes or mid-range servers.

Other Types of Printers

Several other types of specialty printers are available. Some examples are as follows:

- *Thermal:* A *thermal printer* forms characters by heating paper. The printer requires special heat-sensitive paper.

- *Mobile:* A *mobile printer* is a small, battery-powered printer, primarily used to print from a notebook computer.

- *Label and postage:* A *label printer* prints labels of various types and sizes on an adhesive-type paper; a postage printer is a special type of label printer. This type of printer contains a built-in digital scale and prints postage stamps.

- *Plotters/large-format:* Engineers, architects, and graphic artists use *plotters* and *large-format printers* for drawings and drafting output.

Other Output Devices

In addition to printers, other types of output devices exist. Some examples are as follows:

- *Speakers and headsets: Speakers* generate sound, such as music or instructions on how to complete a tutorial. Individuals use headsets to hear the music or other voice output privately.

- *Fax machines and fax modems:* A *fax machine* and *fax modem* transmit and receive documents over a telephone line or through a computer.

- *Multifunction peripherals:* A *multifunctional peripheral* provides a combination of various output options such as printing, scanning, copying, and faxing.

- *Data projectors:* A *data projector* projects the computer image onto a screen; mostly used for presentations.

STEP-BY-STEP 5.2

1. Click the **Start** button on the taskbar, right-click **My Computer** to display the shortcut menu, and point to **Properties**, as shown in Figure 5-24. (If you are using Windows 2000, right-click **My Computer** on the Desktop and point to **Properties**.)

FIGURE 5-24
My Computer shortcut menu

2. Click **Properties**. In the System Properties dialog box, click the **Hardware** tab (see Figure 5-25).

FIGURE 5-25
Hardware tab

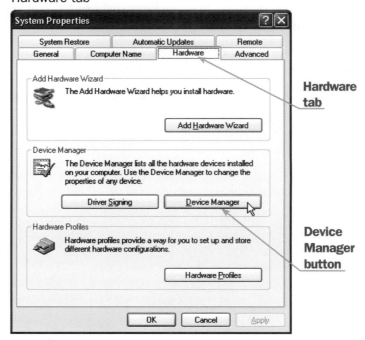

STEP-BY-STEP 5.2 Continued

3. Click the **Device Manager** button. If necessary, click the plus sign to the left of the label for your computer (a minus sign then appears). A list of hardware device categories appears (see Figure 5-26). Your lists and devices most likely will be different from those shown in Figure 5-26 and the other figures in this exercise.

FIGURE 5-26
Device Manager dialog box

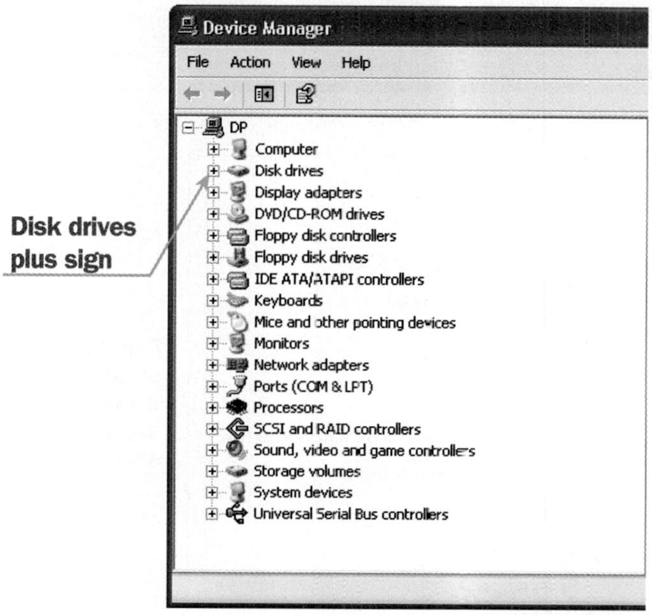

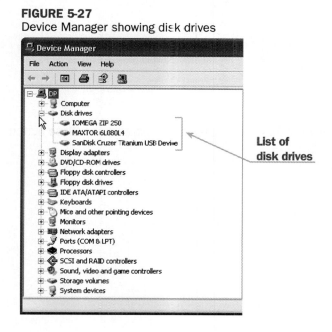

4. Click the plus sign to the left of **Disk drives** (see Figure 5-27). How many disk drives are displayed?

FIGURE 5-27
Device Manager showing disk drives

STEP-BY-STEP 5.2 Continued

5. Click the plus sign to the left of **Display adapters**. What type of display do you have?

6. Click the plus signs to the left of the following and review the information that is displayed: **Floppy disk drives**, **Keyboards**, **Mice and other pointing devices**, **Monitors**, **Ports**, **Sound, video and game controllers**, and **Universal Serial Bus controllers** (see Figure 5-28). If requested to do so, click the **Print** button and give your printout to your instructor. (In Windows 2000, click the **View** menu and then click **Print**.)

FIGURE 5-28
Displaying input and output devices

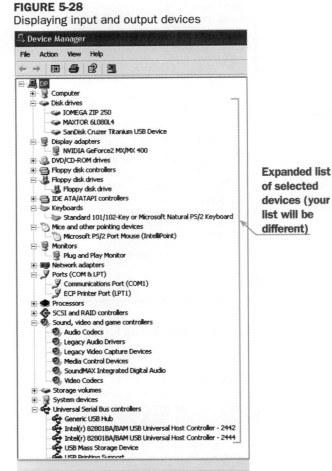

7. Close the Device Manager dialog box, and then click the **Close** button to close the System Properties dialog box.

Connecting Input/Output Devices to the Computer

Input and output devices must be connected to the computer. Some devices connect to the computer through a physical connection, such as a port. For instance, you can plug the cable for a physical device into an existing port located on the back or front of the computer. Some monitors also have ports. See Lesson 4 for a discussion on ports. Wireless devices connect through infrared or radio waves.

SUMMARY

In this lesson, you learned:

- Input devices enable you to input data and commands into the computer.
- The most common input devices are the keyboard and mouse.
- Other types of input devices include the trackball, joystick and wheel, pointing stick, graphics tablet, touch display screen, stylus, voice recognition devices, touchpad, scanner, digital camera, video input, and biometric input.
- To maintain a permanent copy of data, you should store it on some type of storage medium.
- The three categories of storage media are magnetic storage, optical storage, and solid-state storage.
- Monitors and printers are examples of output devices.
- Monitors produce soft copy.
- Printers are used to produce a paper or hard copy of the processed result.
- Criteria for selecting a printer include speed, print quality, and cost.
- Input and output devices must be connected to the computer.
- Some I/O devices communicate with the computer through a physical connection.
- Wireless devices communicate with the computer through infrared or radio waves.

VOCABULARY *Review*

Define the following terms:

Audio input	Input devices	Output
Biometrics	Keyboard	Output devices
Floppy disk	Laser printer	Pointing device
Hard disk	Monitor	Solid-state storage
Inkjet printer	Mouse	Video input
Input	Optical storage	

REVIEW *Questions*

MULTIPLE CHOICE

Select the best response for the following statements.

1. Laser, ink jet, and dot matrix are types of _____.
   A. monitors
   B. printers
   C. storage devices
   D. input devices

2. Monitors and printers are types of _____.
   A. input devices
   B. output devices
   C. storage devices
   D. ports

3. A keyboard that requires fingerprint identification is an example of a(n) _____ input device.
   A. biometric
   B. USB
   C. SCSI
   D. MIDI

4. A DVD is an example of _____ storage.
   A. solid-state
   B. optical
   C. magnetic
   D. floppy

5. _____ mostly is (are) used for making backup copies of data.
   A. CD-R
   B. Hard drives
   C. Magnetic tape
   D. Magnetic disks

TRUE/FALSE

Circle T if the statement is true or F if the statement is false.

T   F   1. Input and output devices perform the same function.

T   F   2. The mouse is a pointing device that rolls around on a flat surface and controls the pointer.

T   F   3. A trackball is a type of output device.

T   F   4. Some devices can function as both input and output devices.

T   F   5. A DVD-RW disc is an example of optical media.

FILL IN THE BLANK

Complete the following sentences by writing the correct word or words in the blanks provided.

1. A(n) _____ is the most widely used device for entering data into the computer.

2. _____ and _____ are the most popular output devices.

3. Input and output devices are connected to computers through _____.

4. Hard disks and floppy disks are types of _____ storage devices.

5. _____ storage contains no mechanical parts.

PROJECTS

CROSS-CURRICULAR—MATHEMATICS

Contact computer vendors, read computer magazines, research the Internet, and use any other resources to collect data concerning the prices of at least five storage devices. Find sales information for the same product from three vendors. Determine the average cost of each device. Prepare a chart to show your findings.

CROSS-CURRICULAR—SCIENCE

There are many styles of keyboards for computers. Many of the designs were developed to address various health issues related to keyboard use. Use appropriate research sources to locate information on various keyboard designs and report on the theory on which they are designed. You also may visit retail stores that sell computers to obtain information and sales documents. Prepare a written report outlining the information you locate.

CROSS-CURRICULAR—SOCIAL STUDIES

Biometric technology is the automated method of recognizing a person based on a physiological or behavioral characteristic. Use the Internet and other sources to research this topic. Make a list of the pros and cons that relate to this technology. Include your personal opinion about this topic.

CROSS-CURRICULAR—LANGUAGE ARTS

Prepare a written report describing at least five input devices. Include a table in your report listing the input device, describing how it could be used, and explaining the device's advantages and disadvantages.

WEB PROJECT

You want to learn more about how solid-state storage works. Your instructor thinks this is a great idea and has asked you to prepare a report and share your findings with the class. Your report should include Web searching methodologies and Web-based resources.

TEAMWORK PROJECT

Your supervisor at work is interested in setting up a teleconference with several of the stores throughout the state. However, she would like to get more information on this capability. She has asked you and the assistant manager to research this technology for her and let her know the steps needed to set up such a conference. Search the Internet and other materials to prepare a step-by-step guide for setting up a teleconference. Include an introduction that gives basic information about teleconferencing and list and describe what input and output devices you would need.

CRITICAL *Thinking*

Review the section in this lesson on solid-state storage devices. Research the Internet and other resources to learn more about this technology. Prepare a report indicating if you think this technology eventually will replace magnetic and optical storage media. Explain why you think this will or will not happen.

OPERATING SYSTEMS AND SOFTWARE

Over the last 50 years, computer technology has changed the world. Thirty or so years ago, only a few workers would have used computers. Customers would not have had ID cards that could be scanned. Accounting was done using ledgers. Online banking was not available. And, the Internet and World Wide Web did not exist. Computers have changed our society drastically.

When most of us think about computers, we think of hardware and how the hardware has changed—that computers have become smaller and faster. If we look at the history of computers, however, we find that the early computers were used for little more than high-speed calculators. This alone would not have had such a major influence on our culture and economy. The reason that computers have had such an impact is through the vision and desire of software developers. These software creators came up with hundreds of ideas and ways in which to use computers. They created programs that affect us in every aspect of our lives.

Hardware vs. Software

You probably have heard the words *software* and *hardware* many times. Sometimes it is difficult to distinguish between these two terms. As was discussed in Lesson 1, hardware refers to the tangible, physical computer equipment that can be seen and touched. This includes objects such as the keyboard, mouse, monitor, printer, chips, disks, disk drives, and DVD/CD recorders.

Software is a set of instructions issued to the computer so that specific tasks are performed. You cannot touch software because it has no substance. Another word for software is *program*.

For example, a computer programmer might write a program that lets the user download music from the Internet. Or suppose a bookkeeper has a problem with his computer. You might hear him say, "The problem lies in the software." This means there is a problem with the program or data, and not with the computer or hardware itself. He also might say, "It's a software problem." A good analogy here is a book. The book, including the pages and the ink, is the hardware. The words and ideas on the pages are the software. One has little value without the other. The same is true of computer software and hardware.

Types of Software

The computer uses two basic types of software: applications software and systems software. Applications software helps you perform a specific task. Systems software refers to the operating system and all utility programs that manage computer resources at a low level. Figuratively speaking, applications software sits on top of systems software. Without the operating system and system utilities, the computer cannot run any applications program.

Applications Software

Applications software often is referred to as productivity software. Applications software comprises programs designed for an end user. Some of the more commonly used application programs are word processors, database systems, presentations, spreadsheets, and desktop publishing programs. Some other applications categories are as follows:

- Education, home, and personal software—reference, entertainment, personal finance, calendars, e-mail, and browsers

- Multimedia software—authoring, animation, music, video and sound capturing and editing, virtual reality, and Web site development

- Workgroup computing software—calendars and scheduling, e-mail, browsers, electronic conferencing, and project management

Applications software programs are covered in detail in Lessons 8 through 14.

Systems Software

Systems software is a group of programs that coordinate and control the resources and operations of a computer system. Systems software enables the many components of the computer system to communicate and is made up of three categories: operating systems, utilities, and language translators.

Operating Systems

An *operating system (OS)* provides an interface between the user or application program and the computer hardware. See Figure 6-1 on the next page. Several brands and versions of operating systems software exist. Each of these is designed to work with one or more particular processors. For example, an operating system like Windows is designed to work with a processor made by Intel. Many IBM PC-compatible computers contain this brand of processor. Most Macintosh computers contain a processor manufactured by Motorola. The Windows operating system does not work with this Motorola processor.

FIGURE 6-1
Operating systems: an interface between users and computers

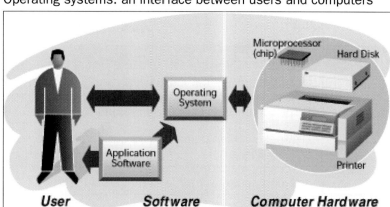

Utilities

Utility programs help you perform housekeeping chores. You use these programs to complete specialized tasks related to managing the computer's resources, files, and so forth. Some utility programs are part of the operating system, and others are self-contained programs. Some examples of utility program functions are as follows:

- You format a disk—a disk formatting utility provides the instructions to the computer on how to do this.

- You copy a file from the hard drive to a USB drive—the file management utility provides the instructions to the computer.

- You back up the hard drive—a backup utility provides the instructions to the computer.

- You want to change files from one format to another—the file conversion utility converts files to the format you select (see Figure 6-2).

FIGURE 6-2
File conversion utility

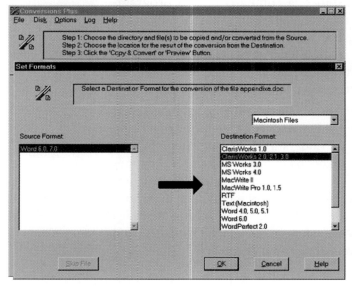

See Table 6-1 for a list of the more commonly used utilities and their purpose.

TABLE 6-1
Utility programs

TYPE OF UTILITY	PURPOSE
Antivirus	Protects the computer system from viruses
Disk formatting	Prepares a disk to have files stored on it
File management	Allows the user to perform tasks such as copying, moving, and deleting files
File recovery	Attempts to recover a file that has been erased
Disk defragmentation	Attempts to place the segments of each file on the hard disk as close to one another as possible
Uninstall	Removes an application that is no longer needed
Diagnostic	Provides detailed information about the computer system and attempts to locate problems
File conversion	Converts a file from one format to another
Disk compression	Frees up storage space on a disk by compressing the existing files
Backup	Makes a duplicate copy of the contents of a secondary storage device

Some of the previously listed utilities are incorporated into the operating system. Other utility programs, such as antivirus programs, are sold as stand-alone programs.

Language Translators

Language translators convert English-like software programs into machine language that the computer can understand. For instance, a company hires a programmer to write a software program to inventory all of the items in the store. The programmer writes the program statements using a high-level programming language such as Microsoft Visual Basic. A program statement directs the computer to perform a specified action.

The computer, however, cannot read the Visual Basic programming statements because they are written in a language that we understand. This is where the language translator takes over. The translator changes each of the Visual Basic programming statements into machine language. A single statement in a high-level language can represent several machine-language instructions. Now the statements can be executed and the company's inventory can be processed.

Extra for Experts

If you have a computer, you should have an emergency boot disk. Sooner or later, your computer might not boot from the hard drive. You can use your emergency boot disk to get your computer started. Each operating system has its own unique way of creating a boot disk. Check your operating system help files for information on how to create this disk. Then be sure to store it in an easy-to-find and safe place.

Microcomputer Operating Systems Interfaces

All computers, big and small, have operating systems. For most of us, however, the computer we most often use is a microcomputer. Our primary focus in this lesson is on microcomputer operating systems.

The *user interface* is the part of the operating system with which we are most familiar. This is the part of the operating system with which we interact when using our computer. The two most common types of user interfaces are command-line interfaces and graphical interfaces.

Command-Line Interfaces

All early computers used command-line interfaces. With this type of interface, you must type the exact command you want to execute. One of the most widely used command-line interfaces for microcomputers is MS-DOS. Using DOS, suppose you want to look at a list of files on your computer's hard drive. You type the DOS command *dir* and press Enter. In Figure 6-3, the *Ping* command is used. This command is used to determine Web site addresses as well as to determine and assist in resolving network issues.

This type of interface is not considered very user friendly. You must memorize the commands and type them without any spelling errors. Otherwise, they do not work.

Internet

The history of Apple Computer, Steve Jobs, and Steve Wozniak is a fascinating story. For an overview of this story and links to some interesting facts about the Macintosh operating system, check out the Web site at *http://inventors.about.com/library/inventors/blapplecomputer.htm.*

Did You Know?

Macintosh popularized the first graphical user interface. However, Apple did not invent the interface. Xerox Corporation developed the idea for a graphical user interface.

FIGURE 6-3
Command-line interface showing example of Ping command

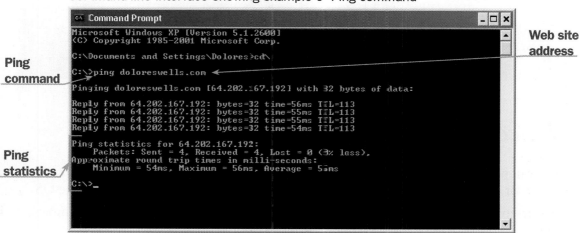

Graphical User Interfaces

As microcomputer technology developed, so did the operating system interface. *Menus* represented the next step in this progression. The user could choose commands from a list.

The big breakthrough in ease of use came with the development of *graphical user interfaces* (*GUIs*). When the user turns on the computer and starts the operating system, a symbolic desktop is displayed. On this desktop are various objects, or icons. These graphical symbols represent files, disks, programs, and other objects. GUIs permit the user to manipulate these on screen icons. Most people use a pointing device such as a mouse to click the icons and execute the commands. Figure 6-4 shows an example of the Windows graphical user interface.

FIGURE 6-4
Graphical user interface

Microcomputer Operating Systems

Several popular operating systems are available for microcomputers. If you are using a Macintosh or a Macintosh clone, you most likely will be using a version of the Mac OS.

If your computer is what is commonly referred to as a PC or an IBM PC-compatible, you most likely are using one of these three operating systems:

- DOS

- A combination of DOS and Windows

- A stand-alone version of Windows

Mac OS

Macintosh's operating system, the *Mac OS*, is used with Apple's Macintosh computers and Macintosh clones. The Macintosh was introduced in 1984. One of the main features of this new computer was a GUI. The GUI was called the Finder and contained icons or symbols that represented documents, software, disks, and so forth. To activate the icon, the user clicked it with a mouse. This operating system also was the first OS to provide on screen help or instructions. In 2005, Macintosh released OS X Tiger, with over 200 new features. The desktop and dashboard widgets are shown in Figure 6-5A and 6-5B.

FIGURE 6-5

A. Desktop

B. Widgets displayed on dashboard

DOS

IBM introduced its first IBM PC in 1981. With the introduction of this new microcomputer came a new operating system. This system was called DOS (Disk Operating System). IBM referred to this operating system as *PC-DOS*. They licensed this software from a small start-up company called Microsoft. But as agreements go, Microsoft retained the rights to market its own version of the OS. Microsoft called their version *MS-DOS*. This OS was the catalyst that launched Microsoft into the multibillion dollar company it is today.

DOS is a character-based operating system. The user interacts with the system by typing in commands. DOS is a single-user or single-tasking operating system because the user can run only one program at a time. DOS still is accessible in all Windows OS versions. In Step-by-step 6.1, you have an opportunity to use some DOS commands. When completing this exercise, keep in mind that the first computers did not have graphical interfaces until the late 1980s, and that this is a version of the original operating system for today's Windows microcomputers. As you work through the steps, consider the term *directory*. In DOS, directory is synonymous with folder in Windows.

STEP-BY-STEP 6.1

1. Click the **Start** menu, point to **All Programs** (or **Programs** in Windows 2000), point to **Accessories**, and then click **Command Prompt**. The Command Prompt dialog box appears, as shown in Figure 6-6. (The information on your screen will be different from that shown in Figure 6-6.) Note the insertion point blinking at the end of the directory location.

FIGURE 6-6
Command Prompt window

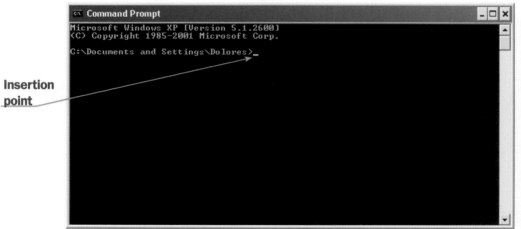

Insertion
point

2. Type **CD** and then press **Enter**. This takes you to the highest directory level—the C:\ root, as shown in Figure 6-7.

STEP-BY-STEP 6.1 Continued

FIGURE 6-7
Root directory

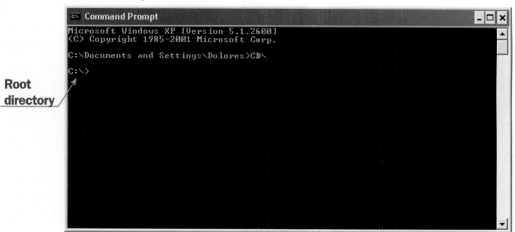

Root
directory

3. Type **CD Windows** (or **CD WINNT** in Windows 2000) and then press **Enter**. You are now in the Windows directory.

4. Type **DIR** and then press **Enter**. A list of files appears—this list (shown in Figure 6-8) contains all of the files and subdirectories within the Windows directory or folder. The list of files scrolled by rather quickly. However, you can use another option to look at the list.

FIGURE 6-8
List of files and directories in Windows directory

List of
files and
directories
in Windows
directory

End of
list

5. Type **dir /p** to list one page of files at a time. Press **Enter** to display the next page (Figure 6-9 on the next page) and continue to press any key until you reach the end of the list.

STEP-BY-STEP 6.1 Continued

FIGURE 6-9
Using dir /p command

Command prompt
dir /p

Press any key to continue

6. When you have finished viewing all of the pages, type **EXIT** and press **Enter** to close the Command Prompt window.

Occasions arise when it is helpful to know some DOS commands. For instance, suppose you are trying to delete a file that is responsible for a computer virus. If you are using Windows, after the file loads into the computer's memory, it is difficult, if not impossible, to delete it. You can, however, load DOS and delete the file.

Technology Careers

SOFTWARE DEVELOPER

A software developer maintains and helps develop new applications and operating systems programs. When you see a job listing for software developer, it could include many requirements.

A company might be looking for someone to develop software using a particular programming language such as Visual Basic, C, or C++. Or a company might be looking for someone to develop add-ons to operating systems programs. This could include enhancements to utility programs, updates to language translators, or new additions to the operating system itself. Many companies seek employees with skills in operating systems programs such as UNIX and Windows NT.

If you go online and look for software developer jobs, you will find that many of them refer to Oracle, a large information technology software company. Oracle products support database technology, data design and modeling, Web applications, and much more.

A variation exists in salaries and educational requirements. Salaries can range from $25,000 to $100,000 plus. Educational requirements range from some college to a bachelor's or master's degree or maybe even a Ph.D. Generally, but not always, the more education you have, the higher your starting salary. Most companies require some experience, but a few have entry-level positions.

Windows

In response to the competition from the Macintosh, Microsoft introduced its own GUI. This OS was called *Windows*. Following is an overview of Windows history, from the first version through the most recent version, which at the time of this writing is scheduled to be released in 2006.

■ Microsoft first began development of the Interface Manager, subsequently called Windows, in 1981. On Nov. 10, 1983, Microsoft announced Windows as an extension of the MS-DOS operating system that would provide a graphical operating environment for PC users.

■ The first versions of Windows (versions 1 and 2) contained a graphical shell and were called *operating environments* because they worked in combination with DOS. The different applications installed on a computer appeared as icons. The user activated the icons by clicking them with a mouse.

■ These early versions of Windows were consecutively numbered beginning with Windows 3.0, Windows 3.1, and so on.

Windows 95 was Microsoft's first true multitasking operating system. *Multitasking* allows a single user to work on two or more applications that reside in memory at the same time. Some advantages of Windows 95 include the following:

■ The graphical interface is improved.

■ Programs run faster than with earlier Windows versions.

■ The software includes support for networking, which allows a group of two more computers to be linked.

■ It uses Plug and Play technology, the goal of which is just to plug in a new device and immediately be able to use it, without complicated setup maneuvers.

Windows 98 was released in June of 1998. Integrated Web browsing and the Active Desktop provided a browser-like interface. Windows 98 was easier to use than Windows 95 and had some additional features, such as Internet integration, a Web browser-look option for Windows Explorer, faster system startup and shutdown, and support for the Universal Serial Bus.

Windows 2000 was an update to the Windows 98 and Windows NT operating systems. Windows NT is Microsoft's platform for high-end systems. It is intended for use on network servers, workstations, and software development machines.

One of the most recent updates is Windows XP, which provides increased stability and improved device recognition. As in previous versions, this version includes utilities to show how much space is available on a storage media device and an error-checking program.

An updated Windows operating system named *Vista* is being developed, and at the time of this writing, it is scheduled for release in 2006. Some new features include the following:

■ WinFS (Windows Future Storage) will help users locate e-mail messages, documents, and multimedia images, no matter what their format.

■ It will contain an integrated antivirus program.

■ A new security technology named Palladium will help protect the computer.

Even though the Windows versions have changed, some features remain consistent, such as the Start menu, taskbar, and desktop.

In Step-by-step 6.2, you have an opportunity to examine some Windows XP features and commands relating to properties on a floppy disk. You can use these same steps to examine any storage media device.

STEP-BY-STEP 6.2

1. Insert your floppy disk into drive A. If you are using a USB drive or another type of storage media, substitute that drive for drive A.

2. Click the **Start** menu and then click **My Computer**. (In Windows 2000, double-click **My Computer** on the desktop.)

3. In the My Computer window, right-click **3½ Floppy (A):** (or your selected storage media) and then point to **Properties** on the shortcut menu, as shown in Figure 6-10.

FIGURE 6-10
Shortcut menu

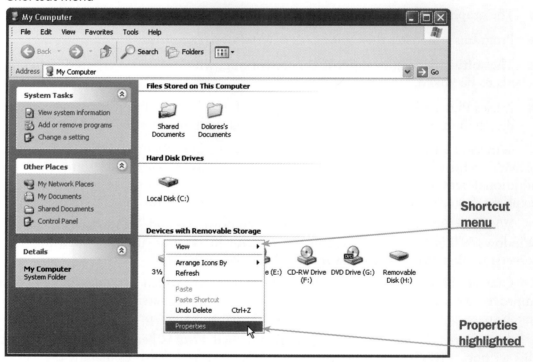

4. Click **Properties** to display the Local Disk (A:) Properties dialog box (or your selected storage media), as shown in Figure 6-11 on the next page. The used and free space on your disk will be different from that shown in the figure.

STEP-BY-STEP 6.2 Continued

FIGURE 6-11
Allocation of space on the disk

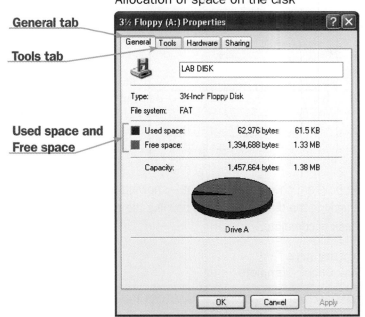

General tab

Tools tab

Used space and
Free space

5. Click the **Tools** tab. See Figure 6-12.

FIGURE 6-12
Tools tab

Tools tab
selected

Check Now

6. Click the **Check Now** button. The Check Disk 3½ Floppy (A:) dialog box appears. (In Windows 2000, the dialog box is just called Check Disk.) Click the check boxes for both Check disk options, as shown in Figure 6-13 on the next page.

STEP-BY-STEP 6.2 Continued

FIGURE 6-13
Check disk options

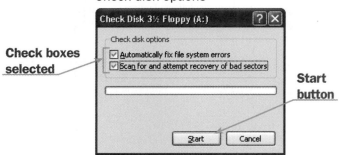

Check boxes selected

Start button

7. Click the **Start** button. The program checks both options—showing phase 1 and phase 2. When the program has completed checking the disk, a message box like the one shown in Figure 6-14 opens, indicating that the disk check is complete.

FIGURE 6-14
Disk Check Complete

8. Click the **OK** button and then close the 3½ Floppy (A:) Properties dialog box. Close the My Computer window.

Embedded Operating Systems

An *embedded operating system* includes technologies and tools that enable developers to create a broad range of devices. This operating system, which resides on a ROM chip, is used on small handheld computers and wireless communication devices. Several embedded operating systems exist, but the three most popular are as follows:

■ *Windows CE* (Consumer Electronics) is a scaled-down Windows operating system, designed for including or embedding in mobile and other devices with limited functionality.

■ *Windows Mobile* works on specific types of PDAs such as Pocket PC and Smartphones. The Pocket PC enables the user to store and retrieve e-mail, contacts, and appointments, play multimedia files and games, exchange text messages, browse the Web, and more. In addition, the user can exchange and synchronize information with a desktop computer.

■ *Palm OS* is a competing operating system with Windows Mobile and runs on Palm handhelds and other third-party devices. Some of the more common built-in applications include an address book, calculator, datebook/calendar, expense list, memo and notepad, to-do list, and the capability to hot sync or integrate with the user's PC.

UNIX

Still another operating system is *UNIX*. This operating system frequently is used by scientists and programmers. UNIX was developed by a group of programmers for AT&T, and is considered a multitasking, portable operating system. This means it can run on just about any hardware platform. Some versions of UNIX have a command-line interface similar to DOS, but most versions provide a graphical user interface such as that shown in Figure 6-15. There are several variants of the language, such as Linux and IBM's AIX.

FIGURE 6-15
UNIX operating system

Both the IBM Aix system and Linux are based on UNIX. Linux, however, is an open source program that is free and one that programmers and developers can use or modify as they wish. Linux has a reputation of being stable and rarely crashing. One Linux user interface is called GNOME (pronounced gah-NOHM) and allows the user to select a desktop similar to Windows or Macintosh. GNOME also includes software applications such as word processing, spreadsheet, database, presentation, e-mail, and a Web browser. Even with these included applications, however, the number of available application programs is far fewer than those for Windows or the Mac OS.

Loading the Operating System

Booting is the process of starting a computer. When you start your computer, operating system commands are loaded into memory. Each operating system boots or starts the computer in its own individual way. Understanding the boot process is the key to diagnosing many computer startup problems.

The steps in this example are based on the Windows operating system. Keep in mind, however, that the boot process is similar for all operating systems.

Did You Know?

Sometimes Windows does not boot properly. Instead, a dialog box indicating that you are in safe mode is displayed on the screen. This means that something did not function properly during the boot process. Safe mode provides functionality to enable the user to do diagnostic testing.

1. Turn on your computer. The first thing that happens is that the *basic input/output system* (*BIOS*) is activated. Next is POST, an acronym for Power-on Self Test. This is a series of diagnostic tests to check RAM and to verify that the keyboard, disk drives, and other devices you might have are physically connected to the computer.

2. Next, the BIOS searches for the boot record—sometimes first on drive A, then on drive C, and/or the CD drive. The BIOS is built-in software that normally is placed on a ROM chip. It contains all of the code that controls the most common devices connected to your computer. This includes the monitor, keyboard, disk drives, and other components. This chip comes with your computer when you purchase it.

3. Now the boot record is loaded into RAM. The boot record contains several files. These files contain programming configuration instructions for hardware devices and software applications that you might have installed on your computer.

4. Software drivers are the next thing loaded. Drivers are what enable you to use your printer, modem, scanner, or other devices. Generally, when you add a new device to your system, you install drivers for that device.

5. After the software drivers are loaded, the GUI is loaded. In this instance, the GUI is Windows. When loading the GUI, the operating system reads the commands for your desktop configuration. It also loads whatever programs you previously have specified into the Windows Startup folder.

6. If everything goes as it should, the GUI appears and the computer is ready to use.

Sharing Files on Different Operating Systems

In many business and educational settings, it is necessary to share files across operating system platforms. A business might have workers using both Macintosh and Windows computers, depending on the task: often artists and designers use Macintosh computers, while accountants and writers might have PCs. In the classroom, all of the computers might be the same type, but students might have different kinds of computers at home for doing homework. These situations require the ability to read disks and share files created on different operating systems. It might even be necessary to run programs on one system that were written only for another system. Hardware and software solutions are available for these problems.

One type of hardware solution is an emulation card that is added to the motherboard of the computer. These cards provide the ability for the computer to run a program that was designed for a different operating system. For example, a card can be added to a Macintosh that will allow it to run Windows programs. Software emulation programs also are available to provide this capability for some programs.

Macintosh computers have software installed that allows them to read disks that were formatted on PCs. Additional software finds a compatible program to run a PC file after the user double-clicks the file's icon.

Another solution to the file-sharing issue is to save files in a format that is readable on different operating systems. One example for word-processing documents is the basic text format (.txt). This format usually is readable by most word-processing programs on different systems. However, documents saved as .txt do not retain complicated formatting. Another text format, called Rich Text Format (.rtf), does retain more formatting commands, such as paragraph breaks, fonts, and styles such as bold and italic. To save a file in Rich Text Format, you use the Save As command in your word-processing program and specifically select Rich Text Format as the file type.

Network Operating Systems

Networks require a multiuser operating system because many users access the server at one time. All networks have some type of network server that manages resources. A *network operating system (NOS)* resides on a network server and is designed specifically to support a network. The NOS program allows a group of computers (also called clients) to be connected and to share resources. One of the main goals of the operating system is to make the resources appear as though they are running from the client computer. Several brands of network operating systems exist. Examples of network operating systems include Windows Server 2003, Novell NetWare, UNIX, and Linux. Networks are discussed in detail in Lesson 7.

 Ethics in Technology

WHAT IS COMPUTER ETHICS?

Ethics is the branch of philosophy concerned with evaluating human action, and a system or code of morals of a particular religion, group, or profession.

Ethical judgments are no different in the area of computing than they are in any other area. The use of computers can raise many issues of privacy, copyright, theft, and power, to name just a few. In 1990, the Institute of Electrical and Electronics Engineers created a code of ethics. Many businesses and organizations have adopted this code as their code. Remember that this is just a code—not a law. People choose to follow it voluntarily. This code is available at *http://onlineethics.org/codes/ IEEEcode.html.* (This Web site address is case-sensitive.)

SUMMARY

In this lesson, you learned:

- Hardware refers to the tangible, physical computer equipment that can be seen and touched.

- Software is a set of instructions that tell the computer what to do; software also is called a program.

- The two basic types of computer software are applications software and systems software.

- Applications software also is known as productivity software.

- Systems software coordinates and controls the resources and operations of a computer system.

- Three major categories of systems software are operating systems, utilities, and language translators.

- Operating systems provide an interface between the user and application program and the computer hardware.

- Utility programs help users complete specialized tasks such as file management.

- Language translators convert English-like software programs into machine language.

- A programmer uses a programming language to write program statements.

- All computers have operating systems.

- The user interface is the part of the operating system with which we are most familiar.

- The two most common user interfaces are command-line interfaces and graphical user interfaces.

- The Mac operating system is used with Apple's Macintosh computers and Macintosh clones.

- Icons are symbols that represent documents, software programs, disks, and so forth.

- DOS was introduced with the IBM PC in 1981 and is a character-based operating system.

- Microsoft introduced the first version of Windows in 1981; this was an operating environment.

- Windows 95 was Microsoft's first true multitasking operating system.

- Windows CE is a scaled-down Windows operating system used for small handheld computers.

- UNIX is a portable operating system.

- Network operating systems allow a group of two or more microcomputers to be connected.

- Several methods are available for sharing files on different operating systems.

VOCABULARY *Review*

Define the following terms:

Applications software	Macintosh OS	UNIX
Booting	MS-DOS	User interface
Graphical user	Multitasking	Utility programs
interfaces (GUIs)	Network operating system	Windows
Language translators	Operating system	Windows CE
Linux	Systems software	Windows Mobile

REVIEW *Questions*

MULTIPLE CHOICE

Select the best response for the following statements.

1. Which is another word for software?
   A. hardware
   B. program
   C. programming statement
   D. interface

2. Which are the two basic types of computer software?
   A. program, applications
   B. productivity, applications
   C. applications, systems
   D. systems, networking systems

3. A group of programs that coordinate and control the resources of a computer system is called _____.
   A. systems software
   B. applications software
   C. language translator
   D. utility program

4. The part of the operating system with which we are most familiar is _____.
   A. formatting utility
   B. programming statement
   C. language translator
   D. user interface

5. DOS was first introduced with the _____.
   A. Apple Macintosh
   B. IBM PC
   C. UNIX operating system
   D. Windows

TRUE/FALSE

Circle T if the statement is true or F if the statement is false.

T F 1. The first version of Windows was a true operating environment.

T F 2. DOS is a multitasking operating system.

T F 3. Apple Computer Company developed the first GUI.

T F 4. Computer hardware is anything you can touch.

T F 5. Networks require a multiuser operating system.

FILL IN THE BLANK

Complete the following sentences by writing the correct word or words in the blanks provided.

1. An embedded operating system resides on a(n) _____ chip.

2. Word processing is an example of _____ software.

3. Novell NetWare is an example of a(n) _____ system.

4. Windows CE is a type of _____ operating system.

5. DOS is a(n) _____-user operating system.

PROJECTS

CROSS-CURRICULAR—MATHEMATICS

Windows Task Manager provides information about computer performance and displays details about programs and processes running on your computer. Use Windows Help and Support and research this utility program. Write a one-page report on the five available tasks within this program—applications, processes, performance, networking, and users. Explain the purpose of each task and provide an example of how you would apply it.

CROSS-CURRICULAR—SCIENCE

Operating systems have come a long way in the last few years. They are much easier to use and support many more features. If you were going to design an operating system for computers for the year 2010, what features would you include? How would your operating system be different from those that are currently available? Use your word-processing program to write a report or give an oral report to the class.

CROSS-CURRICULAR—SOCIAL STUDIES

The more recent versions of operating systems include accessibility options for people with visual or hearing disabilities. Research the operating system on your computer and complete a report on the accessibility options.

CROSS-CURRICULAR—LANGUAGE ARTS

You have been hired to create an icon to represent a new software program that has just been developed. This is an interactive encyclopedia. It also contains games to help reinforce the topics presented in the encyclopedia. Think about the icons on your computer's desktop or that you see in the figures throughout this lesson. Using graph paper or a computer drawing program, create an icon for this new interactive encyclopedia.

 WEB PROJECT

One of the more commonly used DOS commands is *PING*. Use Google or another search engine and search for the DOS command *PING*. Write a report explaining how and why someone would use this command. Next, use the Command Prompt and "ping" three different Web site addresses. Include in your report the results of pinging these Web sites.

 TEAMWORK PROJECT

You and two team members have been given the responsibility for purchasing new computers for your company's front office. One team member wants to purchase an Apple Macintosh with the Macintosh OS X Tiger and the latest software suite; another wants to purchase a PC with the latest version of the Windows OS; and the third wants to purchase a PC with the UNIX operating system. The manager has requested that your team do some research and present her with a report so that she can make the best choice. Your report should include the positives and negatives for each of these operating systems.

CRITICAL *Thinking*

Many people, when they finish using a computer, simply turn it off instead of using the shutdown procedure. Research this topic and then explain why you think this is a good idea or a bad habit. If you agree that it is OK just to turn off the computer, provide details on how you came to this conclusion. If, however, you believe that the shut-down procedure should be followed, explain why and what processes take place when you use it.

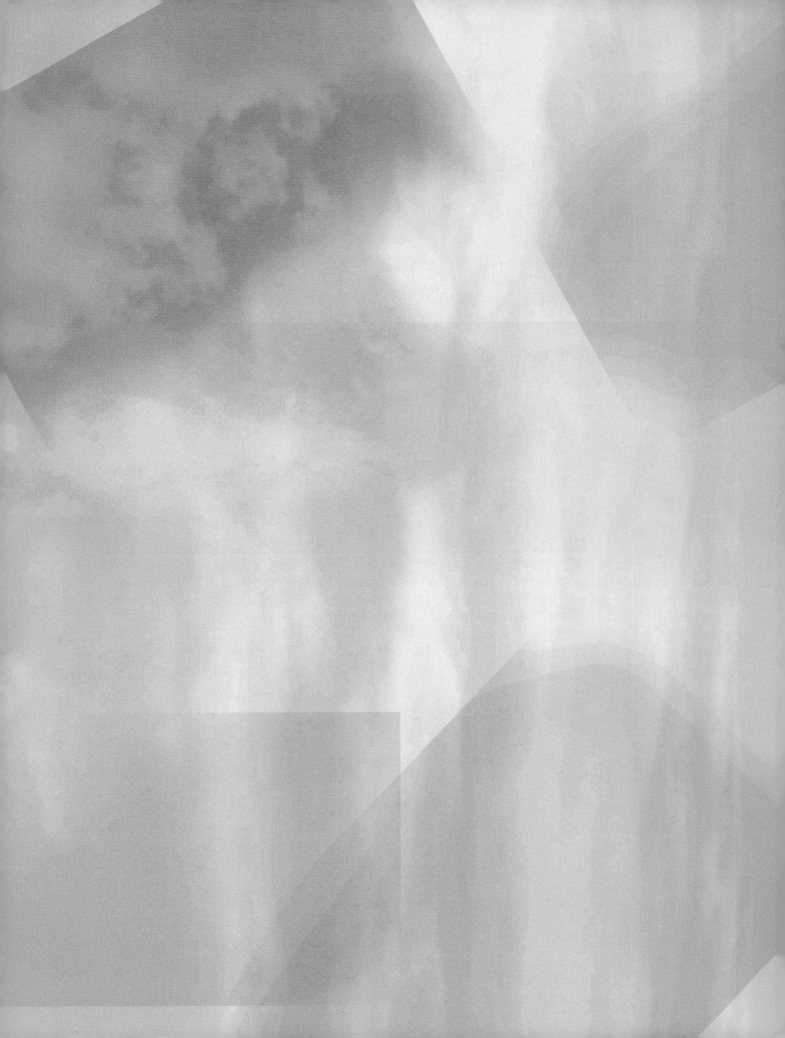

NETWORKS

Telephony, which is the technology associated with the electronic transmission of voice, fax, or other information between distant parties, is nothing new. Early forays into telephony such as the telegraph and telephone have evolved into more complicated devices; now a computer can be networked to the Internet, another PC, or even a home stereo. In this lesson, we look at how networks function and the components necessary to make them function.

Network Building Blocks

When most people think of networks, they envision something fairly complicated. At the lowest level, networks are not that complex. In fact a network, as discussed in Lesson 1, is simply a group of two or more computers linked together. As the size of a network increases and more and more devices are added, installation of devices and management of the network does become more technical. Even so, networking concepts and terminology basically remain the same regardless of size.

Most organizations today rely on computers and the data stored on the computers. In addition, more and more people work and communicate from home. Many times, organizations and individuals find that they need to transmit data or communicate from one location to another. The transmission of data from one location to another is known as *data communications*.

Communication devices are discussed in detail on page 143. Transmittal of data requires the following components, as shown in Figure 7-1:

- A sending device, which generally is a computer

- A communications device that converts the computer signal into signals supported by the communications channel

- A communications channel or path, such as telephone lines or cable, over which the signals are sent

- A receiving device that accepts the incoming signal, which generally is a computer

- Communications software

FIGURE 7-1
Communications components using dial-up modem and telephone lines

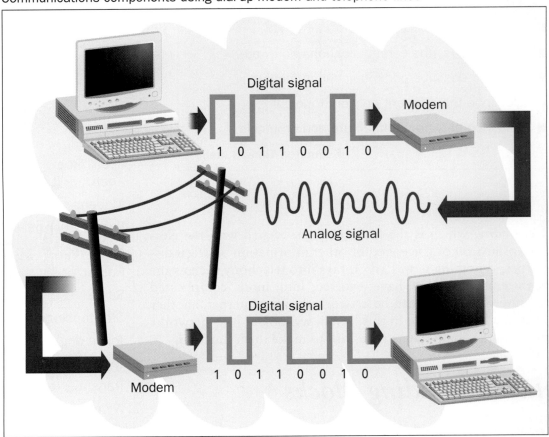

Network Benefits and Disadvantages

To consider the topic of network benefits, you first might think about the biggest network of all—the Internet. Consider some of the many changes that have occurred in our society because of the Internet. Perhaps the most profound of all of these changes is electronic mail. A network provides almost instant communication, and e-mail messages are delivered almost immediately. Other network benefits include the following:

- *Information sharing*: Authorized users can access computers on the network to share information and data. This could include special group projects, databases, and so forth.

■ *Hardware sharing*: It is not necessary to purchase a printer or a scanner or other frequently used peripherals for each computer. Instead, one device connected to a network can serve the needs of many users.

■ *Software sharing*: Instead of purchasing and installing a software program on every single computer, it can be installed on the server. All of the users then can access the program from this one central location. This also saves money because companies can purchase a site license for the number of users. This is less expensive than purchasing individual software packages, and updating software on the server is much easier and more efficient than updating on individual computers.

■ *Collaborative environment*: A shared environment enables users to work together on group projects by combining the power and capabilities of diverse equipment and software.

As with any technology, disadvantages also exist. For instance, data security and the vulnerability to unauthorized access is a primary weakness with many networks. Hackers can access and steal or delete data. Some other disadvantages are as follows:

■ *Malicious code*: Networks are more vulnerable than stand-alone computers to viruses, worms, Trojan horses, and spyware.

■ *Network faults*: Network equipment problems can result in loss of data or resources.

■ *Setup and management costs*: Setting up a network requires an investment in hardware and software; ongoing maintenance and management of the network requires the care and attention of an IT professional or professionals.

Network Types

Several types of networks exist, but the two most common types are local area networks (LANs) and wide area networks (WANs). Five other types of networks are metropolitan area networks (MANs), neighborhood area networks (NANs), personal area network (PANs), home area networks (HANs), and campus area networks (CANs).

Local Area Networks

Most *local area networks (LANs)* connect personal computers, workstations, and other devices such as printers and scanners. The two popular types of LANs are client/server and peer-to-peer. The basic difference between the two is how the network is managed and where the data is stored.

■ *Client/server network*: In this type of architecture, one or more computers on the network act as a *server*. The server manages network resources. Depending on the size of the network, several different servers might be connected. For example, a print server manages the printing, and a database server manages a large database. In most instances, the server(s) is a high-speed computer with considerable storage space. The network operating system software and network versions of software applications are stored on the server. All of the other computers on the network are called *clients*. They share the server resources. Users access the server through a user name and password. See Figure 7-2 on the next page.

FIGURE 7-2
Client/server local area network

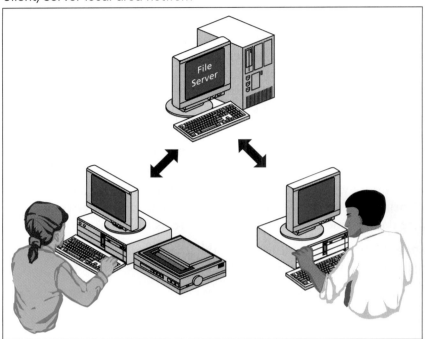

■ *Peer-to-peer network*: In this type of network, all of the computers are equals. There is no computer designated as the server. People on the network each determine what files on their computer they will share with others on the network. This type of network is much easier to set up and manage. Many small offices use peer-to-peer networks. See Figure 7-3A. The *Internet peer-to-peer*, also called P2, is a variation of the peer-to-peer. Users connect directly to each other's storage media and exchange files over the Internet. See Figure 7-3B.

FIGURE 7-3
(A) Peer-to-peer network (B) Internet peer-to-peer network

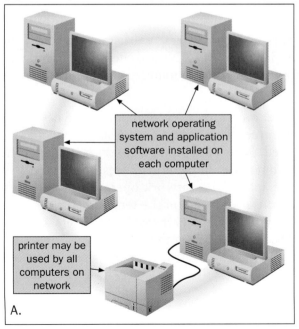
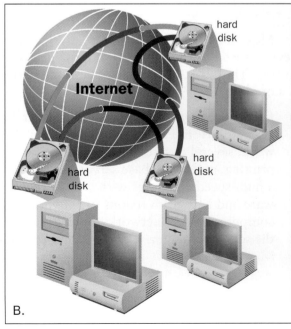

Wide Area Networks

A *wide area network (WAN)* covers a large geographical area. See Figure 7-4. This area might be as large as a state or a country or even the world, because the largest WAN is the Internet. Most WANs consist of two or more LANs and are connected by routers. Communications channels can include telephone systems, fiber optics, satellites, microwaves, or any combination of these.

FIGURE 7-4
Wide area network

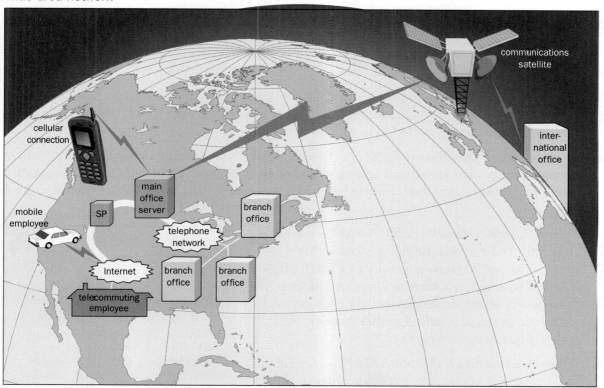

 Ethics in Technology

RISKS OF NETWORKED COMPUTING

The security of a computer network is challenged every day by equipment malfunctions, system failures, computer hackers, and virus attacks.

Equipment malfunctions and system failures can be caused by a number of things, including natural disasters such as floods or storms, fires, and electrical disturbances, such as a brownout or blackout. Server malfunctions or failures mean users lose temporary access to network resources, such as printers, drives, and information.

Computer hackers and viruses represent a great risk to networked environments. People who break into computer systems are called hackers. They break into systems to steal services and information, such as credit card numbers, test data, and even national security data. Some hackers want to harm a company or organization they do not like or support; sometimes, they do it just for the thrill of being able to get into the system.

People create computer viruses and infect other computers for some of the same reasons. Viruses are very dangerous to networked computers—they are usually designed to sabotage files that are shared.

Two variations on a WAN are intranets and extranets. An intranet is designed for the exclusive use of people within an organization. Many businesses have implemented intranets within their own organizations. On such intranets, employees can access files such as handbooks and employee manuals, newsletters, and employment forms.

An extranet is similar to an intranet, but it allows specified users outside the organization to access internal information systems. Like the Internet, intranets and extranets use and support Web technologies, such as hyperlinks and Web pages coded in hypertext markup language (HTML).

MANs, NANs, PANs, HANs, and CANs

Other types of networks have been developed to connect specific regions and users. Following is a list and description of some of the more common networks:

- *Metropolitan Area Network (MAN)*: A MAN interconnects users with computer resources in a geographic area or region larger than that covered by a large local area network, but smaller than the area covered by a wide area network.

- *Neighborhood Area Network (NAN)*: A NAN generally consists of access points, in which networking services are shared among neighboring businesses and residences. This permits a group of neighbors to share a single high-speed expensive line. Some NANs extend to 25 or more miles.

- *Personal Area Network (PAN)*: A PAN is the interconnection of personal digital devices within a range of about 30 feet—generally in a small office. Wireless technologies such as Bluetooth (discussed later in this lesson) let the users wirelessly connect electronic devices including mobile phones, PCs, handheld devices, and printers.

- *Home Area Network (HAN)*: A HAN is contained within a user's home. This network connects digital devices such as computers, telephones, DVD players, televisions, video game players, security systems, smart appliances, and other such equipment.

> ### Did You Know?
>
> In the near future, a PAN could enable wearable computer devices to comr inicate with other nearby computers. For instance, two people, each wearing business-card-size transmitters, could exchange information by shaking hands. In this example, the electrical conductivity of the human body is used as a data network.

- *Campus Area Network (CAN)*: A CAN is a collection of local area networks within a limited geographical space, such as a university campus or a military base.

Network Hardware

As indicated previously, the purpose of a network is to share hardware and software resources. Most networks consist of a network server and/or servers, client computers, a printer, and other peripheral devices. In addition to these hardware components, communications and transmission hardware also are required to accomplish the connections between the various devices.

Communications Devices

Communications devices facilitate the transmitting and receiving of data, instructions, and information. When we think about communications hardware, the first thing that generally comes to mind is the desktop computer and modem. However, many other devices send and receive data. Some examples are: large computers such as supercomputers, mainframe computers, and minicomputers; handheld and laptop computers; and even fax machines and digital cameras. Following is a list and description of common communications devices:

■ *Dial-up modem:* The word *modem* is an acronym for *modulate-demodulate,* which means to convert analog signals to digital and vice versa. A *dial-up modem* enables a computer to transmit data over analog telephone lines. Computer information is stored digitally, whereas information sent over telephone lines is transmitted in the form of analog waves. Both the sending and receiving users must have a modem. See Figure 7-5A.

■ *Cable modem:* A *cable modem* uses coaxial cable to send and receive data. This is the same type of cable used for cable TV. The bandwidth, which determines the amount of data that can be sent at one time, is much greater with a cable modem. A cable modem can be connected directly to your computer or connected to a set-top box used with your television. With a set-top box, you can access and surf the Web from your TV. See Figure 7-5B.

FIGURE 7-5
(A) Computer with dial-up modem attached (B) Computer with cable modem attached

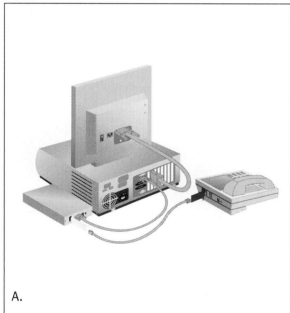
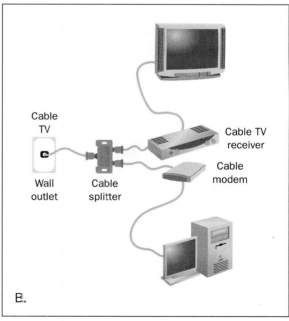

■ *DSL and ISDN modems:* DSL (*digital subscriber line*) and ISDN (*integrated services digital network*) *modems* connect your computer to the Internet.

■ *Network interface cards:* A *network interface card (NIC)* is an add-on card for either a desktop PC or a laptop computer. Each computer on a network must have a NIC. This card enables and controls the sending and receiving of data between the computers in a network. Most computers now come with a network interface built on the motherboard.

■ *Gateway*: A **gateway** is a combination of software and hardware that links two different types of networks that use different protocols. For instance, gateways between electronic mail systems permit users on different systems to exchange messages.

■ *Router*: A **router** is like a traffic policeman—this intelligent device directs network traffic. When you send data through a network, it is divided into small packets. All packets do not travel the same route; instead one might go in one direction and another in a different direction. When the packets reach their final destination, they are reassembled into the original message. A router connects multiple networks and determines the fastest available path to send these packets of data on their way to their correct destination. And, just like our traffic policeman, in the event of a partial network failure, the router can redirect the traffic over alternate paths.

■ *Wireless access point*: A **wireless access point** (**WAP** or **AP**) is a device that connects wireless communication devices together to create a wireless network. See Figure 7-6A. The WAP generally is connected to a wired network and can relay data between devices on each side. Many WAPs can be connected together to create a larger network that allows roaming.

> **Did You Know?**
>
> Bridges also are a communication device. A bridge is a special computer that connects one LAN to another LAN. For the most part, however, bridges are used rarely in modern networks.

■ *Hub*: A **hub** is a place of convergence where data arrives from one or more directions and is forwarded in one or more other directions. For example, a four-port USB hub connects up to four USB devices to a computer. See Figure 7-6B.

FIGURE 7-6
(A) Wireless access point (B) Four-port USB hub

A.

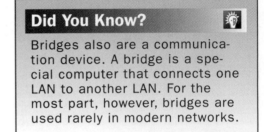

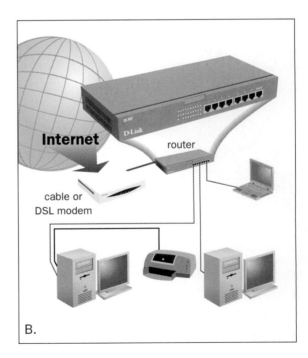

Internet

router

cable or DSL modem

B.

Communications Media

To transfer data from one computer to another requires some type of link through which the data can be transmitted. This link is known as the *communications channel*. The worldwide telephone network is an important part of this channel. The telephone system is actually a collection of the world's telephone networks, including cellular, local, long-distance, and communications satellite networks. Although it originally was designed to handle voice communications, it is now used to transmit data, including fax transmissions, computer-to-computer communications such as e-mail, and live video from the Web. *Bandwidth* is the transmission capacity of a communications channel. High bandwidth media, such as cable, fiber, and DSL, generally are referred to as *broadband*, whereas a standard telephone line generally is referred to as *baseband*.

At one end of the communications channel, you have a sending device, such as a computer or fax machine. A communications device, such as a modem, connected to the sending device converts the signal from the sender to a form that transmits over a standard dial-up telephone line or a dedicated line. A dial-up line provides a "temporary" connection, meaning each time a call is placed, the telephone company selects the line over which to transmit it. A dedicated line, on the other hand, provides a permanent or constant connection between the sending and receiving communications devices. The transmission is moved or "switched" from one wire or frequency to another. A *switch* is a device located at the telephone company's central office that establishes a link between a sender and receiver of data communications. At the receiving end, another modem converts the signal back into a format that the receiving device can understand.

To send the data through the channel requires some type of *transmission media*, which may be either physical or wireless.

Physical Media

Several types of physical media are used to transmit data. These include the following:

■ *Twisted-pair cable* is the least expensive type of cable and is the same type used for many telephone systems. It consists of two independently insulated copper wires twisted around one another. One of the wires carries the signal and the other wire is grounded to absorb signal interference. See Figure 7-7.

FIGURE 7-7
Twisted-pair cable

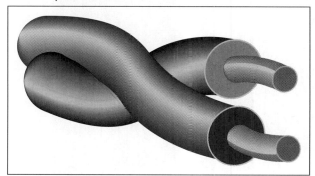

■ *Coaxial cabling* is the primary type of cabling used by the cable television industry, and it is also widely used for computer networks. Because the cable is heavily shielded, it is much less prone to interference than twisted-pair cable. However, it is more expensive than twisted-pair. See Figure 7-8.

FIGURE 7-8
Coaxial cable

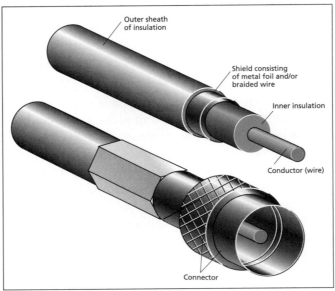

■ *Fiber-optic cable* is made from thin, flexible glass tubing. Fiber optics have several advantages over traditional metal communications lines. The bandwidth is much greater, so it can carry more data; it is much lighter than metal wires; and is much less susceptible to interference. The main disadvantage of fiber optics is that it is fragile and expensive. See Figure 7-9.

FIGURE 7-9
Fiber-optic cable

Wireless Media

Just like physical media, several wireless options also are available. These include the following:

- *Microwaves*: **Microwave** signals are sent through space in the form of electromagnetic waves. Just like radio signals, they also must be sent in straight lines from one microwave station to another. To avoid interference, most microwave stations are built on mountain-tops or placed on the top of large buildings. See Figure 7-10.

FIGURE 7-10
Microwave tower

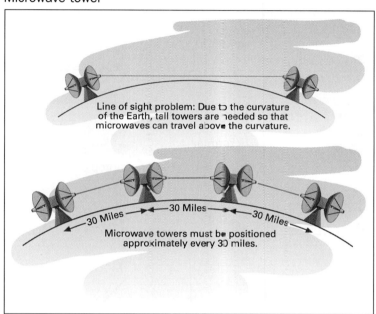

- *Satellites*: Communication **satellites** are placed in orbit 22,300 feet above the surface of the Earth. This allows the satellite to maintain a constant position above one point on the Earth's surface by rotating at the same speed as the Earth. The satellite contains equipment that receives the transmission, amplifies it, and sends it back to Earth. See Figure 7-11.

FIGURE 7-11
Satellites

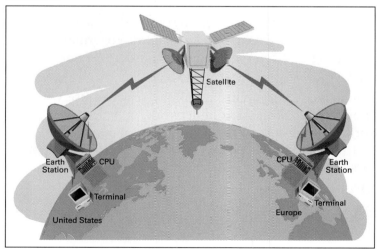

■ *IrDA*: *IrDA* media (also called infrared transmission) send signals using infrared light waves. This type of transmission is used for communication over short distances where the sending and receiving devices are within the line of sight. For example, your television remote control uses infrared to send signals to your TV. Many mobile devices, such as notebook computers, include an infrared port (also called an IrDA port). External devices, such as IrDA keyboards and mice, can be purchased and connected to desktop computers.

■ *Bluetooth*: *Bluetooth* technology uses radio waves to connect mobile devices such as cell phones, PDAs, and notebook computers. See Figure 7-12. The radio receivers embedded into these devices are tiny microchips about a half-inch square. Bluetooth supports short-distance transmission—about 30 feet or less between the devices.

FIGURE 7-12
Short-distance transmission with Bluetooth-enabled devices

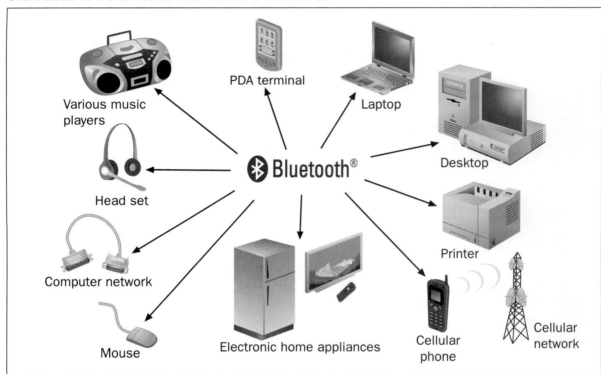

■ *Wi-Fi*: *Wi-Fi,* or wireless fidelity, identifies any network based on the 802.11 family of standards. The *802.11* technology is a family of standards governing wireless transmissions. The standards have progressed from supporting transfer rates of 1 or 2 Mbps up to 54 Mbps and higher.

The communications media an organization may select to use within a network are determined by several different factors: the type of network, the size of the network, and the cost. A network is not limited to one type of media. Most networks mix and match the media types.

The Windows XP operating system provides several informational screens on networking. You will explore these in Step-by-step 7.1.

Internet

For wireless networking terminology, visit *http:// compnetworking.about.com/ od/wirelessterms/.*

STEP-BY-STEP 7.1

1. Click **Start** on the Windows taskbar, and then click **Help and Support**. The Help and Support Center window opens, as shown in Figure 7-13. (Your Help and Support Center window may appear somewhat differently.)

FIGURE 7-13
Help and Support Center window

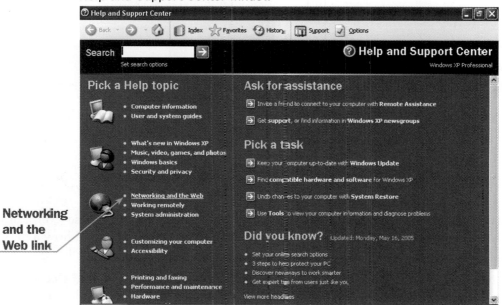

Networking
and the
Web link

2. Click the **Networking and the Web** link in the Pick a Help topic section.

3. Click **Networking** in the left pane, and then click **Getting started**. See Figure 7-14.

FIGURE 7-14
Getting Started window

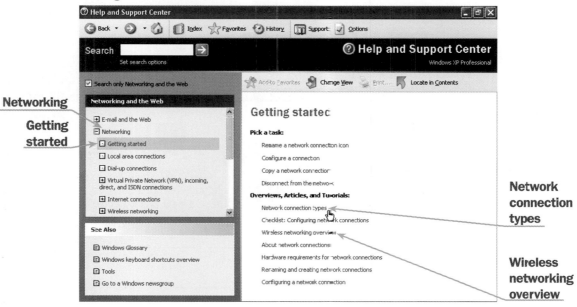

Networking

Getting
started

Network
connection
types

Wireless
networking
overview

STEP-BY-STEP 7.1 Continued

4. In the right pane, click the **Network connection types** link. See Figure 7-14 on the previous page.

5. Read the information in the Help topic. On a sheet of paper, or using your word-processing program, list the five types of network and dial-up connections.

6. Click the **Back** button at the top of the Help and Support Center window, and then click **Wireless networking overview**. Scroll to the bottom of the window.

7. Answer the following questions:

   a. What are the two classifications of wireless network types?

   b. What criteria are used for classification?

8. Close the Help and Support Center window.

Network Topologies

Networks can be designed using a variety of configurations. These configurations are referred to as topologies. A *topology* is simply the geometric arrangement of how a network is set up and connected. The following describes the three basic topologies:

■ *Bus topology*: Within the ***bus topology***, all devices are connected to and share a master cable. This master cable is called the bus or backbone. There is no single host computer. Data can be transmitted in both directions, from one device to another. This type of network is relatively easy to install and inexpensive. See Figure 7-15.

FIGURE 7-15
Bus topology

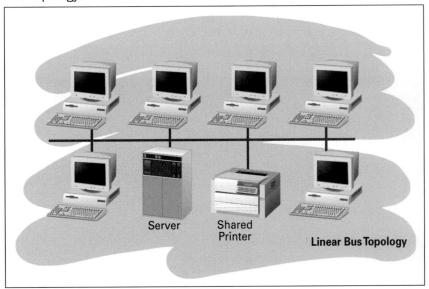

Server

Shared Printer

Linear Bus Topology

■ *Ring topology*: A ***ring topology*** is somewhat similar to a bus. However, the devices are connected in a circle instead of a line. Each computer within the circle is connected to adjoining devices on either side. Data travels from device to device around the ring. This type of topology is more difficult to install and manage and is more expensive. However, it does provide for faster transmission speeds and can span large distances. See Figure 7-16.

FIGURE 7-16
Ring topology

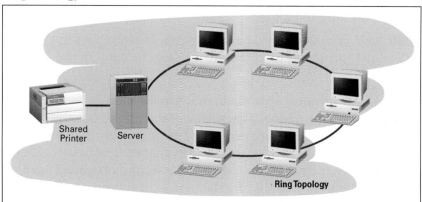

■ *Star topology*: Within a ***star topology***, all devices are connected to a central hub or computer. All data that transfers from one computer to another must pass through the hub. Star networks are relatively easy to install and manage, but bottlenecks can occur because all data must pass through the hub. This type of network requires more cabling than the other types. See Figure 7-17.

FIGURE 7-17
Star topology

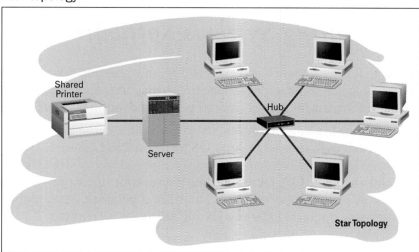

These three topologies also can be mixed or combined to produce hybrid topologies.

Communications Protocols

A protocol is an agreed-upon set of rules and procedures for transmitting data between two or more devices. Some of the features determined by the protocol are as follows:

- How the sending device indicates it has finished sending the message

- How the receiving device indicates it has received the message

- The type of error checking to be used

Many protocols have been developed over the years. However, within networking and LANs, the two most widely used protocols are Ethernet and token ring. On the Internet, the major protocol is TCP/IP.

- *Ethernet*: The **Ethernet** protocol was the first approved industry standard protocol. It is one of the most popular LAN protocols. Ethernet is based on the bus topology, but can work with the star topology as well. It supports data transfer rates of up to 10 megabits per second (Mbps). Two new Ethernet versions are available. The first is called Fast Ethernet and supports data transfer rates of 100 Mbps. The second is called Gigabit Ethernet and supports data transfer rates of 1,000 megabits, or 1 gigabit, per second.

- *Token ring*: The second most widely used LAN protocol is called **token ring**. Within this type of network, all of the computers are arranged in a circle. A token, which is a special signal, travels around the ring. To send a message, a computer on the ring catches the token, attaches a message to it, and then lets it continue to travel around the network.

- *TCP/IP*: TCP/IP is the acronym for Transmission Control Protocol/Internet Protocol. This protocol is used by both LANs and WANs and has been adopted as a standard to connect hosts on the Internet. Network operating systems, such as Microsoft NT and Novell Netware, support TCP/IP.

Network Operating Systems Software

All computers, including network servers, require an operating system. Network operating systems provide features such as administration, file management, print, communications, security, database, management, and other services to personal computer clients.

Two types of operating systems are necessary in computer networking. The first is the desktop operating system, such as Windows or Mac OS (discussed in Lesson 6). The second is the network operating system (also discussed in Lesson 6). Some desktop operating systems, such as Windows, UNIX, and the Mac OS, have built-in networking functions. These functions work adequately within a very limited environment. To utilize a network at its highest capacity, however, full-function network operating systems (NOS) software is required.

SUMMARY

In this lesson, you learned:

- Data communication is the transmission of data from one location to another.

- A network is a group of two or more computers linked together.

- The Internet is the biggest network of all.

- Networks have advantages and disadvantages.

- A local area network generally is confined to a limited geographical area.

- A wide area network is made up of several connected local area networks.

- The two popular types of LANs are the client/server network and peer-to-peer network.

- Other types of specialized networks include metropolitan area networks (MANs), neighborhood area networks (NANs), personal area networks (PANs), home area networks (HANs), and campus area networks (CANs).

- You can use a network for information sharing, hardware sharing, software sharing, and as a collaborative environment.

- The link through which data is transmitted is the communications channel.

- Transmission media can be either physical or wireless.

- Physical media include twisted-pair cable, coaxial cable, and fiber-optic cable.

- Wireless media includes radio signals, microwaves, and satellites.

- Most networks consist of a network server and computer clients.

- Communication devices facilitate the transmitting and receiving of data, instructions, and information.

- Communication devices include dial-up and cable modems, DSL and ISDN modems, network interface cards, gateways, routers, wireless access points, and hubs.

- Network interface cards enable the sending and receiving of data between the PCs in a network.

- A router directs the Internet or network traffic.

- Physical media include twisted-pair cable, coaxial cable, and fiber-optic cable.

- Wireless media includes microwaves, satellites, IrDA, Bluetooth, and Wi-Fi.

- Network topologies include bus, ring, and star.

- A protocol is an agreed-upon set of rules and procedures for transmitting data between two or more devices.

- The Ethernet protocol is one of the most popular LAN protocols. Token ring is the second most widely used LAN protocol.

- TCP/IP is a protocol used by both LANs and WANs to connect to the Internet.

- All computers on a network require an operating system, and networks require network operating systems.

VOCABULARY *Review*

Define the following terms:

Baseband	Ethernet	Server
Broadband	Local area network (LAN)	Star topology
Bus topology	Modem	Token ring
Client/server network	Peer-to-peer network	Topology
Clients	Ring topology	Transmission media
Communications channel	Router	Wide area network (WAN)
Data communications		

REVIEW *Questions*

MULTIPLE CHOICE

Select the best response for the following statements.

1. A _____ is confined to a limited geographical area.
    A. wide area network
    B. local area network
    C. tiny area network
    D. star topology

2. Which of the following is not a network type?
    A. MAN
    B. LAN
    C. FAN
    D. PAN

3. A _____ changes analog signals to digital signals and digital signals to analog.
    A. satellite
    B. NIC
    C. bridge
    D. modem

4. _____ is an example of physical media.
    A. Twisted-pair cable
    B. IrDA
    C. Bluetooth
    D. Bus topology

5. A geometric arrangement of a network is called a _____.
    A. bridge
    B. WAN
    C. LAN
    D. topology

TRUE/FALSE

Circle T if the statement is true or F if the statement is false.

T F 1. The least expensive type of physical communications media is fiber-optic cable.

T F 2. Information sharing is a network benefit.

T F 3. The 802.11 technology is a family of standards governing wireless transmission.

T F 4. An add-on card that allows a computer to connect to a network is called a network interface card (NIC).

T F 5. The token ring protocol was the first approved industry standard protocol.

FILL IN THE BLANK

Complete the following sentences by writing the correct word or words in the blanks provided.

1. _____ is the standard protocol used to connect hosts on the Internet.

2. _____ cable is heavily shielded and is not very prone to interference.

3. In a(n) _____ network, all computers are equal.

4. A(n) _____ network always covers a large geographical area.

5. _____ is the transmission capacity of a communications channel.

PROJECTS

CROSS-CURRICULAR—MATHEMATICS

Assume that you have two computers, a printer, and a scanner that you want to network. Create a report, including a table, listing the hardware and software you would need to purchase, including the cost. How much will your network cost? How will you connect to the Internet, and how much will that cost? List your total cost for the project.

CROSS-CURRICULAR—SCIENCE

Use the Internet and perform a Web search on Bluetooth technology. Find at least one positive and one negative aspect of this technology. Write a one-page report on how this technology is being used. Include your opinion on the future of this technology.

CROSS-CURRICULAR—SOCIAL STUDIES

Assume that you are the system administrator for a local area network. Most networks have a usage policy. Use the Internet and other resources to design a usage policy for your network.

CROSS-CURRICULAR—LANGUAGE ARTS

Select a business that you would like to run from home. Create a report describing your business and how you could market your business using one or more of the following technologies: a network, e-mail, Internet connection, fax modem, and a Web site.

 ## WEB PROJECT

Several popular network operating systems are in use. Search the Web for information on network operating systems. Select at least three of the more popular systems. Prepare a report and chart comparing the features of these three NOSs.

 ## TEAMWORK PROJECT

Your supervisor at work is interested in using the company's network to set up a computerized teleconference with several of the other stores throughout the state. However, she would like to get more information on this undertaking. She has asked you and the assistant manager to research this project and to prepare a report.

CRITICAL*Thinking*

You now have three computers, a scanner, a DVD player, a printer, and a copier spread throughout several rooms in your home. You and your family have decided it is time to network the equipment. Your goal is to determine whether to go wired or wireless. After you decide on the technology you will use, write a one-page report listing why you selected this technology and provide an overview of your network plan.

COMPUTER BASICS

REVIEW *Questions*

FILL IN THE BLANK

Complete the following sentences by writing the correct word or words in the blanks provided.

1. A(n) _____ is an electronic device that receives data (input), processes data, stores data, and produces a result (output).

2. _____ is the technology that enables computers to communicate with each other and other devices.

3. A(n) _____ is a highlighted word or image within a hypertext document which, when clicked, takes you to another place within that document or to another Web site.

4. The _____ in Internet Explorer provides some control over what content can be viewed on the Internet.

5. _____ relates to a search engine's capability to find variations of a word.

6. _____ search engines focus on video, animation, graphics, and music.

7. The _____ contains the CPU, memory, and basic controllers for the system. It also contains ports and expansion slots.

8. _____ is a type of external bus that can connect up to 63 external devices.

9. _____ is instructions issued to the computer so that specific tasks are performed.

10. A(n) _____ is a group of two or more computers linked together.

MULTIPLE CHOICE

Select the best response for the following statements.

1. The _____ is the center of all processing.
   A. monitor
   B. motherboard
   C. control unit
   D. computer system

2. A _____ is a thin plate or board that contains electronic components.
   A. CPU
   B. control unit
   C. circuit board
   D. controller

3. A(n) _____ is an organized collection of data.
   A. Usenet
   B. index
   C. database
   D. spider

4. A(n) _____ is a software program that enables the user to search the Internet using keywords.
   A. search engine
   B. database
   C. modem
   D. operating system

5. A _____ identifies a site on the Internet.
   A. protocol
   B. hyperlink
   C. browser
   D. domain name

6. The original name for the Internet was _____.
   A. FTP
   B. OSP
   C. ARPANET
   D. UNIVAC

7. _____ worked with IBM to develop the operating system for the IBM PC.
   A. Dr. Ted Hoff
   B. Steve Wozniak
   C. Bill Gates
   D. Steve Jobs

8. _____ is the ability to use a computer and its software to accomplish practical tasks.
   A. Compatibility
   B. Computer literacy
   C. Multitasking
   D. Stemming

9. On the Internet, the major protocol is _____.
   A. TCP/IP
   B. MAN
   C. DSL
   D. ISDN

10. The _____ is the most commonly used device for entering numeric and alphabetic data into a computer.
    A. microphone
    B. mouse
    C. keyboard
    D. pointing device

TRUE/FALSE

Circle T if the statement is true or F if the statement is false.

T   F   1.   A browser is a software program that provides a graphical interface for the Internet.

T   F   2.   A mailing list is a group of Internet providers.

T   F   3.   A chat room creates real-time communication between multiple users.

T   F   4.   HTML is a protocol that controls how Web pages are formatted and displayed.

T   F   5.   A host computer stands alone; in other words, it is not part of a network.

T   F   6.   The Internet and the World Wide Web are the same.

T   F   7.   Extranets are systems that allow outside organizations to access a company's internal information system.

T   F   8.   The two basic types of software are application software and system software.

T   F   9.   The type of input device used is determined by the task to be completed.

T   F   10.   A USB Flash drive also is called a jump drive.

PROJECTS

CROSS-CURRICULAR—MATHEMATICS

Use the Internet and other resources to locate information on how computers are being used to teach mathematics. Prepare a two-page report including at least three ways computers are being used. You may find useful information at *www.ask.com* to include in your report.

CROSS-CURRICULAR—SCIENCE

You are interested in learning how to create an effective Web page. You have decided to do some research to gather as much information as possible. Use the Internet and other resources to locate information on Web page creation. Prepare a report to identify qualities of an effective Web page and policies governing Web sites. Add any other information that you find useful. The following sites may be helpful: *http://www.webreference.com/greatsite.html* and *www.useit.com/ alertbox/9605.html*.

CROSS-CURRICULAR—SOCIAL STUDIES

Cell phones are becoming more and more sophisticated almost daily. Can you remember what the early cell phones were like? What were some of their capabilities? Use the Internet and other resources to investigate and prepare a timeline for cell phones showing "new and improved" features. If possible, include pictures of the early cell phones.

CROSS-CURRICULAR—LANGUAGE ARTS

The introduction of e-mail introduced a new form of online communication called "emoticons" or "smileys." These are symbols used to represent a variety of facial expressions to enhance communication. Use the Internet to locate information on this form of communication. Prepare a report to share your findings. Include a list of symbols and explanation of what each represents.

 ### WEB PROJECT

Online courses have become very popular at colleges, universities, and some high schools. Some schools offer entire degrees online. Students taking online courses do not have to physically attend classes; they use the Internet to complete their course requirements. Use the Internet to research information related to online instruction. Prepare a two- to three-page report that includes a description of how online courses are conducted, their advantages and disadvantages, and any other interesting information you find.

 ### TEAMWORK PROJECT

You and a partner have been given an assignment to research information related to safe use of the Internet by young children and teenagers. You have decided to discuss the topic with other students and your local police department in addition to conducting research on the Internet. After you gather information, prepare a document that lists eight to ten "rules" for safety on the Internet. You may find useful information at *www.getnetwise.org*.

SIMULATION

You and a friend are opening a computer consulting business. You will offer in-home consulting services, providing assistance with application software, minor computer operations, and information research.

JOB 1-1

Your first client has called to ask about input devices for someone who has function in only one hand. She is unable to use the standard keyboard.

Use the Internet to research alternative input devices that your client could possibly use. Prepare a report that includes the type and description of each device as well as advantages and disadvantages. Also include cost if available. The client also has asked for your recommendation on the best device for her particular situation. Prepare a written response to her request that explains your recommendation.

JOB 1-2

A client wants to purchase a computer that he can use to write papers for an English Composition course he is taking. His typing skills are very limited. He has contacted your company for help in determining which computer and software he should purchase. He has a budget of $2,500. Use store ads, the Internet, catalogs, and other resources to identify three computers and the type of software that would best meet his needs. Prepare a table that lists information about the hardware and software options. Include items, such as the computer, printer, storage devices, and software. Prepare a written recommendation on the option that you think will work best for your client.

PORTFOLIO *Checklist*

Include the following activities from this unit in your portfolio:

_____ Lesson 1 Mathematics Cross-Curricular Report

_____ Lesson 2 Social Studies Cross-Curricular Report

_____ Lesson 3 Social Studies Cross-Curricular Report

_____ Lesson 4 Science Cross-Curricular Drawing

_____ Lesson 5 Science Cross-Curricular Report

_____ Lesson 6 Language Arts Cross-Curricular Program Icon

_____ Lesson 7 Social Studies Cross-Curricular Network Usage Policy

_____ Unit 1 Review Simulation Job 1-1 Recommendation

_____ Unit 1 Review Simulation Job 1-2 Recommendation

USING THE COMPUTER

Unit 2

 Estimated Time for Unit: 10.5 hours

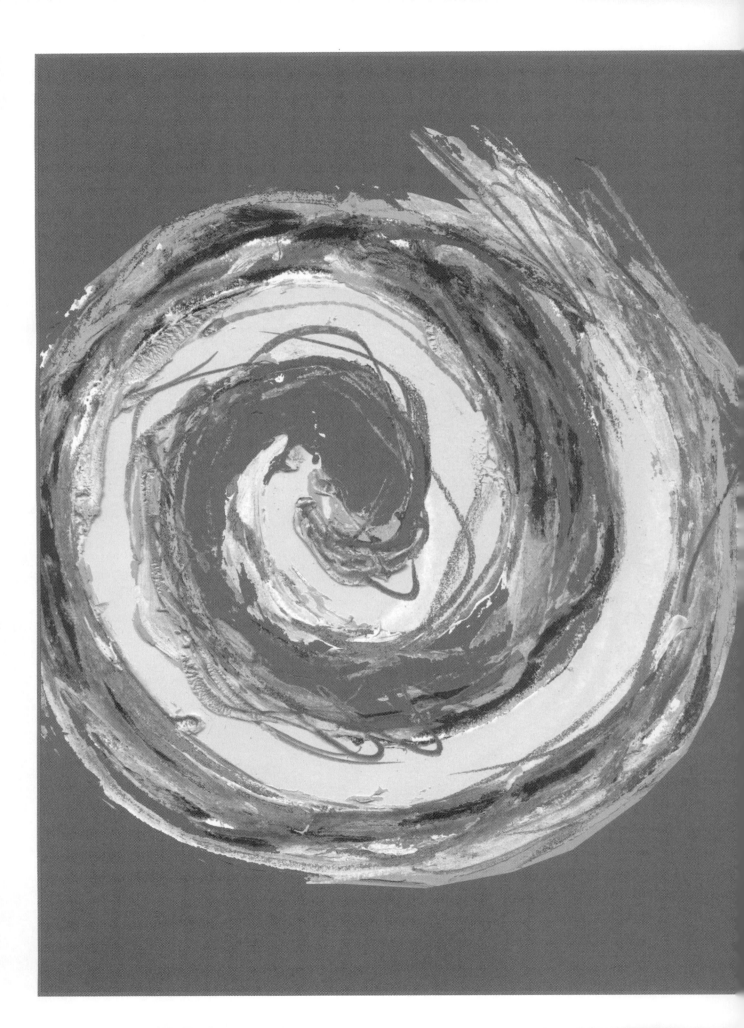

KEYBOARDING

Introduction to Keyboarding

The computer has become a part of our daily life—at work, at home, and at play. Increasingly, we use the computer to complete a variety of everyday tasks, such as composing letters, sending e-mails, managing our finances, and so on. To effectively use the computer requires good keyboarding skills. *Keyboarding* (also called *touch typing*) is the ability to input data by touch using the alphabetic and numeric keys on a computer and/or typewriter keyboard. Using the proper touch system of keyboarding is most important since it determines our speed and accuracy.

Developing good keyboarding skills requires practice and time. Once you have developed your keyboarding skills, you can use word-processing, database, spreadsheet, desktop publishing, presentation, data communications, and other computer software programs more productively. In addition, proper keyboarding techniques can help reduce the risk of carpal tunnel syndrome (CTS). This condition occurs due to an expansion of tendons in the wrist, resulting in pain in the hand and arm.

Learning Correct Keyboarding Techniques

Keyboarding is much like playing a piano or other musical instrument, where the brain and fingers must work together. Several basic techniques are required to learn to keyboard effectively. These include using the correct posture, holding the hands and wrists properly, striking the keys correctly without watching your fingers, and using the "home row" keys properly. Do not worry about speed; if you develop good techniques, the speed will come.

Position

The correct keyboarding position refers to your posture. See Figure 8-1.

FIGURE 8-1
Correct posture is important

- Sit up straight and lean forward slightly from the waist. Your body should be about a hand's length from the front of the keyboard and centered with the keyboard.

- Keep both feet flat on the floor.

- Let your elbows hang naturally at your sides.

- Rest your fingers lightly on the keys.

- Focus your eyes on the book or reference resources unless you are composing at the keyboard; in that case, keep your eyes on the computer screen.

Key Stroking

You must use the correct finger to stroke each key you type. Learning the location of each key and which finger to use to press the key may be the most challenging aspect of learning to keyboard. Keep your fingers curved over the home row. The *home row keys* include *A, S, D, F,* and *J, K, L, ;*. These keys are called the home row because they are the keys to which you return your fingers after you press a key.

On most keyboards, the home row has *bump keys* to assist you in correct placement of your fingers. The bump keys have a small, raised dot in the center of the key or a raised dash at the bottom of the key. They are placed differently on different keyboards and might be on the two index-finger keys or on the middle-finger keys. These keys provide a physical clue to correct finger placement on the home row. Memorizing the location of the keys will help you to develop your keyboarding skill. Do not look at your hands or the keys as you type. See Figure 8-2.

FIGURE 8-2
Correct finger position

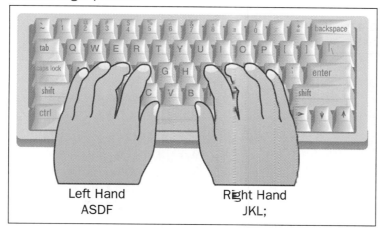

Left Hand
ASDF

Right Hand
JKL;

Your fingers are named for the home row keys on which they rest: *A* finger, *S* finger, *J* finger, and so on. Assigning your fingers names will assist you in making proper moves when reaching for keys. To type the letter "r," for example, you will press the key with the *F* finger, and to type the letter "n," you will press the key with the *J* finger. Figure 8-3 provides a closer look at the fingers you use to press the different keys.

FIGURE 8-3
Fingers you use to press various keys

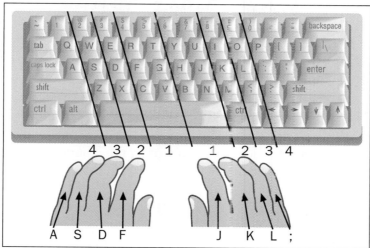

Following are some guidelines for stroking keys:

■ Rest your fingertips lightly on the keys.

■ Keep your fingers slightly curved and upright. Make sure that the palm of your hand does not touch the keyboard or the desk.

■ Press the key with a quick, snappy stroke and return the finger to the home row.

Two additional keys you will learn to use are the Enter key and the spacebar. Figure 8-4 shows the proper finger position for these keys.

FIGURE 8-4
Finger positions for the Enter key and spacebar

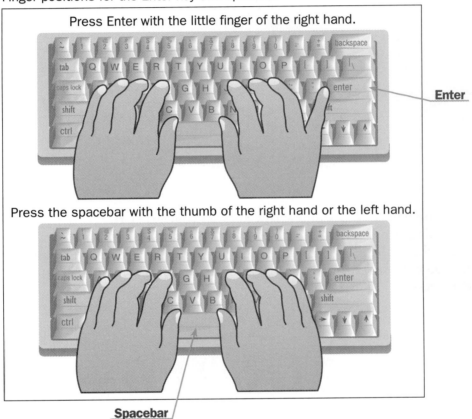

You use the Enter key to move down to the next line. Use the finger on the semicolon key to press the Enter key.

You use the spacebar to insert spaces between words, punctuation marks, and so on. Use the right or left thumb to press the spacebar.

Your Workstation

An organized workstation, which includes your desk, chair, computer, printer, supplies, and reference materials, enhances your productivity. Place reference materials on the right side of the computer and supplies on the left side. Remove any items you are not using.

Keyboard History

The first "writing machine" was developed in the 1800s. These early writing machines came in various sizes and shapes. Many attempts were made to design a keyboard that would allow a typist to type quickly and accurately. Figures 8-5 and 8-6 show examples of two of these early writing machines.

FIGURE 8-5
Early writing machine

FIGURE 8-6
Early writing machine

The *QWERTY* keyboard was the work of inventor Christopher L. Sholes, who developed the prototype for the first commercial typewriter in a Milwaukee machine shop in the 1860s. Pronounced *KWER-tee*, it is named after the first six letters on the top row of alphabetic keys on the standard English computer keyboard. Today, the QWERTY layout is still the most widely used keyboard format for computers. Figure 8-7 shows a typical QWERTY keyboard.

Did You Know?

Many early computers had "blind keys." These keys did not have anything printed on them so it did not help typists to watch their keys when typing.

FIGURE 8-7
The QWERTY keyboard

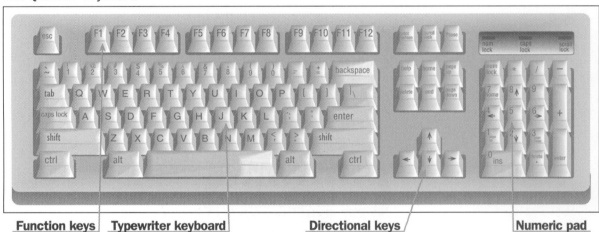

Function keys   Typewriter keyboard   Directional keys   Numeric pad

Some keyboards are designed to relieve stress that can result from repeated and/or longtime use on a keyboard. These are called *ergonomic keyboards*. Figure 8-8 shows an example of an ergonomic keyboard.

Did You Know?

Early typists were called "typewriters."

FIGURE 8-8
An ergonomic keyboard

Even though there are different types of keyboards, they all have the same basic parts. These are identified in Figure 8-9 and described in the following text.

FIGURE 8-9
Computer keyboard parts

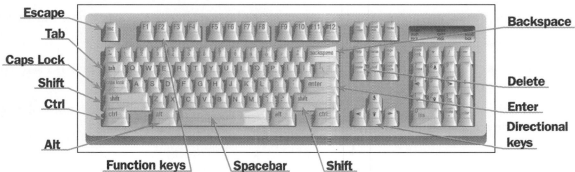

1. The **spacebar** is used to insert a space between words and at the end of a sentence. You press the spacebar with the left or right thumb.

2. The **Alt** (alternate) key can be used alone, or in combination with other keys to do common tasks. Its function is dependent on the specific software program. It is considered a modifier key.

3. The **Ctrl** (control) key, also a modifier key, can be used alone, or in conjunction with other keys to do common tasks. Its function is dependent on the specific software program.

4. Use the **Shift** key to capitalize letters and to type the symbols above the number keys. Hold down the Shift key while you hit the letter you want capitalized. The keyboard contains two Shift keys, usually located on either side and below the home row. Use the right Shift key to capitalize letters that you type with your left hand and vise versa. Use your little fingers to operate the Shift key.

5. Use the **Caps Lock** key to capitalize a series of letters. The Caps Lock key is on the left side of your keyboard. When you press the Caps Lock key, all letters you type will be capitals until you press the key again. It only affects letters, not punctuation symbols or numbers.

6. Use the **Tab** key to move the insertion point to the next tab marker in your document. One of the more common uses of the Tab key is to indent the first line of a paragraph.

7. The **Escape** (Esc) key usually is located to the left of the top row of letter keys on the keyboard. Generally, this key is used to interrupt or cancel an operation. It can be used for other functions, depending on the software program.

8. **Function** keys are a set of programmable keys on a keyboard. They are generally positioned across the top of the keyboard, and labeled F1 through F12. These keys perform different tasks, determined by the software program.

9. Pressing the **Enter** key moves the insertion point to the next line and starts a new line of text.

10. The **Backspace** key removes the character to the left of the insertion point.

11. The **Delete** key removes the character to the right of the insertion point. It also is used to delete any text or object that is currently selected.

12. The **directional keys** are the four keys with arrows on them. They are used to control movement of the insertion point on the screen.

The Computer Screen

In this lesson, you use word-processing software to practice your keyboarding skills. Word-processing software is used primarily for the creation of text documents. The figures in this book show Microsoft Word 2003. After you start your word-processing program, a screen similar to that shown in Figure 8-10 on the next page appears. The parts of the opening screen are described below. (Your screen might differ from the one shown here.)

FIGURE 8-10
Opening screen for Microsoft Word

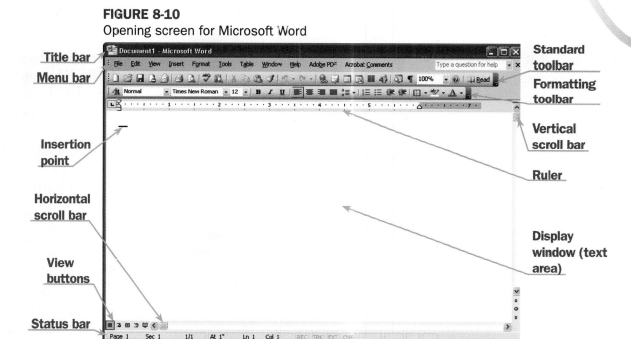

- *Title bar*: Displays the filename you assign to the open document.

- *Menu bar*: Contains menu names; when selected, each menu displays a list of commands.

- Standard toolbar: A *toolbar* contains buttons that you use to quickly execute certain commands; the Standard toolbar has buttons for the more commonly used commands.

- Formatting toolbar: Contains buttons for commands you use to change the appearance of a document.

- *Ruler*: Feature that enables you to control paragraph indentations, margin settings, and tab settings.

- Display window or *text area*: The area in which you type information. As you type in this area, the insertion point continues to move to the right.

- *Insertion point*: The point where the next character keyed appears on the display screen. The insertion point usually is represented by a blinking vertical line.

- Vertical scroll bar: Enables you to scroll vertically through your document.

- Horizontal scroll bar: Enables you to scroll horizontally through your document.

- *Status bar*: Displays information about your document, including current page number, total pages in the document, location of insertion point, and the status of some of the special-purpose keys.

As indicated previously, your word-processing program might have different features. For the most part, however, word-processing programs function in much the same way. For example, the insertion point automatically moves to the next line when it comes to the end of the current line. This is called *word wrap*. The text will "wrap" around the right margin and continue on the next line. You do not need to press the Enter key to get to the next line. You do need to press the Enter key to start a new paragraph.

Developing Beginning Keyboarding Skills

Now that you are familiar with the keyboard layout and the basic components of a word processor's opening screen, you are ready to begin developing keyboarding skills. The most important factor in mastering keyboarding skills is good technique. You build speed and accuracy by applying good technique. At this point, however, do not concern yourself with speed. Concentrate on being accurate, and the speed will come later.

Learning to type all of the keys and to develop accuracy and speed will take several weeks of concentrated study. This lesson does not provide you with comprehensive keyboarding instruction. It introduces you to keyboarding concepts and provides practice drills to help you learn the location of the keys.

You might be instructed to save your practice drills on a floppy disk. Some floppy disks need to be formatted before you can save files to them. *Formatting* a floppy disk is the process of preparing it to receive and store data. Most floppy disks used today are high density, capable of holding 1.44 MB of data. In Step-by-step 8.1, you format a disk. (*Note*: If you are saving files to a different type of storage device, such as a CD or USB drive, or if your floppy disk does not need to be formatted, then you can skip Step-by-step 8.1.)

Important
If you are storing your files on the hard drive, you do not need to perform a format. You never want to format your hard drive!

ADMINISTRATIVE ASSISTANT

An administrative assistant provides administrative support to a manager or group of managers. This support might include coordinating office services and performing typing and transcription duties, compiling data, and preparing various reports and correspondence.

An element of the administrative assistant's job is to operate a computer to access e-mail, electronic calendars, and other basic software, including word processing, spreadsheet, database, and presentation.

A person in this position must have excellent communication skills and the ability to perform typing/word-processing duties. Administrative assistants also are expected to have administrative and supervisory abilities.

An associate's degree in administrative support technology or business or office administration is preferred. It also is helpful to have three to five years of experience. In some instances, additional education may be substituted for years of work experience.

The general salary range for this job is between $25,000 and $35,000. Salary varies depending on location of position, size of organization, and experience level.

S TEP-BY-STEP 8.1

1. Insert a floppy disk. Click the **Start** button on the taskbar and then click **My Computer**.

2. In the My Computer window, right-click the icon for your floppy disk drive.

3. Click **Format** on the shortcut menu, as shown in Figure 8-11. Your shortcut menu may show different commands.

FIGURE 8-11
Select Format on the shortcut menu

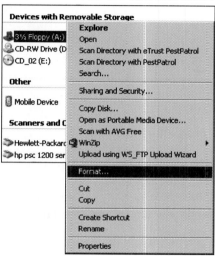

4. The Format dialog box opens, as shown in Figure 8-12. In the Volume label box, type your name.

FIGURE 8-12
Format dialog box

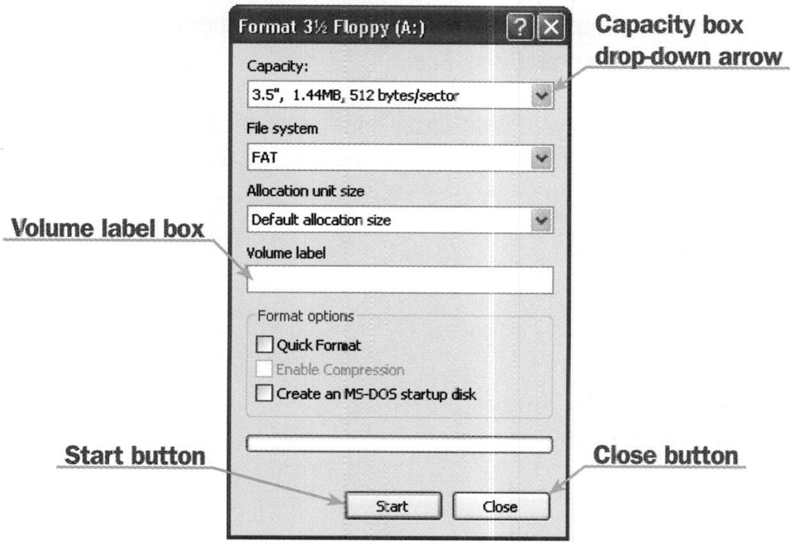

5. Click the Capacity box **drop-down arrow**, and choose either **1.44MB** (which will probably be the one listed) or **720 KB**.

6. Click the **Start** button. A warning box appears. Click the **OK** button.

STEP-BY-STEP 8.1 Continued

7. When the formatting process is completed, a window will open, indicating that the format is complete. Click the **OK** button, and then click the **Close** button to close the window.

8. Close My Computer by clicking the **Close** button at the top-right corner of the window.

In this course, it is assumed that you are using a word-processing program, such as Microsoft Word, to complete the step-by-step exercises. Other programs, including Windows WordPad and Notepad, also can be used.

Practice typing the home row keys in Step-by-step 8.2.

S TEP-BY-STEP 8.2

1. Organize your workstation.

2. Start your word-processing program.

3. Check your posture to be sure you are following the guidelines listed earlier in this lesson.

4. Place your fingers on the home row keys. Curve your fingers so the tips of your fingers are resting on the home row keys. Remember, your fingers are "named" for the home row keys on which they rest: *A* finger, *S* finger, *D* finger, and so on.

5. You will press the spacebar to space between words. Practice using the spacebar. Tap the **spacebar** once (with your right or left thumb); tap it twice; tap it once; tap it twice.

6. You will press the Enter key to move to the next line. This is called a *hard return*. To press the Enter key, extend the "semi" (for semicolon) finger to the Enter key and press lightly. Practice using the Enter key. Reach and press **Enter**. (Remember to return the semi finger to the ; key.) Press the **spacebar** once, twice, once, twice. Press **Enter**.

7. Type the following home row keys. Press **Enter** once after each line and two times after each group of lines. (If time allows, repeat this step several times to get more practice with these keys.)

   ff jj dd kk ss ll aa ;; f j d k s l a ;
   ff jj dd kk ss ll aa ;; f j d k s l a ;

   jj ff kk dd ll ss ;; aa fj a; fj a;
   jj ff kk dd ll ss ;; aa fj a; fj a;

   jk fk kl ds l; sa fj kd sl a; fj a;
   jk fk kl ds l; sa fj kd sl a; fj a;

   aaa lll lll all all sss aaa ddd sad sad
   aaa lll lll all all sss aaa ddd sad sad

   sad sad fad fad ask ask lad lad dad dad
   sad sad fad fad ask ask lad lad dad dad

8. Press **Enter** again and keep the document open for Step-by-step 8.3.

Most keyboarding courses use the same method to teach the rest of the alphabetic keys. After learning the location of the alphabetic keys, you complete drills on the number and symbol keys and begin drills focusing on accuracy and then speed. Drills used to develop speed and accuracy are called *timed writings*. These types of drills and timed writings are beyond the scope of this book. In Step-by-step 8.3, you will practice new key reaches.

S TEP-BY-STEP 8.3

1. Type the following lines. The E key is typed using the *D* finger, and the H key is typed using the *J* finger. Press **Enter** once after each line and two times after each group of lines. (If time allows, repeat this step several times to get more practice with these keys.)

ddd ddd eee eee ded ded ede ede
ddd ddd eee eee ded ded ede ede

hhh hhh jjj jjj jhj jhj hjh hjh
hhh hhh jjj jjj jhj jhj hjh hjh

he he she she shed shed held held
he he she she shed shed held held

he asked; she has; a shed; he has ash
he asked; she has; a shed; he has ash

2. Type the following lines to practice using the Shift, Caps Lock, Tab, and Backspace keys. Press **Enter** once after each line and two times after each group of lines. (If time allows, repeat this step several times to get more practice with these keys.)

[left Shift] j [spacebar] [left Shift] j [spacebar]
Jade Jade Jade Jas Jas Jas Jeff Jeff Jeff

[right Shift] e [spacebar] [right Shift] e [spacebar]
Ed Ed Ed Ada Ada Ada Dale Dale Dale

[Caps Lock] SEE JAMES EAT
JEFF JEFF AL AL ASA ASA [Caps Lock]

[Tab] Jake Jake safe safe Half Half
[Tab] She She He He feed feed all all

she had a lead; shed [Backspace] [spacebar] had a lead;
she asked a lade [Backspace] [spacebar]

3. Complete the following steps to save your work.

   a. Click **File** on the menu bar and then click **Save As**.

   b. In the Save As dialog box, select the location you want to save your work. (If instructed, you can save to the disk you formatted in Step-by-step 8.1.)

   c. In the File name box, type **Practice** as the name of the document.

   d. Click the **Save** button.

Net Fun

Use a search engine such as Google or HotBot to locate information on taking care of your disks.

Printing and Closing

To print a file, complete the following steps:

■ Click File on the menu bar and then click Print.

■ In the Print dialog box, click the OK button.

■ You are returned to your screen while the document is printing.

To close a document, click File on the menu bar and then click Close. When you finish working in a program, you should close the program. To do so, click File on the menu bar and then click Exit.

Retrieving a File

After you save a file, you can open that file to review it, add or delete information, or make other changes.

To open a file:

■ Click File on the menu bar and then click Open.

■ In the Open dialog box, select the drive and folder where your file is located.

■ Click the name of the file you want to open.

■ Click the Open button. A copy of the file appears on your screen.

 Ethics in Technology

PLAGIARISM

"Plagiarism is stealing a ride on someone else's train of thought."
—Author unknown

This definition of plagiarism is very accurate. The basis of plagiarism involves using information as if it were your own.

Why is plagiarism illegal? Even though you might consider it simply borrowing words, pictures, or music from someone, you still are taking something that belongs to someone else. It is his or her possession just like a person's car, house, and so on. Paraphrasing someone else's thoughts also is a form of plagiarism unless you give the originator the credit for the work.

With widespread use of the Internet, incidents of plagiarism have risen at an astonishing rate. It does not take as much time to find information electronically as it does to go through volumes of books to find the same information. A research paper easily can be put together using the cut-and-paste function in your word-processing program.

Easy as it might be, it is also illegal! It is a form of theft. You are taking someone else's work and using it as if it were your own.

How can you avoid plagiarism? You must give credit whenever you use another person's work, or you must ask permission to use their work in your document.

Additional Features

Most word-processing programs offer extensive features for composing and formatting documents. These include spelling and grammar checking, a thesaurus, formatting options, and special characters.

Spell Checking, Grammar, and Thesaurus Features

If you make a spelling error as you are typing a document, you might see a wavy red line under it, identifying that it is a misspelled word. You can correct the error yourself, or you can use the built-in spell checker.

If you want to correct the word yourself, use one of the following methods:

- Press the Backspace key to delete text to the left of the insertion point. For example, if the insertion point is to the right of the "m" in computer and you press the Backspace key, the "m" is deleted.

- Press the Delete key to delete text to the right of the insertion point. For example, if the insertion point is to the left of the "m" in computer and you press the Delete key, the "m" is deleted.

The spell checker in your software typically checks a document for any misspelled words or words that are not in the software's spelling dictionary. Many word-processing programs also include a grammar checker either with the spell checker or as a separate program.

To access the spell checker in most word-processing programs:

- Click Tools on the menu bar and select Spelling and Grammar on the menu (or click the spell checker button on the toolbar).

- The Spelling and Grammar dialog box opens, and is similar to that shown in Figure 8-13. If the program does not recognize the spelling of a word, it is displayed in the dialog box. You have several options from which to choose.

- If the word is mispelled, click the correct word from the list provided, and then click Change. If the word is not misspelled, click Ignore Once or Ignore All.

FIGURE 8-13
Spelling and Grammar dialog box

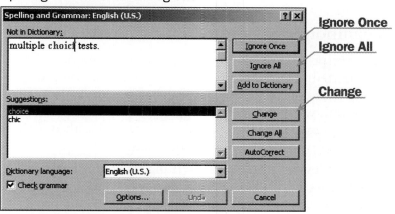

It is important to note that spell checkers do not check for mistakes such as homophone usage. Homophones are words that sound the same but are spelled differently and have different meanings, such as *their* and *there*, or *site*, *cite*, and *sight*. Therefore, it still is necessary to proofread your document carefully.

In Microsoft Word, the thesaurus provides a list of synonyms for the selected word. The grammar checker is a "natural language" grammar checker that flags possible problems by performing a comprehensive analysis of the text. The grammar checker might not look for all types of problems; it is designed to focus on the more typical or frequent errors.

Formatting Documents

After you learn to keyboard, you will type various types of documents, such as letters and reports. You will need to format these documents and adjust margins, spacing, and so on. You might even want to change the font, adjust the size of the text, or bold, underline, or italicize the text. You can apply all of these enhancements, and many more, to your document. This is called *formatting* your document.

You can apply formatting commands before you type the document or you can format your text after you enter it. You access formatting commands in most software programs through a toolbar or a menu. To apply formats before you type, select the formatting commands and then begin typing. To apply formats to text that already is typed, you must first select the text. To do this, click before the first letter and drag to highlight the text you want to format. Then, select the formatting commands to be applied. For example, suppose you want to format the title of a report in bold. Select the title by clicking the first letter, holding down the left mouse button, and dragging to the end of the title. Then, click the Bold button on the Formatting toolbar.

Keyboarding Software

Many different keyboarding software programs are available for learning to keyboard. These programs provide instruction, drills, and testing for developing keyboarding skills. Some of the more popular of these keyboarding software programs include Kid Keys™, Mavis Beacon Teaches Typing®, Letter Chase Typing Tutor, Mario Teaches Typing™, and All the Right Type Three™.

Some of these programs are designed for persons with special needs, such as those who have poor vision or who can use only one hand. Some programs have voice instructions. When using one of these programs, it is important to use appropriate techniques as discussed previously in this lesson.

Speech Recognition Software and Other Input Devices

Several software programs now support speech recognition. You speak through a microphone that is connected to your computer, and the information is displayed on your screen. You will need to train your computer to recognize your voice. This might take some time, but the result of this new skill will be that you can get your work done faster. Studies have shown that voice input easily can exceed 100 words per minute and with practice, 130 words per minute. The average typist can type 40 to 50 words per minute.

Additional input devices include handwriting recognition software, scanners, mobile tablet PCs, personal digital assistants (PDAs), digital pens, and touch screens.

SUMMARY

In this lesson, you learned:

■ Keyboarding (or typing) is the process of inputting text into a device such as a computer by pressing keys on a keyboard.

■ The standard keyboard contains alphanumeric keys, modifier keys, numeric keypad, function keys, cursor movement keys, and special-purpose keys (Esc, Print Screen, Scroll Lock, and Pause/Break).

■ The home row consists of the following keys: *A S D F J K L* and *;*.

■ Bump keys are located on selected keys on some keyboards to assist in the correct placement of your fingers.

■ The primary parts of an opening word-processor screen are the title bar, menu bar, Standard toolbar, Formatting toolbar, ruler, text area, vertical and horizontal scroll bars, and status bar.

■ Using correct techniques is important in developing keyboarding skills. These techniques include posture, key stroking, and the organization of your workstation.

■ You should save your work often.

■ You can retrieve files that have been saved.

■ The spell checker checks a document for words it does not recognize. It gives you several options when incorrectly spelled words are found.

■ You may enhance the appearance of your document by using the formatting features available in most software programs.

■ Keyboarding software is available for learning to keyboard.

■ Speech recognition software allows you to "talk" to your computer to enter data.

■ Digital pens, PDAs, handwriting recognition, mobile tablet PCs, and touch screens are other tools that can be used to input data.

VOCABULARY *Review*

Define the following terms:

Bump keys	Keyboarding	Text area
Ergonomic keyboard	Menu bar	Timed writings
Formatting	Modifier keys	Title bar
Hard return	QWERTY	Toolbar
Home row keys	Ruler	Word wrap
Insertion point	Status Bar	

REVIEW *Questions*

MULTIPLE CHOICE

Select the best response for the following statements.

1. Standard keyboards have the _____ layout.
    A. QWARKY
    B. QWERTY
    C. QWAZXY
    D. QWYTRE

2. The Alt and Ctrl keys are considered _____ keys.
    A. number
    B. modifier
    C. function
    D. directional

3. The _____ displays information about a document, including current page number, total pages in document, location of cursor, and so on.
    A. Formatting toolbar
    B. status bar
    C. vertical scroll bar
    D. horizontal scroll bar

4. The home row keys include _____.
    A. a, b, c, d, k, l, ; ,
    B. q, w, e, r, t, y
    C. a, s, d, f, j, k, l, ;
    D. y, r, t, q, k l, j

5. You press the _____ key to move the insertion point to the next line.
    A. Backspace
    B. Enter
    C. spacebar
    D. Tab

TRUE/FALSE

Circle T if the statement is true or F if the statement is false.

T F 1. Keyboarding is much like playing a piano, where the brain and fingers work together.

T F 2. Ergonomic keyboards relieve stress that can be incurred from repeated and/or longtime use on a keyboard.

T F 3. Bump keys are located at the very top of the keyboard.

T F 4. Slouching in the chair while keyboarding affects your keyboarding skill in a positive way.

T F 5. You will need to train your computer to recognize your voice when using voice recognition software.

FILL IN THE BLANK

1. Keyboarding is sometimes referred to as _____ typing.

2. The _____ keys are usually located in a row at the top of the keyboard.

3. The correct keyboarding position refers to your _____.

4. PDAs, digital pens, and voice recognition software are examples of _____ devices.

5. The _____ is used to insert spaces between words and punctuation marks.

PROJECTS

CROSS-CURRICULAR—MATHEMATICS

Mathematical word problems can be fun to solve. Use the Internet to find examples of mathematical word problems. Prepare a report describing three types of word problems. Give two examples of each type you find and provide step-by-step instructions on how to solve them.

CROSS-CURRICULAR—SCIENCE

This lesson described several electronic devices used for inputting data. Use the Internet and other resources to research some of the electronic devices identified in this lesson. Prepare a report describing these devices, how they are used, and the approximate cost of each.

CROSS-CURRICULAR—SOCIAL STUDIES

You learned in this lesson that Christopher Sholes is given credit for designing the first typewriter. However, there were many attempts to invent a writing machine in the early 1800s. Use the Internet and other resources and write a two-page report on the history of the typewriter. Include the name of each early typewriter you discover, a description, the date, the inventor, and the cost.

CROSS-CURRICULAR—LANGUAGE ARTS

The author of a book on technology careers is visiting your facility in two weeks. Prepare a list of seven technology-related questions that you would like to ask the author at the reception following the presentation.

WEB PROJECT

Many jobs require keyboarding skills. Some examples include administrative assistant, data-entry technician, receptionist, newspaper reporter, author, and secretary. Access *www.hotbot.com* and other Internet sites to locate information regarding these and other jobs and careers that involve or require keyboarding skills. Prepare a report on two of these careers. Include the duties performed, the level of skill required, and the starting salary.

TEAMWORK PROJECT

Ergonomics is a growing concern for persons using computers. Users can develop physical discomforts and conditions. Partner with a classmate to research ergonomics as it relates to computer users. Prepare a report to define ergonomics, identify at least five specific problems for computer users, identify causes of each, and propose solutions for each.

CRITICAL *Thinking*

This lesson discussed the development of the QWERTY keyboard and the layout of the keys on the keyboard. Other keyboard layouts have been developed over the years, one of the more popular being the Dvorak keyboard. Proponents of the Dvorak keyboard argue that the layout is much more efficient and easier to learn, and that the user can type faster. More recently, Microsoft released the Microsoft Keyboard Layout Creator (MSKLC) program, which lets the user define his or her own keyboard layout. This program is free to download from the Web at *www.microsoft.com/globaldev/tools/msklc.mspx.*

Consider these alternatives to the traditional QWERTY keyboard. Do you think another keyboard layout eventually will replace the QWERTY keyboard? Do you think the MSKLC program will become widely used? Would you prefer to stay with the traditional QWERTY keyboard or try something new? Explain your answers in a one-page report.

WINDOWS AND FILE MANAGEMENT

Files, folders, and disks—these are your key system resources. Windows provides two tools for browsing, accessing, and managing these resources: My Computer and Windows Explorer. You can access My Computer from the Start menu, and Windows Explorer by clicking All Programs, clicking Accessories, and then clicking Windows Explorer.

File Management Defined

You most likely will use your computer to create many files and documents. As you create and save files, it is important to understand file organization. The process of organizing and keeping track of your files is called *file management*. Before you can appreciate and use either of the Windows file management tools, you first must understand the foundation on which they are built: files, folders, and disks.

Files

Imagine large file drawers for paper files. If papers simply were stacked in the drawer, not separated or grouped in any way, finding what you wanted would be difficult. If, however, one folder contained reports, another letters, and another memos, then you would be able to find what you wanted much faster with less searching. The same principle applies to storing computer data.

In terms of paper documents, a file may describe a wide range of documents. In computer terms, a file describes a wide range of objects. For example, a *file* can be the instructions the computer needs to operate (called program files or executable files); it may contain a text document you can read (often referred to as a document file); or a file may contain an image.

Folders

Think of your computer as a virtual file cabinet. The drawers in the cabinet are folders, and the folders in the drawers are subfolders. A *folder* is a container, used to store and organize your files. Folders are stored on a disk. Now consider your computer's filing system. Your files are stored in a folder or subfolder, which is located on a designated disk.

For example, you can organize a disk to have a folder that contains only files relating to application programs, another folder for correspondence, another for reports, and so on. Similar to paper folders, disk folders organize files into manageable groups, and subfolders further separate groups of files within a folder.

Disks

Files, folders, and subfolders are stored on media such as floppy disks, hard disks, CDs and DVDs, Zip disks, PC Cards, and mobile storage devices such as USB flash drives and memory cards or sticks. Lesson 5 contains an overview of these various storage devices.

The My Computer Window

As you learned earlier, you start My Computer from the Start menu. Most computer systems also display a My Computer icon on the desktop from which you can start the program.

Figure 9-1 shows the My Computer window in Tiles view from two different computers. (Other views are discussed later in this lesson.) The right pane in the My Computer window contains a list of the storage media on the computer and two document folders—Shared Documents and a user folder. Files stored in the Shared Documents folder or its subfolders are available to other users on your computer, on a network, or on the Web. Selecting different tasks or features from one pane generally changes the available features in the other pane. In Figure 9-1, the top window contains a variety of devices, including fixed and removable storage devices. In the bottom window, the removable storage devices are a USB disk and a mobile device, such as a PocketPC.

FIGURE 9-1
My Computer window

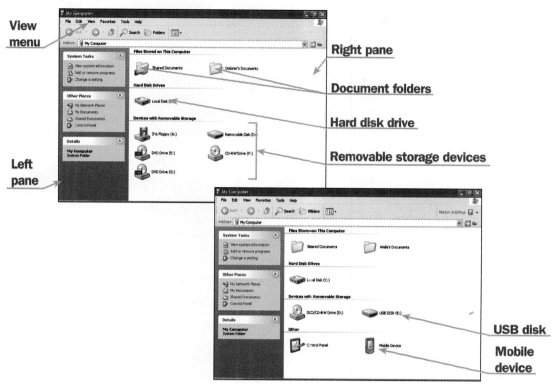

Identifying the Icons in the My Computer Window

As you can see in Figure 9-1, the My Computer window contains two types of icons: disk drive icons and folder icons.

Disk drive icons identify (by letter and type) the drives available on your system. Thus, the icons vary depending on the computer system. Most likely, your system displays drives different from those shown in Figure 9-1. Note that the icons representing the drives also vary.

The drives are named by a letter. For most computers:

- Drives A and B generally are floppy drives, although drive B is not used often.

- Drive C typically represents the hard disk. Some computers have more than one hard disk, and some computers have partitioned hard disks.

- Additional partitioned hard disks and other disks, such as CDs and DVDs, USB disks, Zip disks, and mobile devices, usually are labeled D, E, F, and so on.

Complete Step-by-step 9.1 on the next page to open the My Computer window.

STEP-BY-STEP 9.1

1. Click the **Start** button and then point to **My Computer**, as shown in Figure 9-2.

FIGURE 9-2
Start menu with My Computer highlighted

2. Click **My Computer**. The My Computer window opens. Keep the My Computer window open for Step-by-step 9.2.

Accessing Disk Drives

When My Computer is displayed in the Address bar, each disk drive available is represented by an icon in the right pane. To select a disk, click the appropriate drive icon; the disk drive then is highlighted, as shown in Figure 9-3. Information on the selected object appears in the Details section on the lower-left side of the window. If necessary, click the Details expand/collapse arrow to display disk information. You also can access a disk drive by clicking the arrow on the Address bar and selecting it from the list menu or by double-clicking its icon in the right pane of the My Computer window.

FIGURE 9-3
Selecting a disk drive

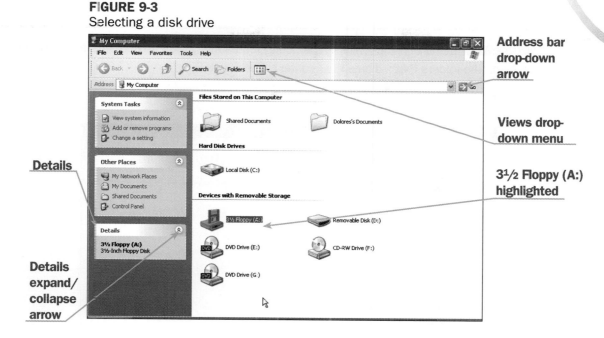

Displaying Files and Folder Views

When viewing your files and folders, you have a number of display options. You can change the view through the View menu or the Views drop-down menu on the My Computer toolbar.

- *Arrange in Groups*: Allows you to group your files by any detail of the file, such as name, size, type, or date modified. To show your files in groups, click the View menu, point to Arrange Icons by, and then click Show in Groups.

- *Thumbnails*: Displays the files and folders within a folder as small images, with the file-name or folder name displayed beneath each.

- *Tiles*: Displays a large icon identifying the file with the filename or folder name, the type of file, and the size of the file displayed below the filename.

- *Icons*: Displays files and folders as icons. The filename is displayed under the icon; sort information is not displayed.

- *List*: Displays the contents of a folder as a list of file or folder names preceded by small icons. These typically are arranged in vertical rows.

- *Details*: Displays the contents of the open folder and provides detailed information about each file, including name, type, size, and date modified. To choose the details you want to display, click the View menu and then click Choose Details.

- *Filmstrip*: Filmstrip view is available in picture folders. Your pictures appear in a single row of thumbnail images.

Complete Step-by-step 9.2 to practice displaying the various available views.

STEP-BY-STEP 9.2

1. Click the **View** menu and then click **Icons**. Icons representing folders and files are displayed with images on the folders that indicate their content. See Figure 9-4.

FIGURE 9-4
Icons view

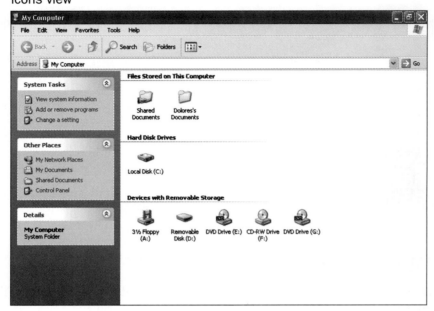

2. Click the **View** menu and then click **Thumbnails**. Large icons representing folders and files are displayed with images that indicate their content.

3. Click the **View** menu and then click **Tiles**. A horizontal arrangement of large icons is displayed.

4. Click the **View** menu and then click **List**. A vertical arrangement of folders and files is displayed, represented by icons and titles.

5. Click the **View** menu and then click **Details**. A list of each file and folder is displayed and includes details such as name, size, and type of file, and date and time created or last modified. See Figure 9-5 on the next page. Remain in this screen for Step-by-step 9.3.

STEP-BY-STEP 9.2 Continued

FIGURE 9-5
Details view

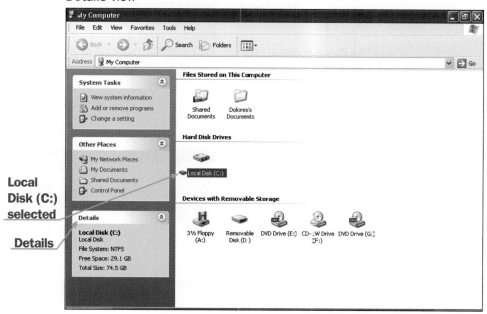

Managing Folders and Files

As you have learned, you use folders to organize files on a disk. When you want to create a folder to store files, your first decision is the folder location and then the folder name. You can create folders on any of your computer's storage media. To create a subfolder, decide under which *parent folder* you will create the subfolder.

Naming Folders and Files

The files and folders that you save on your disk must have names so that you will be able to find them. It is best to make your filenames relevant to the content so that you easily can identify the file when you want to retrieve it.

Filenames can have up to 255 characters. In addition to the name of the file, files also have extensions, which consist of three characters. A period separates the filename and the extension. Extensions identify the type of file, such as *doc* for a Microsoft Word document or *xls* for an Excel spreadsheet file. The program in which you are working assigns a default extension. You can change the file type and, therefore, the extension when you save the file using the Save As dialog box.

Creating Folders

In Windows, you can create folders and subfolders in the Windows Explorer program, in individual software programs, such as Word and Excel, and in My Computer. In Step-by-step 9.3, you use the My Computer window to create and name folders and subfolders.

S TEP-BY-STEP 9.3

1. The My Computer window should still be open. Insert a floppy disk in the floppy disk drive. (*Note*: If you are saving files and folders to another storage device, then you should substitute that device for the floppy disk drive used in this exercise.)

2. In the My Computer window, double-click the **3½ Floppy (A:)** icon (or the icon representing the storage device to which you are saving files and folders). The A:\ is displayed in the Address bar, and the left pane options change, as shown in Figure 9-6.

FIGURE 9-6
My Computer window

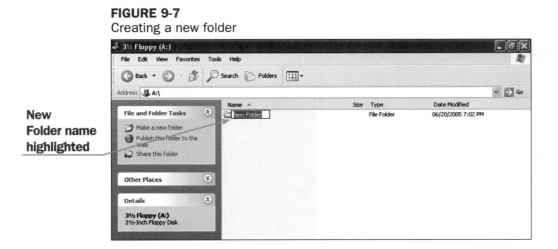

A:\ is displayed
in Address bar

Make a new
folder task

File and
Folder Tasks
pane

3¹/₂ Floppy (A:)

3. Click the **Make a new folder** link. A new folder is created on the disk. The default name, New Folder, is assigned and highlighted, as shown in Figure 9-7.

FIGURE 9-7
Creating a new folder

New
Folder name
highlighted

4. Type the folder name **Reports** and then press **Enter**. The folder name is changed from New Folder to Reports, as shown in Figure 9-8 on the next page.

STEP-BY-STEP 9.3 Continued

FIGURE 9-8
Naming a folder

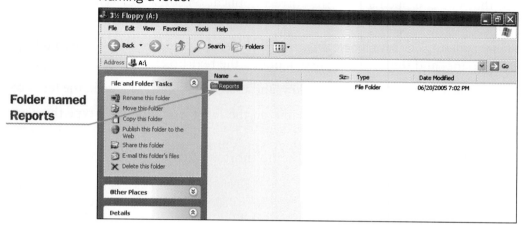

Folder named Reports

5. Next, create three subfolders in the Reports folder:

   a. Double-click the **Reports** folder icon to open it.

   b. Click the **Make a new folder** link. A new folder is created on the disk with the default name, *New Folder*.

   c. Type **Monthly** for the subfolder name and then press **Enter**.

   d. Click anywhere in the window to deselect the folder.

6. Repeating the instructions in Steps 5b–5d, create two additional subfolders in the Reports folder; name the subfolders **Quarterly** and **Final**. (See Figure 9-9.) Leave this window open for Step-by-step 9.4.

FIGURE 9-9
Three subfolders in the Reports folder

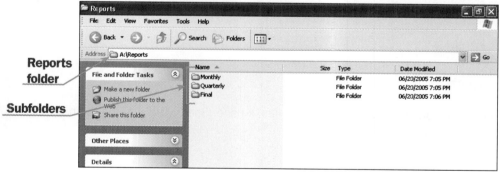

Reports folder

Subfolders

Renaming a File or Folder

Sometimes you might want to change the name of a file or folder—maybe to describe its content better or simply to correct spelling. When renaming a file, you should keep the same filename extension so that you can open it with the correct application software. Renaming a file or folder is a simple process in My Computer. Four options are available:

- Click the folder or file to select it, click *Rename this folder* (or *Rename this file*) in the File and Folder Tasks pane, and then type the new name in the text box.

- Click the folder or file to select it, press the F2 key, and then type the new name in the text box.

- Click the folder or file to select it, choose Rename on the File menu, and then type the new name in the text box.

- Right-click the folder or file, choose Rename on the shortcut menu, and then type the new name in the text box.

In Step-by-step 9.4, you rename a folder.

STEP-BY-STEP 9.4

1. Click the **Up** button on the toolbar, as shown in Figure 9-10, to close the Reports folder and return to the A:\ window.

FIGURE 9-10
Up button icon

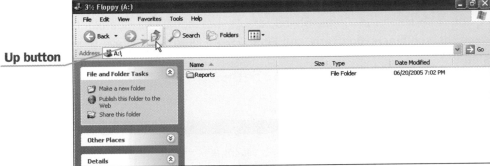

2. Click the **Reports** folder in the A:\ window.

3. Click **Rename this folder** in the File and Folder Tasks pane. See Figure 9-11 on the next page.

STEP-BY-STEP 9.4 Continued

FIGURE 9-11
Renaming a folder

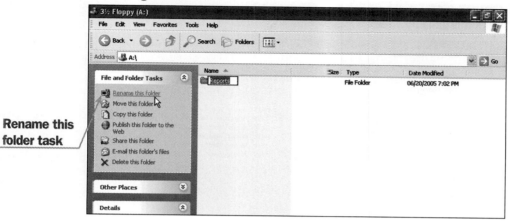

Rename this folder task

4. Type the new name **Status Reports**, and then press **Enter**. Leave this window open for Step-by-step 9.4.

Deleting a File or Folder

Windows provides four options to delete a file or folder:

- Click the file or folder to select it, and then select *Delete this folder* (or *Delete this file*) from the File and Folder Tasks pane.

- Click the file or folder to select it, and then select Delete on the File menu.

- Right-click the folder name, and then click Delete on the shortcut menu.

- Click the folder to select it, and then press the Delete key.

Use extreme caution when deleting a folder. When you delete a folder or subfolder, you also delete all the files in the folder. To verify this is what you really want to do, Windows displays a Confirm Folder Delete or Confirm File Delete dialog box. When you delete a file or folder from a floppy disk, it is deleted permanently. When you delete a folder or file from a hard disk, it goes to the Windows Recycle Bin, from which it can be recovered until the Recycle Bin is emptied.

Selecting Files with Windows Explorer

Windows Explorer is another option that permits you to control how your files are organized by allowing you to move and copy files between disks and folders and to delete files. The first step in performing any of these functions is to select the files.

To select a single file, click it. To select two or more files that are adjacent to one another, click the first file in the series, press and hold down the Shift key, and then click the last file in the series. See Figure 9-12.

FIGURE 9-12
Selecting adjacent files

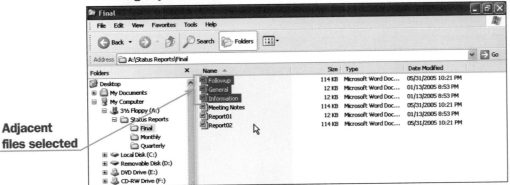

To select files that are not adjacent, press and hold down the Ctrl key and then click each of the files. See Figure 9-13. You can select all the files in a folder with the Select All command accessed through the Edit menu in the Windows Explorer or the My Computer window.

FIGURE 9-13
Selecting nonadjacent files

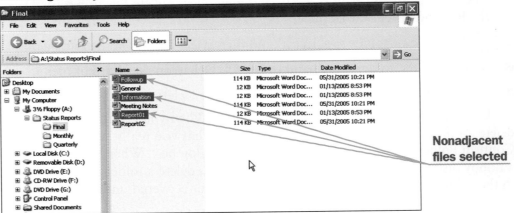

You can use the scroll bars to move around the display window when selecting files. Do not worry if the selected object moves out of view. An object will remain selected until you select another object or cancel the selection. When you want to cancel all the selections in a window, click a blank area in the window.

Copying and Moving Files

One of the key advantages of using Windows is the ease with which you can copy, delete, or move files from one location to another. You move or copy files from a source location to a destination. The *source* is the file to be copied, and the *destination* is the location (folder or disk) where the copied or moved file then will reside. Whenever you need to move or copy files, both the source and destination locations should be visible. In this way, you can see what you are moving or copying and where it is going. In Windows Explorer, you can view the source in the Contents pane and the destination in the left pane. Alternately, you can use the My Computer option to make the source and destination windows visible at the same time by changing the browsing option in the Folder Options dialog box to *Open each folder in its own window*. You access the Folder Options command by clicking Tools on the My Computer menu bar.

Copying Files and Folders

When you copy a file or folder, you place a duplicate of it in a different location and the original remains in place. To copy a file or folder to a new location on a *different* disk, select it, and then drag the file or folder from its source location to its destination location. To copy a file or folder to a new location on the *same* disk, select it, and hold down the Ctrl key as you drag to the new location. You can select more than one file to copy using the techniques you learned earlier. You also can select a folder to copy.

Moving Files and Folders

The moving process is similar to the copying process. When you move a file or folder, however, you remove it from its source location and place it in the destination location. To move a file or folder to a new location on a *different* disk, simply select it and drag it to the destination. To move a file or folder to a new location on the *same* disk, you must hold down the Shift key as you drag it to the destination.

Rather than try to remember when to hold down the Shift or Ctrl key, an alternate method of moving and copying files is to drag the file or folder using the right mouse button. When the file or folder is dropped in the destination, a menu appears giving you the options to *Copy Here* or *Move Here*. If you attempt to copy or move a file to a destination where an identically named file exists, Windows displays a message box asking you to confirm that you want to replace it. Click the Yes button to replace the existing file; click No to cancel the copy or move.

Take special care when moving, copying, deleting, or renaming files and folders so that they are not lost. You may inadvertently move a file or folder to a location or rename it and then forget the name or location. Another common error occurs when you rename a file using different application software than that used to create the original file, so the file is no longer associated with that original file. You also may find that you can no longer open the renamed file in either the original or the new application. Common problems associated with manipulating and working with files include lost files and file or disk corruption. You can avoid these problems by naming and storing files systematically, backing up data files regularly, and checking compatibility.

Expanding and Collapsing Drives and Folders

In Windows Explorer, the *Folders pane* on the left side of the window displays the drives and folders on your computer in a hierarchy. The *Contents pane* on the right side displays the contents of the disk or folder you selected in the Folders pane. You can display the same view in the My Computer window by clicking the Folders button on the My Computer toolbar. See Figure 9-14.

FIGURE 9-14
Hierarchy of drives, folders, and files

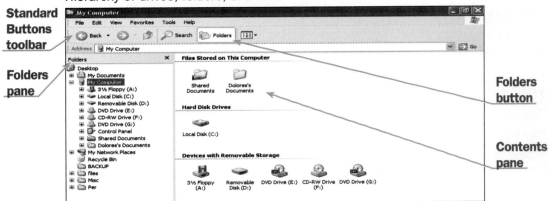

At the top of the hierarchy in the Folders pane is the Desktop, followed by My Documents, My Computer, My Network Places, and Recycle Bin icons. You will notice icons containing either a plus sign (+) or a minus sign (–) to the left of the folders and the storage media listed in the Folders pane. The plus sign indicates additional subfolders or drives exist within this folder or disk. Some folders have subfolders that also have a plus sign to the left. To view these additional folders and drives, click the plus sign. The plus sign then changes to a minus sign, and this *expands* the folder. When a minus sign appears to the left of a folder or disk, this indicates no additional levels of folders within the selected disk or folder. Click the minus sign to *collapse* an expanded folder. To display and view the contents of the folder in the Contents (right) pane, click the folder icon or name.

In Step-by-step 9.5, you practice expanding and collapsing folders.

STEP-BY-STEP 9.5

1. Click the **Up** button on the Standard Buttons toolbar and then click the **Folders** button. See Figure 9-14 above. The Folders pane is displayed.

2. In the Folders pane, click the **plus sign** to the left of My Documents. The folder expands and additional subfolders are displayed in the Folders pane, as shown in Figure 9-15 on the next page. The contents in the right pane do not change. Most likely, your computer will display different folders.

STEP-BY-STEP 9.5 Continued

FIGURE 9-15
My Documents folder expanded

Minus sign appears next to expanded folder

My Documents folder expanded

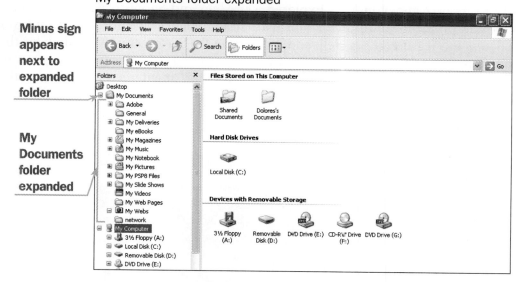

3. Click the **My Music** subfolder icon or another folder icon in the My Documents folder. The folder expands and the folder contents are displayed in the right pane. The My Music subfolder contains additional subfolders, as shown in Figure 9-16.

FIGURE 9-16
Contents of My Music subfolder

My Music subfolder expanded

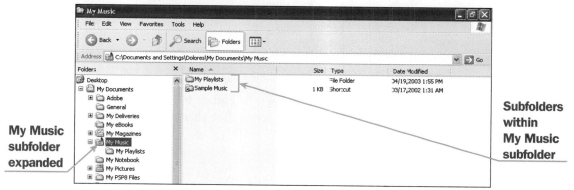

Subfolders within My Music subfolder

4. Click the **minus sign** at the left of the My Music folder (or the folder you expanded). The folder collapses, but the content remains in the right pane.

5. Practice expanding and collapsing other folders. Some subfolders will have additional subfolders. When you are finished, close the My Computer window.

Getting Help and Support in Windows

Windows provides you with online assistance to most problems you might encounter when working with My Computer and Windows Explorer. The Help and Support feature can assist you in troubleshooting problems and provide you with an abundance of information on tasks and features. To access this feature, select Help and Support on the Start menu. A window for the Help and Support Center opens, similar to that shown in Figure 9-17. In this window, you can click one of the links displayed, use the Index button on the toolbar, or enter a search word in the Search box to locate the Help information you desire.

FIGURE 9-17
Help and Support Center

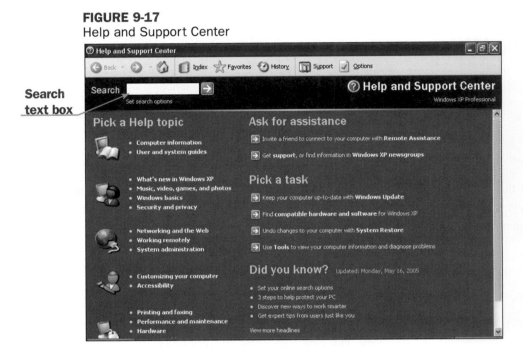

The *What's new in Windows XP* topic is shown in Figure 9-18 on the next page. Your Help and Support Center window may vary somewhat from that shown in Figures 9-17 and 9-18.

FIGURE 9-18
Help and Support Center

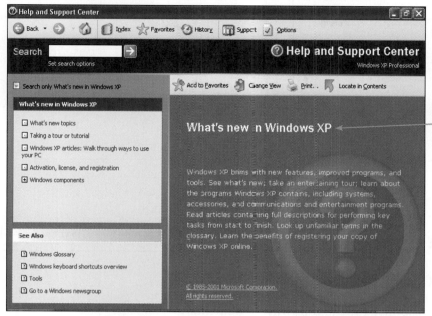

What's new in Windows XP is displayed

SUMMARY

In this lesson, you learned:

■ My Computer is a file management program.

■ Folders are used to store and organize files on a disk.

■ My Computer's View menu lets you control how files and folders are displayed in the Contents pane. The viewing options are Arrange in Groups, Thumbnails, Tiles, Icons, List, Details, and Filmstrip.

■ In the Folders pane, you can collapse to hide folders and subfolders or expand to display folders at all levels.

■ Filenames can have up to 255 characters. They include a three-character extension, which identifies the application in which the file was created.

■ Once a file or folder is deleted from a floppy disk or other removable media, it is gone forever; however, if you delete a file or folder from a hard disk, it is placed in the Recycle Bin where it can be recovered.

■ You can rename a file or folder in My Computer. You also can move and copy files and folders.

■ The Windows Explorer window is another option that you can use to select, copy, and move folders and files.

■ The Help and Support Center feature provides assistance and information on Windows features and programs.

VOCABULARY *Review*

Define the following terms:

Arrange in Groups	File	Icons view
Collapse	File management	List view
Contents pane	Filmstrip view	Source
Destination	Folder	Thumbnails view
Details view	Folders pane	Tiles view
Expands		

REVIEW *Questions*

MULTIPLE CHOICE

Select the best response for the following statements.

1. A filename can have up to _____ characters.
   A. 150
   B. 28
   C. 255
   D. 25

2. Removing a file from a folder is called _____.
   A. copying
   B. formatting
   C. renaming
   D. deleting

3. When a folder is expanded in the Folders pane, a _____ is displayed.
   A. plus sign
   B. minus sign
   C. period
   D. greater than symbol (>)

4. The _____ menu allows you to choose how your folders and files will be displayed in My Computer.
   A. Save As
   B. View
   C. Details
   D. Thumbnails

5. The _____ command allows you to change the name of a file or folder.
   A. Move
   B. Help and Support
   C. Rename
   D. Delete

TRUE/FALSE

Circle T if the statement is true or F if the statement is false.

T   F   1. My Computer is a tool for browsing, accessing, and managing files, folders, and disks.

T   F   2. You can drag folders to move them to another location.

T   F   3. The Folders pane displays folders and disks in a hierarchy.

T   F   4. Files only can be stored on your computer's hard disk.

T   F   5. A new folder can be created in the Save As window.

FILL IN THE BLANK

Complete the following sentences by writing the correct word or words in the blanks provided.

1. The process of organizing and keeping track of your files is called _____.

2. The _____ pane displays the drives and folders on your computer in a hierarchy.

3. Collapsed folders are identified by the _____ sign.

4. To copy a file to a location on the same disk, you must hold down the _____ key while dragging it to the destination.

5. A commonly used letter designation for the _____ disk drive is C.

PROJECTS

CROSS-CURRICULAR—MATHEMATICS

The Details view in Windows Explorer gives you information regarding the size of files. View several of the folders on your disk to determine the size of various files located in the folders. Create a list of the files and sizes contained within five folders.

CROSS-CURRICULAR—SCIENCE

Some files are very large and use a large amount of space on the disk. This space can be reduced by compressing files. Use the Internet and other resources to investigate compressing files, and write a one- to two-page report on how this process works.

CROSS-CURRICULAR—SOCIAL STUDIES

Use the Internet and other resources to compare how file management was handled in early versions of the computer operating system. Include Windows 95, Windows 98, Windows 2000, and Windows XP.

CROSS-CURRICULAR—LANGUAGE ARTS

Create a chart listing the different options located on the View menu in Windows Explorer or My Computer. Include the following in your chart: the name of the view, a description, a sample, and the advantages or disadvantages of this option.

 ## WEB PROJECT

Use the Internet to research information on various types of data storage media, such as USB drives, for computers. Prepare a one-page report to identify at least five data storage media. In your report, include the amount of storage space, and advantages and disadvantages of each type of media.

 ## TEAMWORK PROJECT

Your instructor has given you and your team an assignment to form a lawn service business. As part of the assignment, you will need to store information using your computer. Working with your partner, identify the types of information you will need to store. Design a folder structure to organize your files by creating a parent folder with the name of the company, and add folders and subfolders to include at least two levels.

CRITICAL *Thinking*

You are a member of an organization that has been in existence for about one year. During that time, officers have created numerous files on the organization's main computer and saved them without organizing them. You have been asked to organize the files so that each officer has his or her own folder. The president, secretary, treasurer, and vice president are the officers. Their files include agendas, reports, minutes, membership lists, budgets, member addresses, and membership dues. Create a folder structure with the parent folder being the name of the organization. Create at least two levels of folders for each officer. You may add additional folders as you think necessary. Create your folders on a formatted floppy disk or on another storage device.

WORD PROCESSING

Estimated Time: 2.5 hours

OBJECTIVES

Upon completion of this lesson, you should be able to:

- Identify the components of the word-processor window.
- Save, open, and print a document.
- Select commands using menus and toolbars.
- Create and edit a document.
- Correct spelling and grammar in a document.
- Select synonyms from the Thesaurus.
- Apply character, paragraph, and document formatting.
- Insert and modify pictures and drawn objects.
- Create, edit, and format a table.
- Use the Word Help system.

VOCABULARY

Alignment
Editing
Font
Font style
Footer
Format Painter
Formatting
Header
Insertion point
Leaders
Line spacing
Margins
Points
Sans serif
Selecting
Serif
Sizing handles
Styles
Tab stop
Table
Word wrap

Word-Processing Software Defined

Microsoft Word is a powerful, full-featured word processor. You can use Word to create reports, tables, letters, memos, Web pages, and much more. This lesson introduces you to word-processing features that enable you to prepare documents efficiently. You also learn how to edit documents and enhance their appearance.

Create a New Document

You start Microsoft Word by launching it from the Start menu. The opening Word screen appears, similar to that shown in Figure 10-1.

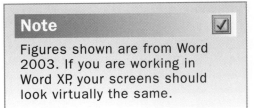

Note ☑

Figures shown are from Word 2003. If you are working in Word XP, your screens should look virtually the same.

FIGURE 10-1
Opening Word window

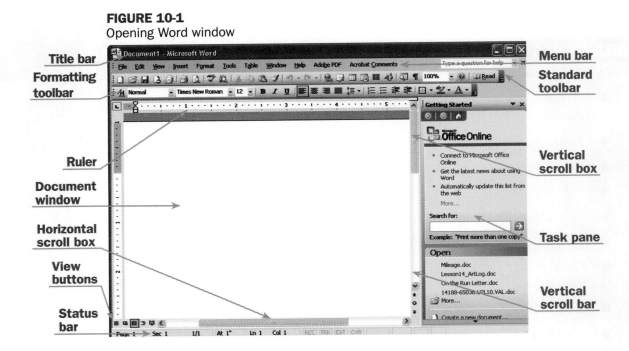

The following list describes the components you see in most word-processing programs.

- *Title bar*: Displays the name of the software program. It also displays the name of the document on which you are working after you have named and saved the document.

- *Menu bar*: Displays menu names. A menu is a list of options or choices. Click the menu name to open the menu and display its list of commands.

- *Standard and Formatting toolbars*: Contain icons, or buttons, for the more frequently used commands, such as printing and saving.

- *Ruler*: Shows the positioning of text, tabs, margins, and any other elements on the page.

- *Document window*: Area where you type and work with a document.

- *View buttons*: Allow you to switch among Normal view, Print Layout view, Web Layout view, and Outline view.

- *Vertical and horizontal scroll bars*: Allow you to scroll through a document that is too large to fit in the document area.

- *Task pane*: Displays recently used documents as well as frequently used features. Click one of the listed options to select it. To close the pane, click its Close button.

- *Status bar*: Displays the page number and section number of the current page, the total number of pages in the document, and the position of the insertion point. It also indicates the on/off status of several Word features such as overtype mode and spelling and grammar checking.

Entering Text

When you type in the blank document window, the *insertion point* moves across the screen indicating where the next character will be placed, as shown in Figure 10-2.

FIGURE 10-2
The insertion point shows your location in the document

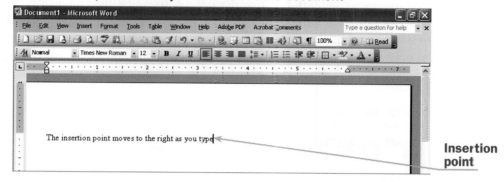

The insertion point moves to the right as you type

Insertion point

Most word-processing programs come with a *word wrap* feature. When your text reaches the end of a line, the insertion point automatically moves, or wraps, to the next line. If you want to start a new line of text manually, you must press the Enter key.

Saving a File

To store a document permanently, you need to save it. When you save a file, you give it a file-name, and indicate where you want to save the file. To save a file, open the File menu and click Save (or Save As). The Save As dialog box opens, as shown in Figure 10-3. Click the drop-down arrow on the Save in box and select the disk and/or folder to which you want to save the document. Click in the File name box, type the name for the document, and then click the Save button.

FIGURE 10-3
Save As dialog box

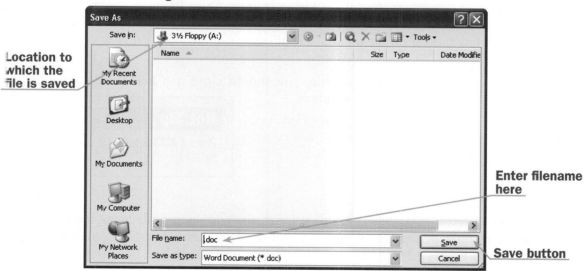

Location to which the file is saved

Enter filename here

Save button

As you work in a document, it is a good idea to save it regularly. You can do this by clicking the Save button on the Standard toolbar, or by using the Save command on the File menu.

Printing and Closing a File

Often, you will want to print a hard copy of a file. You can print an entire document, a single page, or selected pages. You can print a document by clicking the Print button on the Standard toolbar. The document is sent to the printer using the default print settings (for example, paper size, paper orientation, and number of copies). If you want to change default settings, you should use the Print command on the File menu. This option displays the Print dialog box where you can view and change print settings. See Figure 10-4.

FIGURE 10-4
Print dialog box

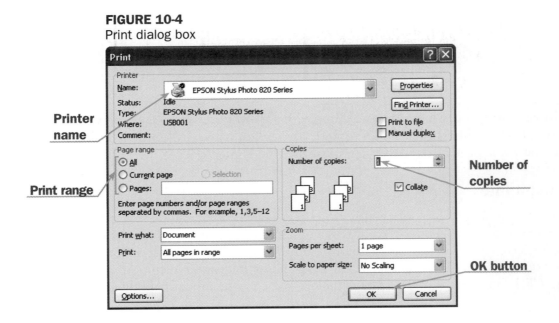

Before you print a document, you should view it in the Print Preview screen. This gives you an image of how the document will look when it prints. To switch to the Print Preview screen, click the Print Preview button on the Standard toolbar or use the Print Preview command on the File menu.

When you are finished working on a file, you should close it. Click the document's Close window button or select Close on the File menu.

When you are finished working in a program, you should exit it. Click the program's Close button or use the Exit command on the File menu.

> **Hot Tip**
> Press **CTRL+F4** to close a file quickly.

Opening an Existing File

You can open saved files to view, edit, or print them. You open a file using the Open button on the Standard toolbar or the Open command on the File menu. The Open dialog box is displayed, as shown in Figure 10-5. Click the down arrow on the Look in box to display the disks and folders on your computer. Click the folder in which the saved document is located. A list of files is displayed. Click the name of the file you want to open and then click the Open button. The document appears on your screen.

FIGURE 10-5
Open dialog box

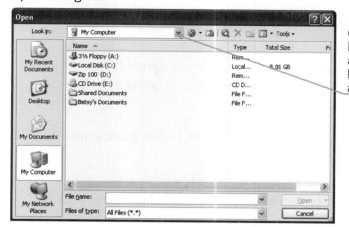

Click the Look in
box drop-down
arrow to display a
list of disks
and folders

In Step-by-step 10.1, you practice entering text in a document by composing a letter. You then save the file.

STEP-BY-STEP 10.1

1. Start Word 2003 by clicking the **Start** button, pointing to **All Programs**, pointing to **Microsoft Office**, and then clicking **Microsoft Office Word 2003**. (Start Word XP by clicking the **Start** button, pointing to **Programs**, and then clicking **Microsoft Word**.)

2. Press **Enter** eight times. This will place the insertion point approximately 2.5 inches from the top of the page. Check this location on the status bar.

3. Type the current date.

4. Press **Enter** four times.

5. Type the following lines, pressing **Enter** once after each line except the third line. Press **Enter** two times after the third line.

Mrs. Dierdra Smith

1948 Tundrah Lane

Atlanta, GA 30307

6. Type the salutation, **Dear Mrs. Smith** followed by a comma. Press **Enter** two times.

7. You are now ready to type the body of the letter. Type the following text and note how the text automatically wraps to the next line:

On the Run is a new fitness center that is opening in your area. You are invited to attend our Open House on Monday at 6:00 p.m.

8. Press **Enter** two times.

STEP-BY-STEP 10.1 Continued

9. Type the following paragraphs, pressing Enter twice after the first paragraph:

There will be prizes, food, and lots of fun at the Open House. You also will have an opportunity to use the center's equipment, so come dressed "not to impress," but to work out! There will be several drawings for great prizes, including various products and two free six-month memberships!

Mark the date on your calendar and join us for this grand affair.

10. Press **Enter** two times.

11. Type **Sincerely** followed by a comma. Press **Enter** four times.

12. Type **Dolly Kincaid** and press **Enter**.

13. Type **Manager**.

14. Click the **Save** button on the Standard toolbar. Click the **drop-down arrow** on the Save in box and select the location to which you are saving files. Type **On the Run Letter** in the File name box. Click **Save**. Leave the document open for Step-by-step 10.2.

Selecting Text

If you want to modify text in a document, you first have to identify the text. You do this by *selecting* the text. To select text, click at the beginning of the text you want to change and drag to the end of the text you want to change. You can double-click a word to select it. Triple-click to select an entire paragraph. Once the text is selected, you can edit it or format it. Editing and formatting are covered later in this lesson. To deselect a block of text, click anywhere on the screen or press any arrow key.

You also can copy or cut selected text and then paste it to another location. You do this by using the Cut, Copy, and Paste buttons on the Formatting toolbar. These same commands are on the Edit menu. When you cut or copy text, it is placed on the Clipboard, which is a temporary storage area. Click in the location you want to paste the cut or copied text, and then click the Paste button.

Editing Text

After creating a document, you can make changes to it without having to retype the document. Making changes to an existing document is called *editing*. Once you select the text, you can edit it by deleting it, replacing it, moving it, copying it, and so on.

You can move the insertion point to any position in a document in order to make corrections or to insert text. You move it with either the arrow keys or by clicking the mouse.

The following list includes some easy-to-use methods for quickly correcting text:

■ Use the *Backspace* key to delete text to the left of the insertion point. Each time you press Backspace, a character of text or blank space is deleted. For example, if your insertion point is to the right of the "r" in *computer* and you press Backspace, the "r" is deleted.

- Use the *Delete* key to delete text to the right of the insertion point. Each time you press Delete, a character or space in front of the insertion point is deleted. For example, if the insertion point is to the left of the "p" in *computer* and you press Delete, the "p" is deleted.

- Most word-processing applications function in *Insert mode* by default. This means that wherever you place the insertion point, the text that you type enters at that point and the text to the right of the insertion point moves to the right. Pressing the Insert key changes the mode to *Overtype mode*, in which new text overwrites the old.

- Many word-processing programs have a feature called *AutoCorrect*. The program automatically corrects certain errors, such as commonly misspelled words. For example, if you accidentally type "teh," the software automatically changes it to "the." You can customize this feature to include words that you often misspell.

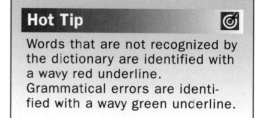

Hot Tip

If you delete text by mistake, immediately click the **Undo** button on the Standard toolbar to restore the deleted text.

Using Spell Check

In addition to the AutoCorrect feature, Word comes with a spell check tool. You can check the spelling of one word at a time, a group of words, or the entire document.

Using the spell check feature does not eliminate the need to proofread a document carefully. The spell check tool cannot check for correct word usage. For example, if you type *cite* in a document when you should have used *site*, the spell checker would not detect the error.

To use the spell checker, click Tools on the menu bar, and then click Spelling and Grammar. The Spelling and Grammar dialog box opens, as shown in Figure 10-6.

Hot Tip

Words that are not recognized by the dictionary are identified with a wavy red underline. Grammatical errors are identified with a wavy green underline.

FIGURE 10-6
Spelling and Grammar dialog box

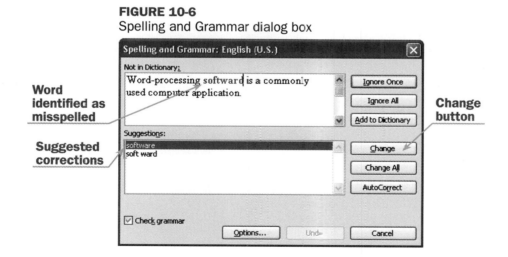

The first spelling error is identified in the top box, and suggestions for replacing it are provided in the box below. If the correct word is in the list of suggestions, click it. Several buttons are located on the right side of the dialog box. Click the Change or Change All button to accept the highlighted word in the Suggestions box. If the word is spelled correctly, click the Ignore or Ignore All button. After you click one of these buttons, Word continues to check the document.

In addition to proofreading your document for misspelled words, you need to check the grammar. When you check for grammar in a document, you read for content to verify that you have used correct punctuation and capitalization, complete sentences, the right tense, and so forth.

Use the Spelling and Grammar feature to make corrections. This process is similar to correcting spelling errors.

Using the Thesaurus

The Word Thesaurus feature allows you to look up synonyms for words. To use the Thesaurus, select the word that you want to change. Click Tools on the menu bar, point to Language, and then click Thesaurus. The Research task pane opens. As shown in Figure 10-7, the word for which you want to find a synonym appears in the Search for box. Synonyms for the selected word are listed in the box below. Point to a synonym and a drop-down arrow appears beside the word. Click the drop-down arrow and then click Insert to replace the word in your document. Click the Close button on the task pane to remove it from the screen.

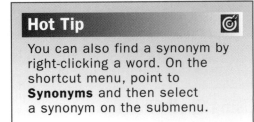

Hot Tip

You can also find a synonym by right-clicking a word. On the shortcut menu, point to **Synonyms** and then select a synonym on the submenu.

FIGURE 10-7
Using the Thesaurus

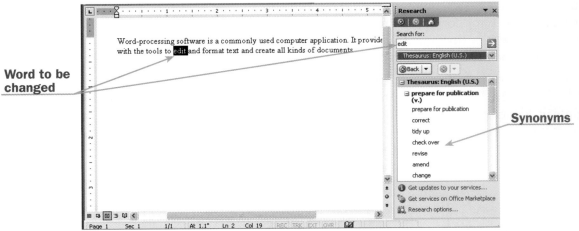

In Step-by-step 10.2, you edit the document.

STEP-BY-STEP 10.2

1. The On the Run document should still be open. At the end of the first paragraph, change the time to **7:30**.

2. In the first sentence of the second paragraph, double-click the word **food** to select it, and then type **appetizers and drinks**.

3. In the last paragraph, double-click the word **grand** to select it. Click **Tools** on the menu bar, point to **Language**, and then click **Thesaurus**.

STEP-BY-STEP 10.2 Continued

4. In the Research task pane, click a synonym of your choice and then click **Insert**.

5. Click the **Close Window** button to close the *On the Run Letter* document. When the message box opens asking if you want to save your changes, click **Yes**.

Formatting Text

You can enhance the appearance of a document by using Word formatting features. *Formatting* refers to the appearance and layout of text. Using different fonts, font sizes, colors, and styles in a document can make it look more professional. You can format characters, paragraphs, or the entire document.

- Character formats include font size and font color and attributes such as bold, italics, and underlining. These are applied to selected characters.

- Paragraph formats include line spacing and indents. These are applied to an entire paragraph; they cannot be applied to a portion of a paragraph.

- Document formats apply to an entire document. These include margins and paper size.

Character Formatting

Using different fonts, font sizes, and font styles is a quick way to enhance the appearance of a document. A *font* is the design of a typeface. Different *font styles* will have different effects on various documents. Adding color, italics, underlining, and other available effects allows you to create impressive documents. Some of the more commonly used fonts are Times New Roman, Arial, and Courier.

This is Times New Roman.

This is Arial.

This is Courier.

Fonts are either *serif* or *sans serif*. Serif fonts have extra strokes at the ends of the letters. Sans serif fonts do not have these extra strokes. Generally, you use serif fonts for the body of text because they are easier to read in large blocks of text. Times New Roman is a serif font. Sans serif fonts often are used for headings. Arial is a sans serif font.

The size of fonts is measured in *points*—72 points equal one inch. Sizes vary from one font to the next; 10 point in one font might look bigger than 12 point of another font. The most common font size for text is a 12-point font. Sizes over 18 points are good for headlines and banners.

This is 10-point font size.

This is 12-point font size.

This is 14-point font size.

This is 18-point font size.

This is 36-point font size.

You also can add attributes such as bold, underline, italics, and color to characters. These attributes can be applied as you type the text or after you have finished typing.

You can bold your text.

<u>You can underline your text.</u>

<u>You can double underline your text</u>.

You can type your text in italics.

You can add ***<u>more than one attribute</u>*** to your text.

You can add color to your text.

You can outline your text.

You can apply these and other options using buttons on the Formatting toolbar or by selecting Font on the Format menu. The Font dialog box opens, as shown in Figure 10-8. You can apply several formats at one time such as the font size, style, color, and so forth.

FIGURE 10-8
Font dialog box

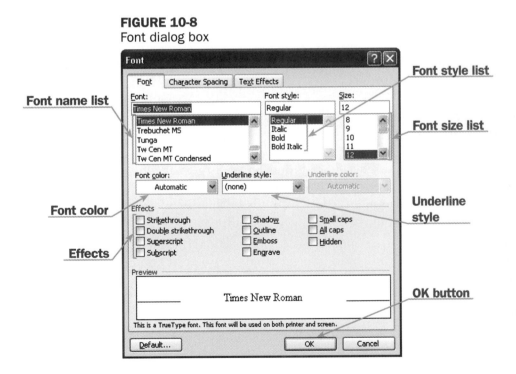

To apply the same formatting to different text within a document, such as making all headings 18-point Arial bold, you can use the *Format Painter*. This tool provides a time-saving way to apply formats consistently throughout a document. Select the text whose formatting you want to copy, click the Format Painter button on the Standard toolbar, and then select the text to which you want to apply the formatting.

In Step-by-step 10.3, you format a document.

S TEP-BY-STEP 10.3

1. Word should still be open. Click the **New Blank Document** button on the Standard toolbar to open a new document.

2. Type your birth month and press **Enter** two times.

3. Select the name of your birth month. Click the **Bold** button on the Formatting toolbar.

4. Click on the line below your birth month. Click the **Underline** button on the Formatting toolbar. Type the name of your Zodiac sign. It will be underlined as you type.

5. Click the **Underline** button to turn off underlining. Press **Enter** two times.

6. Click the **Italic** button on the Formatting toolbar. Type the name of the city and state in which you live.

7. Select your birth month. Click **Format** on the menu bar and then click **Font**. In the Font box, scroll to and click **Arial**. In the Size box, scroll to and select **18** and then click **OK**.

8. Select the name of your Zodiac sign. Click **Format** or the menu bar and then click **Font**. In the Font box, click the **Text Effects** tab. In the Animations list box, click **Sparkle Text** and then click **OK**.

9. Place the insertion point at the end of the text on the page and click the **Italics** button to turn off italics. Press **Enter** two times. Type the following paragraph:

   Word-processing software is used to produce documents such as letters, reports, flyers, and envelopes. Word-processing software also will allow you to enter text in a document and later make changes to the text. This is called editing.

10. Double-click the word *editing* and click the **Bold** button on the Formatting toolbar.

11. The word *editing* should still be highlighted. Click the **Format Painter** button on the Standard toolbar. The pointer changes to a paintbrush icon.

12. Highlight the first occurrence of the term, **Word-processing**. Release the mouse button. *Word-processing* should now be bold. Use the same process to apply bold to the next occurrence of *Word-processing*.

STEP-BY-STEP 10.3 Continued

13. Save the document as **Formatting Drill**. Your document should look similar to that shown in Figure 10-9. If instructed to do so, print the document and then close the document.

FIGURE 10-9
Formatted document

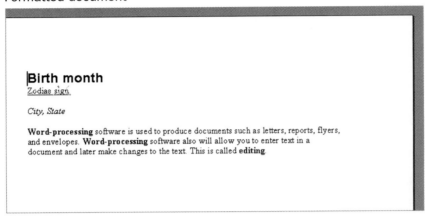

Line and Paragraph Formatting

Most documents are organized into paragraphs. A paragraph is defined by pressing Enter after the last word in the paragraph. You can adjust the alignment and line spacing within the paragraph. You also can indent lines within the paragraph, add bullets and numbered lists, and place a border around a paragraph.

Line spacing controls the amount of space between lines of text. Single-spacing is the default setting.

The following is an example of single-spaced text:

Word-processing software is one of the more commonly used computer applications.

The following is an example of double-spaced text:

Word-processing software is one of the more commonly used

computer applications.

To change line spacing, select the text, click Format on the menu bar, and then click Paragraph. The Paragraph dialog box opens, as shown in Figure 10-10 on the next page. Click the arrow on the Line spacing box, choose the line spacing you want to apply, and then click OK.

FIGURE 10-10
Indents and Spacing tab in Paragraph dialog box

Alignment

Indentation

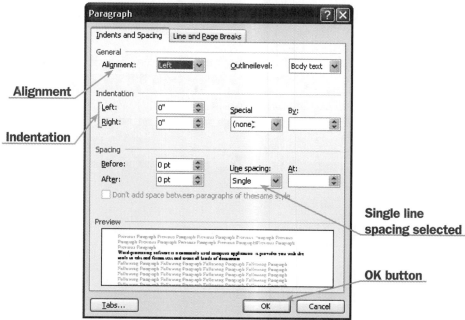

Single line spacing selected

OK button

Alignment refers to the placement of text between the margins. Text can be aligned at the left or right margin; it can be centered between the margins; or it can be justified where it is flush with both margins.

To set alignment, select the text and click one of the Alignment buttons on the Formatting toolbar. Or, you can open the Format menu and click Paragraph. Refer to the Paragraph dialog box shown in Figure 10-10. Click the arrow on the Alignment box and select the alignment you desire.

You also can set indents using the Paragraph dialog box. By default, you can indent a line one-half inch from the left margin by pressing the Tab key. You manually can set the length of the indent in the Indentation section of the Paragraph dialog box. See Figure 10-10. You can indent a paragraph from the left margin, from the right margin, or from both margins.

> **Hot Tip**
>
> You also can use keyboard shortcuts to set alignment: Ctrl+L for left alignment, Ctrl+E for center alignment, Ctrl+R for right alignment, and Ctrl+J for justified alignment.

Bullets and Numbering

You can emphasize and organize a list in a document by numbering it or applying bullets. Bullets are available in a variety of styles. You can add bullets and numbers using the Bullets and Numbering buttons on the Formatting toolbar or by using the Bullets and Numbering command on the Format menu. The Bullets and Numbering dialog box opens, as shown in Figure 10-11. The Bulleted tab displays various styles of bulleted lists. The Numbered tab provides various options for numbering lists.

FIGURE 10-11
Bullets and Numbering dialog box

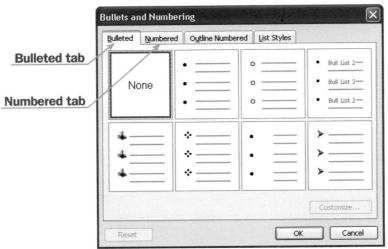

In Step-by-step 10.4, you adjust spacing, alignment, and indents in a document.

STEP-BY-STEP 10.4

1. Word should still be open. Click the **Open** button on the Standard toolbar.

2. In the Open dialog box, navigate to and open **Step10-4** from the data files supplied for this course.

3. Save the document as **Insurance**.

4. Indent the first line of each paragraph by clicking in front of the first character and pressing the **Tab** key. (Do *not* indent the four items listed in all capital letters in the middle of the document.)

Hot Tip

Click the **Show/Hide ¶** button on the Standard toolbar to show where paragraphs begin.

5. Select the title of the document and then click the **Center** button on the Formatting toolbar.

6. Select the first two paragraphs after the title, click **Format** on the menu bar, and then click **Paragraph**. In the Paragraph dialog box, click the **drop-down arrow** on the Line spacing box, click **Single**, and then click **OK**.

7. Select the list of four items below the second paragraph. Click the **Bullets** button on the Formatting toolbar.

STEP-BY-STEP 10.4 Continued

8. Select the remaining two paragraphs and change the line spacing to **Single**.

9. Save the document. If instructed, print a copy and then close the file. Leave Word open for Step-by-step 10.5.

Document Formatting

You can format your document so that all pages have the same formatting.

Margins are the white space around the edges of the page. The margins "frame" the document. The margins can be adjusted to be wider or smaller, and you can adjust the top, bottom, left, and right margins individually. By default, the top and bottom margins are set at 1 inch and the left and right margins are set at 1.25 inches.

To set margins, click File on the menu bar and then click Page Setup. The Page Setup dialog box opens, as shown in Figure 10-12. In the Margins section, use the arrow buttons to set the margin size, or type the size in the text boxes.

FIGURE 10-12
Page Setup dialog box

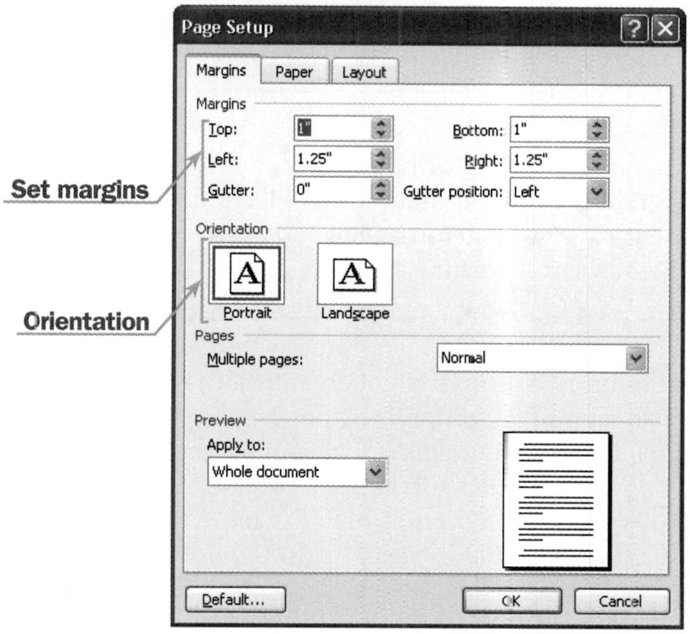

You also can set the orientation of the document in the Page Setup dialog box. You can print a page in Portrait orientation, where the top of the page is oriented to the shorter side of the paper. Or, you can print in Landscape orientation, where the top of the page is oriented to the longer side of the paper.

On the Layout tab of the Page Setup dialog box (see Figure 10-13), you can adjust the vertical alignment of text in the document. In Figure 10-13, Top vertical alignment is selected.

FIGURE 10-13
Layout tab of Page Setup dialog box

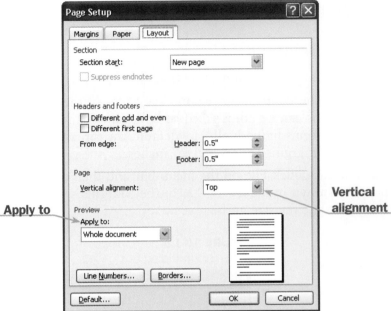

You can set text to be aligned at the top or bottom, centered, or justified on the page. Click the arrow on the Vertical alignment box and make your selection. In the Apply to box, you can select the part of the document to apply the alignment. For example, you might want to center the text on only the first page of the document.

Often, you will create multipage documents. Word automatically moves text to the next page, based on the margins. You can manually determine where text breaks occur by inserting a page or section break. A section is a portion of a document that is separated from the rest of the document. You can format a section break differently than the rest of the pages in the document. To insert a page or section break, position the insertion point at the location you want the break, click Insert on the menu bar, and then click Break. The Break dialog box opens, as shown in Figure 10-14. Click the break you want; a section break is indicated by a double-dotted line in the document, and a page break is indicated by a single dotted line.

FIGURE 10-14
Break dialog box

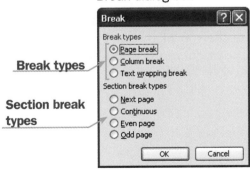

The header and footer feature allows you to insert information on every page, either at the top or bottom. The information at the top of the page is called a *header*, and the information at the bottom of the page is called a *footer*. You can type any information in the header or footer, such as the title of the document, date it was written, author, page number, and so forth.

To insert a header and/or footer, click in the first page of the document. Click View on the menu bar and then click Header and Footer. The Header and Footer toolbar is displayed, and the insertion point appears in the header of the page, as shown in Figure 10-15. To add a header, type the header text in the header area; to add a footer, click the Switch Between Header and Footer button and type the footer text. You can use the buttons on the Header and Footer toolbar to automatically insert text, such as page number, current date, or other text, from the Insert AutoText list box. Click the Close button on the toolbar to close it.

FIGURE 10-15
Adding a header and footer

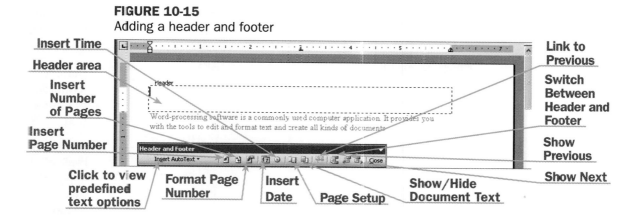

You also can add page numbers to a document by using the Page Numbers command on the Insert menu. To insert page numbers in this manner, place the insertion point at the beginning of the document. Click the Insert menu and then choose Page Numbers. The Page Numbers dialog box opens, as shown in Figure 10-16. Select the position and alignment for your page numbers by clicking the down arrows on the Position and Alignment boxes. Click OK.

FIGURE 10-16
Page Numbers dialog box

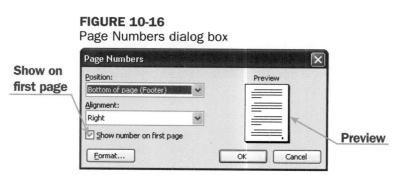

Other Formatting Features

Styles are predesigned formats. Word comes with a number of styles; you also can create your own styles. Using styles can save you time and ensure consistency of formatting throughout the document. To apply styles, select the text to which to apply a style. Click Format on the menu bar, and then click Styles and Formatting, or click the Styles and Formatting button on the Formatting toolbar. The Styles and Formatting task pane opens, as shown in Figure 10-17. The styles already in use in the document are listed in the *Pick formatting to apply* section. Click the style you want to apply.

FIGURE 10-17
Styles and Formatting task pane

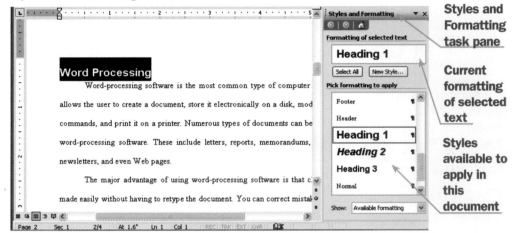

Borders and Shading

Borders and shading can add emphasis to a document and call out important information. You can apply a border or shade or both to a portion of the document or to the entire document. Select the text to which you want to add the border or shading, click Format on the menu bar, and then click Borders and Shading. The Borders and Shading dialog box opens, as shown in Figure 10-18 on the next page. You can select from a variety of border styles and thicknesses. You also can apply color to a border. Click the Shading tab in the dialog box to select a fill color for the selected text. When you apply shading, choose a shade that is light enough so that the text can be easily read.

FIGURE 10-18
Borders and Shading dialog box

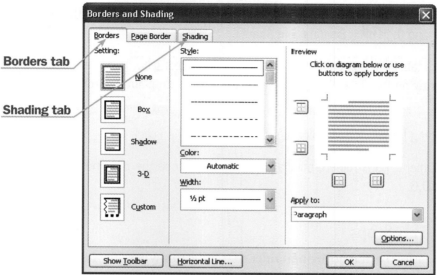

In the Step-by-step 10.5, you adjust the margins, and add a page break, a header, and formatting to a document.

STEP-BY-STEP 10.5

1. Open the document **Step10-5** from the data files supplied for this course.

2. Save the file as **Computer Software**.

3. Click **File** on the menu bar, and then click **Page Setup**. The Page Setup dialog box opens. If necessary, click the **Margins** tab.

4. Click the **Top** margin text box and enter **1.5**. Do the same for the left margin. Change the right margin to **1** inch. Click **OK**.

5. Click in front of the first subheading, *Word Processing*, click **Insert** on the menu bar, and then click **Break**.

6. In the Break dialog box, make sure the **Page break** option is selected, and click **OK**.

7. Click **View** on the menu bar and then click **Header and Footer**. In the Header pane, type your name and press **Tab** two times. Click the **Insert Date** button on the Header and Footer toolbar, and then click **Close**.

8. Select the subheading **Word Processing**.

9. Click **Format** on the menu bar and then click **Styles and Formatting**.

10. In the Styles and Formatting task pane, scroll through the list of styles and click **Heading 1**. Repeat this for each of the remaining subheadings.

STEP-BY-STEP 10.5 Continued

11. Select the title of the document and the text below it, **Prepared by Carnell L. Cherry**. Click **Format** on the menu bar, and then click **Borders and Shading**.

12. On the Borders tab, click **Box** under the Border section. Select a border style of your choice. Click the **drop-down arrow** on the Color box and click **Red**. Click the **drop-down arrow** on the Width box, and then click **1½**.

13. Click the **Shading** tab, click a fill color of your choice, and then click **OK**.

14. Save the document. If instructed, print a copy and then close the document. Leave Word open for Step-by-step 10.6.

Setting Custom Tab Stops

A *tab stop* is a location on the horizontal ruler that indicates where the insertion point will stop when you press the Tab key. Tab stops are used to indent text and align columns in a document.

You can set Left, Right, Center, Bar, or Decimal tab stops. Table 10-1 describes the various tabs.

TABLE 10-1
Tab stops

TAB NAME	FUNCTION
Left	The default tab stop, it aligns text at the left
Right	Aligns text at the right; used for aligning numbers
Center	Centers text; useful for titles or headings over columns
Decimal	Aligns text on the decimal point; used for numbers containing decimals
Bar	Places a vertical line at the tab stop

You also can add *leaders*, which are characters that fill in blank spaces between columns. Leaders can be periods, dashes, or underlines.

To set tabs, position the insertion point at the point where the tabs are to begin. Select Tabs on the Format menu. The Tabs dialog box opens, as shown in Figure 10-19 on the next page. Clear all old tabs by clicking Clear All. Enter the tab stop position and select the type of tab you want. Click Set. Use the same steps to set additional tabs. Once all tabs are set, click OK.

Hot Tip

You also can set tabs directly by using the tab button to the left of the horizontal ruler. Click the button until the type of tab you want appears on the button and then drag from the button to the position on the ruler where you want the tab to stop.

FIGURE 10-19
Tabs dialog box

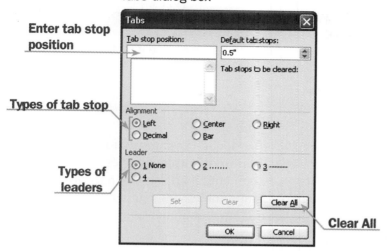

In Step-by-step 10.6, you set tabs in a document.

STEP-BY-STEP 10.6

1. Click the **New Blank Document** button on the Standard toolbar. A new document window opens.

2. Type the title **SPRING CLASS ENROLLMENTS**. Bold and center the title.

3. Press **Enter** three times. Click the **Align left** button on the Formatting toolbar.

4. Click **Format** on the menu bar and then click **Tabs**. The Tabs dialog box opens.

5. Click the **Clear All** button.

6. Click in the **Tab stop position** text box and type **2.25**. Click the **Center** button, and then click **Set**. Follow the same steps to set a right tab stop at **4.0** inches and another right tab stop at **5.75** inches.

7. Click **OK**.

8. Enter the information shown in Figure 10-20. Press **Tab** to move to the next tab stop. Apply bold as shown in the figure.

FIGURE 10-20
Typing data in columns

Division	Course	Sections	Enrollment
Business	Accounting	10	235
Business	Economics	4	79
Business	Computer Concepts	19	295
Biology	General Biology	12	262
Biology	Human Anatomy	7	163
TOTALS		**52**	**1,034**

STEP-BY-STEP 10.6 Continued

9. Save the document as **Tab Practice**.

10. If instructed, print a copy of the document and then close it. Leave Word open for Step-by-step 10.7.

Graphics

Adding graphics and other images to a document can provide visual appeal and also help to communicate a message. Clip art is a collection of graphic images that comes with the Word program and which you can insert into a document. You also can add photos, symbols, and drawings to a document. Many software programs come with a gallery of graphics that can be used in your documents. After you insert a picture into a document, you can move it, resize it, and make other modifications.

To insert clip art, click Insert on the menu bar, point to Picture, and then click Clip Art. The Insert Clip Art task pane opens.

In the Search for box, type a word or two that describes the type of clip art you want to insert and

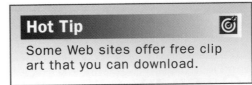

Hot Tip

Some Web sites offer free clip art that you can download.

then click the Go button (see Figure 10-21). Word will search in the default *All collections* for the specified art. The matches are displayed as thumbnail images in the results box. Click a picture to insert it into the document.

FIGURE 10-21
Clip Art task pane

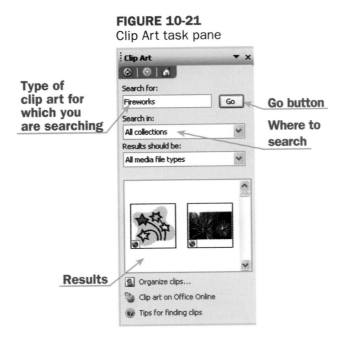

Select the image to move it or resize it. When the image is selected, small squares, called *sizing handles,* appear on its border, as shown in Figure 10-22 on the next page. Drag a handle to resize the picture. When an image is selected, the Picture toolbar opens. This toolbar, shown on the next page, contains buttons for making additional changes to the image.

FIGURE 10-22
Graphic with sizing handles

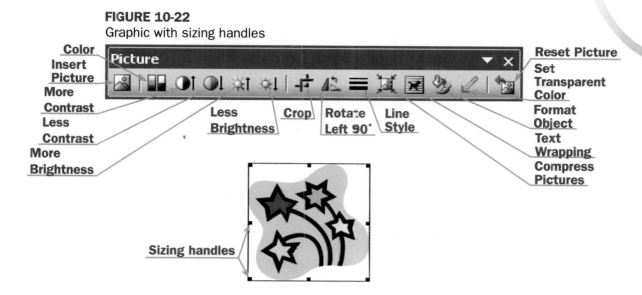

Symbols are special characters, such as mathematical symbols or currency symbols, which can be inserted in documents. To insert a symbol, click Insert on the menu bar and then click Symbol. The Symbol dialog box opens, similar to that shown in Figure 10-23. Select the font and a category (such as mathematical operators or currency) of symbols. Then, select the symbol you want, click the Insert button, and then click Close. The symbol is inserted at the position of the insertion point.

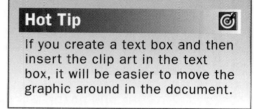

Hot Tip

If you create a text box and then insert the clip art in the text box, it will be easier to move the graphic around in the document.

FIGURE 10-23
Symbol dialog box

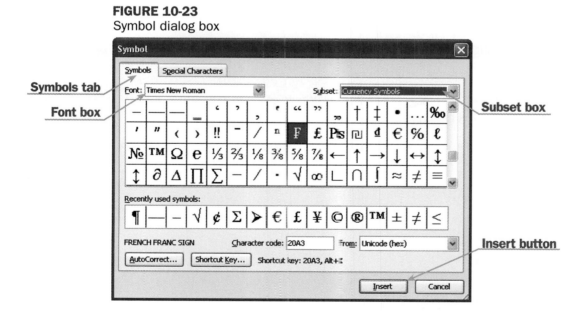

In addition to clip art and symbols, you also can use Word's Drawing toolbar to insert drawn objects into a document. The tools include lines, ovals, circles, rectangles, and more. Display the Drawing toolbar by clicking the Drawing button on the Standard toolbar or by clicking View on the menu bar, pointing to Toolbars, and then clicking Drawing. The Drawing toolbar appears, as shown in Figure 10-24. Click the tool you want to use. Depending on the tool selected, the pointer changes to a crosshair. Position the crosshair where you want the object to appear. Click and hold the left mouse button and drag to draw the object the size you want.

FIGURE 10-24
Drawing toolbar

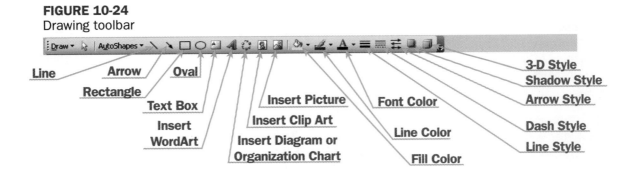

Complete Step-by-step 10.7 to insert a graphic into a document.

STEP-BY-STEP 10.7

1. Click the **New Blank Document** button on the Standard toolbar.

2. Type **ON THE RUN BOARD MEETING**. Select the title and change the font size to **24**, apply bold formatting, and center it. Press **Enter** three times.

3. Click **Insert** on the menu bar, point to **Picture**, and then click **Clip Art**.

4. Type **meeting** in the Search for text box and click the **Go** button.

5. Scroll through the displayed images and click to select one of your choice. It appears in your document at the insertion point.

6. Click to select the image. Drag its sizing handles so it is approximately 2 inches by 2 inches, and then center it on the page.

7. Click anywhere outside the image and press **Enter** three times. Set the font size to **14** and type the following:

   Tuesday, April 23

   2:30 p.m.

   Room B210

   Important business will be discussed.

8. Click **File** on the menu bar and then click **Page Setup**. Click the **Layout** tab, click the **drop-down arrow** on the Vertical alignment box, and click **Center**. Click **OK**.

STEP-BY-STEP 10.7 Continued

9. Save the document as **Board Meeting**. Your document should look similar to that shown in Figure 10-25.

10. If instructed, print the document and then close it. Leave Word open for Step-by-step 10.8.

FIGURE 10-25
Document with graphic inserted

ON THE RUN BOARD MEETING

Tuesday, April 23
2:30 p.m.
Room B210
Important business will be discussed.

Creating a Simple Table

A *table* is an arrangement of information in columns and rows. A cell is the point at which a row and a column meet or intersect. In tables, rows go across while columns go down.

To create a table, click the Insert Table button on the Standard toolbar. A grid appears, as shown in Figure 10-26. Click in the first cell and drag across to indicate the number of columns, and drag down to indicate the number of rows you want in your table. The empty table structure is inserted in the document. Click in a cell to enter text in it. Use the Tab key to move to the next cell.

> **Net Fun** ☀
>
> Visit *www.free-graphics.com/index2.shtml* to view clip art images that you can download for free.

FIGURE 10-26
Insert Table button and menu

Insert Table button

Column

Row

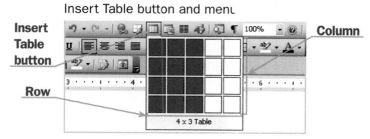

4 x 3 Table

Formatting and Modifying a Table

You can modify the structure of a table and format the text in the cells. The following describes formatting and modification options:

- *Insert rows and columns*: You can insert a row to the left or right and a column above or below the selected cell. Click the cell, click the Table menu, click Insert, and then select the row or column option.

- *Delete rows and columns*: Click in a cell in the row or column you want to delete, click the Table menu, click Delete, and then select Rows or Columns on the submenu.

- *Merge cells*: Use this feature to merge the contents of a group of cells into one. Select Merge Cells on the Table menu.

- *Split cells*: Use this feature to split a cell into more than one cell. Select Split Cells on the Table menu.

- *Increase column width and row height*: Drag the column or row borders to adjust the width and height.

- *Borders and shading*: Select the cell(s) to which you want to add a border or shading, and select Borders and Shading on the Format menu.

- *AutoFormatting*: With this feature, you can apply a predesigned format to the table. Use the Table AutoFormat option on the Table menu.

In Step-by-step 10.8, you create a table in a document.

STEP-BY-STEP 10.8

1. Click the **New Blank Document** button on the Standard toolbar.

2. Type **MILEAGE FOR LOUISA CORTEZ**. Select the title and change the point size to **18**, apply bold formatting, and center it.

3. Press **Enter** two times. Change the font size to **12**, deselect the **Bold** button, and then click the **Align Left** button.

4. Click the **Insert Table** button on the Standard toolbar.

5. Click in the first box and drag to the last box in the lower-right corner. A table with four rows and five columns is inserted.

6. You are going to enter data in the table, as shown in Figure 10-27 on the next page. Notice that you will need one more row. Click any cell in the first row of the table, click the **Table** menu, click **Insert**, and then click **Rows Above**.

STEP-BY-STEP 10.8 Continued

7. Enter the data as shown in Figure 10-27. Press **Tab** to move from cell to cell.

FIGURE 10-27
Text to enter in table

Month	Campus A	Campus B	Campus C	Total Mileage
July	235	151	521	907
August	213	54	212	479
September	189	256	151	596
Total	637	461	884	1,982

8. Select the first row by pointing to the first cell and dragging to the last cell. Click the **Bold** button.

9. Select the last row and then click the **Bold** button. Click the arrow on the **Font Color** button on the Formatting toolbar and click **Red**.

10. Select all the cells containing numeric data (this should include all cells except those in the first column and first row). Click the **Align Right** button on the Formatting toolbar.

11. Save the document as **Mileage**. Your document should look like that shown in Figure 10-28.

12. If instructed, print the document. Close it and exit Word.

FIGURE 10-28
Document with table inserted

MILEAGE FOR LOUISA CORTEZ

Month	Campus A	Campus B	Campus C	Total Mileage
July	235	151	521	907
August	213	54	212	479
September	189	256	151	596
Total	637	461	884	1,982

Getting Help

Word comes with a Help feature that provides quick access to information on Word features and step-by-step instructions on how to use the features. To use the Help system, click Help on the menu bar and then click Microsoft Office Word Help. Click in the Search for box in the Word Help task pane (see Figure 10-29). Type a word or two describing the feature for which you need help. Click the Start searching button to start the search. If your computer is connected to the Internet, Help also will search the Office Online site and display results in the task pane. Click a result to view the Help information.

FIGURE 10-29
Word Help task pane

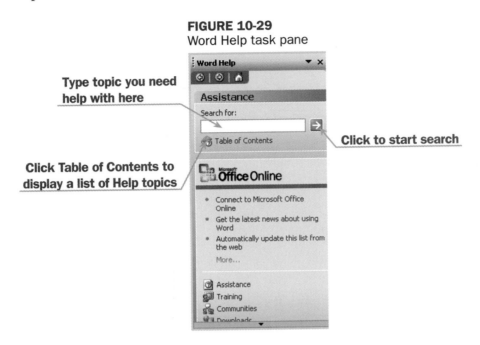

Notice the other search options in the task pane. You can click the Table of Contents option to display a list of Help topics. In the Microsoft Office Online section of the task pane, you can click a link to go to other sources of help and information on Word and other Microsoft products.

SUMMARY

In this lesson, you learned:

- Word-processing software is used to create documents such as letters, reports, memos, brochures, and Web pages.

- Commands for using the features of a word-processing program are selected from menus and toolbars. You also can use keyboard shortcuts to execute some commands.

- Word-processing programs come with powerful editing tools. You can make changes quickly and easily to text, cut or copy text, and delete it.

- The spell checker checks documents for possible misspelled words. Word also has a grammar-checking tool that identifies grammatical mistakes and a Thesaurus, which displays synonyms for a selected word.

- You can apply formatting to characters, paragraphs, or the entire document. Word comes with a variety of formatting tools that enable you to enhance the appearance of documents.

- Clip art can be added to documents to enhance their visual appearance.

- Tables are used to present information in an organized manner.

- Word's Help system offers a variety of resources for getting help and information on features and tools.

VOCABULARY *Review*

Define the following terms:

Alignment	Header	Selecting
Editing	Insertion point	Serif
Font	Leaders	Sizing handles
Font style	Line spacing	Styles
Footer	Margins	Tab stop
Format Painter	Points	Table
Formatting	Sans serif	Word wrap

REVIEW *Questions*

MULTIPLE CHOICE

Select the best response for the following statements.

1. Which of the following is used to access commands?
   A. menu bar
   B. title bar
   C. scroll bar
   D. status bar

2. Which Word feature corrects errors as you type?
   A. AutoCorrect
   B. Spelling and Grammar
   C. Thesaurus
   D. Undo and Redo

3. Times New Roman, Arial, and Courier are types of _____.
   A. templates
   B. commands
   C. fonts
   D. formatting

4. To place the name of a document at the top of every page in the document, create a
_____.
   A. margin
   B. justification
   C. header
   D. footer

5. You can tell that a graphic is selected by small squares on its border. These squares are
called _____.
   A. sizing handles
   B. borders
   C. symbols
   D. Clip art

TRUE/FALSE

Circle T if the statement is true or F if the statement is false.

T   F   1. In a table, rows go across and columns go down.

T   F   2. Editing documents means making changes to existing text.

T   F   3. It is possible to apply more than one formatting attribute to the same text.

T   F   4. You cannot modify the default tab stops set for a document.

T   F   5. Styles are used to ensure consistency of formatting in documents.

FILL IN THE BLANK

Complete the following sentences by writing the correct word or words in the blanks provided.

1. The _____ are the white space at the edges of a document.

2. The _____ feature automatically moves text to the next line when you reach the end
of the current line.

3. Use the _____ feature to find a synonym for a word.

4. Left, right, center, bar, and decimal are types of _____ in Word.

5. _____ are predesigned sets of formatting options that add consistency to documents.

PROJECTS

CROSS-CURRICULAR—MATHEMATICS

Use the Internet and other resources to research five to ten roller coaster rides at amusement parks in the United States. Gather information to include the name of the ride, a brief description, the name and location of the amusement park, and the height, length, and speed of the roller coaster. Present your data in a Word table. Format your table using Word's formatting features.

CROSS-CURRICULAR—SCIENCE

Use the Internet and other resources to identify five women who have received the Nobel Prize for Science. Use your word-processing program to prepare a written report. Include the name of the scientist, her birth country, her contribution to science, and the year in which she received the award. The report will be shared with your classmates, so make it attractive by inserting one or two clip art images.

CROSS-CURRICULAR—SOCIAL STUDIES

Black History Month is fast approaching, and your class has been assigned the task of "introducing" African-American inventors at the opening session. You are to provide your classmates with a copy of your introduction. Use the Internet and any other resources to gather information to use in your introduction. Your introduction should include the name of the inventor, birthplace, date of birth, education, a picture of the invention, a description of the invention and why it was important, and what life would be like without the invention. You may decide on the setup of your findings. Use various formats to enhance the appearance of your report.

CROSS-CURRICULAR—LANGUAGE ARTS

Most word-processing programs have features that are especially useful to writers, such as styles and formatting, and comments. Use the Internet, software manuals, and any other resources to identify these and other features that are useful to writers. Prepare a report that includes the name of each feature and why it is useful.

WEB PROJECT

Computer crimes have increased rapidly over the last few years. These crimes involve illegal use of or the unauthorized entry into a computer system or computer data to tamper, interfere with, damage, or manipulate the system or data. Use the Internet and other resources to research and prepare a report on various security devices to guard against computer crime. Include graphics in your report if possible.

TEAMWORK PROJECT

Do you like trying to solve mysteries? Work with a partner to investigate the mystery of the Bermuda Triangle. Many planes and boats have mysteriously disappeared there! Along with a partner, use the Internet and any other resources to find information on the Bermuda Triangle. You might want to include some background information such as its location, documented disappearances, and unexplained events; thoughts of other researchers; and your conclusion. Prepare a report with your findings. Be sure to format it attractively.

CRITICAL *Thinking*

Many instructors require students to use a style guide when preparing a report. One of the more popular guides is the *MLA Handbook for Writers of Research Papers*. It includes information on writing and formatting research papers. You probably have used this tool in some of your report assignments. Use the Internet and any other resources to research the MLA guidelines for formatting a research paper. Use those guidelines and Word features to prepare a one- to two-page report on your findings.

PRESENTATION GRAPHICS

Presentation Software Defined

Presentation software is a computer program you use to organize and present information, normally in the form of a slide show. Through the use of sequential slides enhanced with a variety of special effects and features, a presentation is an effective and professional way to communicate topics and ideas. In addition, presentation software provides options for generating notes for the presenter and handouts for the audience. Equipment requirements for the presentation include a projector and computer. See Figure 11-1.

FIGURE 11-1
A presentation using a computer and presentation graphics

Presentation software is a form of multimedia software because it enables you to combine multiple types of media, such as text, graphics, and video clips, in a single slide show, and even in a single slide! In general, *multimedia* is defined as the use of text, graphics, audio, and video in some combination to create an effective means of communication and interaction. Multimedia technology is a very effective tool in applications such as Microsoft PowerPoint, as well as in Web-based communications. Presentations can be saved in Web page format or as hyperlinks.

Presentation programs are excellent for creating on-screen shows, but t' at is not the only output option. Other options include the following:

- *Self-running presentation*: Job fairs, demonstrations, and conventions are a few examples of where you might see a self-running presentation. When the presentation is completed, it automatically restarts.

- *Online meetings*: Using a program like Microsoft NetMeeting, you can share a presentation in real time (occurring immediately) with colleagues in another state or even another country.

- *Presentation broadcasting*: You can use the Web to broadcast your presentation to locations all over the world.

- *Web presentation*: You can save a presentation as a Web or HTML document, and upload it on your organization's Web site or to your own personal Web site.

- *Overhead transparencies*: If you do not have access to a computer and projector for your presentation, you can create and print either black-and-white or color transparencies. This requires using plastic transparency acetate sheets in your printer.

- *35mm slides*: Each screen can be saved as a separate slide and then converted to 35mm slides.

- *Audience handouts*: Printed handouts support your presentation. Smaller versions of your slides can be printed two, three, six, or nine to a page.

Several software companies produce presentation graphics programs. Some of the more popular of these include Microsoft PowerPoint—both Macintosh and Windows versions—Corel Presentations, and Lotus Freelance.

Effective Presentation Guidelines

You can use presentation tools to make any presentation more effective and interesting. However, beware! Presentation programs contain many features and many options, so it might be difficult to avoid getting carried away. Often, the first-time user is tempted to add distracting sounds, animations, and excessive clip art to each slide. Before you create a presentation, therefore, you need to plan and outline the message that you want to communicate. As you develop the outline for your presentation, consider who your audience is, and determine the presentation's purpose, the location in which it will be given, and the equipment you will need.

Follow these guidelines to create an effective presentation:

- Keep the text simple—use the "6 by 6 rule," which is six lines of text, six words per line.

- Use no more than 50 words per slide, including titles and subtitles.

- Do not clutter your slide with large paragraphs displayed in a small font size. Use one-sentence comments and fill in the details orally.

- Use bullets, not numbers, unless providing specific step-by-step instructions. Bullets indicate no significant order, while numbers indicate rank or sequence.

- Cover only one topic per slide.

- Use readable typefaces and fonts. Use serif fonts for body text and sans serif fonts for titles.

- Choose color carefully.

- Use simple tables to present numbers.

- Add clip art sparingly and only where appropriate.

- Don't try to dazzle your audience with graphics, sound, transitions, and other available effects.

> **Net Fun**
>
> Visit *www.presentations.com* for tips, tools, and techniques for creating and delivering effective presentations.

Creating a Presentation

As mentioned earlier, several presentation programs are on the market. This lesson uses Microsoft PowerPoint. You start PowerPoint by launching it from the Start menu. The opening PowerPoint screen looks like that shown in Figure 11-2. By default, PowerPoint opens in *Normal view*. You should already be familiar with the toolbars, menu bar, and task pane. The other parts of the window in Normal view are described in the following paragraphs.

FIGURE 11-2
PowerPoint window

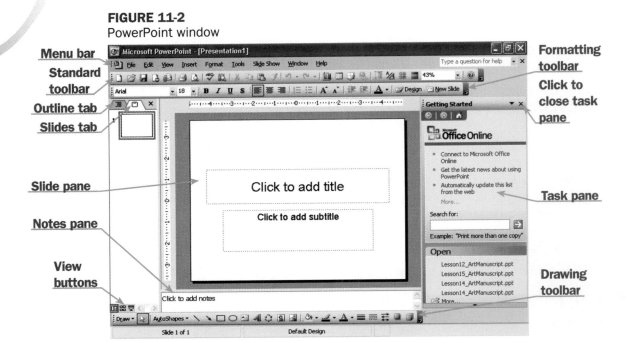

Outline and Slides tabs: The **Slides tab** displays thumbnail images of each slide in the presentation. Click an image to display that slide in the Slide pane. The **Outline tab** displays slide text in an outline format. You can easily enter and edit text on this tab. (The names of the tabs might appear next to the icons that represent each tab.)

Slide pane: The currently selected slide is displayed in the **Slide pane**. You can enter and edit text, insert graphics, images, or audio and video clips, apply formats, and so forth in the Slide pane.

Notes pane: The **Notes pane** is used to enter notes and other slide details to which the presenter might refer as the presentation is being delivered.

View buttons: In addition to Normal view, you can view slides in Slide Sorter view and Slide Show view. These views are discussed later in the lesson.

To create a new presentation, click New on the File menu. Or, scroll to the bottom of the task pane and click Create a new presentation. The New Presentation task pane opens, as shown in Figure 11-3.

FIGURE 11-3
New Presentation task pane

The options for creating a new presentation are described below:

Blank presentation: Lets you add slides one at a time to the presentation, selecting from various layouts for the text and other content.

From design template: Lets you select a preformatted design that is applied to each slide you add to the presentation. The template includes formats for text as well as the slide background.

From AutoContent wizard: Guides you through the steps of creating certain types of presentations, such as one for an employee orientation or a brainstorming session.

From existing presentation: Lets you create a presentation that is based on an existing presentation.

Applying a Design Template

A *design template* is a predesigned set of slide layouts and formatting that can be applied to a presentation to maintain consistency and give it a professional, finished look. Design templates save you the time involved in setting up the layout of each individual slide and then formatting it. PowerPoint comes with several design templates; you also can access templates online. In most cases, you should use only one template throughout a presentation. You can modify a template if you choose to do so.

In Step-by-step 11.1, you create a new presentation using a design template.

STEP-BY-STEP 11.1

1. Start PowerPoint by clicking the **Start** button. Point to **All Programs**, point to **Microsoft Office**, and then click **Microsoft Office PowerPoint 2003**. (Start PowerPoint XP by clicking the **Start** button, pointing to **Programs**, and then clicking **Microsoft PowerPoint**.)

2. In the Getting Started task pane, point to the arrow at the bottom of the pane to scroll if necessary, and click **Create a new presentation**.

3. Click **From design template**. The Slide Design task pane shown in Figure 11-4 is displayed at the right of your screen. You will see many designs from which to choose. If necessary, scroll to the *Available For Use* section of the task pane, and then scroll to view the design templates. Point to a template to display a ScreenTip with its name.

FIGURE 11-4
Slide Design task pane

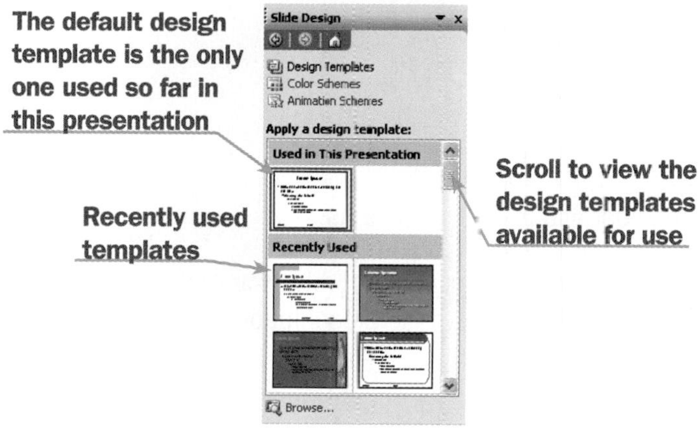

The default design template is the only one used so far in this presentation

Recently used templates

Scroll to view the design templates available for use

STEP-BY-STEP 11.1 Continued

4. Click the **Capsules** design template. The design is applied to the blank slide, as shown in Figure 11-5.

FIGURE 11-5
Applying the Capsules design template

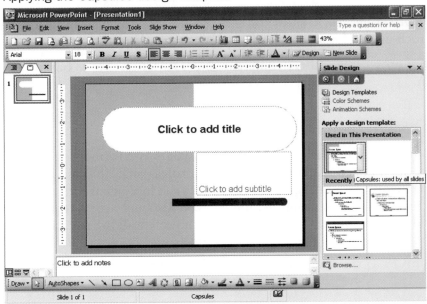

5. To change the color scheme of the design, click **Color Schemes** at the top of the Slide Design task pane. Several color schemes appear in the task pane. Point to the second scheme in the right column, as shown in Figure 11-6, click the down arrow, and then click **Apply to All Slides**.

FIGURE 11-6
Selecting a color scheme

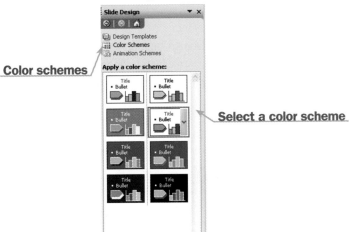

6. Click **File** on the menu bar and then click **Save As**.

7. In the Save As dialog box, select the location to which you are saving files, enter **PowerPoint Tips** in the File name box, and click **Save**. Leave the presentation open for Step-by-step 11.2.

Entering Text on Slides

You can enter text on a slide by typing directly on the Outline tab. Or, you can enter text directly on the slide in the Slide pane. In most cases, you should select a slide layout for the slide before you enter text or any other content. The *slide layout* refers to the way that text and other objects are arranged on the slide. These layouts include *placeholders* for text, titles, and/or other content, such as pictures, tables, charts, and so forth.

To select a layout for a slide, display the Slide Layout task pane. You can do this by clicking the Other Task Panes arrow on the task pane title bar and clicking Slide Layout, or by selecting Format on the menu bar and then Slide Layout. The Slide Layout task pane looks like that shown in Figure 11-7.

FIGURE 11-7
Slide Layout task pane

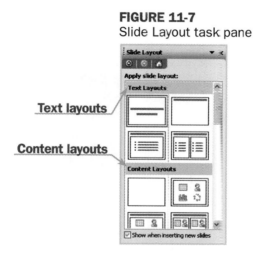

In most cases, the first slide of every presentation is the title slide. In Figure 11-8, the Title Slide layout has been applied to the slide. Notice that there are placeholders for a title and a subtitle. Click in a placeholder and type the text.

FIGURE 11-8
Placeholders on the title slide

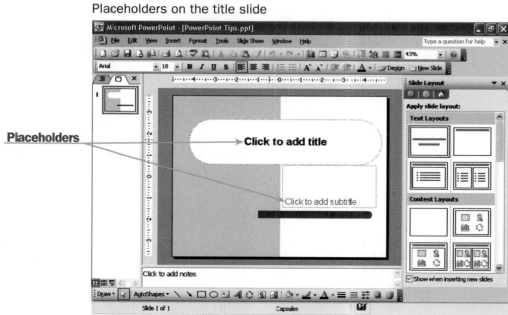

Inserting New Slides

To add slides to your presentation, click the New Slide button on the Formatting toolbar. The design template you selected for the presentation is automatically applied to the new slide. Select the layout for the slide from the Slide Layout task pane. Continue in this manner to add slides to your presentation.

Working in Different Views

As was discussed earlier, you can look at a presentation in three different views—Normal, Slide Sorter, and Slide Show. You are already familiar with Normal view.

In *Slide Sorter view*, the slides are displayed as thumbnails, as shown in Figure 11-9. In this view, you can easily change the order of slides in the presentation.

FIGURE 11-9
Slide Sorter view

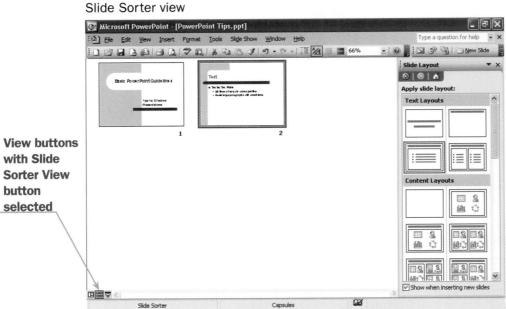

View buttons with Slide Sorter View button selected

In *Slide Show view*, the current slide fills the computer screen. In this view, you can click to progress through your slides and see your presentation as your audience will see it.

In Step-by-step 11.2, you enter text on a slide and change views.

STEP-BY-STEP 11.2

1. Click inside the title placeholder and type **Basic PowerPoint Guidelines**.

2. Click inside the subtitle placeholder and type **Tips for Effective Presentations**.

3. Click the **New Slide** button on the Formatting toolbar to insert a new slide.

4. In the Text Layouts section of the Slide Layout task pane, click the second layout in the left column (**Title and Text**), if necessary.

STEP-BY-STEP 11.2 Continued

5. Click in the title placeholder and type **Text**.

6. Click in the text placeholder, type **Six by Six Rule**, press **Enter**, and then press **Tab**.

7. The next bullet is indented. Type **Six lines of text; six words per line** and then press **Enter**.

8. Type **Avoid large paragraphs with small fonts**.

9. Change to Slide Sorter view by clicking the **Slide Sorter View** button in the lower-left corner of the Slides tab.

10. Click the **Normal View** button in the lower-left corner.

11. Click the **Save** button on the Standard toolbar and leave the presentation open for Step-by-step 11.3.

Adding Clip Art to a Presentation

Adding clip art to your presentation enhances its visual appeal and makes your presentation look professional. Microsoft Office has a Clip Organizer, which is a collection of clip art and other media files, including photographs, movies, and sound clips. You can insert these professionally designed media objects in your presentation. You also can obtain clip art from other sources such as the Internet.

Hot Tip

Use photos, clip art, and graphics instead of words for a more powerful presentation.

You can edit and manipulate a clip art image or other object after it is placed on a slide. Click to select it. Eight small squares, called sizing handles, appear on the border of the object. Once an object is selected, you can cut, copy, paste, delete, or move it. You also can use the handles to resize the object.

In Step-by-step 11.3, you insert clip art on a slide.

STEP-BY-STEP 11.3

1. Click the **New Slide** button to insert a third slide.

2. In the Text and Content Layouts section of the Slide Layout task pane, click the first layout (**Title, Text, and Content**). See Figure 11-10.

STEP-BY-STEP 11.3 Continued

FIGURE 11-10
Title, Text, and Content layout

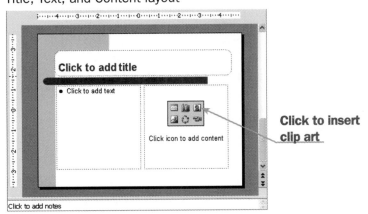

3. Click in the title placeholder and type **Graphics**.

4. Click in the text placeholder and type **Use clip art sparingly and where appropriate**. (Do not type a period at the end of the line.) Press **Enter**.

5. Type **Do not try to dazzle your audience with art and images**.

6. In the content placeholder, click the **Insert Clip Art** button. The Select Picture dialog box opens, as shown in Figure 11-11. The clip art images that appear on your screen might be different from those shown in the figure.

FIGURE 11-11
Select Picture dialog box

7. Click in the **Search text** box, type **alphabet**, and then click **Go**. PowerPoint will search the Clip Organizer for all pictures related to this word and display them in Select Picture dialog box.

8. Scroll through the results to find clip art of the letter "G." Select the image and then click **OK**. The clip art is inserted on the slide, as shown in Figure 11-12. (The image you selected might be different from the one shown in the figure.)

STEP-BY-STEP 11.3 Continued

FIGURE 11-12
Inserting clip art

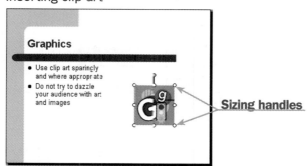

9. The graphic should be selected with the sizing handles displayed. Point to the sizing handle at the upper-left corner of the image. When the pointer changes to a two-headed arrow, drag the sizing handle up and to the left to make the picture larger.

10. Point to the center of the image. The pointer changes to a four-headed arrow. If desired, drag the image to reposition it.

11. Click the **Save** button to save your changes and leave the presentation open for Step-by-step 11.4.

Adding WordArt to a Presentation

You can add pizzazz to the text on a slide by applying special text effects. The *WordArt* feature provides a variety of text designs that you can apply to a slide title or use to call out other text.

In the following exercise, you insert WordArt in a presentation.

STEP-BY-STEP 11.4

1. Click the **New Slide** button on the Formatting toolbar.

2. In the Content Layouts section of the Slide Design task pane, click the **Blank** layout.

3. Click **Insert** on the menu bar, point to **Picture**, and then click **WordArt**. The WordArt Gallery dialog box opens, as shown in Figure 11-13.

STEP-BY-STEP 11.4 Continued

FIGURE 11-13
WordArt Gallery

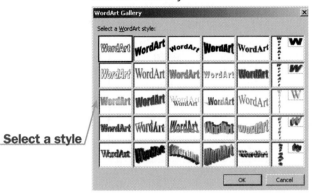

Select a style

4. Click the third option in the third row and then click **OK**. The Edit WordArt Text dialog box opens, as shown in Figure 11-14.

FIGURE 11-14
Edit WordArt Text dialog box

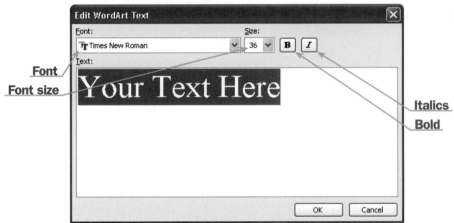

Font
Font size

Italics
Bold

5. Type **Presentations** and then click **OK**. The WordArt design is applied to the word *Presentations*.

6. Drag a sizing handle to enlarge the WordArt to fill more of the slide.

7. Click the **Save** button to save your changes and leave the presentation open for Step-by-step 11.5.

Adding a Chart to Your Presentation

Presentations often include statistical and financial data that is best presented in a chart. *Charts* can help an audience analyze and assess numerical information and simplify complex data.

In the following exercise, you add a chart to a presentation.

S TEP-BY-STEP 11.5

1. Click the **New Slide** button to insert a new slide.

2. If necessary, scroll to the Other Layouts section of the Slide Layout task pane, and click the **Title and Chart** layout. The slide layout looks like that shown in Figure 11-15.

FIGURE 11-15
Title and Chart slide layout

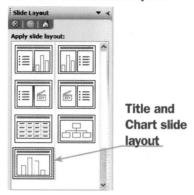

Title and
Chart slide
layout

3. Click in the title placeholder and type **Presentation Software Sales**.

4. Double-click the **chart icon** on the slide. This displays a datasheet, which is a table in which you enter the raw data that will be charted. See Figure 11-16.

FIGURE 11-16
Datasheet

Datasheet

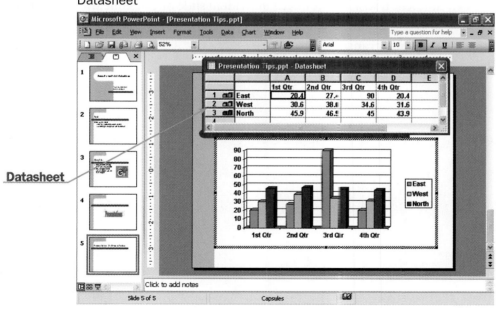

STEP-BY-STEP 11.5 Continued

5. In the datasheet, click the cell that contains the word *East*, then type **Store 1** and press **Enter**. Notice that the change is reflected in the chart.

6. Type **Store 2**. Press **Enter** and type **Store 3**.

7. Enter the rest of the data in the datasheet, as shown in Figure 11-17. You can use the arrow keys to move from cell to cell or click the cell in which you want to type.

FIGURE 11-17
Data to enter in datasheet

		A	B	C	D	E
		1st Qtr	2nd Qtr	3rd Qtr	4th Qtr	
1	Store 1	92,045	89,390	90,055	98,732	
2	Store 2	109,333	105,649	106,807	110,300	
3	Store 3	70,059	65,755	66,980	74,218	

Presentation Tips.ppt - Datasheet

8. When you are done, click the **Close** button in the datasheet window.

9. Click the **Save** button to save your changes and leave the presentation open for Step-by-step 11.6.

Adding Transitions to Slides

You can determine how each slide moves in and out of view in your presentation by assigning transitions. *Transitions* are special visual and sound effects that lead the audience from one slide to the next. You can assign different transitions for each individual slide or the same transition to all the slides in the presentation.

In Step-by-step 11.6, you add transitions to slides.

S TEP-BY-STEP 11.6

1. On the Slides tab, click the first slide.

2. Click **Slide Show** on the menu bar, and then click **Slide Transition**. The Slide Transition task pane is displayed, as shown in Figure 11-18. The AutoPreview option at the bottom of the task pane should be checked. (You might need to scroll to bring this option into view.)

FIGURE 11-18
Slide Transition task pane

3. The available transitions are listed in the *Apply to selected slides* section. Scroll down the list and click various options to see how they affect the slide. When you are done experimenting, select the **Shape Circle** transition.

4. In the Modify transition section, you can change the speed of the transition and add sound to the slide as it comes into view during the presentation. Click the arrow on the **Speed** box and click **Medium**. Do not change Sound.

5. In the Advance slide section, you determine how the slides will advance. You can have the slide advance upon the click of the mouse or automatically at intervals of time that you specify. If necessary, select the **On mouse click** option.

6. Click the **Apply to All Slides** button.

7. Make sure the first slide is selected on the Slides tab and click the **Slide Show** button in the task pane. Remember, you must click the mouse to advance to the next slide.

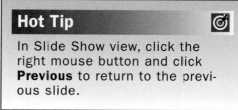

Hot Tip

In Slide Show view, click the right mouse button and click **Previous** to return to the previous slide.

STEP-BY-STEP 11.6 Continued

8. When you get to the end of the show, click to exit and return to Normal view.

9. Save the presentation and leave it open for Step-by-step 11.7.

Did You Know?

You also can open the Slide Transition task pane by clicking the down arrow at the top of the task pane and choosing **Slide Transition** on the menu.

Adding Animation to Slides

You can animate objects on a slide to help make a presentation more engaging. PowerPoint comes with a variety of *animation* effects that add movement to the object selected. The object can be text, titles, or graphics. You can also attach sounds to animations. You can apply an animation scheme to a slide or to all slides, or to you can apply it to only a certain object on a slide.

In Step-by-step 11.7, you add animation to slides.

STEP-BY-STEP 11.7

1. If necessary, select the first slide on the Slides tab. Click the slide title to select it.

2. Click **Slide Show** on the menu bar, and then choose **Custom Animation**. The Custom Animation task pane is displayed, as shown in Figure 11-19. Verify that the AutoPreview button at the bottom of the task pane is checked.

FIGURE 11-19
Custom Animation task pane

3. Click the **Add Effect** button, point to **Entrance**, and click **Fly In**.

4. In the Modify section of the task pane, click the arrow on the **Speed** box and click **Medium**. Do not change the Start and Direction options.

STEP-BY-STEP 11.7 Continued

5. Click slide **4** on the Slides tab.

6. Select the *Presentations* Word Art. Click the **Add Effect** button in the task pane, point to **Emphasis**, and then click **Spin**. Do not change the Start, Amount, and Speed options.

7. Click slide **1** on the Slides tab and then click the **Slide Show** button in the task pane to view the presentation. Because you kept the "start" of the animations set to occur on the mouse click, you must click to activate the animations as well as to advance to the next slide.

8. At the end of the show, click to exit and return to Normal view.

9. Save the presentation and leave it open for Step-by-step 11.8.

Checking Spelling in the Presentation

As you continue to add information to your presentation, you need to review and proofread your slides for errors. You can use the Spelling and Grammar feature. Remember, you still must proofread for punctuation and word usage because this feature recognizes only misspelled words, not misused words.

In Step-by-step 11.8, you check the spelling in the presentation.

STEP-BY-STEP 11.8

1. At the bottom of the Slides tab, click the **Slide Sorter View** button, and then click slide **1** if necessary.

2. Click **Tools** on the menu bar, and then click **Spelling**.

3. If your presentation contains a misspelled word, the Spelling dialog box opens, as shown in Figure 11-20. The misspelled word appears in the Not in Dictionary box. Suggestions for correct spellings are listed in the Suggestions box, with the best choice listed in the Change to box. If you want to use the highlighted word, click **Change**. If the word is spelled correctly, click **Ignore**. Once all spell checking is complete, click **OK**. (If your presentation does not contain any misspelled words, a message box appears indicating that the spelling check is complete.)

FIGURE 11-20
Spelling dialog box

4. Save the presentation and leave it open for Step-by-step 11.9.

Printing the Presentation

PowerPoint provides several options for printing a presentation. For example, you can print your entire presentation—the slides, outlines, notes, and audience handouts—in color, grayscale, or black and white. You also can print specific slides, notes pages, or outline pages.

In the following exercise, you print handouts of the slides.

STEP-BY-STEP 11.9

1. Click **File** on the menu bar, and then click **Print**. The Print dialog box opens, as shown in Figure 11-21.

FIGURE 11-21
Print dialog box

Click the arrow to select Handouts from the drop-down list

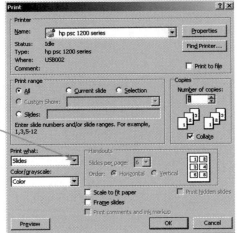

2. Click the arrow on the **Print what** box, and then click **Handouts**.

3. In the Handouts section, make sure **6** is entered in the Slides per page box.

4. Click **OK** to print the handouts.

5. Save and close the presentation. Exit PowerPoint.

Viewing the Presentation

Once you have created the slides, you can view your presentation. Your slides will be displayed with the transitions and animations that you applied. To view a presentation:

1. With PowerPoint running, click the Slide Show View button.

2. Click the left mouse button to advance the slides.

3. Click the right mouse button, and then click Previous to see the previous slide.

PowerPoint has a feature that allows you to "write" on slides while the show is playing. Right-click a slide. On the shortcut menu, point to Pointer Options. See Figure 11-22. Select an option on the submenu. Depending on your choice, a cot or block will appear on the slide. Move the mouse to write or highlight text. You can erase text with the Eraser option. You can choose whether to save the pen annotations or discard them when you close the presentation preview.

FIGURE 11-22
Pointer options

Technology Careers

PRESENTATION EXPERT

Presentations are an organization's most direct communication effort. Many times, a presentation can make or break a sale or prevent a company from landing that big contract. As more and more employees are using computers and presentation graphics programs, companies are beginning to realize the importance of this media.

A growing trend in large companies is to hire a presentation expert to oversee the creation and delivery of presentations within the organization. Depending on the size of the company and the number of presentations required, this person might work alone or work as part of a media department. The media department generally functions as a service bureau for the rest of the company. The presentation manager might also be responsible for design. They must keep updated and be aware of technological advances in the areas of multimedia. This position will most likely require additional education such as workshops, conferences, and classes.

Many large companies have a set of master slides and templates. All employees are expected to use these standards. The presentation manager might be responsible for creating these masters and templates and might even be responsible for teaching physical presentation delivery skills or coaching frequent speakers.

Because there are no certifications or degrees for presentation managers, many people employed in this field have graphics design and/or Web design backgrounds. They may or may not have a four-year degree. It is not unusual to find someone with a community college two-year degree in design or someone with design certifications employed in this type of job.

Salaries are varied and can range from as little as $20,000 to as much as $80,000 or more.

Delivering the Presentation

Many people fear public speaking. Most of us, however, will, at one time or another, find ourselves in a position where we must talk to a group or give an oral presentation. Several professional organizations train people in presentation skills. Even with training, most people will not become professional speakers overnight. There are, however, some special techniques you can use. If you practice and use some of the following suggestions, you might find that you actually enjoy public speaking:

Plan: Know the purpose of your presentation, plan your content, and know your audience.

Prepare: Have an attention-getting opener, be positive, and develop a memorable closing.

Outline your main points: Outlining helps you stay focused, but do not be afraid to skip some points or move ahead if that is what your audience wants.

Talk: Do not talk too slow or too fast; watch your audience and take your cue from them.

Present: Make eye contact, be natural and sincere; involve your audience.

Take questions: Be sure to leave time at the end of your presentation to answer questions.

SUMMARY

In this lesson, you learned:

■ You use presentation software to illustrate a sequence of ideas in a slideshow format.

■ Use presentation software for on-screen shows, self-running presentations, online meetings, presentation broadcasting, Web presentation, overhead transparencies, audience handouts, and 35mm slides.

■ Some of the more popular presentation programs are Microsoft PowerPoint, Corel Presentations, and Lotus Freelance.

■ Some general presentation rules to consider are: keep each slide's content simple; use words or phrases; don't clutter; and use art and images appropriately.

■ Most presentation programs come with a collection of professionally designed templates.

■ The addition of clip art, transitions, and animations can make your presentation more entertaining.

■ Techniques to help you give a better presentation include planning, preparing, outlining, talking at a moderate rate, following cues from the audience, and leaving time for questions.

VOCABULARY *Review*

Define the following terms:

Animation	Notes pane	Slide Show view
Charts	Outline tab	Slide Sorter view
Design templates	Presentation software	Slides tab
Multimedia	Slide layout	Transitions
Normal view	Slide pane	WordArt

REVIEW *Questions*

MULTIPLE CHOICE

Select the best response for the following statements.

1. With a presentation program, you can _____.
   A. create slides
   B. create handouts
   C. create overhead transparencies
   D. all of the above

2. Online meetings are conducted _____.
   A. in real time
   B. in late time
   C. after 12 noon
   D. before 12 noon

3. In which view are the Outline and Slides tabs displayed?
   A. Normal view
   B. Slide Sorter view
   C. Print Preview
   D. Slide Show view

4. _____ are special effects that are displayed when you move from slide to slide.
   A. Animations
   B. Programs
   C. Formats
   D. Transitions

5. A tool for creating special text effects is called _____.
   A. animation
   B. WordArt
   C. shadowing
   D. AutoShapes

TRUE/FALSE

Circle T if the statement is true or F if the statement is false.

T F 1. Each slide in your presentation should contain a lot of detail.

T F 2. You should rarely use visuals in your presentation.

T F 3. Outline view shows an outline of the presentation's text.

T F 4. The only output option for presentation graphics programs is on-screen shows.

T F 5. You can add slides to a presentation by clicking the Add Effect button in the task pane.

FILL IN THE BLANK

Complete the following sentences by writing the correct word or words in the blanks provided.

1. In _____ view, thumbnails of each slide are displayed.

2. _____ are special visual or sound effects that you can add to text or to an object on a slide.

3. To present an on-screen presentation, you need the software, a computer, and a(n) _____.

4. A(n) _____ presentation is one that automatically restarts when it reaches the end.

5. You can generate _____ of the slides in a presentation to distribute to your audience.

PROJECTS

CROSS-CURRICULAR—MATHEMATICS

Many women have made great contributions in the field of mathematics. Use the Internet and other resources to research the life and contributions of a woman mathematician. Prepare a presentation with four or five slides on your findings. Include various layouts, graphics, transitions, and animations in your presentation.

CROSS-CURRICULAR—SCIENCE

DNA has become a very sought-after tool to determine the fate of those accused of crimes. Conduct research on this "alphabet of life" and prepare a five- to six-slide presentation that covers what it is, how it works, how it is used, and other pertinent information. Include animation, sound, graphics, and other objects that will make the presentation interesting to other students. Print handouts to be distributed to the class.

CROSS-CURRICULAR—SOCIAL STUDIES

What were the headlines 10 years ago today, or 20, or 30 years ago? Research an event that happened on a particular day in history and create a seven- to eight-slide presentation about it. Include as many PowerPoint features as necessary to create a self-running presentation.

CROSS-CURRICULAR—LANGUAGE ARTS

Your civic organization has volunteered to work at the local adult education center. The students at the center are all high school dropouts who are working to pass the GED test so that they will be able to either continue their education or find desirable employment. The members of your group will provide tutoring in math, computer skills, English, and writing. You have been asked to work with a group that is learning to write papers. You want to make this subject interesting to the students so you decide to develop a presentation. Include at least five slides, using graphics, sound, animation, and transitions. Print a set of speaker's notes that you will use as you discuss each step in writing a paper. Print audience handouts for the students to use.

 WEB PROJECT

You have just returned from a year abroad as an exchange student. You have been asked to prepare a slide presentation of your experience. Prepare an eight- to ten-slide presentation. Include information regarding the country and its culture, the school you attended, the family with whom you lived, and any other interesting information. Research a country on the Web for information to use in your presentation. Use various slide layouts, animations, and graphics.

 TEAMWORK PROJECT

Work with a teammate to research "Juneteenth." Use the Internet and any other resources. This is a holiday that has been around for more than 125 years, but until recently it was not widely celebrated. Together, prepare an eight- to ten-slide presentation that will include the history, purpose, festivities, the decline and resurgence, and any other interesting information regarding this holiday. Include as many features as necessary to make this an interesting presentation.

CRITICAL *Thinking*

The presentation you worked on in this lesson covered some of the basic tools and features you can use to prepare an effective presentation. Following is an outline that provides more comprehensive information. Use the outline to create a new presentation. You also can use the Internet to gather more information on how to design an effective presentation and integrate this information into your presentation. Use a design template of your choice, and add graphics, transitions, and animations as desired. Be sure to spell check your presentation. Save it as **Presentation Basics**.

TITLE: Basic PowerPoint Guidelines

SUBTITLE: Tips for Effective Presentations

I. Text

- 6 by 6 Rule: 6 lines of text; 6 words per line

- No more than 50 words per slide, including titles and subtitles

- Avoid large paragraphs with small fonts

II. Fonts

   - Use at least 16-point size font

   - Limit to no more than three fonts

   - Use serif for body text

   - Use sans serif for titles

III. Graphics

   - Support point of current slide

   - Use only high-quality photographs or graphics

   - Use one graphic element per slide

   - Use appropriate size graphic elements

IV. Presentation Tips

   - Show one slide per minute

   - Avoid reading your slides

   - Identify additional materials

SPREADSHEETS

OBJECTIVES

Upon completion of this lesson, you should be able to:

- Understand the purpose and function of a spreadsheet.
- Identify the parts of a spreadsheet window.
- Enter labels, values, formulas, and functions in a spreadsheet.
- Use the AutoSum feature to enter the SUM function.
- Understand relative and absolute cell references.
- Change column width and row height.
- Format data in a spreadsheet.
- Insert and delete cells, rows, and columns.
- Save and print a spreadsheet.
- Add headers and footers in a spreadsheet.
- Sort data in a spreadsheet.
- Create a chart from spreadsheet data.

Estimated Time: 1.5 hours

VOCABULARY

Absolute cell reference
Active cell
AutoFormats
Cell
Cell reference
Chart
Footer
Formula
Formula prefix
Function
Header
Label
Order of evaluation
Range
Relative cell reference
Spreadsheet
Value
Workbook
Worksheet

Spreadsheet Software Defined

A *spreadsheet* is a row and column arrangement of data. Electronic spreadsheet software programs like Microsoft Excel allow you to calculate, manipulate, and analyze numbers. The feature of an electronic spreadsheet that updates calculations automatically makes this type of software very effective for numerous applications, such as preparing budgets, financial statements, payrolls, and sales reports, and managing inventory. Spreadsheet software also is used to make forecasts and identify trends.

The Anatomy of a Spreadsheet

A spreadsheet looks much like a page from a financial journal. It is a grid with columns and rows. This grid in Excel is referred to as a *worksheet*. The terms *spreadsheet* and *worksheet* are used interchangeably. The Excel worksheet window is shown in Figure 12-1. The columns are identified by letters of the alphabet, and the rows are identified by numbers. The point at which a column and a row intersect or meet is called a *cell*. Each cell has a name, called the *cell reference* (or cell address), which is represented by the column letter and the row number. For example, the first cell in a worksheet is cell A1. It is located in column A and in row 1. The *active cell* is the cell in which you are working currently. It is surrounded by a thick border. Note that cell A1 is the active cell in Figure 12-1. Individual worksheets are stored within a *workbook*. By default, a workbook contains three worksheets.

FIGURE 12-1
The Excel window

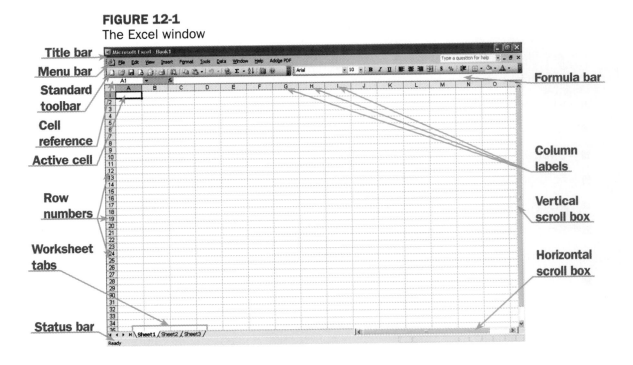

Selecting Cells

To enter data in a spreadsheet, you first select the cell. You select the cell by using the mouse or the keyboard. To select a cell with the mouse, simply point to the cell and click. You can select a group of cells by clicking the first cell and dragging the mouse to the last cell of the group. When you select a group of cells, the group is called a *range*. It is identified by the address of the cell in the upper-left corner, followed by a colon, and then the cell in the lower-right corner; for example, A1:D5 identifies all the cells between cell A1 and cell D5. When you select a range, the first cell in the range is not shaded, yet the others in the range are shaded. You can select an entire column by clicking the column letter at the top of the spreadsheet or an entire row by clicking the row number.

If you want to select a cell that is not on the screen currently, you can use the vertical and horizontal scroll bars or scroll boxes to display the area of the spreadsheet that contains the cell(s) you want to select. You also can use keyboard shortcuts to move around the spreadsheet and select cells. Table 12-1 lists some shortcuts for moving around the spreadsheet.

TABLE 12-1
Keyboard shortcuts

PRESS THIS KEY	TO MOVE
Arrow keys	Up, down, left, or right one cell
Page Up	The active cell up one full screen
Page Down	The active cell down one full screen
Home	The active cell to column A of the current row
F5 (function key)	Opens the Go To dialog box, in which you enter the cell address of the cell you want to make active
Tab	To the next cell
Ctrl + right arrow	To the last cell with data in a row
Ctrl + left arrow	To the first cell in a row
Ctrl + End	To the cell after the last cell with data in the document
Ctrl + Home	To the beginning of the spreadsheet, or cell A1

Entering Data in a Spreadsheet

The data that is entered in a spreadsheet will be one of four types—a label, a value, a formula, or a function. A *label* is alphabetical text and aligns at the left side of the cell. It also can contain numerical data not used in calculations, such as zip codes, telephone numbers, dates, and so on. A *value* is a number and aligns at the right side of the cell. A *formula* is an equation that performs a calculation. A *function* is a built-in formula that is a shortcut for common calculations, such as totaling numbers or finding the average. Each type of data has a particular use and is handled in a unique way.

When you press Enter, the next cell down in the column becomes the active cell. You also can press the Tab key to enter the data and move to the next cell in the row. Or you can press one of the arrow keys to enter the data and move to the next cell in the direction of the arrow.

You can edit data in a cell by selecting the cell and then typing the new data. You also can double-click the cell and then move the insertion point to where you want to edit the data. Use the Delete or Backspace keys or retype the data as desired.

In Step-by-step 12.1, you start a workbook file and enter values and labels in the worksheet.

Hot Tip

You can enter data in a cell by typing it in the active cell and pressing Enter or by clicking the green checkmark on the Formula bar.

Did You Know?

You can use the Undo command to undo your most recent actions. You can use the Redo command to reverse the Undo command.

STEP-BY-STEP 12.1

1. Start Excel by clicking the **Start** button, pointing to **All Programs**, pointing to **Microsoft Office**, and then clicking **Microsoft Office Excel 2003**. (If you are using Windows 2000, start Excel by clicking the **Start** button, pointing to **Programs**, and then clicking **Microsoft Excel**.)

2. Click cell **A1** and then type **Sisters Wrap**. Press **Enter** to move to cell A2. (Do not be concerned if data extends into the nearby cells.)

3. Type **Part-time Employees**. Press **Enter** to move to cell A3.

4. Type **Weekly Payroll**. Press **Enter** to move to cell A4.

5. Type **Week Ending July 1, 200_** (enter the current year). Press **Enter**.

6. Type **Employee**. Press the right arrow key to move to cell B5.

7. Type **MON**. Press the right arrow key.

8. Enter the rest of the data as shown in Figure 12-2. Again, do not be concerned if cell data extends into the next cell or is cut off. You will learn how to adjust column width later in this lesson. Correct any errors by selecting the cell and entering the correct data, or by double-clicking the cell and using the Backspace or Delete keys, or retyping the data as necessary.

FIGURE 12-2
Part-time payroll spreadsheet

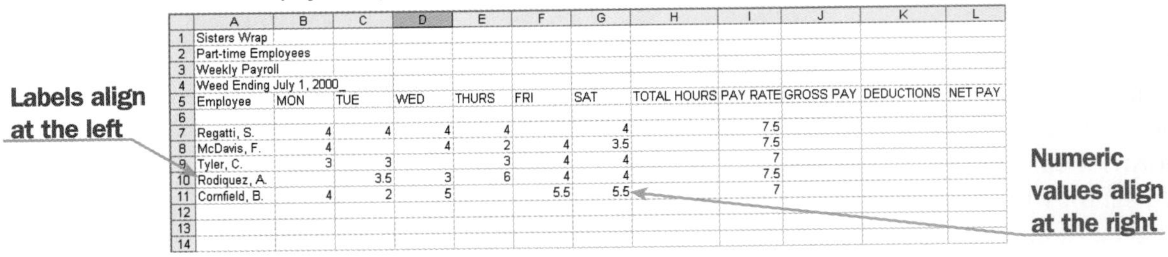

Labels align at the left →

Numeric values align at the right →

	A	B	C	D	E	F	G	H	I	J	K	L
1	Sisters Wrap											
2	Part-time Employees											
3	Weekly Payroll											
4	Weed Ending July 1, 2000_											
5	Employee	MON	TUE	WED	THURS	FRI	SAT	TOTAL HOURS	PAY RATE	GROSS PAY	DEDUCTIONS	NET PAY
6												
7	Regatti, S.	4	4	4	4		4		7.5			
8	McDavis, F.	4		4	2	4	3.5		7.5			
9	Tyler, C.	3	3		3	4	4		7			
10	Rodiquez, A.		3.5	3	6	4	4		7.5			
11	Cornfield, B.	4	2	5		5.5	5.5		7			
12												
13												
14												

9. Click **File** on the menu bar and then click **Save As**. In the Save As dialog box, select the location to which you are saving files from the Save in box. Enter **Part-time Payroll** in the File name box, and then click **Save**. Leave the workbook open for Step-by-step 12.2.

Entering Formulas and Functions

A formula performs calculations, such as adding, subtracting, averaging, and multiplying. You can type a formula directly in a cell or in the formula bar. To enter a formula in a cell, you must first type an equal sign (=). This symbol, called the *formula prefix*, identifies the data as a formula and not a label. For the formula, you can enter cell references, arithmetic operators, and/or functions. The arithmetic operators indicate the desired arithmetic operations. These include addition (+), subtraction (-), multiplication (*), and division (/). These keys are on the numeric keypad as well as the keyboard.

Formulas that contain more than one operator are called complex formulas. When there is more than one operator, the *order of evaluation* determines the sequence of calculation. Formulas are evaluated as follows:

■ Multiplication and division are performed before addition and subtraction.

■ Calculations are performed from the left side of the formula to the right side.

■ You can change the order of evaluation by using parentheses. Calculations enclosed in parentheses are performed first.

Figure 12-3 provides examples to illustrate the order of evaluation.

FIGURE 12-3

Examples of order of evaluation

Multiplication is performed first and then addition	Formula	Result	
	= 6 + 3 * 3	6 + 9 = 15	
	= 6 * 3 + 3	18 + 3 = 21	**Values in parentheses are calculated first**
	= (6 + 3) * 3	9 * 3 = 27	
Division is performed first and then subtraction	= 6 - 3 / 3	6 - 1 = 5	
	= 6 / 3 - 3	2 - 3 = -1	
	= (6 * 3) - (3 / 3)	18 - 1 = 17	

For even more complex calculations, you can use Excel functions. A function is a prewritten formula that automatically calculates a value based on data you insert. Excel comes with a variety of functions that range from simple, such as the SUM function that calculates a total, to complex, like the PMT function, which calculates the payment for a loan based on constant payments and a constant interest rate. Table 12-2 shows a list of commonly used functions.

TABLE 12-2

Common functions

FUNCTION NAME	DESCRIPTION
AVERAGE	Gives the average of specified values
COUNT	Counts the number of cells in a range
IF	Specifies a logical test to perform, then performs one action if test result is true and another if it is not true
MAX	Identifies the maximum value in a range of cells
MIN	Identifies the minimum value in a range of cells
ROUND	Rounds the value to the nearest value in one of two ways—with the specified number of decimal places or to the nearest whole number
MEDIAN	Gives the middle value in a range of cells
SUM	Totals a range of cells

To enter a function, you type the equal sign (=), the name of the function (such as SUM, AVERAGE, and so forth), an opening parenthesis, the value(s), cell, or range of cells to be calculated in the function (referred to as the *argument*), and then the closing parenthesis. The argument for a range of cells consists of the cell address of the first cell in the range, followed by a colon (:), and then the address of the last cell in the range. For example, to use the SUM function to total the values in cells B9 through G9, you would type *=SUM(B9:G9)*. You also can insert a function by clicking Insert on the menu bar and then selecting Function.

As you type a formula or a function, it is displayed in the formula bar. After you press Enter, the formula is displayed in the formula bar and the result of the formula is displayed in the active cell.

You can use the AutoSum feature as a shortcut for entering the SUM function. Click the cell where the result is to appear, and then click the AutoSum button on the Standard toolbar. Excel will display an outline around the group of cells in the column above the highlighted cell or row of cells adjacent to the highlighted cell. If the highlighted cells are not the ones that you want, click the first of the group you want and drag to the last cell in the range you want to add. Press Enter or click the AutoSum button again.

Be careful when entering formulas. Typing the incorrect cell reference, using a semicolon instead of a colon to identify a range, or even misspelling a function could cause your result to be incorrect. However, if you enter a formula incorrectly, you can make the correction in the formula bar. Just click the cell in which the formula appears, place the insertion point at the point of the correction in the formula bar, and make the correction.

In Step-by-step 12.2, you enter formulas in a worksheet.

> **Hot Tip**
>
> A useful feature of spreadsheet software is a macro, a recorded series of keystrokes that can be replayed as needed. For example, all of the keystrokes necessary to print a spreadsheet to a certain printer can be recorded as a macro.

STEP-BY-STEP 12.2

1. Click cell **H7** and type **=B7+C7+D7+E7+F7+G7** to calculate the total hours worked by Regatti, S. (*Hint:* Even though cell F7 is blank, you should include it in the formula in case data is entered in it at a later time.) Press **Enter** to move to cell H8.

2. Type **=B8+C8+D8+E8+F8+G8** to calculate the total hours worked by McDavis, F. Press **Enter** to move to cell H9.

3. Type **=**, click cell **B9**, type **+**, click cell **C9**, type **+**, click cell **D9**, type **+**, click cell **E9**, type **+**, click cell **F9**, type **+**, and then click cell **G9** to calculate the total hours worked by Tyler, C. Press **Enter** to move to cell H10.

4. Type **=SUM(B10:G10)** to calculate the total hours worked by Rodiquez, A. Press **Enter**.

5. Type **=SUM(B11:G11)** to calculate the total hours worked by Cornfield, B.

6. Click cell **B13**. Type **=SUM(B7:B11)** to calculate the total hours worked on Monday by each employee.

7. Click cell **C7** and drag to cell **C13**. Click the **AutoSum** button on the Standard toolbar to automatically calculate the total hours worked on Tuesday by each employee. Click elsewhere in the worksheet to deselect the cells.

8. Your worksheet should resemble the one shown in Figure 12-4 on the next page. Click the **Save** button on the Standard toolbar to save the workbook. Leave the workbook open for Step-by-step 12.3.

FIGURE 12-4
Formulas entered

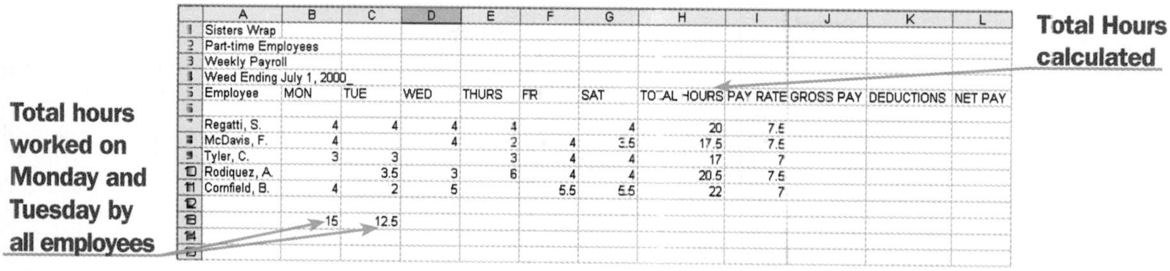

Total Hours calculated

Total hours worked on Monday and Tuesday by all employees

	A	B	C	D	E	F	G	H	I	J	K	L
1	Sisters Wrap											
2	Part-time Employees											
3	Weekly Payroll											
4	Weed Ending July 1, 2000											
5	Employee	MON	TUE	WED	THURS	FRI	SAT	TOTAL HOURS	PAY RATE	GROSS PAY	DEDUCTIONS	NET PAY
6												
7	Regatti, S.	4	4	4	4		4	20	7.5			
8	McDavis, F.	4		4	2	4	3.5	17.5	7.5			
9	Tyler, C.	3	3		3	4	4	17	7			
10	Rodiquez, A.		3.5	3	6	4	4	20.5	7.5			
11	Cornfield, B.	4	2	5		5.5	5.5	22	7			
12												
13		15	12.5									
14												
15												

Copying Data

In the previous exercise, you entered a fairly lengthy formula to calculate the total hours worked for the week by employees S. Regatti, F. McDavis, and C. Tyler. Instead of entering that formula for each employee, you can copy the formula. Excel provides several ways to copy data. You can use the Copy and Paste commands, the drag-and-drop method, or the Fill command.

To use the Copy and Paste commands:

■ Click the cell to be copied.

■ Click the Copy button on the Standard toolbar.

■ Click the cell into which you want to paste the data. You also may select a range of cells in which to paste the data.

■ Click the Paste button on the Standard toolbar.

To use the drag-and-drop method:

■ Select the cell or range of cells you want to copy.

■ Hold down the Ctrl key.

■ Drag to the location to which you want to copy the data.

■ Release the mouse button.

To use the Fill command:

■ Click the cell to be copied. The active cell has a black square at its lower-right corner. This black square is called a fill handle. See Figure 12-5.

FIGURE 12-5
Fill handle on a selected cell

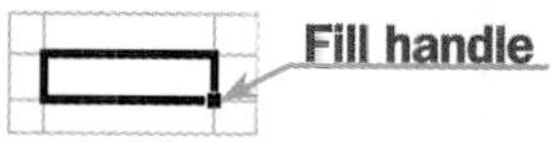

Fill handle

■ Move the mouse pointer over the fill handle. When the pointer changes shape to a plus sign, drag the fill handle, highlighting the cells into which you want the data to be copied.

■ Release the mouse button. Note that filling works only when you want to copy to adjacent cells.

Relative and Absolute Cell References

When you copy cells that contain formulas, the cell references change to accommodate the new location. This is called a **relative cell reference**. If you want the value of a cell referenced in a formula to remain constant when copied, then you need to make it an **absolute cell reference**. This means that the content of the cell will not change when copied to another cell.

To create an absolute cell reference, type a $ before the column letter and a $ before the row number in the cell reference you want to remain the same. For example, A4 is an absolute cell reference for cell A4.

In Step-by-step 12.3, you use various methods to copy data.

S TEP-BY-STEP 12.3

1. Click cell **C13**. Notice that the formula bar contains the formula =SUM(C7:C12).

2. Click the **Copy** button on the Standard toolbar.

3. Click cell **D13** and click the **Paste** button on the Standard toolbar. Notice in the formula bar how the cell references changed in reference to the new location of the copied formula.

4. Cell D13 should still be selected. Drag its fill handle to cell **H13**.

5. Click cell **J7**. Type **=H7*I7** and press **Enter** to determine Gross Pay for Regatti, S.

6. Use either the Copy and Paste commands or the Fill command to copy the formula in J7 to **J8:J11**.

7. Click cell **K7**. Type **=J7*.27** and press **Enter** to determine the amount of deductions taken from Regatti's pay. (The amount of deductions is 27% of gross pay.)

8. Copy the formula in K7 to **K8:K11** to determine deductions for the other four employees.

9. Click cell **L7**. Type **=J7-K7** and press **Enter** to determine net pay for Regatti, S.

10. Copy the formula in L7 to **L8:L11** to determine net pay for the other four employees.

11. Select **J7:J13** and then click the **AutoSum** button to total the gross pay for all employees.

12. Copy the formula in cell J13 to cell **K13** and cell **L13**. Your worksheet should resemble the one shown in Figure 12-6.

13. Save the workbook and leave it open for Step-by-step 12.4.

FIGURE 12-6
Payroll with copied data

	D	E	F	G	H	I	J	K	L
1									
2									
3									
4									
5	WED	THURS	FRI	SAT	TOTAL HOURS	PAY RATE	GROSS PAY	DEDUCTIONS	NET PAY
6									
7	4	4		4	20	7.5	150	40.5	109.5
8	4	2	4	3.5	17.5	7.5	131.25	35.4375	95.8125
9		3	4	4	17	7	119	32.13	86.87
10	3	6	4	4	20.5	7.5	153.75	41.5125	112.2375
11	5		5.5	5.5	22	7	154	41.58	112.42
12									
13	16	15	17.5	21	97		708	191.16	516.84
14									

Copied formulas

Formatting a Spreadsheet

The appearance of the spreadsheet is almost as important as the accuracy of the data that it contains. You can use formatting to emphasize specific entries, enhance the appearance of the spreadsheet, and make the information easier to read and understand. In Figure 12-7, you see how formatting can affect the appearance of the data.

FIGURE 12-7
(A) Unformatted data, (B) Various formats applied, (C) Excel AutoFormat applied

	A	B	C	D	E	F	G	H	I	J	K	L
1	Sisters Wrap											
2	Part-time Employees											
3	Weekly Payroll											
4	Weed Ending July 1, 2000_											
5	Employee	MON	TUE	WED	THURS	FRI	SAT	TOTAL HOURS	PAY RATE	GROSS PAY	DEDUCTIONS	NET PAY
6												
7	Pegatti, S.	4	4	4	4		4	20	7.5	150	40.5	109.5
8	McDavis, F.	4		4	2	4	3.5	17.5	7.5	131.25	35.4375	95.8125
9	Tyler, C.	3	3		3	4	4	17	7	119	32.13	86.87
10	Podiquez, A.		3.5	3	6	4	4	20.5	7.5	153.75	41.5125	112.2375
11	Cornfield, B.	4	2	5		5.5	5.5	22	7	154	41.58	112.42
12												
13		15	12.5	16	15	17.5	21	97		708	191.16	516.84

A.

	A	B	C	D	E	F	G	H	I	J	K	L
1						Sisters Wrap						
2						Part-time Employees						
3						Weekly Payroll						
4						Weed Ending July 1, 200_						
5												
6	Employee	MON	TUE	WED	THURS	FRI	SAT	TOTAL HOURS	PAY RATE	GROSS PAY	DEDUCTIONS	NET PAY
7												
8	Pegatti, S.	4	4	4	4		4	20	7.5	150.00	40.50	109.50
9	McDavis, F.	4		4	2	4	3.5	17.5	7.5	131.25	35.44	95.81
10	Tyler, C.	3	3		3	4	4	17	7	119.00	32.13	86.87
11	Fodiquez, A.		3.5	3	6	4	4	20.5	7.5	153.75	41.51	112.24
12	Cornfield, B.	4	2	5		5.5	5.5	22	7	154.00	41.58	112.42
13												
14	TOTAL	15	12.5	16	15	17.5	21	97		708.00	191.16	516.84
15												
16												

B.

	A	B	C	D	E	F	G	H	I	J	K	L
1	Sisters Wrap											
2	Part-time Employees											
3	Weekly Payroll											
4	Weed Ending July 1, 200_											
5												
6	Employee	MON	TUE	WED	THURS	FRI	SAT	TOTAL HOURS	PAY RATE	GROSS PAY	DEDUCTIONS	NET PAY
7												
8	Pegatti, S.	4	4	4	4		4	20	7.5	150.00	40.50	109.50
9	McDavis, F.	4		4	2	4	3.5	17.5	7.5	131.25	35.44	95.81
10	Tyler, C.	3	3		3	4	4	17	7	119.00	32.13	86.87
11	Fodiquez, A.		3.5	3	6	4	4	20.5	7.5	153.75	41.51	112.24
12	Cornfield, B.	4	2	5		5.5	5.5	22	7	154.00	41.58	112.42
13												
14	TOTAL	15	12.5	16	15	17.5	21	97		708.00	191.16	516.84
15												

C.

Changing Column Width and Row Height

When you enter data in a cell that is too long for the width of the cell, one of the following will happen: a series of # characters appear in the cell, the text might spill over into the next cell, or some of the characters might be cut off.

To adjust the column width:

- Position the pointer on the vertical line between the column letters at the top of the worksheet. The pointer changes shape to a double-headed black arrow.

- Click and drag to the right to widen the column. Drag to the left to decrease the column width.

- Adjusting the row height improves readability. To adjust row height:

- Position the pointer on the line between the row numbers at the left of the worksheet. The pointer changes shape to a double-headed arrow.

- Click and drag upward to increase the height of the row and drag downward to decrease the height of the row.

Formatting Data

The appearance of the data in a spreadsheet can have an impact on how well the information is understood. Following is a list of some of the formatting tools you might apply to data in a worksheet.

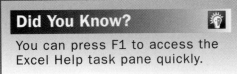

Did You Know?

You can press F1 to access the Excel Help task pane quickly.

- *Alignment*: By default, text is aligned to the left in a cell and numeric data is aligned to the right. You can change alignment using the Align Left, Center, Align Right, and Merge and Center buttons on the Formatting toolbar. The Merge and Center format is ideal for worksheet titles and subtitles.

- *Rotating and Wrapping*: Data in cells can be rotated or wrapped to make it fit better within the cell. Select Cells on the Format menu to open the Format Cells dialog box. Click the Alignment tab and select the wrapping or rotating feature you want to use.

- *Font*: You can change the font, font size, font style, and font color of data just as you would in a word-processing document. Use buttons on the Formatting toolbar or options in the Format Cells dialog box.

- *Format Painter*: The Format Painter provides a time-saving way to apply formats consistently throughout a worksheet. With this tool, you can copy the formats applied to a cell or range to another cell or range. Select the cell(s) whose formatting you want to copy, click the Format Painter button on the Standard toolbar, and then select the cell(s) to which you want to apply the formatting.

Inserting and Deleting Cells, Rows, and Columns

As you work on a worksheet, you might find it necessary to insert a cell or range of cells, or even an entire row or column to accommodate new data.

- To insert a cell, click Cells on the Insert menu. The Insert dialog box opens in which you select whether you want cells to shift to the left or down in order to insert the desired cell(s).

- To insert a row, click Rows on the Insert menu. One row is inserted above the row in which the cell pointer is located.

■ To insert a column, click Columns on the Insert menu. One column is inserted to the left of the column in which the cell pointer is located.

You can delete cells, rows, and columns by selecting them and then using the Delete command on the Edit menu or by pressing the Delete key.

Formatting Numbers

Much of the data you enter in a worksheet will be numeric. This data is more meaningful if it is formatted correctly. For example, monetary values should be formatted as currency and dates should be formatted in a recognized date format. You can format numbers to have a set number of decimal places, to have a comma (signifying the thousands separator), or to display as a percentage. Some of the more commonly used formats can be applied using buttons on the Formatting toolbar. Others can be selected on the Number tab of the Format Cells dialog box, shown in Figure 12-8.

FIGURE 12-8
Number tab in the Format Cells dialog box

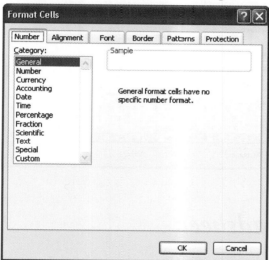

 Ethics in Technology

PHYSICAL SECURITY

With all the concern about major computer crime, the subject of internal security might be overlooked. It is usually fairly easy for an unauthorized person to access systems by simply going to a valid user's desk.

Machines and consoles should be kept in a secure place. Only a limited number of persons should have access. A list of persons with access should be kept up to date. Some organizations have security guards to monitor computer rooms and control entry.

Remember that limited access means less opportunity for computer equipment and/or data to be stolen. That is why alternative methods for getting into a computer room should not be available. This includes hidden spare keys in an unsecured place.

Some organizations have taken computer safety an extra step by securing equipment physically to desks and tables. This might seem like overkill, but you should protect your investment and your data by whatever means necessary.

AutoFormat

You can use an Excel AutoFormat to quickly apply professional-looking formatting to worksheet data. *AutoFormats* are customized preset styles that come with Excel. To apply an AutoFormat, select the data that you want to format, click Format on the menu bar, and then click AutoFormat. The AutoFormat dialog box opens, as shown in Figure 12-9. Select a format and click OK. After you have applied an AutoFormat, you can continue to format individual cells and ranges as desired.

FIGURE 12-9
AutoFormat dialog box

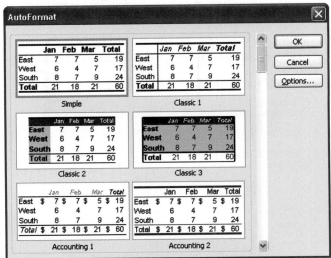

Printing a Spreadsheet

Often, you will want to print a copy of your spreadsheet. You can preview the spreadsheet to see how it will look before you print it. Click the Print Preview button on the Standard toolbar.

You can adjust several print settings in the Page Setup dialog box. To open it, click File on the menu bar and then click Page Setup. For example, you might want to include the row numbers and column letters on the printout. Or, you might want the gridlines to print to make it easier to read the data. You specify these settings on the Sheet tab of the Page Setup dialog box, as shown in Figure 12-10.

FIGURE 12-10
Page Setup dialog box

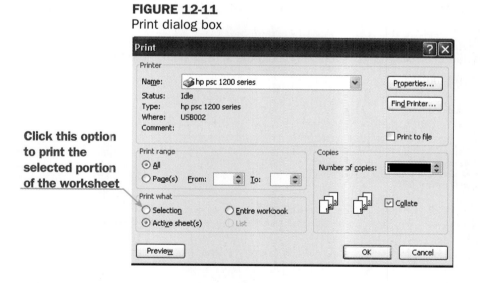

Page tab

Sheet tab

Select this
option to print
row numbers and
column letters

Click to print
gridlines

You also can determine the orientation in which the spreadsheet prints. In portrait orientation, the page is oriented toward the short side of the paper. In landscape orientation, the page is oriented toward the long side of the paper. You set orientation on the Page tab of the Page Setup dialog box.

In some cases, you might want to print only a portion of the spreadsheet. You can define the part you want to print by selecting it first. Then, click Print on the File menu. In the Print dialog box, click the Selection option in the Print what section. as shown in Figure 12-11.

FIGURE 12-11
Print dialog box

Click this option
to print the
selected portion
of the worksheet

To print the entire spreadsheet, click Print on the File menu and then click OK in the Print dialog box.

In Step-by-step 12.4, you add formatting to the spreadsheet and print it.

STEP-BY-STEP 12.4

1. Select the range **A1:L1**.

2. Click the **Merge and Center** button on the Formatting toolbar. Do the same for the ranges **A2:L2**, **A3:L3**, and **A4:L4**.

3. Select **A5:L5**. Click the **Center** button and then click the **Bold** button on the Formatting toolbar.

4. The range **H5:L5** should still be selected. Click **Cells** on the **Format** menu. Click the **Alignment** tab in the Format Cells dialog box, and then click the **Wrap text** check box. Click **OK**.

5. Position the pointer on the vertical line between column A and column B. Drag the pointer to the right until column A is wide enough to display the complete names in the cells. Do the same to adjust column K so that it is wide enough to display the word *DEDUCTIONS* on one line.

6. Select **J7:L13** and then click the **Currency Style** button on the Formatting toolbar.

7. To insert a blank row between the titles at the top of the worksheet and the payroll data, click a cell in row 5. Click **Insert** on the menu bar and then click **Rows**.

8. Click **Page Setup** on the **File** menu. In the Page Setup dialog box, click the **Page** tab, if necessary, and click the **Landscape** option. Click the **Sheet** tab and then click **Gridlines**, if necessary.

9. Click the **Print** button on the Sheet tab and then click **OK** to print the spreadsheet.

10. Select the range **A1:L14**. Click **Format** on the menu bar and then click **AutoFormat**. Scroll to and click the **3D Effects 2** format, and then click **OK**. Your spreadsheet should resemble that shown in Figure 12-12.

11. Click the **Print** button on the Standard toolbar to print the spreadsheet. Save the workbook and leave it open for Step-by-step 12.5.

FIGURE 12-12
Formatted spreadsheet

	A	B	C	D	E	F	G	H	I	J	K	L
1	Sisters Wrap											
2	Part-time Employees											
3	Weekly Payroll											
4	Week Ending July 1, 200_											
5												
6	Employee	MON	TUE	WED	THURS	FRI	SAT	TOTAL HOURS	PAY RATE	GROSS PAY	DEDUCTIONS	NET PAY
7												
8	Regatti, S.	4	4	4	4		4	20	7.5	$150.00	$ 40.50	$109.50
9	McDavis, F.	4		4	2	4	3.5	17.5	7.5	$131.25	$ 35.44	$ 95.81
10	Tyler, C.	3	3		3	4	4	17	7	$119.00	$ 32.13	$ 86.87
11	Rodiquez, A.		3.5	3	6	4	4	20.5	7.5	$153.75	$ 41.51	$112.24
12	Cornfield, B.	4	2	5		5.5	5.5	22	7	$154.00	$ 41.58	$112.42
13												
14	TOTAL	15	12.5	16	15	17.5	21	97		$708.00	$ 191.16	$516.84
15												

Working with Other Spreadsheet Tools

You can make spreadsheets more useful and attractive by inserting headers and footers, and other objects. You can sort the data in a spreadsheet according to the data in a specified column or columns. You also can hide data that might be sensitive or classified. These features are discussed in the next sections.

Headers and Footers

Use *headers* and *footers* to place information at the top or bottom of the spreadsheet. If your spreadsheet is more than one page long, the header and footer information will appear on every page. For example, you might include the date the spreadsheet was prepared and the name of the person who prepared it in a footer that appears on each page of the spreadsheet. Excel comes with several standard headers and footers from which you can choose. To select one, click View on the menu bar and click Header and Footer. The Page Setup dialog box opens with the Header/Footer tab displayed. Click the drop-down arrow on the Header or Footer box to display the standard options. Figure 12-13 shows some of the standard Excel footers.

FIGURE 12-13
Excel headers and footers

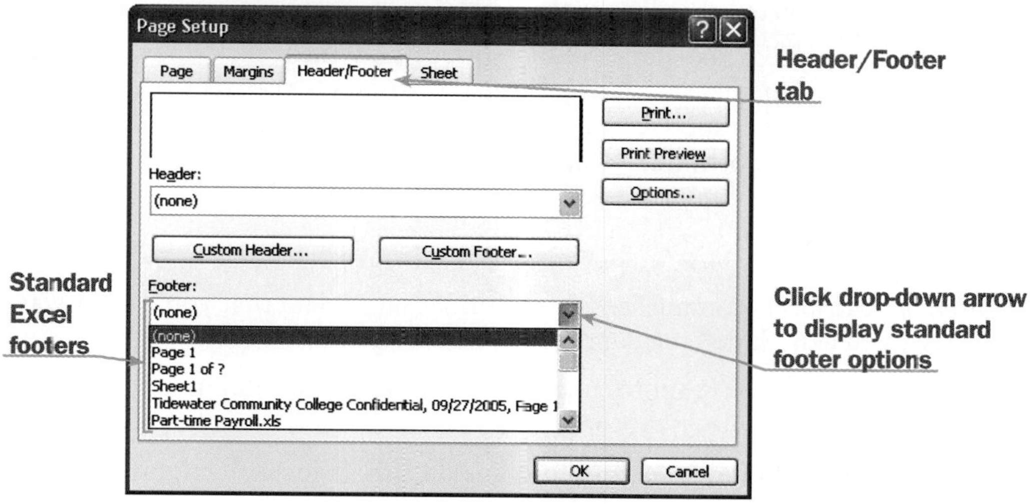

You also can create your own custom headers and footers. On the Header/Footer tab of the Page Setup dialog box, click the Custom Header or Custom Footer button. A dialog box opens from which you can select the items to insert in the header or footer, such as date, page number, filename, and so forth. Figure 12-14 on the next page shows the Header dialog box. You also can determine where the item is placed (left, center, or right) in the header or footer.

FIGURE 12-14
Creating a custom header

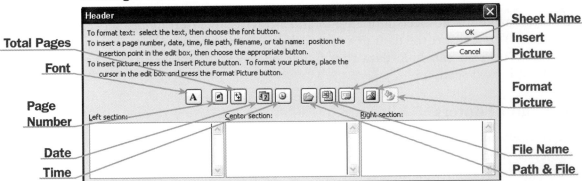

Sorting Spreadsheet Data

Sorting is organizing or rearranging data in either ascending or descending order. When you sort data in ascending order, the alphabetic information is arranged in ABC order and numeric information sorts from the lowest to the highest number. When you sort data in descending order, alphabetic information is sorted from Z to A and numbers from highest to lowest. You can sort data in a worksheet according to the data in one column or more than one column.

To sort data, select the range to be sorted, and then click the Sort Ascending or Sort Descending button on the Formatting toolbar. This sorts the data by the first column in the range. You can sort by a specific column or columns by using the Sort dialog box. To open the Sort dialog box, select Sort on the Data menu.

Hiding Data

Often, spreadsheets contain sensitive information or data that you do not want others to see. In this case, you can "hide" the data. To hide a column:

■ Select the column you want to hide by right-clicking the column letter and then clicking Hide. The column will disappear.

■ To unhide the column, select the columns on either side of it, right-click, and then select Unhide.

Adding Objects to a Spreadsheet

You can add clip art, photos, and other objects to a spreadsheet to enhance its appearance. You can use tools on the Drawing toolbar to insert objects, such as text boxes, WordArt, arrow shapes, and so forth.

To insert clip art:

■ Click Insert on the menu bar, point to Picture, and then click Clip Art. The Clip Art task pane opens.

■ Enter the type or category of clip art that you want in the Search for box and then click Go. The results are displayed in the task pane, as shown in Figure 12-15 on the next page.

FIGURE 12-15
Clip Art task pane

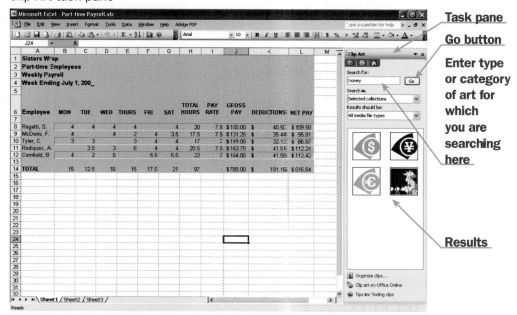

■ Scroll through the displayed pictures using the vertical scroll bar at the right of the task pane.

■ Once you locate the picture you want, click it to display it in the spreadsheet.

To insert a drawn object in a spreadsheet:

■ Open the Drawing toolbar (see Figure 12-16) by clicking the Drawing button on the Standard toolbar.

FIGURE 12-16
Drawing toolbar

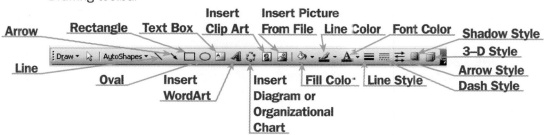

■ Click the button representing the object you want to insert.

■ Click in the worksheet where you want to insert the object.

In Step-by-step 12.5, you use additional spreadsheet tools to enhance the worksheet.

STEP-BY-STEP 12.5

1. Select the range **A8:L12**.and then click the **Sort Ascending** button on the Formatting toolbar.

2. Right-click the column letter **I**, which shows the employees' pay rates, and then click **Hide** on the shortcut menu. The column is removed from view.

3. Select columns **H** and **J**, right-click, and then click **Unhide** on the shortcut menu to redisplay the pay rate data.

4. Create a footer with your name, page number, and date of completion:
   a. Select **View** on the menu bar and then click **Header and Footer**. In the **Page Setup** dialog box, click **Custom Footer**.
   b. Click in the Left section panel and type your first and last name.
   c. Press **Tab** to move to the Center section panel and click the **Page Number** icon.
   d. Press **Tab** to move to the Right section panel and click the **Insert Date** button.
   e. Click **OK** and then click **OK** again to close the Page Setup dialog box.

5. Insert a clip art picture related to money:
   a. Click **Insert** on the menu bar, point to **Picture**, and then click **Clip Art**.
   b. In the Clip Art task pane, type **money** in the Search for box and click **Go**.
   c. Scroll through the pictures and click one of your choice.
   d. If necessary, click one of the handles on the clip art to resize it so it is about 1 inch by 1 inch in size.
   e. Position the clip art in the upper-right corner of the worksheet. Click elsewhere in the worksheet to deselect the clip art.

6. Your worksheet should look similar to that shown in Figure 12-17. Click the **Print Preview** button on the Standard toolbar to view the worksheet.

FIGURE 12-17
Sorted spreadsheet with clip art inserted

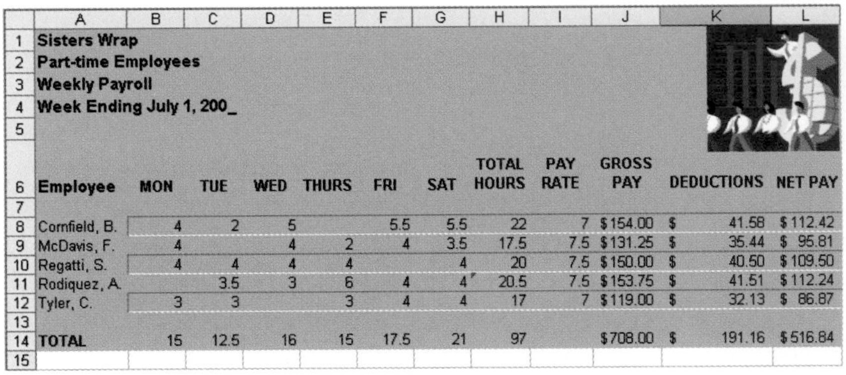

	A	B	C	D	E	F	G	H	I	J	K	L
1	Sisters Wrap											
2	Part-time Employees											
3	Weekly Payroll											
4	Week Ending July 1, 200_											
5												
6	Employee	MON	TUE	WED	THURS	FRI	SAT	TOTAL HOURS	PAY RATE	GROSS PAY	DEDUCTIONS	NET PAY
7												
8	Cornfield, B.	4	2	5		5.5	5.5	22	7	$154.00	$ 41.58	$112.42
9	McDavis, F.	4		4	2	4	3.5	17.5	7.5	$131.25	$ 35.44	$ 95.81
10	Regatti, S.	4	4	4	4		4	20	7.5	$150.00	$ 40.50	$109.50
11	Rodiquez, A.		3.5	3	6	4	4	20.5	7.5	$153.75	$ 41.51	$112.24
12	Tyler, C.	3	3		3	4	4	17	7	$119.00	$ 32.13	$ 86.87
13												
14	TOTAL	15	12.5	16	15	17.5	21	97		$708.00	$ 191.16	$516.84
15												

7. Click the **Close** button to return to Normal view. Make any changes you think are necessary.

8. Save the workbook and then print it. Leave the workbook open for Step-by-step 12.6.

Creating Charts

A *chart* is a visual representation of spreadsheet data. Charts can help make the data more interesting and easier to understand. Before creating a chart, you need to plan the information you want your chart to show and how you want it to look. Excel provides options for creating a variety of chart types, including pie charts, column charts, bar charts, and line charts. The chart type that you select will depend on the data you want to represent. Table 12-3 lists some of the Excel chart types and a description of the types of data best illustrated with each chart.

TABLE 12-3
Chart types

CHART TYPE	DESCRIPTION
Area	Effective for emphasizing trends because it illustrates the magnitude of change over time
Bar	Helpful when you want to make comparisons among individual items
Column	Useful in showing changes over a period of time, or for making comparisons among individual items
Pie	Compares the sizes of portions as they relate to the whole unit and illustrates that the parts total 100%; effective when there is only one set of data
Doughnut	Also shows comparisons between the whole and the parts, but enables you to show more than one set of data
Line	Illustrates trends in data at equal intervals
Scatter	Illustrates scientific data, specifically showing even intervals—or clusters—of data

You can use the Excel Chart Wizard to create a chart. The wizard guides you through the steps of selecting the chart type, adding chart titles and labels, and determining if the chart appears on the same worksheet as the data being charted or on its own sheet. Before you begin the Chart Wizard, select the range containing the data you want in the chart.

 Technology Careers

DATA WAREHOUSE DEVELOPER

The data warehouse developer is responsible for translating business requirements into computer solutions. This is accomplished by understanding the users' needs and assisting in the design of physical databases to address those needs. The data warehouse developer also provides secondary technical support. This position requires teamwork skills. The qualifications include a bachelor's degree in Computer Technology, Computer Science, or Engineering. Excellent oral and written communication skills are also required. Salary range varies depending on location, responsibilities, and qualifications.

In Step-by-step 12.6, you create a chart in the payroll spreadsheet that displays the net pay of employees.

STEP-BY-STEP 12.6

1. Select the range **A8:A12**. Hold down the **Ctrl** key and then select the range **L8:L12**. (Both ranges of data will appear on the chart.)

2. Click the **Chart Wizard** button on the Formatting toolbar. The Chart Wizard – Step 1 of 4 dialog box opens, as shown in Figure 12-18.

FIGURE 12-18
Chart Wizard – Step 1 of 4 – Chart Type dialog box

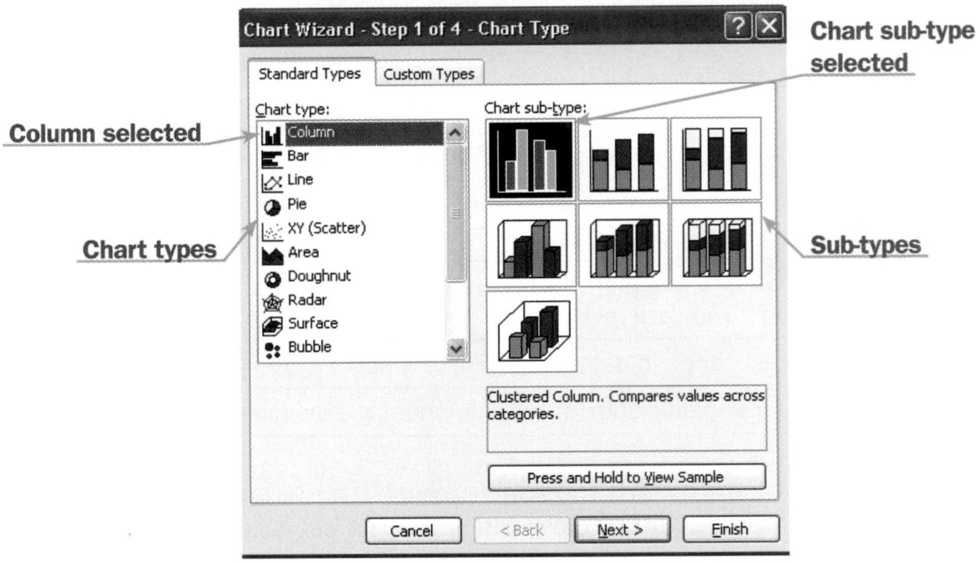

3. Click **Column** in the Chart type list, and then select the first chart sub-type in the second row (**Clustered column with a 3-D visual effect**). Click the **Press and Hold to View Sample** button in the dialog box. You will see how your chart will look.

4. Release the mouse button and click **Next**. The Chart Wizard – Step 2 of 4 dialog box opens, as shown in Figure 12-19 on the next page. You see a preview of the chart. Click the **Rows** option button and note how the preview changes.

STEP-BY-STEP 12.6 Continued

FIGURE 12-19
Chart Wizard – Step 2 of 4 – Chart Source Data

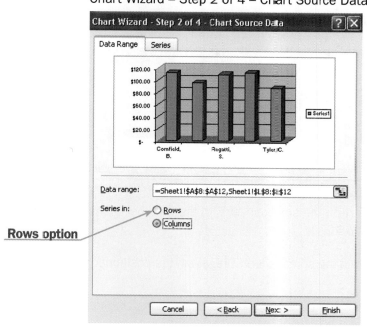

Rows option

5. Click the **Next** button. The Chart Wizard – Step 3 of 4 dialog box opens, as shown in Figure 12-20.

FIGURE 12-20
Chart Wizard – Step 3 of 4 – Chart Options

Axes tab

Chart title text box

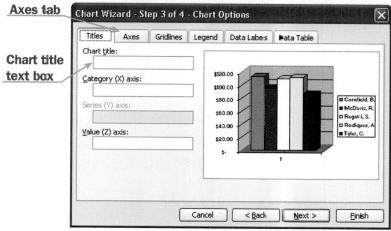

6. Click in the **Chart title** text box and type **Net Pay for Employees**.

7. Click the **Axes** tab and click the **Category (X) axis** box to deselect it. This will remove the "1" that appears below the X axis.

STEP-BY-STEP 12.6 Continued

8. Click the **Next** button. The Chart Wizard – Step 4 of 4 dialog box opens, as shown in Figure 12-21.

FIGURE 12-21
Chart Wizard – Step 4 of 4 – Chart Location

This option places the chart on its own sheet

This option places the chart on the same worksheet as the data

Finish button

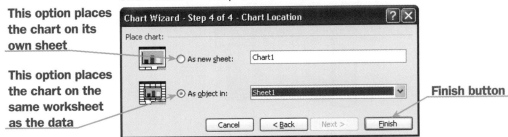

9. You will embed the chart on the spreadsheet with the data being charted, so click **As object in** if necessary, and then click **Finish**.

10. The chart is embedded in the spreadsheet. Drag it so it is positioned below the data, as shown in Figure 12-22.

FIGURE 12-22
Spreadsheet with chart

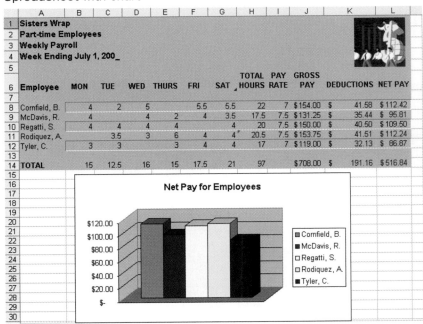

11. Print the spreadsheet. Then save and close the workbook.

12. Exit Excel by clicking **File** on the menu bar and then clicking **Exit**.

SUMMARY

In this lesson, you learned:

- The primary use of Excel spreadsheets is to enter, calculate, manipulate, and analyze numbers.

- Columns in spreadsheets are identified by letters, and rows are identified by numbers.

- The point at which a row and a column intersect is a cell.

- A cell that has been selected (highlighted or outlined with a black border) is referred to as the active cell.

- A range of cells is a group of closely situated cells.

- Alphabetic information in cells is referred to as labels; numeric information in cells that can be calculated is referred to as values.

- A formula is a type of data that performs a calculation. To enter a formula in a cell, you must first type an equal sign.

- A function is a built-in formula that performs calculations ranging from simple to complex.

- You can copy data by using the Copy and Paste commands, the drag-and-drop method, or the Fill command.

- A relative cell reference refers to cells that change when they are copied into other locations. An absolute cell reference refers to cells that do not change when they are copied into other locations.

- The AutoSum feature enables you to quickly add a range of cells.

- You can change the appearance of data by using a variety of formatting tools and options or by applying one of the Excel AutoFormats.

- Selected data in a spreadsheet can be hidden so it will not be displayed or printed.

- The contents of a spreadsheet can be displayed in chart format. A chart displays the spreadsheet data visually so that data can be understood more easily.

VOCABULARY *Review*

Define the following terms:

Absolute cell reference	Formula	Relative cell reference
Active cell	Formula prefix	Spreadsheet
AutoFormats	Function	Value
Cell	Header	Workbook
Cell reference	Label	Worksheet
Chart	Order of evaluation	
Footer	Range	

REVIEW *Questions*

MULTIPLE CHOICE

Select the best response for the following statements.

1. A collection of related worksheets is called a(n) _____.
   A. volume
   B. spreadsheet
   C. AutoFormat
   D. workbook

2. Which of the following would not be placed in a header or footer?
   A. current date
   B. filename
   C. page number
   D. worksheet chart

3. A formula in a selected cell is displayed in the _____.
   A. Standard toolbar
   B. formula bar
   C. menu bar
   D. Formatting toolbar

4. Pie, bar, column, and line are examples of types of _____.
   A. spreadsheets
   B. worksheets
   C. charts
   D. cells

5. Labels, values, formulas, and functions are types of _____ that can be entered in a spreadsheet.
   A. fonts
   B. data
   C. formats
   D. headings

TRUE/FALSE

Circle T if the statement is true or F if the statement is false.

T   F   1. A worksheet is the same as a spreadsheet.

T   F   2. By default, a workbook contains three worksheets.

T   F   3. A spreadsheet program is used primarily to type letters.

T   F   4. Charts can be embedded in a spreadsheet.

T   F   5. AutoFormat is used to give spreadsheets a professional look.

FILL IN THE BLANK

Complete the following sentences by writing the correct word or words in the blanks provided.

1. A cell address consists of a(n) _____ letter and a(n) _____ number.

2. Four types of data entered in a spreadsheet are _____, _____, _____, and _____.

3. To identify a cell as absolute, type a(n) _____ before the letter and number in the cell address.

4. All formulas entered in a cell should begin with a(n) _____.

5. SUM, AVERAGE, IF, and COUNT are examples of _____.

PROJECTS

CROSS-CURRICULAR—MATHEMATICS

You have volunteered to research the cost of three possible two-week vacation locations for your family. Prepare a spreadsheet that will show the cost of each trip, including line items for transportation, hotel, car rental, meals, activities, and any miscellaneous costs. Apply an AutoFormat to the data. Chart the information for each vacation location.

CROSS-CURRICULAR—SCIENCE

Prepare a spreadsheet that will display your weight on different planets. Use the Internet and other resources to find information on how to determine relative gravity. The spreadsheet might have columns labeled "Planet," "Relative Gravity," "Current Weight," and "Planet Weight." Include clip art in the spreadsheet and format it as desired.

CROSS-CURRICULAR—SOCIAL STUDIES

Use the Internet and other resources to research national monuments. Prepare a spreadsheet that shows the name, location, date erected, current age, height, and distance from where you live for each monument. Format the spreadsheet using AutoFormat. Sort the spreadsheet to show the list from tallest to shortest, from oldest to youngest, and from closest to and farthest from you. Print the spreadsheet after each sort.

CROSS-CURRICULAR—LANGUAGE ARTS

You have been asked to prepare a report on teen drug abuse. Use the Internet and other sources for your research. Include statistical data as part of the written report. Present the statistical data in a spreadsheet. It should include the top five drugs used by teenagers, the amount of money spent on drugs yearly, the number of deaths yearly, and any other statistics that would support your report. Include a footer containing the name of the report, the page number, and the date. Include clip art, and format the spreadsheet as desired.

WEB PROJECT

Your civic organization is planning its national conference in Hampton, Virginia next year. As vice president, you have been asked to gather information about the hotels in the area that are convenient to the Hampton Convention Center. Use the Internet to research information and present it in a spreadsheet. Your spreadsheet should include the name of the hotel, age of the hotel, number of rooms, number of nonsmoking rooms, number of restaurants, daily parking cost, distance to the convention center, and cost of rooms. Format the spreadsheet as desired. Create a chart to show hotels' distances from the convention center.

TEAMWORK PROJECT

You and a classmate are to gather information regarding the top-ten careers for the next decade. You should collect data on projected need, current salary, expected salary, training needed, and cost of training. Enter this information in a spreadsheet. Sort the data according to the projected need. Format the spreadsheet as desired.

CRITICAL *Thinking*

You have been given the responsibility of maintaining scores for your bowling team. Enter the following information in a spreadsheet.

TEAM MEMBER	WEEK 1	WEEK 2	WEEK 3	WEEK 4
Donnell Taborn	215	175	142	187
Grace DeBrew	90	85	114	105
Mark Lawson	240	210	180	195
Don Roberts	105	100	125	281
Ty Nguyen	158	281	132	189

Add a column to the right of the Week 4 column and enter a formula to determine the monthly average for each player. Enter weekly averages for the team on the row beneath the last team player. Include appropriate column and row headings for the data. Add a title to the spreadsheet. Format the data as desired and insert clip art or a drawing that you create using the Drawing tools. Create a chart that will illustrate the monthly average information.

DATABASES

Upon completion of this lesson, you should be able to:

- Define the purpose and function of database software.

- Identify uses of databases.

- Identify and define the components of a database.

- Plan a database.

- Create a table using a wizard.

- Enter records in a table.

- Add a fom using a wizard.

- Create a query using a wizard.

- Create a report using a wizard.

Estimated Time: 1.5 hours

VOCABULARY

Data

Database

Database management system (DBMS)

Database window

Datasheet

Datasheet view

Design view

Fields

Forms

Information

Object

Primary key

Query

Records

Report

Table

Views

Effective information management is the core of a successful business or organization and is important in one's personal life. *Data* is unorganized text, graphics, sound, or video. *Information* is data that has been organized and processed so that it is meaningful and useful. Every organization and most individuals need a method to store data and convert it into accurate, relevant, and timely information when needed.

Database Software Defined

A *database* is a collection of related information organized in a manner that provides for rapid search and retrieval. A *database management system (DBMS)* is a software program that is used to create, maintain, and provide controlled access to data. A database and spreadsheet are somewhat similar. Like spreadsheets, database tables are composed of rows and columns. Both programs enable you to organize, sort, and calculate the data. A database, however, provides more comprehensive functions for manipulating the data. Microsoft Access 2003 is a powerful software application program that offers many features. This lesson introduces you to some of the basic features for entering, organizing, and reporting data in Access. As you continue to learn and use Microsoft Access, you will have the building blocks you need for utilizing this software for more advanced applications.

Before you begin to design and develop a database, you should do some planning. Consider what data you will include and what information you want to create. After you have made these decisions, you are ready to create your database.

Database Structure

To use Access effectively, you first need to understand some basic terminology. In Access, a database can consist of one table or a collection of tables. A *table* is composed of columns and rows, referred to as fields and records in Access. Figure 13-1 shows a sample database table for customers of the Flower Store.

FIGURE 13-1
Sample database

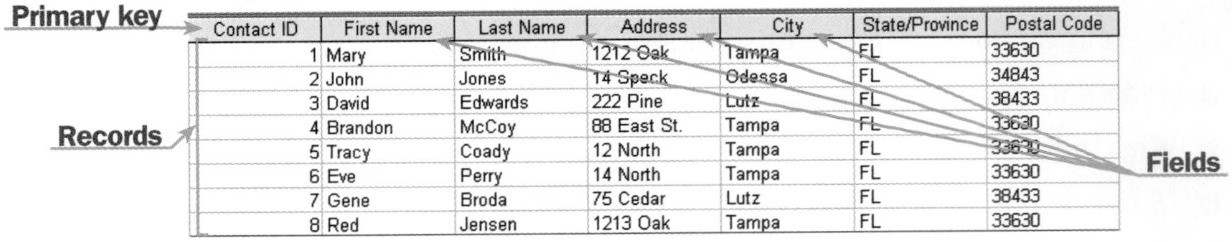

Contact ID	First Name	Last Name	Address	City	State/Province	Postal Code
1	Mary	Smith	1212 Oak	Tampa	FL	33630
2	John	Jones	14 Speck	Odessa	FL	34843
3	David	Edwards	222 Pine	Lutz	FL	38433
4	Brandon	McCoy	88 East St.	Tampa	FL	33630
5	Tracy	Coady	12 North	Tampa	FL	33630
6	Eve	Perry	14 North	Tampa	FL	33630
7	Gene	Broda	75 Cedar	Lutz	FL	38433
8	Red	Jensen	1213 Oak	Tampa	FL	33630

Primary key · **Records** · **Fields**

Following is a description of the three table components identified in Figure 13-1:

The rows in the table are call *records*. Each record is a group of related fields, such as all of the information regarding each member in a membership database or each customer in a customer table.

The columns in the table are called *fields*. Each field contains a specific piece of information within a record. In the table in Figure 13-1, for example, the Postal Code field contains the zip code of the area where the customer lives.

The *primary key*, which is assigned to a field, uniquely identifies each record in a table. It tells the database program how your records will be sorted, and it prevents duplicate entries. In Figure 13-1, the primary key is the Contact ID field.

Creating a New Database

When you start Access, the screen you see is similar to other Office XP applications in several ways—it displays a title bar, a menu bar, and a status bar. Unlike Word, Excel, and PowerPoint, however, Access does not have a standard document view. The Access screen changes based on the *object* you are using as you work with the database. Furthermore, many of the menu options and toolbar buttons are unique to Access.

Using the data stored in the table, you can use Access to create the following objects: queries, forms, and reports. A *query* asks a question about the data stored in the table. The database program searches for and retrieves information from a table or tables to answer the question. You use *forms* to enter data in a table, and a *report* is a printout of selected data. All of these objects—tables, forms, queries, and reports—are stored in a single file, which is the database.

In Step-by-step 13.1, you start Access and create a database file.

STEP-BY-STEP 13.1

1. Start Access by clicking the **Start** button, pointing to **All Programs**, pointing to **Microsoft Office**, and clicking **Microsoft Office Access 2003**. (If you are using Windows 2000, click the **Start** button, point to **Programs**, and then click **Microsoft Access**. The Access window opens, as shown in Figure 13-2. Your opening window may look somewhat different than that shown in the figure.

FIGURE 13-2
Microsoft Access window

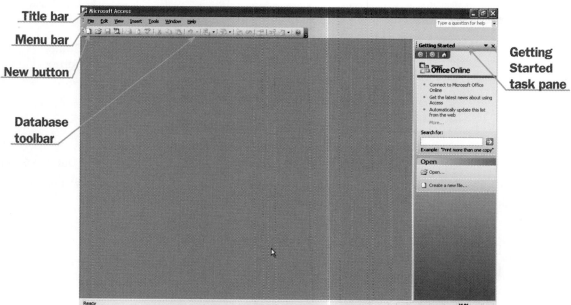

2. Click the **New** button on the Database toolbar. The New File task pane is displayed, as shown in Figure 13-3.

FIGURE 13-3
New File task pane

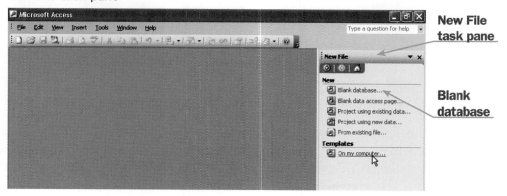

3. Click **Blank database** in the New File task pane. The File New Database dialog box is displayed. Type **Flower Shop** in the File name text box, Click the **Save in** drop-down arrow and locate the drive and folder where you will store your file. In Figure 13-4 on the next page, 3½ Floppy (A:) is selected.

STEP-BY-STEP 13.1 Continued

FIGURE 13-4
File New Database dialog box

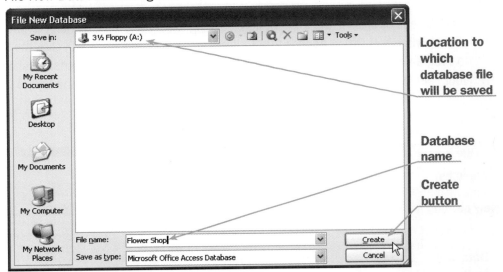

4. Click the **Create** button to create the database. The database is created, and the Database window appears, as shown in Figure 13-5. The Objects bar is displayed on the left. The task pane is not displayed. Leave Access open for Step-by-step 13.2.

FIGURE 13-5
Database window

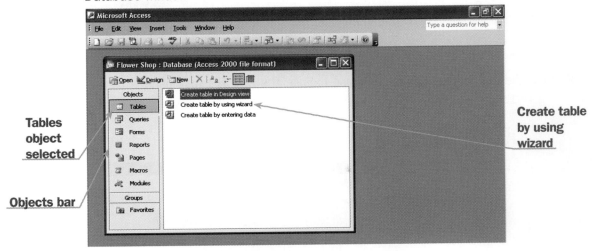

As you see in Figure 13-5, the *Database window* is the command center for working with Access objects. Three of these objects—forms, queries, and reports—are discussed later in this lesson. The other objects (pages, macros, and modules) are beyond the scope of this lesson.

Tables

After you create and save a new database, the next step is to create the tables. *Tables* are the primary objects in a database because they contain the data. In this lesson, you create one table in the database. Most databases, however, contain multiple tables.

Creating a Table

Access provides several ways to create a table, including the following:

■ Create a table in Design view, where you can add fields, define how each field appears or handles data, and create a primary key. Recall that a primary key uniquely identifies each record in a table.

■ Enter data directly in a blank table, called a datasheet.

■ Use the Table Wizard to choose the fields for your table from a variety of predefined tables such as business contacts, household inventory, or medical records.

The Table Wizard walks you through each step by asking a series of questions about how you want to design the table. The table is formatted automatically based on your answers. The Table Wizard contains 25 business and 20 personal sample tables from which you can select fields for your table. In Step-by-step 13.2, you use the wizard to create the table for your database.

S TEP-BY-STEP 13.2

1. Double-click **Create table by using wizard**. The Table Wizard dialog box is displayed, as shown in Figure 13-6. The Business option button is selected, so the sample tables from which you can select will be business oriented.

FIGURE 13-6
Table Wizard dialog box

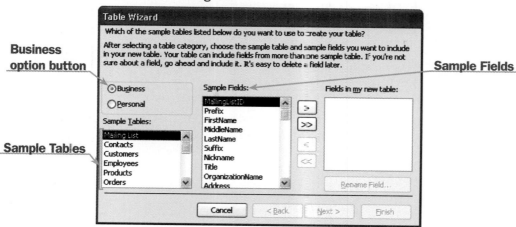

2. Click **Contacts** in the Sample Tables list. *ContactID* should be highlighted in the Sample Fields list, as shown in Figure 13-7 on the next page.

STEP-BY-STEP 13.2 Continued

FIGURE 13-7
Contacts and ContactID selected

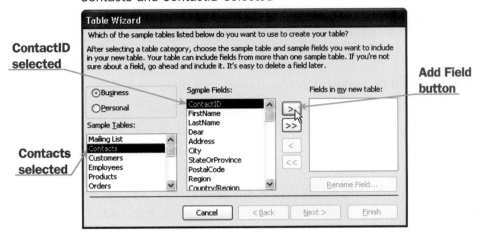

3. Click the **Add Field** button to add the ContactID field to the Fields in my new table box, as shown in Figure 13-8.

FIGURE 13-8
ContactID added to the Field in my new table box

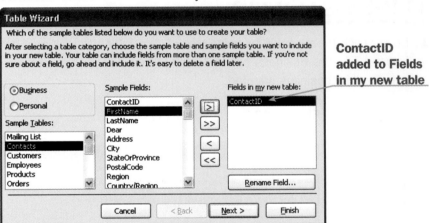

4. Repeat Step 3 to add the following fields: **FirstName**, **LastName**, **Address**, **City**, **StateOrProvince**, and **PostalCode**. See Figure 13-9 on the next page.

STEP-BY-STEP 13.2 Continued

FIGURE 13-9
Adding fields to the table

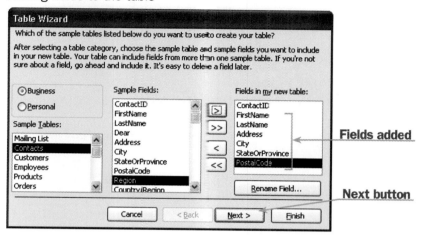

5. Click the **Next** button.

6. The next Table Wizard dialog box opens, providing the option to name the table. The default name *Contacts* is displayed and highlighted. Type **Customers**. If necessary, click the **Yes, set a primary key for me** option button. (See Figure 13-10.)

FIGURE 13-10
Naming the table

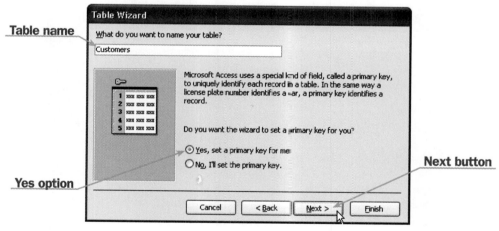

7. Click the **Next** button to display the Table Wizard dialog box shown in Figure 13-11 on the next page. If necessary, click the **Enter data directly into the table** option.

STEP-BY-STEP 13.2 Continued

FIGURE 13-11
Last Table Wizard dialog box

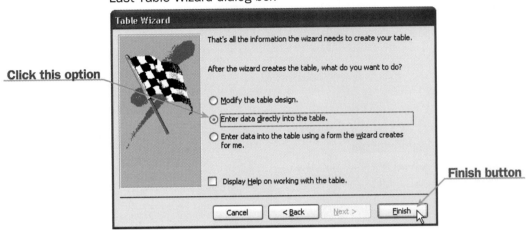

8. Click the **Finish** button. The table is created and the columns display the field names in Datasheet view, as shown in Figure 13-12. The Table Datasheet toolbar is displayed. Click the **Save** button. Leave the database open for Step-by-step 13.3.

FIGURE 13-12
Field names listed in Datasheet view

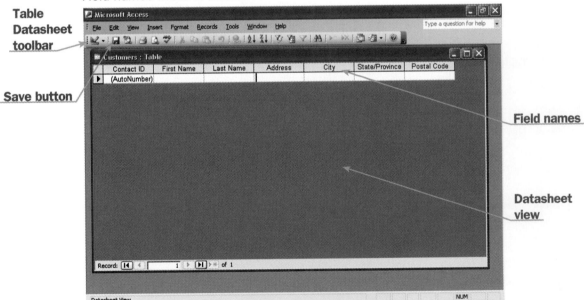

Adding Records to a Table

Creating and saving a table is the first step in a two-step process. The next step is to populate or add records to the table. When adding or editing records in a table, you can create a form or use Datasheet view. *Views* are formats used to display and work with the various objects. Access contains two basic views:

■ *Design view*: Used to create a table, form, query, and report.

■ *Datasheet view*: Displays a row-and-column view of the data in tables, forms, and queries; the table is called a *datasheet*.

You can switch between views by clicking the View button arrow on the toolbar. See Figure 13-13.

FIGURE 13-13
Changing views

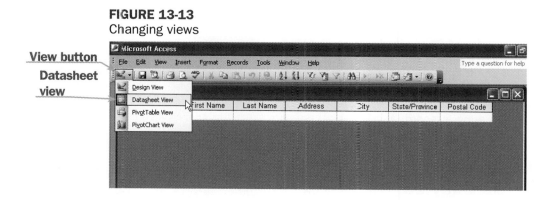

When data is entered in a cell, it is called an entry. To move from one cell to another, you can use the mouse to click in a cell or you can use the keyboard to navigate in a table. Table 13-1 contains a list of keyboard navigations.

TABLE 13-1
Keys for navigating in Datasheet view

KEY	DESCRIPTION
Enter, Tab, or right arrow	Moves the insertion point to the next field
Left arrow or Shift + Tab	Moves the insertion point to the previous field
Home	Moves the insertion point to the first field in the current record
End	Moves the insertion point to the last field in the current record
Up arrow	Moves the insertion point up one record and stays in the same field
Down arrow	Moves the insertion point down one record and stays in the same field
Page Up	Moves the insertion point up one screen
Page Down	Moves the insertion point down one screen

You learn how to create and use a form to add records later in this lesson. In Step-by-step 13.3, you use Datasheet view to enter records in the table.

STEP-BY-STEP 13.3

1. Click the first empty cell (the *First Name* field), and type **Mary**. Notice that as you enter the text, Access automatically assigns the primary key *1* in the Contact ID field.

2. Press **Tab** to move from field to field, and complete the entry by typing the following information in the respective fields. When you are done, the table should look like that shown in Figure 13-14.

> Last Name: **Smith**
>
> Address: **1212 Oak**
>
> City: **Tampa**
>
> State/Province: **FL**
>
> Postal Code: **33630**

FIGURE 13-14
Entering a record

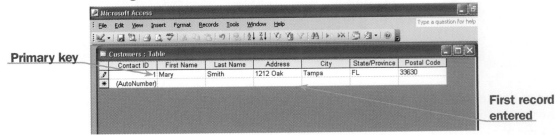

3. Press **Tab** two times to move to the First Name field in the next row. Refer to Figure 13-15 and enter the data for records 2 through 8.

FIGURE 13-15
List of records

Contact ID	First Name	Last Name	Address	City	State/Province	Postal Code
1	Mary	Smith	1212 Oak	Tampa	FL	33630
2	John	Jones	14 Speck	Odessa	FL	34843
3	David	Edwards	222 Pine	Lutz	FL	38433
4	Brandon	McCoy	88 East St.	Tampa	FL	33630
5	Tracy	Coady	12 North	Tampa	FL	33630
6	Eve	Perry	14 North	Tampa	FL	33630
7	Gene	Broda	75 Cedar	Lutz	FL	38433
8	Red	Jensen	1213 Oak	Tampa	FL	33630

4. Your screen should resemble Figure 13-16 on the next page. Click the **Save** button to save the changes. Leave the database open for Step-by-step 13.4.

FIGURE 13-16
Records entered in a table

Records added to Customers table

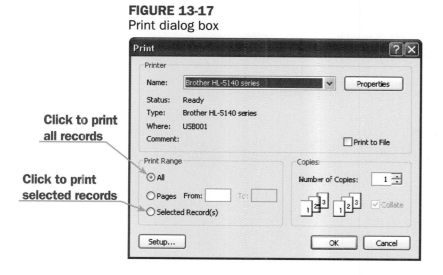

Datasheet view

Contact ID	First Name	Last Name	Address	City	State/Province	Postal Code
1	Mary	Smith	1212 Oak	Tampa	FL	33630
2	John	Jones	14 Speck	Ocassa	FL	34843
3	David	Edwards	222 Pine	Lutz	FL	38433
4	Brandon	McCoy	88 East St.	Tampa	FL	33630
5	Tracy	Coady	12 North	Tampa	FL	33630
6	Eve	Perry	14 North	Tampa	FL	33630
7	Gene	Broda	75 Cedar	Lutz	FL	38433
8	Red	Jensen	1213 Oak	Tampa	FL	33630
(AutoNumber)						

Printing a Table

You can print the table from Datasheet view. To print the table in landscape mode (in which the lines of text are parallel to the long dimension of the page), select Page Setup on the File menu to display the Page Setup dialog box. Click the Page tab and then click the Landscape option button. Click the OK button to close the dialog box.

Click File on the menu bar and then click Print to display the Print dialog box, as shown in Figure 13-17. You have a choice of printing all records or selected records.

FIGURE 13-17
Print dialog box

Click to print all records

Click to print selected records

Sorting a Table

The data in a table can be sorted in ascending or descending order. In ascending order, the records are sorted from A to Z, or smallest to largest. In descending order, the records are sorted from Z to A, or largest to smallest. In Datasheet view, click the field name that you want sorted; the column is highlighted. Click the Sort Ascending or Sort Descending button on the Datasheet toolbar. You may sort on any field. In Figure 13-18, the Last Name field is highlighted so the data will be sorted according to that field.

FIGURE 13-18
Selecting a field to sort by

Field on which the data will be sorted

Sort Descending button

Sort Ascending button

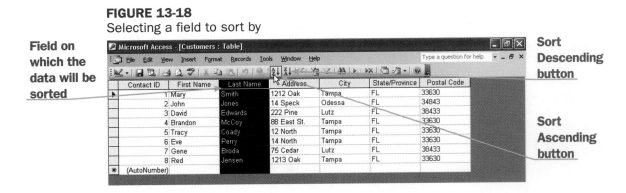

Table Navigation

Quite often data changes after it is entered in a database. For example, one of your customers changes their address or phone number. Or, you want to add a new customer to the database. Access provides a navigation toolbar that makes it easy for you to move from record to record or locate a particular record in a table. Figure 13-19 shows the navigation buttons that are displayed at the bottom of a table in Datasheet view. These navigation buttons are especially useful when you are working in a large database with hundreds or even thousands of records.

FIGURE 13-19
Navigation buttons

Next record

Last record

First record

Previous record

Record number box

New record

Total number of records

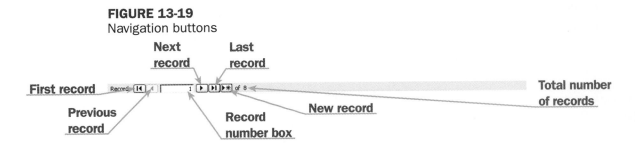

Modifying a Table Structure

After you have created a table, you can modify it by adding and deleting columns (fields) and rows (records). When you delete a column or a row from the table, all the data contained in the column or row is deleted from the database. Delete columns or rows from a table when they are no longer needed to store data. You can add/delete rows and columns in Datasheet view.

If necessary, click the arrow on the View button and select Datasheet View.

To insert a column, right-click the field name that is to the right of the new field, and then click Insert Column on the shortcut menu. To delete a column, right-click the field name, and then click Delete Column.

To add a record, right-click the selected row, and then click New Record. You also can add a record by clicking in the last field of the last record and then pressing Tab or Enter. To delete a row (or record), select the row. Right-click the selected row, and then click Delete Record on the shortcut menu.

Creating a Table in Design View

The sample tables that you can access through the Table Wizard are an excellent tool to help you get started and understand the different views and features in Access. These tables, however, might not necessarily fit your needs. You can create a table from scratch using Design view.

When creating a table in Design view, you determine the structure of the table by defining the fields it will contain. Each field must have a unique name. In addition, you assign the data type for the field and enter a description of it. The *data type* indicates to Access the type of data the field will contain. Table 13-2 lists and describes the data types.

TABLE 13-2
Data type descriptions

DATA TYPE	DESCRIPTION
Text	Can contain any characters; entries can be up to 255 characters in length
Memo	Used for alphanumeric data with more than 255 characters
Number	Numeric data used in mathematical calculations
Date/Time	Used to hold dates and times
Currency	Contains only monetary data—values are displayed with currency symbols, such as dollar signs, commas, and decimal points, and with two digits following the decimal point
AutoNumber	A unique sequential number assigned by Access for each record entered
Yes/No	Stores one of two values—the choices are Yes/No, True/False, or On/Off
OLE Object	Used for more advanced features, such as storing or linking objects in a table
Hyperlink	Stores a hyperlink to an URL, other document, or other object
Lookup Wizard	Creates a field that can be used to choose a value from another table or query

After you have assigned a data type, you also can set properties for the field. Field properties are specifications that allow you to customize the data type settings. The field properties available depend on the data type selected. One of the most common field properties is the field size. The default size is 50 characters, but you can specify that the field allows up to 255 characters. Another common field property is format. The format specifies how you want Access to display numbers, dates, times, and text.

Following are the steps for creating a table in Design view:

1. In the Database window, click Tables on the Objects bar.

2. Double-click Create table in Design view.

3. Define the fields in the table by entering a field name, selecting the data type, and typing a description, if desired.

4. Save the table. It now appears in the Database window with other table objects.

5. To open the table from the Database window, make sure Tables is selected on the Objects bar, and then double-click the table.

6. The table is displayed in Datasheet view, ready for you to enter records (similar to the Customers table shown in Figure 13-12 on page 296.).

Forms

In addition to adding and viewing records in Datasheet view, you also can create and use a data-entry form. A form provides a convenient way to enter and view records in a table. When you create a form, you are adding a new object to the database. You can create the form manually or use the Form Wizard. The wizard asks you questions and formats the form according to your preferences.

Use the Form Wizard to create a form in Step-by-step 13.4.

Technology Careers

DATABASE DEVELOPER

A database developer writes and modifies databases. Data in a database can be reorganized, dispersed, and accessed in several ways. Databases are important to companies and organizations because they contain records or files, such as sales transactions, product catalogs and inventories, and customer profiles.

Database developers create management systems to provide effective and efficient access to information stored in databases. They provide expertise and guidance in the design, implementation, and maintenance of database management systems. An important part of this work involves implementing and controlling security procedures to protect the database from accidental or intentional damage or loss.

These individuals must be good at communicating not only in computer languages, but with people as well. They write descriptions about programs, prepare manuals, create help screens, and explain new systems to users. In addition to excellent communication skills, they must have extensive experience with hardware, software, and systems and processes.

To become a database developer, an individual should have a Bachelor of Science degree in Computer Science, as well as specific computer certifications. Prior experience also is recommended. The salary for this position will vary depending on the location and size of the organization and an individual's experience.

STEP-BY-STEP 13.4

1. Click the arrow on the **New Object** button on the Table Datasheet toolbar and then point to **Form**, as shown in Figure 13-20.

FIGURE 13-20
New Object button on Table Datasheet toolbar

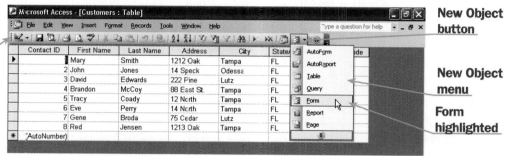

2. Click **Form** to display the New Form dialog box, and then click **Form Wizard**, as shown in Figure 13-21.

FIGURE 13-21
Form Wizard highlighted

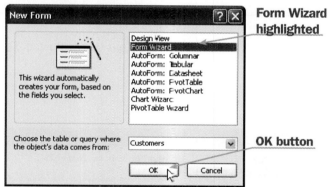

STEP-BY-STEP 13.4 Continued

3. Click the **OK** button. The Form Wizard dialog box shown in Figure 13-22 is displayed. Note that the list of Available Fields shows the same fields as those that you selected in Step-by-step 13.2 when you created the table.

FIGURE 13-22
Form Wizard dialog box

Table name

Select All button

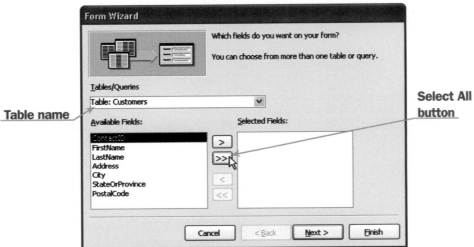

4. Click the **Select All** button. All of the fields are copied to the Selected Fields box, as shown in Figure 13-23.

FIGURE 13-23
Fields to be added to form

Selected Fields

Next button

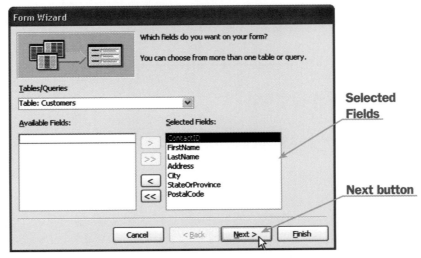

5. Click the **Next** button. In the Form Wizard dialog box, you select the layout for the form. If necessary, click the **Columnar** option and then click **Next**.

6. In the next Form Wizard dialog box, you select the style for the form. Click the **SandStone** style, as shown in Figure 13-24 on the next page.

STEP-BY-STEP 13.4 Continued

FIGURE 13-24
SandStone style highlighted

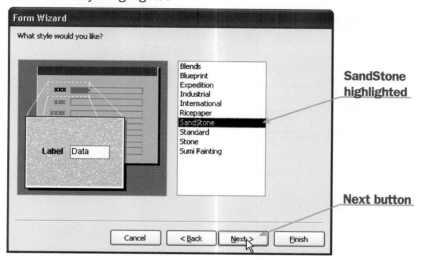

7. Click the **Next** button. The Form Wizard displays *Customers* as the default title. Type **Flower Shop Customers**, as shown in Figure 13-25. Verify that the **Open the form to view or enter information** option is selected.

FIGURE 13-25
Entering a name for the form

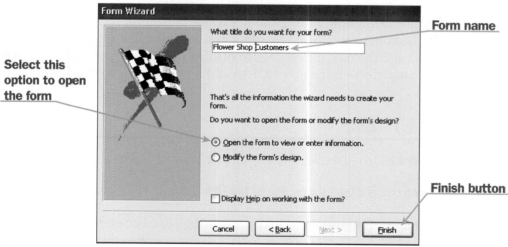

8. Click the **Finish** button. A form is displayed on your screen, as shown in Figure 13-26 on the next page. Maximize the screen by clicking the **Maximize** button in the upper-right corner of the form window. This form contains the Mary Smith data, which you entered earlier in this lesson. Note the controls at the bottom of the form. These are the same controls located in the table's Datasheet view. Leave the form open for the next exercise.

STEP-BY-STEP 13.4 Continued

FIGURE 13-26
Completed form

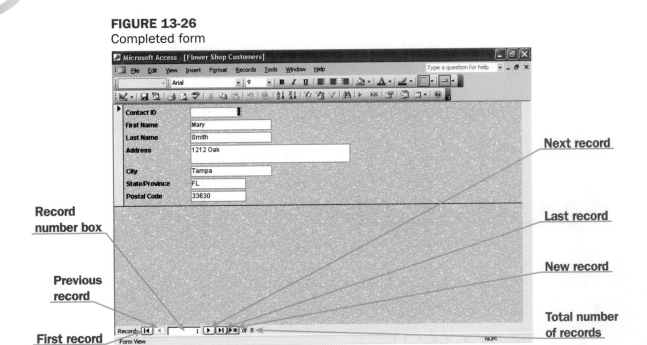

Entering and Editing Data in a Form

Entering data in a form is similar to entering data in a table in Datasheet view. You use the same keys to move the insertion point among the fields. Furthermore, the same navigation buttons are available at the bottom of the form. To add a new record, click the New Record button. To edit an existing record, use the navigation keys to display the record and make the changes in the fields on the form. Complete Step-by-step 13.5 to add a new record to the database.

STEP-BY-STEP 13.5

1. Click the **New Record** button to display a blank form, as shown in Figure 13-27 on the next page.

2. Click the **First Name** box and type **Karen**. Press **Tab** to move to the Last Name box.

3. Type **Williams** and press **Tab**. Use the following information to complete the rest of the fields for this record:

   Address: **601 Walnut**

   City: **Lutz**

   State/Province: **FL**

   Postal Code: **38433**

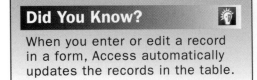

Did You Know?

When you enter or edit a record in a form, Access automatically updates the records in the table.

STEP-BY-STEP 13.5 Continued

FIGURE 13-27
Blank form

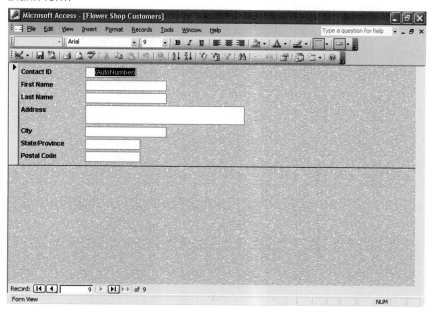

4. The form should look like that shown in Figure 13-28. Click the **Save** button and then click the form's **Close** button. If the table datasheet is still open, click its **Close** button to close it. Keep the Database window open for Step-by-step 13.6.

FIGURE 13-28
New record entered in a form

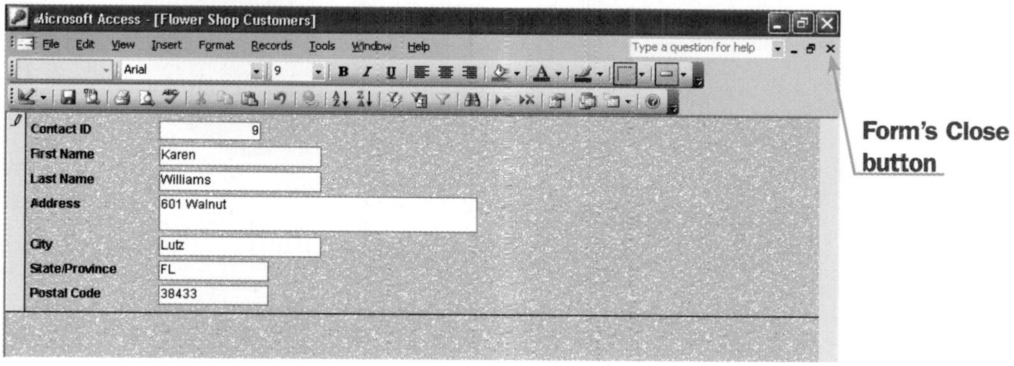

Form's Close button

Queries

A query enables you to locate records that match specified criteria by providing a way for you to ask a question about the information stored in a database table or tables. Access searches for and retrieves data from the table(s) to answer your question.

Suppose, for example, that you want a list of all customers within a specified zip code. When you create a query, you determine what fields you want displayed in the query results. Often, you only need to see certain fields in the query results instead of all the fields in the table. In the preceding example, for instance, you might want only the customer's last name and the zip code displayed. The order in which you select the fields will determine the order in which the information is displayed in the query results.

In Step-by-step 13.6, you create a query to display specified fields.

STEP-BY-STEP 13.6

1. Click the arrow on the **New Object** button and then point to **Query**, as shown in Figure 13-29.

FIGURE 13-29
Query selected

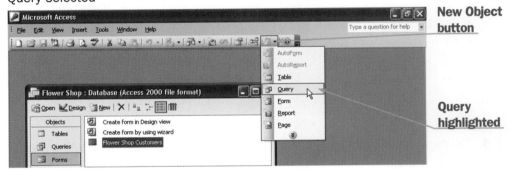

2. Click **Query** to display the New Query dialog box. Select **Simple Query Wizard**, as shown in Figure 13-30.

FIGURE 13-30
New Query dialog box

3. Click **OK** to display the Simple Query Wizard dialog box. Click **PostalCode** and then click the **Add Field** button. Click **LastName** and then click the **Add Field** button. See Figure 13-31 on the next page.

STEP-BY-STEP 13.6 Continued

FIGURE 13-31
Selecting fields for the query

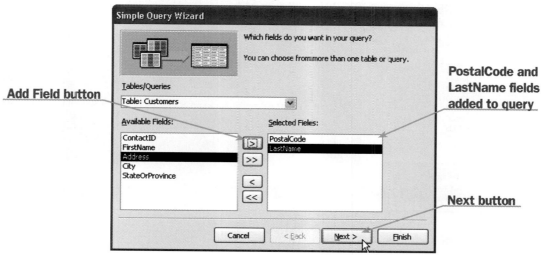

4. Click the **Next** button. Type **Postal Codes** for the title of the query, as shown in Figure 13-32. Verify that the **Open the query to view information** option is selected.

FIGURE 13-32
Naming the query

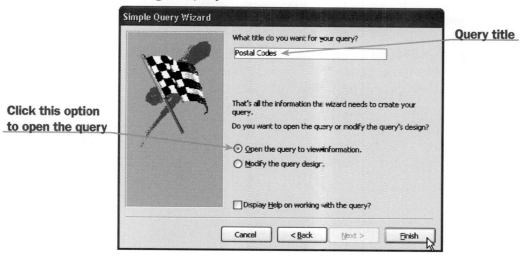

STEP-BY-STEP 13.6 Continued

5. Click the **Finish** button. The query is displayed, as shown in Figure 13-33.

FIGURE 13-33
Query results

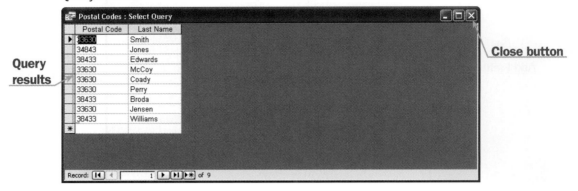

Query results

Close button

6. Click the **Close** button in the query results window. Leave the Database window open for Step-by-step 13.7.

Reports

An important feature of database management software is the ability to generate sophisticated reports that contain the contents of the database. A report is a database object that allows you to organize, summarize, and print all or a portion of the data in a database. You can create a report based on a table or a query. You can decide what formatting you want to use, such as headings, spacing, and graphics. After the report has been generated, you can decide which records you want included in the report, you can sort the report, and you can insert a picture in the report.

Although you can produce a report manually, the Report Wizard provides an easy and fast way to design and create one. The wizard asks questions about which data you want to include in the report and how you want to format the data.

In the following exercise, you use the Report Wizard to create a report.

S TEP-BY-STEP 13.7

1. In the Database window, click **Reports** on the Objects bar, and then click **Create report by using wizard**, as shown in Figure 13-34.

FIGURE 13-34
Reports object in Database window

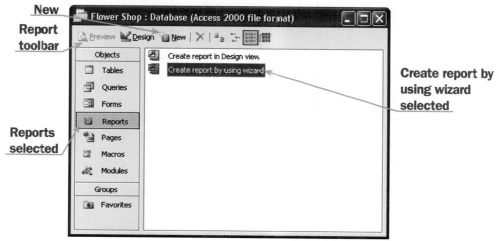

2. Click **New** on the Reports toolbar. The Report Wizard dialog box is displayed. Click **Report Wizard**, as shown in Figure 13-35.

FIGURE 13-35
Report Wizard dialog box

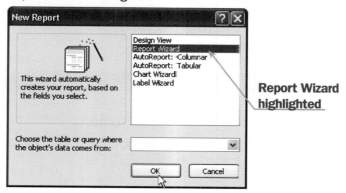

STEP-BY-STEP 13.7 Continued

3. Click the **OK** button to display the Report Wizard dialog box. Click the **Select All** button to move all of the Available Fields to the Selected Fields box, as shown in Figure 13-36.

FIGURE 13-36
All fields selected

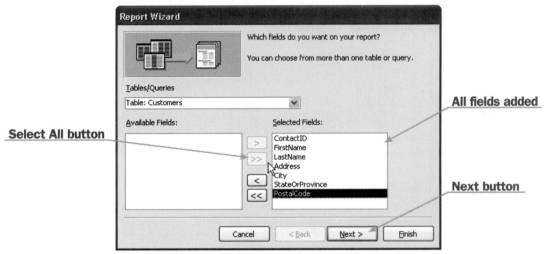

Select All button

All fields added

Next button

4. Click the **Next** button. A dialog box is displayed and has options for grouping a report by fields. No grouping is applied to this report. Click the **Next** button.

5. The Report Wizard dialog box opens with options for the sort order of the records. Click the down arrow on the first box and click **LastName**, as shown in Figure 13-37.

FIGURE 13-37
Report Wizard sorting options

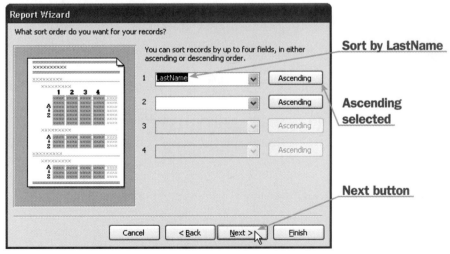

Sort by LastName

Ascending selected

Next button

6. Click the **Next** button. The Report Wizard dialog box displays options for the layout and orientation for the report. Click the **Justified** option, as shown in Figure 13-38 on the next page.

STEP-BY-STEP 13.7 Continued

FIGURE 13-38
Justified layout option selected

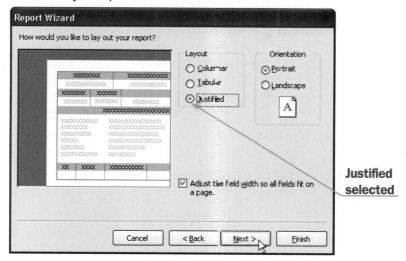

7. Click the **Next** button to display the Report Wizard dialog box with options for report styles. Click **Casual**, as shown in Figure 13-39.

FIGURE 13-39
Report Wizard style options

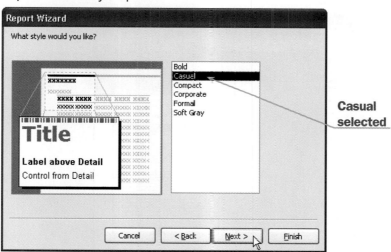

8. Click the **Next** button to display the Report Wizard dialog box in which you enter a title for the report. Type **Flower Shop Customers**. Verify that the **Preview the report** option is selected as shown in Figure 13-40 on the next page.

STEP-BY-STEP 13.7 Continued

FIGURE 13-40
Entering a title for the report

Report title

Click this option to preview the report

9. Click **Finish** to display the report. Click the arrow on the **Zoom** box and select **Fit**, as shown in Figure 13-41. If instructed to do so, click the **Print** button to print a copy of the report.

FIGURE 13-41
Report view

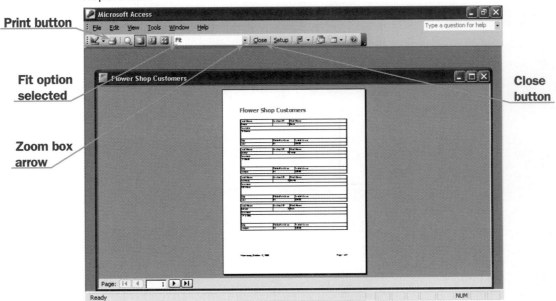

Print button

Fit option selected

Zoom box arrow

Close button

10. Click the **Close** button to close the Report window. Close Access by clicking its **Close** button.

SUMMARY

In this lesson, you learned:

- Databases allow for organizing, storing, maintaining, retrieving, and sorting data.
- The components of a database are objects. These include tables, queries, forms, and reports.
- You should plan the database structure first and then create it.
- After the table structure is created, you add records to the table.
- Records can be sorted in ascending or descending order.
- You can create a form to enter records in a table. Forms are designed to simplify data entry.
- You can design a query to find records that meet specified criteria.
- A report is a formatted display of table records. In a report, you can organize, summarize, and print all or a portion of the data.

VOCABULARY *Review*

Define the following terms:

Data	Datasheet view	Primary key
Database	Design view	Query
Database management	Field	Records
system (DBMS)	Forms	Report
Database window	Information	Table
Datasheet	Object	Views

REVIEW *Questions*

MULTIPLE CHOICE

Select the best response for the following statements.

1. The rows in a table are called _____.
   A. records
   B. fields
   C. columns
   D. primary

2. A(n) _____ is a single piece of information in a database.
   A. field
   B. record
   C. entry
   D. table

3. The _____ uniquely identifies each record in a table.
   A. field name
   B. memo field
   C. primary key
   D. file

4. A(n) _____ is a group of records.
   A. field
   B. table
   C. database
   D. entry

5. _____ view displays the table data in a row-and-column format.
   A. Table
   B. Design
   C. Normal
   D. Datasheet

TRUE/FALSE

Circle T if the statement is true or F if the statement is false.

T   F   1. You can add records to a table at any time.

T   F   2. Databases are similar to spreadsheets and used for the same purpose.

T   F   3. Data in a table may be sorted in ascending or descending order.

T   F   4. It is unnecessary to plan your database structure.

T   F   5. Access has wizards that guide you through the process of creating database objects.

FILL IN THE BLANK

Complete the following statements by writing the correct word or words in the blanks provided.

1. A(n) _____ is a collection of records.

2. The _____ key, which uniquely identifies each record in a table, is assigned to a field.

3. A(n) _____ is a question you ask about the data stored in a database.

4. Text, numeric, date, and memo are examples of _____.

5. The _____ object allows you to organize, summarize, and print all or a portion of the data in a database.

PROJECTS

CROSS-CURRICULAR—MATHEMATICS

Use the Internet and other resources to locate statistical information on five NFL teams. Create a database named **NFL** and a table named **Stats**. The table will consist of statistical information from the previous season for at least five teams. Determine the fields in the table. These might include Team Name, Games Played, or Games Won, for example. Enter the data in the table. Print the table. Now, gather information for two additional teams and add them to the table using a form. Prepare and print a report using the data in the table. Create a query that shows the teams that won fewer than five games during the season.

CROSS-CURRICULAR—SCIENCE

Create a database named **Plants**. Use the Table Wizard and select **Plants** from the Personal sample tables. Include a minimum of five of the Sample Fields in the table. Name the table **Local Plants**. Add a minimum of 10 records to the table. Use the Internet and other resources to gather your data. Create a report using the data in the table. Add grouping levels if applicable. Print a copy of the report if instructed to do so.

CROSS-CURRICULAR—SOCIAL STUDIES

Create a database named **Brown's Cab Company**. Use the Table Wizard and select **Employees** from the Business sample tables. Include a minimum of seven of the Sample Fields in the table. Name the table **Employees**. Add a minimum of 10 records to the table. Sort the table on two fields. Create a query, specifying criteria that apply to the sample fields you chose. Create a report using all the data in the table. Add grouping levels if applicable. Print a copy of the query results and a copy of the report if instructed to do so.

CROSS-CURRICULAR—LANGUAGE ARTS

Create a database named **Writers**. Create a table named **Shakespeare** with the following fields: **Title**, **Type**, **Date**, and **Subject**. Include records for at least 15 of Shakespeare's works. Use the Internet and other resources to gather your data. Print a query that shows one type of his work. Print the table sorted by Date.

WEB PROJECT

You are investigating various schools, colleges, and universities. You have decided what you want to study and now need to find the best school for that field of study. However, there are other features to be considered, such as tuition, distance from home, required SAT score, student population, and so on. Create a database with a table to record college features. The table should have at least five fields. Research at least six schools. Create a report and three printouts showing different sorts, such as all colleges with tuition under a certain amount or schools in a certain state.

TEAMWORK PROJECT

You are the chairman of the Environmental Cleanup Committee in your service organization. You and your co-chair are busy signing up other groups in your community to participate in the Adopt-a-Highway project. You have decided to use a database to organize and manage the information for this project. Create a database named **Environmental Cleanup**. Create a table named **Adopt-a-Highway**. Consider the following and any additional fields you think will be useful: Organization, Contact, Telephone, Highway Location, Begin Date, and Application Submitted. Create a form to enter at least eight records. Print the table sorted by Organization. Prepare and print a report grouped by organization.

CRITICAL *Thinking*

Decide how using database software could assist you in school, work, or other activities. Examples would be to organize your CD collection or create a family directory. Prepare a database file to address a selected need. Use the various capabilities of the software to perform a query, prepare a report, and print at least two sorted lists.

E-MAIL AND ELECTRONIC COMMUNICATION

Microsoft Outlook is a *personal information management (PIM)* program that you can use to organize your schedule, keep track of your contacts, and manage e-mail. E-mail, or electronic mail, one of the most popular services on the Internet, is the focus of this lesson.

You can use e-mail to stay in touch with your family and friends, conduct business, and send attachments such as text and image files. Similar to Microsoft Outlook, *Outlook Express* is an Internet e-mail and news reader program included with Microsoft Internet Explorer. Outlook Express does not have the task- and contact-management capabilities of Microsoft Outlook, nor can it handle e-mail other than Internet mail. The e-mail features of Outlook, however, are very similar to the features of Outlook Express. After you practice using Outlook e-mail in the exercises in this lesson, you will find that you also are able to use Outlook Express. (*Note*: If you currently have Outlook Express set up as your default mail program, some of the commands and buttons might not be available in Outlook.)

Electronic Mail

Electronic mail (e-mail) is the transmission of files and data using a computer network. It is not that different from regular mail. You have a message, an address, and network protocols that route it from one location to another. You may send e-mail to other people on a network at an organization, or you can use an Internet service provider to send e-mail to any connected computer in the world.

When you send someone an e-mail message, it is broken down into small chunks called *packets*. These packets travel independently from server to server. You might think of each packet as a separate page within a letter. When the packets reach their final destination, they are reassembled automatically into their original format. Unless a technical problem occurs, this process allows e-mail to travel much faster than regular mail (sometimes referred to as "snail mail"). In fact, some messages can travel thousands of miles in less than a minute.

Microsoft Outlook also addresses accessibility issues for a wide range of users, including those who have limited dexterity, low vision, or other disabilities. Keyboard shortcuts, increased text size, and color and sound options are all available. The user can customize toolbars and menus and assign preferred accelerator keys as needed.

E-Mail Access

E-mail has become a prevalent way of communicating in our business and personal lives. The methods used to access e-mail have multiplied. A number of Web sites and Internet service providers offer e-mail for a monthly fee; some provide the service at no charge. America Online, Hotmail, and Yahoo! are examples of companies that provide Web-based e-mail services. After you set up an e-mail account with one of these services, you easily can access your account through the organization's Web page by entering your account name (usually your e-mail address) and a password. Most e-mail programs provide you with the capabilities to read mail, send messages, and manage your electronic communication.

Other programs, such as Microsoft Word, PowerPoint, and Excel, also have an E-mail button on the Standard toolbar. Clicking this button opens Microsoft Outlook (or Outlook Express) and lets the user send a message with a file attachment.

Wireless communication also has expanded the ways in which e-mail is transmitted and retrieved. Many people have cell phones or handheld computers that they can use to send and receive e-mail.

Microsoft Outlook

In addition to sending e-mail, Outlook is a versatile application that also can help you organize appointments, keep track of tasks and to-do lists, and maintain addresses. In this lesson, you concentrate on sending, receiving, and managing e-mail with Outlook. You will, however, have the opportunity to experience a short tour of the other program features at the end of this lesson.

Outlook stores information in folders. You can organize different types of information in each Outlook folder. This makes it easy to store many types of personal and business data and then display it at the click of a button. An *item* is a particular piece of information stored in an Outlook folder.

When you start Outlook, a screen similar to the one shown in Figure 14-1 is displayed. The default opening window is the Outlook Today window, which gives you an option to select any of the other features: Calendar, Contacts, or Tasks. Outlook provides several formats for composing and editing e-mail messages. Composing formats include HTML, Rich Text, and Plain Text. Editing options include using Microsoft Word to edit and read e-mail and Rich Text messages. The figures in this lesson use the HTML option to compose and edit.

FIGURE 14-1
Outlook default window

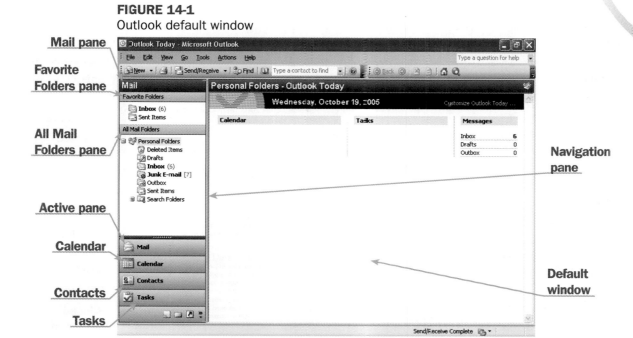

The default task selected in the Navigation pane is Mail. The name of the selected task (*Mail*) appears in the task banner at the top of the Navigation pane. The expanded Mail pane contains a Favorite Folders and All Mail Folders section. The Favorite Folders section in Figure 14-2 includes two standard folders—Inbox and Sent Items. The All Mail Folders pane contains the same folders as in the Favorite Folders section, plus additional folders such as Junk E-mail. Your program might display different folders. The plus and minus signs to the left of a folder indicate that you can expand and collapse the folder. To move a copy of a folder from the All Mail Folders into the Favorite Folders list, click the folder and drag it to the Favorite Folders pane.

When you select a folder in Mail, such as the Inbox, the names of items in the folder appear in the Navigation pane, as shown in Figure 14-2. Click an item in the Navigation pane to see the full text in the Reading pane. In the other Outlook tasks, such as the calendar, the task window opens directly in the Reading pane.

FIGURE 14-2
Navigation pane and Reading pane in Mail window

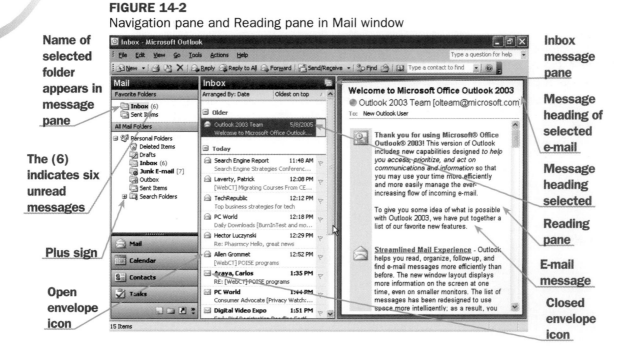

Setting Up an E-Mail Account

If you do not have an e-mail account, it is suggested that you create one; otherwise, you will not be able to complete the exercises in this lesson. Two Web sites that provide free e-mail accounts are Yahoo! at *http://mail.yahoo.com/* and MSN Hotmail at *http://hotmail.com*. Check with your instructor if you are to create an e-mail address using one of these Web sites or if you have access to another option.

After your computer is set up to handle e-mail, you can use the Inbox folder in Outlook to send and receive e-mail messages. An advantage to using Outlook as your e-mail application is that, as you create messages, you have easy access to the other Outlook folders. You quickly can address the message to someone on your contacts list, check your calendar to make sure you are available for a meeting, or add a task to your task list when a message requests further action. In addition to sending just a text message, you can include attachments such as pictures or documents.

E-Mail Addresses

When you send postal mail to someone, you must know the address. The same thing is true for e-mail. An *e-mail address* consists of three parts:

- The user name of the individual
- The "@" symbol
- The user's domain name

For instance, David Edward's e-mail address could be *dedwards@msn.com*.

Starting Outlook

When Outlook starts, it sends a request to your mail server. If you have messages, Outlook receives them and stores them in a folder in the All Mail Folders pane. The number of unread messages is displayed in parentheses. The Inbox displays message headers for any new messages. The message header indicates the sender's name, the subject of the message, and the date and time received. Clicking the header (Figure 14-3) displays the Reading pane and the actual text of the message. If you have a number of messages, you can read each one by clicking its message header to display the message text in the Reading pane.

FIGURE 14-3
Message displayed in Reading pane

As previously indicated, the figures in this lesson use the HTML option to compose and edit. Complete the following exercise to start Outlook and to change your Mail Format options to HTML if necessary.

STEP-BY-STEP 14.1

1. Click **Start** on the taskbar, point to **All Programs**, point to **Microsoft Office**, and then click **Microsoft Outlook 2003** (or your version).

2. If necessary, maximize the Outlook Today window. Click the **Inbox** folder to display message headers for any messages you might have received. (You might not have any messages in your Inbox when you open the Inbox folder in this exercise.)

STEP-BY-STEP 14.1 Continued

3. Click **Tools** on the menu bar and then click **Options**. Click the **Mail Format** tab and verify that **HTML** is selected for the *Compose in this message format*. If another option is selected, click the down arrow and select **HTML**. Click **OK** or click **Apply** to close the Options dialog box. If either the *Use Microsoft Office Word 2003 to edit e-mail messages* or *Use Microsoft Office Word 2003 to read Rich Text e-mail messages* boxes are checked, deselect them. Keep Outlook open for Step-by-step 14.2.

> **Did You Know?**
>
> The *Cc* in the e-mail window is the abbreviation for *carbon copy*. This originated with the old-fashioned typewriter. To send someone a copy of a letter or to create a file copy required that the typist use a sheet of carbon paper between each sheet of paper.

Creating, Receiving, and Sending Messages

Creating and sending an e-mail is as easy as identifying the recipients, typing your message, and sending it. To display the Untitled Message dialog box, click New on the Standard toolbar. Enter an e-mail address or addresses in the To text box, either by typing the address or by inserting an address from your Contacts list (discussed later in this lesson). Separate e-mail addresses of multiple recipients with a semi-colon (;).

You can type additional e-mail addresses in the Cc text box if you are sending copies of the message to other recipients. You also can enter e-mail addresses for recipients who are to be "blind" copied, meaning the primary addressee(s) will not see that others are copied on the message. To do this, you must display the Bcc field. Click View on the menu bar and then click Bcc Field. If more than one person uses the computer and/or if you have more than one e-mail address, you also can designate an e-mail address by adding the From field to the message. To add the From field, click View on the menu bar and then click From Field.

E-mail etiquette requires that you include a subject for your mail message. The subject should be brief, yet descriptive. Enter this in the Subject text box. Figure 14-4 on the next page shows the Untitled Message window with the fields previously discussed.

FIGURE 14-4
Message window

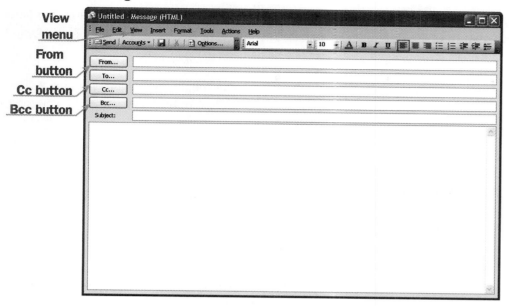

After you have completed the fields in the message header, type your message. Then click the Send button on the toolbar to send the e-mail message.

In the following exercise, you will practice creating an e-mail message that you will send to yourself or to someone else in your class. If necessary, check with your instructor regarding the e-mail address (or addresses) to be used for the exercises in this lesson.

STEP-BY-STEP 14.2

1. Click the **New Mail Message** button on the Standard toolbar. The Untitled Message window appears. The window contains a menu bar and two toolbars—Standard and Formatting.

2. If necessary, click the **To** box. Type your e-mail address (or the e-mail address of the person to whom you are sending the message). If you do not know what e-mail address you should use, check with your instructor.

3. Click the **Subject** box and type **Caribbean cruise**.

4. Click in the message area. The title of the window changes to *Caribbean cruise*.

STEP-BY-STEP 14.2 Continued

5. Type the following message: **I am looking forward to going on the cruise next month. Our ports of call are Grand Cayman, Belize, and Cozumel. The Web site is www.cruise.com.** Press **Enter** two times and type your name. Your screen should look similar to Figure 14-5.

Notice that when you type the Web site address, it is underlined. It also might appear in a different color. Some e-mail programs require you to click, double-click, or hold down the CTRL key and click to activate the link and open the associated Web page.

FIGURE 14-5
Completed message form

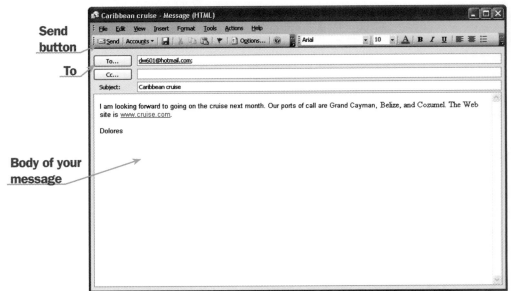

6. Click the **Send** button on the toolbar to send the message. Leave Outlook open for Step-by-step 14.3.

Receiving and Opening E-Mail Messages

Now that you have sent a message to yourself (or someone in your class has sent you a message), you should receive it in the Inbox. You use the Send/Receive button on the Standard toolbar to check for messages. In the following exercise, you check for messages and then open the message you sent to yourself or a message you received from another student. In some instances, your instructor might have sent you a message.

Did You Know?

After you send a message, Outlook closes the message window and temporarily stores the message in the Outbox folder. After the message is sent, Outlook moves the message to the Sent Items folder.

STEP-BY-STEP 14.3

1. Click the **Send/Receive** button on the Standard toolbar. The Inbox receives the message and the message header is displayed, like that shown in Figure 14-6.

FIGURE 14-6
Receiving a message

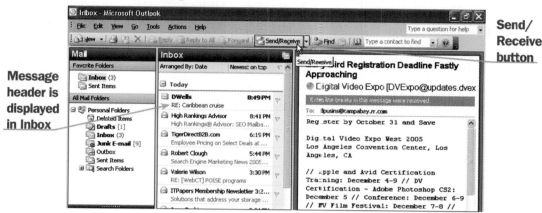

Message header is displayed in Inbox

Send/
Receive
button

2. Click the message header in the Inbox pane. The message is displayed in the Reading pane, as shown in Figure 14-7. Leave Outlook open for Step-by-step 14.4.

FIGURE 14-7
Displaying a message

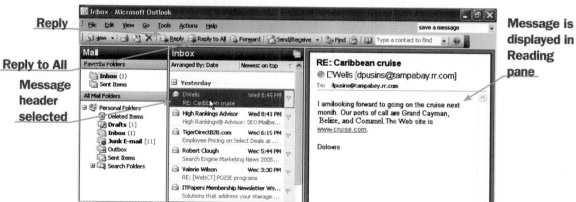

Reply

Reply to All

Message header selected

Message is displayed in Reading pane

Saving a Message

When you receive a message, Outlook automatically saves the message in the Inbox or another designated folder until you delete the message. You can save a message, however, as a text file, an HTML document, or a template. To save a message in one of these formats, click File on the menu bar and then select the Save As command. When the Save As dialog box is displayed, type a name in the File name text box, and then select the format by clicking the Save as type text box arrow. Click the Save button to save the file.

Replying to a Message

When replying to a message, first select the message. Then click the Reply or Reply to All button on the Standard toolbar, type your message, and click the Send button. With this format, the original message is included along with your reply message. Suppose, for example, you received an e-mail from a friend and the friend sent a cc of the message to several other people. To reply to the friend, click the Reply button. To reply to the friend and send a copy of the message to the others who were sent a cc, use the Reply to All button. Using the Reply or Reply to All option is appropriate when you are answering a question or responding to specifics in the original message.

When you reply to a message, a Message window is displayed. This window is similar to the window that was displayed when you created a new message. When you use this format to reply to an e-mail message, the recipient(s) normally sees the letters "Re" preceding the text in the subject line to indicate that it is a reply message.

Formatting a Message

The Formatting toolbar contains many of the same features as those in your word-processing program and other similar software. You can change the font type, font size, and text color of an e-mail message. You also can add bold, italics, and an underline to text as well as center it and add bullets.

Attaching a File to an E-Mail Message

Attachments are documents, images, figures, and other files that you can attach to your e-mail messages. To attach a file to a message, click Insert on the menu bar and then click File, locate the file or document you want to attach in the Insert File dialog box, and then click the Insert button.

In the following exercise, you reply to a message. You change the font and text color, attach a file, and then send the message. Use a file you created in one of the other lessons in this course or as directed by your instructor for the attachment. Outlook should be open and a message should be displayed in the Reading pane.

S TEP-BY-STEP 14.4

1. Click the **Reply** (or **Reply to All**) button on the Standard toolbar. The message window is displayed, similar to that shown in Figure 14-8 on the next page. The menu bar and Standard and Formatting toolbars are displayed. The e-mail address is displayed automatically in the To box, and the insertion point is blinking in the message area.

STEP-BY-STEP 14.4 Continued

FIGURE 14-8
Replying to a message

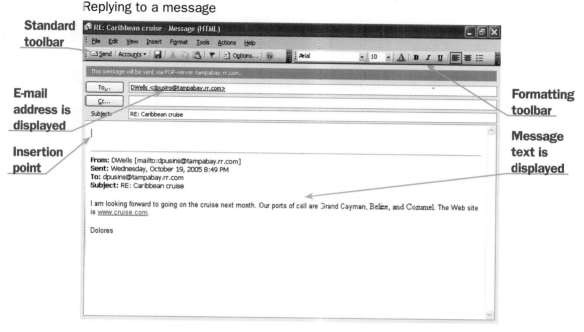

Standard toolbar

E-mail address is displayed

Insertion point

Formatting toolbar

Message text is displayed

2. Type the following:

Dolores, (substitute the name of your recipient, and then press **Enter** two times).

Good to hear from you. I also am preparing for the cruise and look forward to seeing you. I have attached some information for you. Press **Enter** two times and type your name.

3. Select the text of your message. Use the buttons on the Formatting toolbar to change the font to a style of your choice and the font size to 12. Change the color to one of your choice. Format all of the text in bold.

STEP-BY-STEP 14.4 Continued

4. Click **Insert** on the menu bar and then click **File**, as shown in Figure 14-9. The Insert File dialog box is displayed.

FIGURE 14-9
Attaching a file

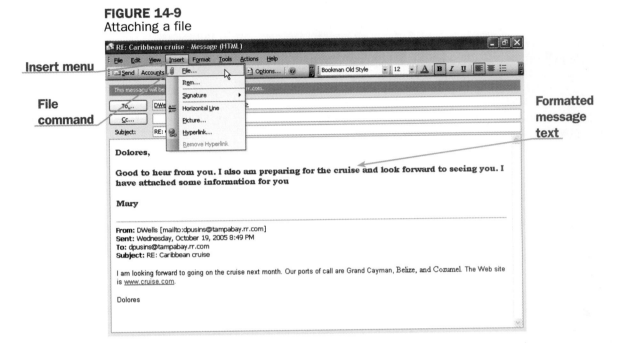

5. Locate and select the file that you want to attach, and then click the **Insert** button. The file is attached, as shown in Figure 14-10. An Attachment Options pane might open. If so, read the information and then close the pane.

FIGURE 14-10
File is attached

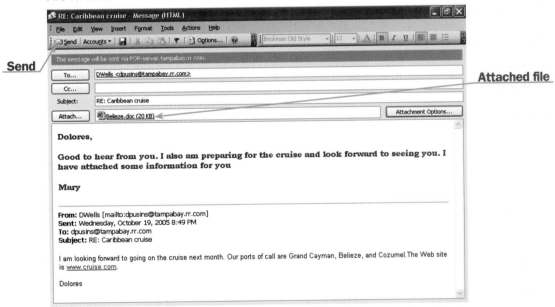

6. Click the **Send** button. The message is sent. Leave Outlook open for Step-by-step 14.5.

E-Mail Troubleshooting

Occasionally, when you send an e-mail with an attachment, you receive a return message indicating that the message cannot be sent. This happens because some e-mail service providers limit the size of e-mail attachments. Even if your e-mail provider and program can send a large attachment, you might find that the recipient cannot receive the message or open the attachment.

Other technical problems can prevent messages from being sent or received. This generally means that the recipient's address was entered incorrectly or no longer exists. Other errors, however, might be caused by a problem with the server that handles the mail for your e-mail provider or for that of the recipient.

If you receive a message that says your e-mail could not be delivered or sent, check the address and try to send it again. Sometimes the problems with a server are temporary, and the message can be sent successfully on the second try.

Organizing and Managing E-Mail

E-mails require file management similar to any other references (electronic or hard copy) you want to keep and manage. Most of the time, you will want to reply to messages you receive, and save important messages for future reference. On the other hand, you probably will want to delete unneeded messages and spam. *Spam* is unsolicited e-mail, essentially electronic junk mail. In many instances, spam is used to advertise products and services. Other spam messages might contain bogus offers.

> **Did You Know?**
>
> When Outlook is open, you can check your e-mail at any time. Just click the Send/Receive button on the Standard toolbar.

Some messages might contain viruses—most of the time in the form of an attachment. If you have an anti-virus program, generally the program will identify the message as having a virus. Many Internet service providers use firewalls to protect their customers from viruses. Do not open an attachment if you suspect that it has a virus, and immediately delete the message to which it is attached.

Managing the Inbox

When you receive an e-mail message, you have several options. You can send a reply as you did in the previous exercise, forward the message to someone else, save the message to a specified location, delete the message, or select a combination of the aforementioned options. Before you can perform an action on a message, you first must select it by clicking the header in the Inbox pane.

- *Forwarding a message*: This is similar to replying to a message. Forwarding messages helps cut down on the time you spend retyping a message. It also is a quick way to share information with several people. When you forward a message, the recipient(s) normally sees the letters "Fw" preceding the text in the subject line to identify it as a message that is being forwarded.

■ *Saving a message*: You can save an e-mail message in various formats (including text and HTML formats) to disk so that you can open and read it later or keep it for follow-up or reference. You also can save and organize e-mail messages in folders within your e-mail program. In Outlook, for example, you can create folders within your local folders (Inbox, Outbox, Sent Items, and Deleted Items) to organize your messages further. To move a message into a folder, simply right-click the message header, select the Move to Folder option, and then select the folder in the Move Items dialog box to which you want to move or copy the message.

■ *Deleting a message*: You can delete an e-mail message by selecting it and then pressing the Delete key or clicking the Delete button on the e-mail program's toolbar. In some e-mail programs, such as Outlook, this moves the message into a deleted mail folder. To delete it permanently, you must delete it from this location.

Message Icons

Icons in the message headers listed in the Navigation pane offer clues about each message. For example, an icon that looks like the back of a sealed envelope indicates a message that has been received but not read; an exclamation point icon means the sender considers it an urgent or high-priority message; a paper clip icon indicates that the message has an attached file. You also can manually mark a message as read or unread, or add a flag icon as a reminder to follow up on the message.

In the following exercise, you create a folder, move a message from one folder to another, forward a message, and print a message. Outlook should be open and the Inbox displayed.

S TEP-BY-STEP 14.5

1. Click **File** on the menu bar, point to **New**, and then click **Folder** to display the Create New Folder dialog box. Type **Cruise** in the Name text box. Click **Personal Folders** in the *Select where to place the folder* box. If necessary, click the plus sign to the left of Personal Folders to display the subfolders. The dialog box should look like that shown in Figure 14-11.

FIGURE 14-11
Create New Folder dialog box

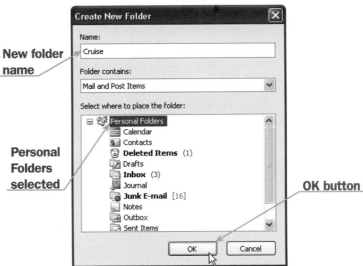

STEP-BY-STEP 14.5 Continued

2. Click the **OK** button. The folder is displayed as a subfolder in the Personal Folders folder, as shown in Figure 14-12.

FIGURE 14-12
New folder created

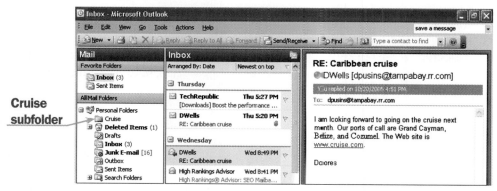

3. You should have two messages in your Inbox regarding the cruise. Click the **first Cruise message**; hold down the **Ctrl** key and click the **second Cruise message**. Both messages are selected. (If you are creating other messages and/or do not have two cruise messages, select any other two messages.)

4. Right-click the selected messages to display the shortcut menu. Point to **Move to Folder**, as shown in Figure 14-13.

FIGURE 14-13
Move to Folder selected in the shortcut menu

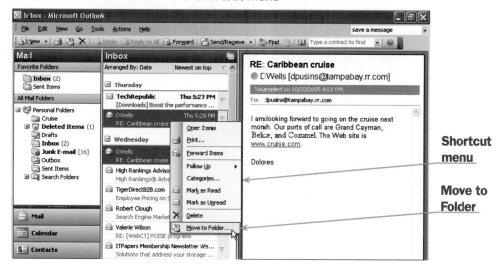

STEP-BY-STEP 14.5 Continued

5. Click **Move to Folder** to display the Move Items dialog box. If necessary, select the Cruise folder, as shown in Figure 14-14.

FIGURE 14-14
Move Items dialog box

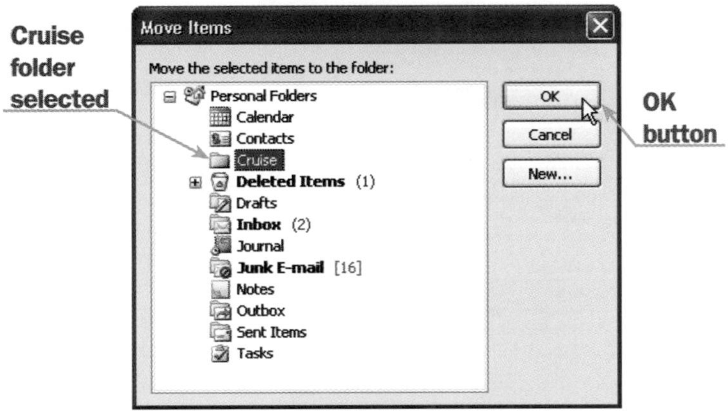

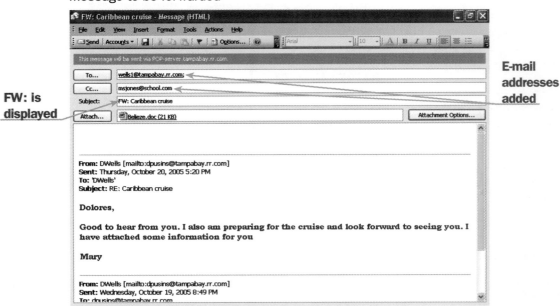

6. Click the **OK** button. Click the **Cruise** folder to display the two messages.

7. Right-click the **first message** to display the shortcut menu. Click **Forward**. The message is displayed with *FW:* indicated in the Subject box.

8. Type your e-mail address or one of your classmates' in the To box. Type your instructor's e-mail address (or an e-mail address to another classmate) in the Cc box. (See Figure 14-15.)

FIGURE 14-15
Message to be forwarded

STEP-BY-STEP 14.5 Continued

9. Click the **Send** button.

10. Right-click the first cruise message to display the shortcut menu. Click **Print** to print a copy of the message. Leave Outlook open for Step-by-step 14.6.

Special E-Mail Features

Most e-mail programs come with a variety of features and options that make it easy to send a copy to multiple recipients, generate an automatic reply, block messages from specific senders, and customize the look and feel of your messages.

Copying to Multiple Recipients

As previously indicated, you can insert more than one address in the To, Cc, and Bcc boxes. The message will go to all the addressees at the same time. If you are sending or copying an e-mail to more than one person, each e-mail address should be separated by a semicolon.

Automatic Message Responses

It is possible to configure e-mail programs such as Outlook to deal automatically with e-mail messages you receive. The automatic controls you can set in Outlook include the following:

- *Automatic "out of the office" response*: Automatically replies to all received e-mail messages when you are unable to reply to messages yourself. This feature requires a Microsoft Exchange Server e-mail account and might not be available on your system.

- *Forwarding command*: Automatically redirects your mail to another e-mail address; this feature is accessed through the Rules and Alerts command on the Tools menu.

- *Block Senders List*: Prevents messages from designated addresses from being placed in your Inbox; this is particularly useful to block unwanted advertisements that often are sent repeatedly to the same e-mail address.

- *Safe Senders List*: Similar to the Block Senders list, selecting this option indicates to Outlook to accept all e-mails from the sender names contained in the list. A similar feature is the Safe Senders Domain List, which contains a list of all safe domains (*@msn.com*, for example) that you want to accept.

The Block Senders and Safe Senders lists are accessed through the Junk E-mail command on the Actions menu. Use the Outlook Help feature to find out more about how to block, forward, or automatically respond to messages. Use the key terms *automatic message* and *block senders* to generate a list of topics in Help.

Adding a Signature and Stationery to a Message

Earlier in this lesson, you formatted your message text by changing font style and font color. Outlook also includes other options that add visual interest. You can change backgrounds by adding stationery and special signatures for new messages and for replies and forwarded messages.

A *signature* consists of text and/or pictures that you create and automatically is added to the end of any outgoing messages. You can create unique signatures for different addresses. For instance, you might want a signature for friends and family and another signature for business purposes.

In the following exercise, you create a special signature for your personal e-mail messages and then add a background image.

STEP-BY-STEP 14.6

1. Outlook should be open. Click **Tools** on the menu bar, click **Options**, and then click the **Mail Format** tab, as shown in Figure 14-16.

FIGURE 14-16
Options dialog box

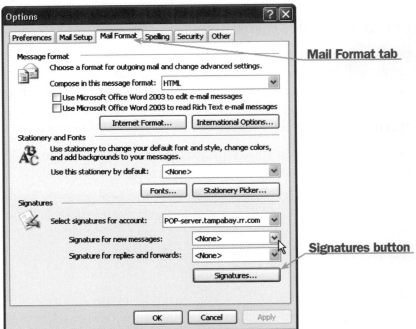

2. Click the **Signatures** button to display the Create Signature dialog box, as shown in Figure 14-17 on the next page.

STEP-BY-STEP 14.6 Continued

FIGURE 14-17
Create Signature dialog box

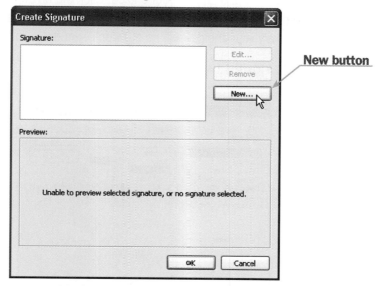

New button

3. Click the **New** button to display the Create New Signature dialog box. Type your name. (See Figure 14-18.)

FIGURE 14-18
Create New Signature dialog box

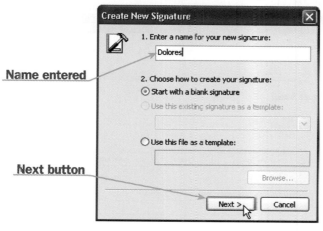

Name entered

Next button

STEP-BY-STEP 14.6 Continued

4. Click the **Next** button to display the Edit Signature dialog box. Click the **Font** button to display the Font dialog box and select a font type of your choice. Click the arrow on the **Color** box and change to a color of your choice. Click **Bold** in the Style box. Change the font size to a size of your choice. (See Figure 14-19.) Most likely your choices will be different from those in Figure 14-19.

FIGURE 14-19
Font dialog box

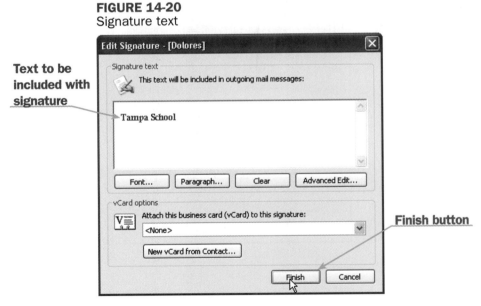

Bold selected

Calisto MT
font selected

OK button

Size 10
selected

Red selected

5. Click the **OK** button to redisplay the Edit Signature dialog box. Type any additional information you might want to include. (See Figure 14-20.)

FIGURE 14-20
Signature text

Text to be
included with
signature

Finish button

6. Click the **Finish** button to return to the Create Signature dialog box. Click the **OK** button to redisplay the Options dialog box. Click the arrow on the **Signature for new messages** box and select your name, as shown in Figure 14-21 on the next page.

STEP-BY-STEP 14.6 Continued

FIGURE 14-21
Name is selected

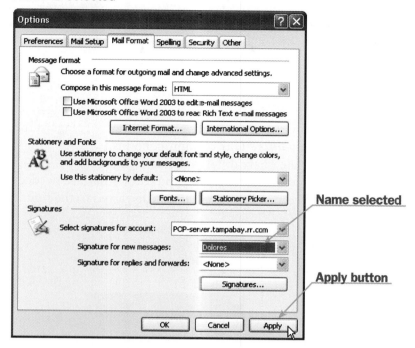

7. Click the **Apply** button and then click the **Stationery Picker** button to display the Stationery Picker dialog box. Scroll through the list of Stationery options and select one of your choice. In Figure 14-22, Sunflower is selected. Some choices might not be displayed. This is determined by the Microsoft Office installation on your computer.

FIGURE 14-22
Stationery selected

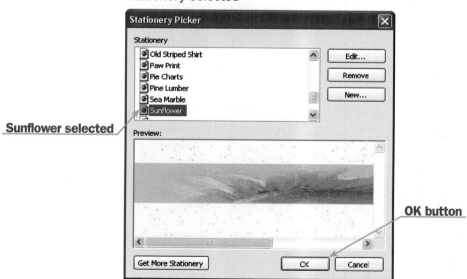

STEP-BY-STEP 14.6 Continued

8. Click the **OK** button to return to the Options dialog box. The stationery name you selected is shown in the Stationery and Fonts section. Verify that this is correct, and then click the **OK** button to return to Outlook. Leave Outlook open for Step-by-step 14-7.

> **Did You Know?**
>
> The Junk E-mail filter in Outlook is turned on by default. This filter automatically evaluates whether unread messages should be saved in the Junk E-mail folder. You can change the default settings to your own personal settings through the Options command on the Tools menu.

Flagging and Sorting

Located to the right of the message heading in the Inbox is the *Flag Status column*. This column contains flags that can be assigned one of six different colors. You can use the flags as reminder notices or other indicators that are needed for your personal or business use. For instance, in Figure 14-23, a red flag is displayed to the right of a message as a reminder.

FIGURE 14-23
Red flag displayed

After flagging messages, you can sort the messages by flag color. Click View on the menu bar, and point to the Arrange By command to display the submenu, as shown in Figure 14-24 on the next page. Note also in Figure 14-24 that you can sort messages in numerous other formats, including Date, Type, and Subject.

FIGURE 14-24
Arrange By commands

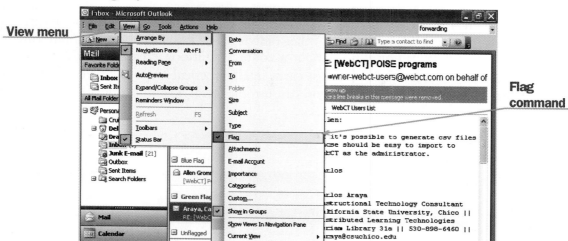

Encoding or Encrypting E-Mail

The process of *encrypting* information in a message is accomplished by "scrambling" it so that it cannot be read. When the intended recipient opens the message, he or she uses a key for *decryption* that unscrambles the information and returns it to the original text. To use this feature requires that certificates for digital signing and encryption from a certificate authority be obtained.

Ethics in Technology

E-MAIL/E-ACHES

Although e-mail is one of the more popular services of the Internet, its widespread use has created several problems. One of the more time-consuming problems it causes is the overflow of e-mail messages many users find in their Inboxes. Similar to your telephone number, marketers and news groups can locate your e-mail address, enabling them to send you many unwanted e-mails.

E-mail communications also can lead to confusion and misinterpretation. Receivers often are guilty of not thoroughly reading an e-mail message before they reply, or they might not use the Reply All option correctly. It is important to pay close attention to whom you are sending your messages and replies. You do not want to reply automatically to all addressees if the content of the message is not relevant to everyone.

Managing an Address Book

The *Contacts* feature in Outlook allows you to create an address book to store information about friends, family, work associates, and other individuals with whom you communicate on a regular basis. As you insert information about a contact, Outlook creates an address card for that individual. Outlook arranges the address cards in alphabetical order so you easily can locate each one by scrolling through the list, or you can use the numeric/alphabetical list finder at the right side of the window. (See Figure 14-25.)

FIGURE 14-25
Contacts window

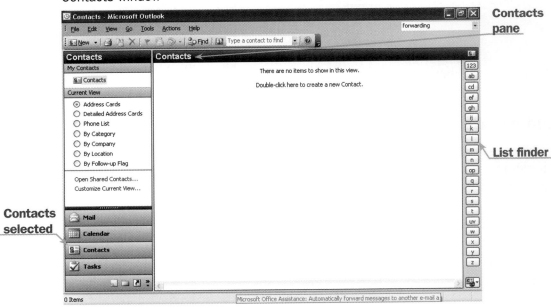

Adding and Deleting Contacts

To add a new contact, click the New button. Outlook displays the Contact dialog box, which contains a number of tabs—General, Details, Activities, Certificates, and All Fields. You can add as much or as little information as you choose. As a minimum, you should include the full name and e-mail address of the contact. After you fill in the contact information in the dialog box, Outlook adds a new address card to the Contacts folder.

In the following exercise, you will add a contact and create an e-mail message to the contact. A fictitious name and e-mail address is used in the Step-by-step instructions. Use the name of one of your contacts or check with your instructor as to what name you should use.

S TEP-BY-STEP 14.7

1. Click the **Contacts** button in the Navigation pane to open the Contacts folder.

2. Click the **New** button on the toolbar to display the Untitled – Contact dialog box.

STEP-BY-STEP 14.7 Continued

3. Click in the **Full Name** box and type **Tracy Coady** (or the name of one of your own contacts).

4. Press **Tab** to move the insertion point to the next box. Notice that the *File as* box automatically fills in *Coady, Tracy.* Click the **Job title** box and type **Office Manager.**

5. Click the **Addresses** box arrow and select **Home**. Click the **This is the mailing address** box. Type the following in the Address box (or substitute this with the address of your own contact):

444 East Street

Tampa, FL 33630

6. Click the **E-mail** box, type **tcoady@msn.com**, and then press **Tab**. (See Figure 14-26.)

FIGURE 14-26
Contact information entered

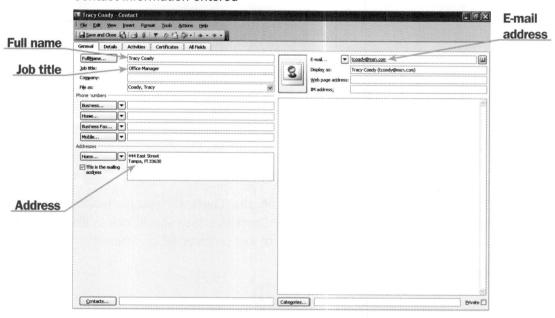

STEP-BY-STEP 14.7 Continued

7. When you have finished entering the information, click the **Save and Close** button. The form closes and the contact information appears in the Contacts window Reading pane. (See Figure 14-27.)

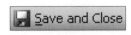

FIGURE 14-27
Contacts window

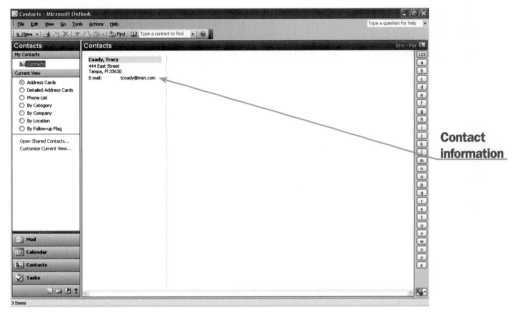

8. Repeat Steps 2 through 7 and add two more contacts. Check with your instructor as to what names you should use. After adding the contacts, your Contacts screen should look similar to that shown in Figure 14-28. Most likely, however, the names of your contacts will be different.

FIGURE 14-28
Contacts window with additional names

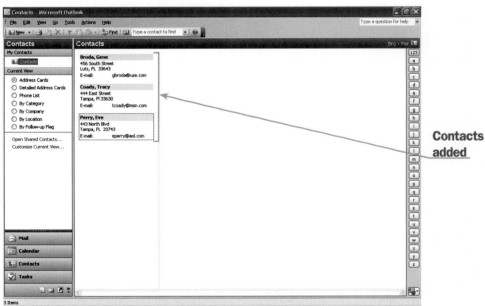

Notice that the Address Card view in Figure 14-28 on the previous page does not show all the details for the contact you just added. You can view them with the Detailed Address Cards view. On the Contacts Navigation pane, select Detailed Address Cards.

To send a message to a contact stored in the Contacts folder, click Mail in the Outlook bar, and then click New on the Standard toolbar. When the message dialog box is displayed, click the To button. A dialog box opens to allow you to select a contact name, as shown in Figure 14-29.

FIGURE 14-29
Contacts window with additional names

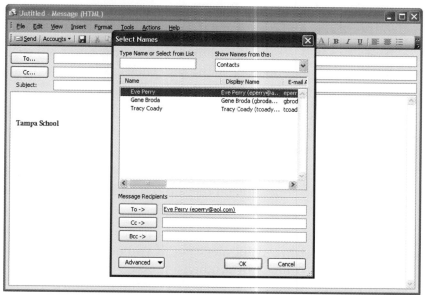

You stored the e-mail address for that contact in the Contacts folder, so you do not have to retype the address. The contact's name appears in the To text box, and the message will automatically be sent to the e-mail address you previously stored.

If you want to send a copy of the message to another person, click the Cc button to open the dialog box with contact names again. If an e-mail address is not in your address book, you can also type it in the Cc box.

You easily can remove an address card from the contacts list. Right-click the name to be removed and then select Delete from the shortcut menu.

Professional and Effective Electronic Communication

E-mail has become a common form of communication for both personal and business users. While it can be informal in nature—much like a telephone conversation—e-mail communication should be courteous and professional, especially among business users. E-mail messages can be printed and saved, so they can serve as "written proof" of what has transpired, much like a signed letter or other official document. Keep in mind the following elements of professional and effective electronic communication when you compose your e-mail messages:

- Proofread your messages before sending them. Most e-mail programs have spell checkers that can help identify spelling and grammatical mistakes.

- Limit your use of emoticons (keyboard symbols used to show emotion, such as :-o to show surprise), humor, and jokes in your messages. They easily can be misunderstood and misinterpreted.

- Keep your messages short and to the point. If you are soliciting a response from the receiver of the message, you will find that a brief message with a pointed list of questions is most effective in getting that response.

- Try to limit each message to a single subject. For work-related communications, your message might become part of someone's file on the subject, and it is easier to track the information if it is subject specific.

- Double-check the addresses in the To and Cc/Bcc text boxes before sending a message to avoid sending inappropriate or irrelevant messages. If you use the Reply All feature, you might accidentally embarrass yourself by sending a message to the wrong person or inconvenience the recipient with unwanted and unneeded communications.

- Remember that e-mail sent through company networks or Internet e-mail sites is not private.

- Use the appropriate mail format to send your messages. Sometimes excessive formatting in a specific word-processing format or in HTML format can prevent the receiver from reading a message if they do not have the appropriate application to view it.

Other Features Tour

As indicated earlier, this lesson focuses on using the Outlook mail feature. However, in Step-by-step 14.8, you take a short tour of Outlook by opening two other Outlook folders. You can customize most Outlook folders to display the information in a folder in several different ways. When you open a folder, you will see the view that was used the last time that folder was opened.

S TEP-BY-STEP 14.8

1. If necessary, start Outlook.

2. Click **Calendar** in the navigation pane. This feature is used to set up appointments and meetings. If no one has entered any meetings in Outlook yet, this folder will be empty.

STEP-BY-STEP 14.8 Continued

3. Click **Tasks** in the Navigation pane. A grid used to organize information about tasks you want to accomplish is displayed in the Reading pane. If no one has entered any tasks in Outlook yet, this folder will be empty.

4. Close Outlook.

If you have the opportunity, use the Help feature to find out more about how you can use the application to organize many aspects of your work and personal tasks effectively.

Other Forms of Electronic Communications

As mentioned previously, it is now possible to send e-mail using a cell phone, a personal digital assistant, or hand-held computer. There are also other forms of text messaging available besides e-mail, and these methods are available on many kinds of electronic devices. *Instant messaging* is a popular medium for correspondence in business as well as social settings. The Instant Messaging feature in Outlook, for example, enables you to send messages in real time. In other words, you can send and receive messages while you and the contact are both logged on to the Internet. Each contact must have an instant messaging account available.

Instant messaging is set up through the Options command on the Tools menu. In the Options dialog box, select the Other tab. Click the check boxes to Enable the Person Names Smart Tag and Display Presence Status in the From field.

SUMMARY

In this lesson, you learned:

■ Microsoft Outlook includes features to manage appointments, tasks, and e-mail. The Outlook bar displays shortcuts that give you quick access to each of the Outlook folders.

■ Electronic mail is similar to regular mail because it requires an address, a message, and a carrier to get it from the sender to the receiver.

■ E-mail messages are broken into smaller portions of electronic data called packets, which are sent independently and then reorganized into the original message.

■ You can access e-mail on a computer using a program like Microsoft Outlook, or you can send and receive e-mail messages using a Web site with a built-in e-mail program, such as America Online or Hotmail.

■ Wireless communication makes it possible to send and receive e-mail using a handheld computer or cell phone with e-mail capabilities.

■ E-mail addresses consist of three parts: the user name, the "@" symbol, and the domain name.

■ An e-mail message header includes the address of the recipient, the subject of the message, and information about to whom the message is sent as a copy.

■ You can use the Inbox folder in Outlook to send and receive e-mail messages.

- An attachment is a file that is sent with an e-mail message and can be opened by the recipient.

- You can reply to an e-mail message, forward a message to a new recipient, delete a message, or save a message.

- Spam, or junk e-mail, consists of unsolicited messages that take up space in your Inbox unnecessarily.

- E-mail messages are organized in folders of incoming messages, sent messages, deleted messages, and junk e-mail. You also can create additional folders to organize your own e-mail.

- Special e-mail features let you add an automatic signature to messages, block messages from certain addresses, create personalized stationery for your messages, and set up an automatic response or forward your messages to another address.

- Professional electronic communication requires courtesy and brevity. Always check that the spelling and grammar is correct, and that the message is being sent to the intended recipient(s).

- The Contacts folder is designed to store information about business and personal contacts with whom you often communicate.

- You can create address cards that hold information such as name, address, phone number, e-mail address, and so on. Address cards are listed in alphabetical order in the Contacts folder.

- Other forms of electronic communication are available such as instant messaging, which allows you to send messages in real time.

VOCABULARY *Review*

Define the following terms:

Attachments	Encrypting	Packets
Contacts	Flag Status column	Personal information
Decryption	Instant messaging	management (PIM)
E-mail address	Item	Signature
Electronic mail (E-mail)	Outlook Express	Spam

REVIEW *Questions*

TRUE/FALSE

Circle T if the statement is true or F if the statement is false.

T F 1. Each Outlook folder organizes a different type of information.

T F 2. The first part of an e-mail address is called the domain name.

T F 3. As you add contacts to your address book, Outlook arranges them in alphabetical order.

T F 4. You can sort e-mail messages by subject or by date received.

T F 5. Long messages are appropriate for e-mail if you cover several topics in one message.

FILL IN THE BLANK

Complete the following sentences by writing the correct word or words in the blanks provided.

1. An e-mail address consists of three parts: the user name, the @ symbol, and the user's _____.

2. Some e-mail providers limit the size of e-mail _____.

3. A(n) _____ is an electronic list of contacts.

4. _____ enables you to send messages in real time.

5. _____ is unsolicited messages.

MATCHING

Match the correct term in Column 2 to its description in Column 1.

Column 1	**Column 2**
___ 1. To send an e-mail message on to another recipient	A. Emoticon
___ 2. A file sent with an e-mail message	B. Spam
___ 3. A keyboard symbol used to convey a tone or feeling in an electronic communication	C. Packet
	D. Blind copy
___ 4. A small chunk into which an e-mail message is broken as it is sent to the recipient	E. Attachment
___ 5. Junk e-mail marketing a product or service	F. Instant message
	G. Forward

PROJECTS

CROSS-CURRICULAR—MATHEMATICS

Microsoft's Rules and Alerts option was discussed briefly in this lesson. Use Microsoft's Help and Support Center to learn more about this option. Then use Google or another search engine to locate Web sites that contain information on how to use this option. You might want to start with these two Web sites: *http://oit.uta.edu/cs/email/outlook/pc/rules_alerts/rules_alerts.html* or *http://www.uwec.edu/help/Outlook03/rules.htm.*

After you complete your research, write a one- to two-page report explaining how this option works and ways in which you personally can use this feature.

CROSS-CURRICULAR—SCIENCE

Microsoft has several free audio courses that are accessible through your browser. A list of these courses is available at *http://office.microsoft.com/en-us/FX010857931033.aspx*. Access this Web site and then scroll down to the Training section and the list of audio courses. Click the link for "Help protect yourself: Security in Office" and complete the course. When you are finished with the course, write a report listing what you learned about passwords and password protection, and about viruses and macros.

CROSS-CURRICULAR—SOCIAL STUDIES

Access the Web site *http://websearch.about.com/od/whatistheinternet/a/usewww_2.htm* to read an article on "The Impact of the World Wide Web On Society-Communication-Email-Snail Mail." After you read the article, write a report expressing your opinion about the article. Do you agree or disagree with the author's statements? Explain why you agree or disagree.

CROSS-CURRICULAR—LANGUAGE ARTS

Access the Microsoft Web site at *http://office.microsoft.com/clipart/* where you can download clip art and other media files. Select at least three clip art images to download. Send an e-mail to your instructor with one of the clip art images attached. Include a message that you downloaded the file from the Microsoft Web site.

 WEB PROJECT

Spam was discussed briefly in this lesson. Use Google and other search engines to research the topic "spam" to learn about ways that you can stop spam. Prepare a report discussing your findings.

 TEAMWORK PROJECT

Individuals who use e-mail for frequent communication often are annoyed by unsolicited e-mail called spam. Spam can be obnoxious, offensive, and a waste of your time. Some countries have laws against spam. Your Internet service provider might try to block spam before it reaches your mailbox. However, you still might be inconvenienced by junk e-mail. Working with a partner, research spam to learn more about what it is used for, how marketers get addresses, how effective spam is, and ways that you can stop spam. Prepare a report on your findings. Include information on both good and bad instances of spam; if it is a nuisance or problem; and how you can stop it before it reaches your e-mail Inbox. At the end of your report, answer the following questions: Is spam ever useful? Should there be laws to restrict spam? Do you think you can block all spam from reaching your Inbox?

CRITICAL *Thinking*

A number of Web sites provide free access to e-mail. If you do not have a computer, public libraries, schools, and even some "Internet cafes" offer free or inexpensive computer access to the World Wide Web that you can use to check incoming messages and send your own e-mail. What kind of features would you like to have for a personal e-mail account? You might want to investigate some Web sites, such as *www.hotmail.com*, *www.usa.net*, or *www.yahoo.com*, to find out about the options available and then list the ones you think are most important. Why do you believe you would need these features for your e-mail account?

USING THE COMPUTER

REVIEW Questions

FILL IN THE BLANK

Complete the following sentences by writing the correct word or words in the blanks provided.

1. A(n) _____ walks you through the steps of a process by asking a series of questions.

2. A(n) _____ is an object you use to input, maintain, and print records in a database one record at a time.

3. A(n) _____ template contains color schemes with custom formatting and styled fonts, all designed to create a special look for slides.

4. The process of organizing and keeping track of your files is called _____ management.

5. _____ a floppy disk is the process of preparing it to receive and store your files.

6. The ability to input data by touch using the alphabetic and numeric keys on a computer and/or typewriter keyboard is called _____.

7. Some keyboards have _____ keys to assist in the correct placement of your fingers.

8. Making changes to an existing document is called _____ the document.

9. In a spreadsheet, the point at which a column and row intersect or meet is called a(n) _____.

10. Microsoft _____ is a program that includes features to manage appointments, tasks, and e-mail.

MULTIPLE CHOICE

Select the best response for the following statements.

1. Use _____ software to prepare a budget.
   A. word-processing
   B. database
   C. spreadsheet
   D. keyboarding

2. Use _____ software to maintain a list of club members.
   A. word-processing
   B. database
   C. spreadsheet
   D. keyboarding

3. A(n) _____ is a shortcut for entering a formula to calculate data in a spreadsheet.
   A. function
   B. value
   C. formula
   D. order of evaluation

4. A(n) _____ is a visual representation of spreadsheet data.
   A. chart
   B. footer
   C. label
   D. workbook

5. A _____ is a predesigned formatting option that makes it easy to control the way your text looks and assures consistent formatting throughout your document.
   A. word wrap
   B. serif
   C. format painter
   D. style

6. The home row keys include _____.
   A. q w e r t y
   B. a s d f j k l ;
   C. a s d g j k l :
   D. a s d f n k l ;

7. _____ are used to store and organize your files and documents.
   A. Folders
   B. Jump drives
   C. Formats
   D. Thumbnails

8. Filenames can have up to _____ characters.
   A. 33
   B. 55
   C. 255
   D. 52

9. When you send someone an e-mail message, it is broken down into small chunks, called _____.
   A. packets
   B. attachments
   C. contacts
   D. instant messages

10. Slides in a presentation that would provide participants with a means to write notes can be printed as _____.
    A. outlines
    B. speaker notes
    C. audience handouts
    D. individual slides

TRUE/FALSE

Circle T if the statement is true or F if the statement is false.

T F   1. Windows Explorer is a file management program.

T F   2. You cannot change the name of a file once it has been saved.

T F   3. Slide presentations only can be used to present slide shows.

T F   4. E-mail addresses consist of three parts: the user name, the @ symbol, and the domain name.

T F   5. AutoSum instantly formats an entire spreadsheet with borders, shading, and data formatting.

T F   6. Assistance is always available through the software's Help system.

T F   7. A cell in a spreadsheet that has been selected (highlighted or outlined with a black border) is referred to as an active cell.

T F   8. You can use WordArt in presentations to create special text effects.

T F   9. The first step in designing a database is planning.

T F 10. In Windows applications, the status bar always displays the names of the menus available in that application.

PROJECTS

CROSS-CURRICULAR—MATHEMATICS

You are the treasurer of the local Little League baseball team. The team has won the regional championship title and now will compete for the state title. The championship will be held in your state's capital. The 16-member team, two coaches, and four chaperones will attend the state championship games. Prepare a spreadsheet to create a budget indicating the amount of money that will be needed for everyone to fly (at the cheapest fare) to the state games. (You will need to check with airlines to find the cheapest fare.) The special hotel rate is $104 per night plus 11.9% tax. Determine the cost of the stay in the hotel for three nights. (Two persons will share a room.) Registration for each person is $25. (You are to make up the names of the team members, coaches, and chaperones.) Each person will be given $55 per day for food for three days. Your spreadsheet should include the total cost for transportation, the total cost of registration, the total cost of food, the total cost for each person, and the total cost of the entire trip for everyone. *Note*: A third coach has decided to drive instead of fly. He will be allotted 37 cents per mile to drive his car. You will need to determine the distance from your city to your state's capital. Format the spreadsheet appropriately; be sure to add a title. Create a chart showing the distribution of the various budgeted items.

CROSS-CURRICULAR—SCIENCE

There have been many newspaper articles and television reports of widespread misuse of steroids by professional athletes to enhance their performance. Use the Internet and other resources to research steroids and athletes. Prepare a two-page report that addresses this misuse. Include a definition of steroids, an explanation of how they work, side effects, and any other relevant information. You may include the names of athletes who were featured in articles or reports and information regarding their "case."

CROSS-CURRICULAR—SOCIAL STUDIES

Use your social studies textbook, the Internet, and any other appropriate resources to research how a bill becomes a law. Prepare a slide presentation to show the steps for a bill to become a law in the United States. Your presentation should include at least six slides. Be sure to use as many features as necessary to make this an effective presentation. Print handouts for your audience.

CROSS-CURRICULAR—LANGUAGE ARTS

Use the Internet to research information regarding the greatest movies of the past decade. Create a "Greatest Movies" database that will contain information for at least 10 movies. Create a table named **Movies**. Include fields such as Title, Year, Category, Date, Subject, Star, Award, Award Year, and any other fields you think are important. After you have created the table, create a form named **Movies** and then enter the records. Print a copy of the table in alphabetical order by name of the movie. Print another copy of the table in alphabetical order by year. Create a report named **Category** and print it grouped by category.

 WEB PROJECT

You have decided that you need to determine your career path. You are not completely sure which career you want to pursue and have been told that you can take a personality survey to help determine which job best suits your personality. Visit a Web site, such as *http://www.questcareer.com*, *http://a.livecareer.com*, or *www.careerkey.org/english/* to determine which career would be the best for you. After you identify the career for you, use the Internet to further research the career. Prepare a two-page report on your career of choice that includes the nature of the work, qualifications, possible earnings, and projected vacancies. Include a graphic of your career choice if available.

 TEAMWORK PROJECT

You are a member of the Computer Club. The club will be sponsoring a conference in about three weeks, and you have been asked to work with another member of the club to prepare a presentation on the early history of computing. Use the Internet and any other resources to identify contributors and contributions to the evolution of computing. One of you will present information about one person's contribution, an event, a timeline, or a thing that made or was a significant contribution to the history of computing. You may select which topic you want to present. You are to prepare a two- to three-page written report or develop a slide presentation with a minimum of six slides to present your findings.

SIMULATION

JOB 2-1

Use the following list of customers to create a database. Determine the fields from the list. Name the database **Computer Help OnCall**. Name the table **Customers**. After you have created the table and entered the records, print the entire table in alphabetical order according to the customers' last names.

Jerome Biggs
1967 Jamesville Road
Norfolk, VA 23510
555-1234

Darrell Williams
104 Center Street
Norfolk, VA 23502
555-5678

Flonnie Slade
371 Butt Station Road
Norfolk, VA 23513
555-5210

Georgia D'Marior
3821 Windsor Lake Drive
Norfolk, VA 23513
555-2978

Paul Veerman
130 Ivy Drive, #5
Chesapeake, VA 23322
555-2301

Hilton Wallace
909 Harbor View Way
Virginia Beach, VA 23456
555-4567

Courtney Henley
5157 Central Mew
Portsmouth, VA 23702
555-3456

Molly Cage
13 Wavy Boulevard
Norfolk, VA 23402
555-7354

Clinton Mendez
777 Commerce Road
Chesapeake, VA 23323
555-1180

Matthew Lukes
2005 Diploma Crescent
Virginia Beach, VA 23462
555-7085

JOB 2–2

Your company, Computer Help OnCall, offers the following services: computer setup, network support, virus detection and removal, software installation, laptop computer repair, printer services, data backup and restore, and wireless network setup. Use your word-processing software to prepare a flyer announcing these services. You may use fictitious information for the address, telephone number, and other information. Use clip art, various fonts, and color to make the flyer attractive.

JOB 2–3

Prepare your disk with the folder structure for files that you will be using for Computer Help OnCall. You will begin with the following folders: Customers, Services, Budget, and Miscellaneous. Move your current files into the appropriate folder. Save future files in the appropriate folder.

PORTFOLIO*Checklist*

Include the following activities from this unit in your portfolio:

_____ Lesson 8 Teamwork Report

_____ Lesson 9 Web Report

_____ Lesson 10 Science Cross-Curricular Report

_____ Lesson 11 Critical Thinking Presentation Basics PowerPoint Presentation

_____ Lesson 12 Language Arts Cross-Curricular Report and Spreadsheet

_____ Lesson 13 Critical Thinking Database for Personal Use

_____ Lesson 14 Science Cross-Curricular Report

_____ Unit 2 Review Mathematics Cross-Curricular Spreadsheet

_____ Unit 2 Review Teamwork Report/Slide Presentation

_____ Unit 2 Review Job 2-2 Flyer

COMPUTERS AND SOCIETY

Unit 3

Estimated Time for Unit: 5 hours

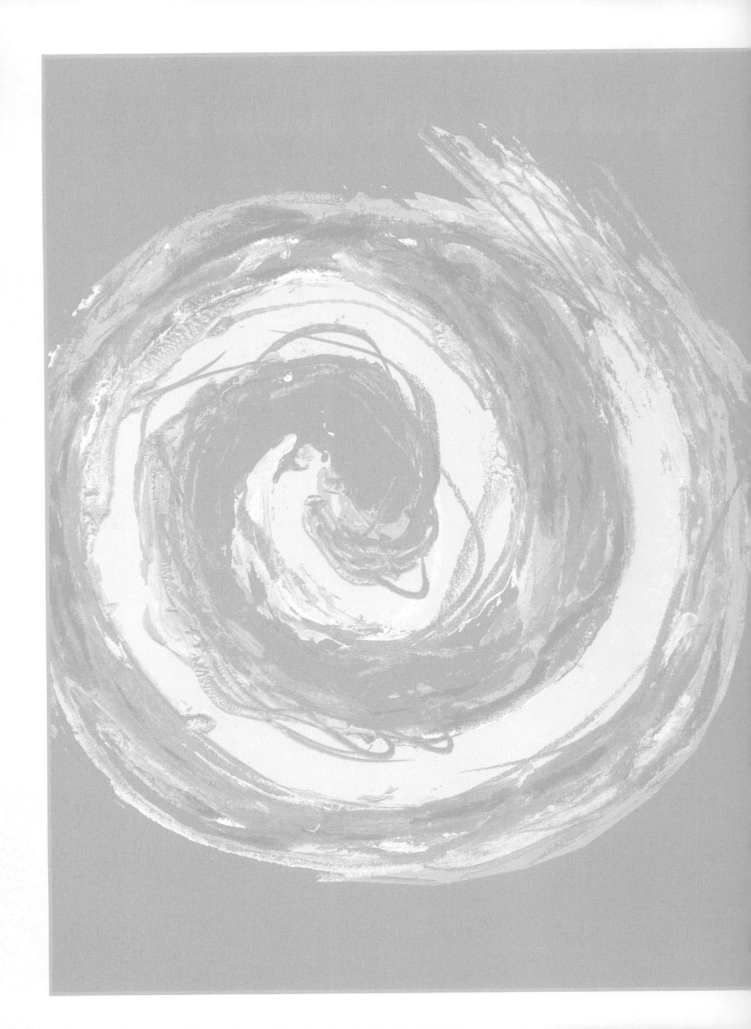

EVALUATING ELECTRONIC INFORMATION

OBJECTIVES

Upon completion of this lesson, you should be able to:

- Identify reasons for evaluating Internet resources.
- Identify criteria for evaluating electronic information.
- Describe software piracy.
- Identify Internet resources.
- Understand the rules of copyright.
- Identify false information, including hoaxes and urban legends.
- Cite Internet resources appropriately.
- Explore other legal and ethical issues concerning information you obtain from the Internet.

Estimated Time: 1.5 hours

VOCABULARY

Copyright

Currency

Hoax

Navigation

Patent

Public domain

Shareware

Software license

Software piracy

Sponsored site

Trademark

Urban legends

Information is only as good as the source. Anyone, anywhere, can put anything on the Internet. It might be true; it might not be true. How can you determine if the information is legitimate? Developing the ability to evaluate information critically on the Internet is important today because so many people depend on electronic resources in so many areas of their lives. For example, you might have used information you found on the Internet to research a paper for a science class, and of course you want to ensure that the data you use is accurate. But consider some other types of information you might depend on, such as consumer reports on the safety of a certain make of automobile, unbiased news about candidates running for office in your city or state, guidelines for training your pet, or information about your health. You do not want to be steered wrong in any of these areas, and you must carefully assess the wealth of information available.

Criteria for Evaluating Electronic Resources

The Internet provides opportunities for students, teachers, scholars, and anyone needing information to find it from all over the world. It is fairly easy to locate information and to publish it electronically. However, because anyone can put information on the Internet, it is not always accurate or reliable. Anyone using information obtained from the Internet needs to develop skills to evaluate what they find.

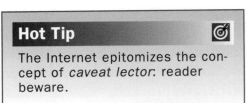

Hot Tip

The Internet epitomizes the concept of *caveat lector*: reader beware.

Pages on the Web have many different looks. Some pages are filled with pictures, sounds, animations, links, and information. Some are very exciting; others just might be plain. Sometimes the appearance of the page alone might draw you to a site and, after reading it, you realize it is not the site you need.

Following are some questions you might want to ask when you view a Web page:

- Did the page take a long time to load?
- Are the graphics on the page related to the site?
- Are the sections on the page labeled?
- Who wrote the information on this page?
- How can you communicate with the author?
- When was the page last updated?
- Are there appropriate links to other Web pages?
- Is it easy to follow the links?
- Can you tell what the page is about from its title?
- Is the information useful to you?
- How old is the information?
- Does any of the information contradict information you found somewhere else?
- Did the author use words like *always, never, best, worst*?
- Do you think the author knows the information he or she is sharing?

These questions represent just the beginning of the process involved in evaluating electronic information.

Did You Know?

Links that are no longer active are called "dead links."

Determining Authorship

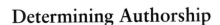

A well-developed resource identifies its author and/or producer. You should be given enough information to be able to determine whether the originator is a reliable source. What expertise or authority does the author have that qualifies him or her to distribute this information? Be sure to look for a name and e-mail address of the person who created or maintains the information (see Figure 15-1 on the next page). This person generally is the Web site developer.

FIGURE 15-1
Determining a Web site author

If you cannot find information at the site regarding the author or originator, you should use a search engine to search by the author's name. This also could lead to other information by the same author. If an e-mail address is visible, use it to request information regarding the author's credentials and expertise.

The domain portion of the URL also will give you information concerning the appropriateness of the site for your area of study. Examples are:

■ .edu for educational or research information

■ .gov for government resources

■ .com for commercial products or commercially sponsored sites

■ .org for nonprofit organizations

■ .mil for military branches

Relevance and Reliability

Do not take any information presented on the Internet at face value. Is the purpose of the Web site stated? Is the information accurate? Does the information provide enough content? Has the information been reviewed? The source of the information should be clearly stated—whether it is original or borrowed from somewhere else. Make sure you understand the agenda of the site's owner. Is the site trying to sell a product or service? Is it trying to influence public opinion? As you read through the information, pay close attention to determine whether the content covers a specific time period or an aspect of a topic, or if it is broader. Check other resources, such as books or journals at the local library, which contain similar information.

Timely Content

A very important consideration of an effective site is its *currency*, which refers to the age of the information, how long it has been posted, and how often it is updated. Some sites need to be updated more often than others to reflect changes in the kind of information. Medical or technological information, for instance, needs to be updated more often than historical information. Out-of-date information might not give you the results you need. Does the site contain dead links—links that are no longer active? Dead links are a clue that the information on the Web site might not be up to date.

Validity and Bias

The style of writing and the language used can reveal information about the quality of the site. If the style is objective, the chances are the information is worthy of your attention. However, if it is opinionated and subjective, you might want to give second thought to using it. Ideas and opinions supported by references are additional signs of the value of the site. Determine the validity of the site by checking other resources that contain similar information.

The overall layout of the page also is important. The page should be free of spelling and grammatical errors. Even if the page appears to contain valuable information, misspelled words and incorrect grammar usage tend to bias a reader regarding the validity of the information.

Site Navigation

Navigation is the ability to use links to move through a site. Being able to move quickly through the links on a Web site is a very important element. Having the information laid out in a logical design so you can locate what you need easily adds to the efficiency of the site. The consistency of the layout from page to page adds to the ability to navigate easily. The first page of a Web site indicates how the site is organized and what options are available. Some sites also contain a site map that gives you a good idea of the overall organization of the site.

You move through a site by clicking links on the page. Some pages consist of many links; others might only contain a few. Regardless, the links should be:

- Easy to identify

- Grouped logically

- Pertinent to the subject of the original page

Each page should contain a link that will take you back to the home page and a link that allows you to e-mail the author. Figure 15-2 on the next page shows an example of multiple types of links.

Ethics in Technology

RESTRICTING INTERNET ACCESS

In various situations, people might want to block access to specific Internet sites or to sites that contain certain content. For instance, parents often want to prevent their children from visiting sites with adult-oriented material. Or companies might want to deny their employees access to online shopping and entertainment sites that are not business-related.

Several tools exist that can be used to restrict site access. A low-tech solution is simply to have someone oversee computer users and what is on their monitors. At the other end of the spectrum, there are software programs that can be installed on a computer or network that will automatically block access to user-specified sites or to sites with specified content.

FIGURE 15-2
Web site navigation

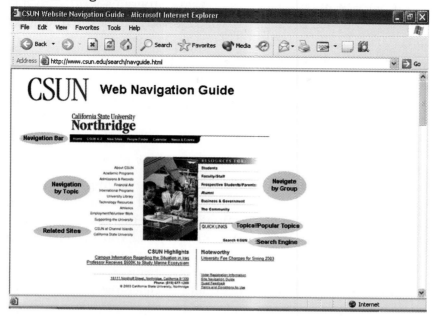

Types of Internet Resources

The types of electronic resources include the following:

- Journals and journal articles
- Magazines and magazine articles
- Newspapers and newspaper articles
- E-mail
- Mailing lists
- Commercial sites
- Organizational sites
- Subject-based sites

Some of these are presented in complete form; others are only portions of the document. Regardless of the type, the site should give information concerning:

- Identity of the publisher
- Reviewers of the article
- Special hardware requirements to use the site
- Availability of older copies of the article, newspaper, or journal
- Currency of the site

Search Engines

Search engines, discussed in detail in Lesson 3, are programs written to query and retrieve information stored in a database. They differ from database to database and depend on the information stored in the database itself. Examples of search engines are AltaVista, Excite, Yahoo, and Google. If you used one of the many search engines available to locate information on the Internet, you need to know:

■ How the search engine decides the order in which it returns information requested. The top spaces (the first sites listed) are sold to advertisers by the search engines. Therefore, the first sites listed are not always the best sites or the most accurate and reliable.

■ How the search engine searches for information and how often the information is updated.

You might be surprised to find that even the most academic subjects result in sponsored sites in your search results. A *sponsored site* is a site that has paid the search engine a fee in exchange for being listed in the "Sponsored Sites" section on many of their pages. Sponsored sites are unlikely to provide balanced and impartial information, and you should consider the intent of the sites when judging the reliability of information provided on them. In addition, if information in a search result appears to be out of date or irrelevant, consider trying the search again with a different search engine and compare the results when assessing the information. See Figure 15-3 for an example of sponsored sites.

FIGURE 15-3
Sponsored sites in a Google™ search for copyright law

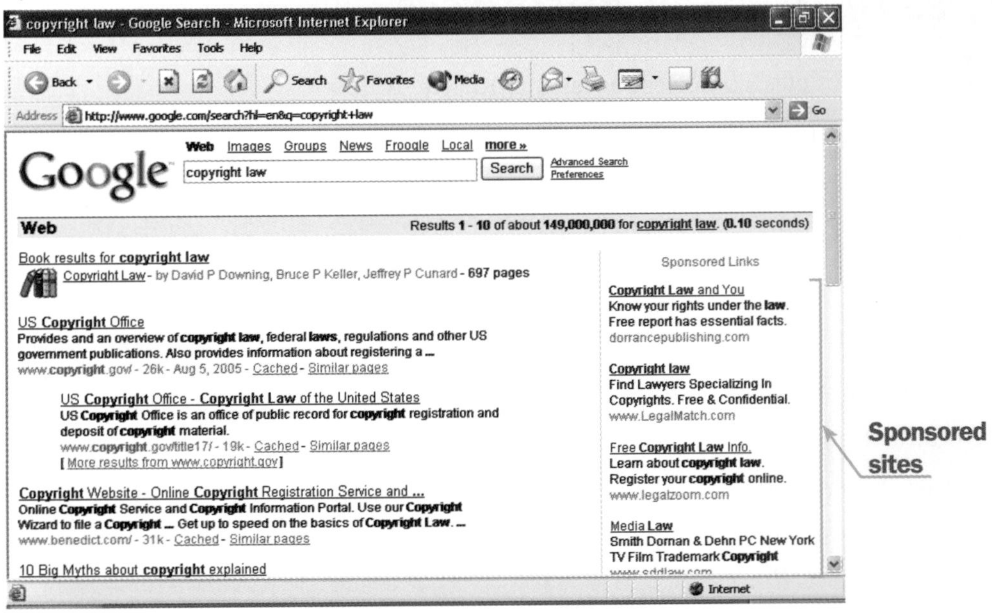

Web Sites and Copyright Rules

For the most part, information displayed on an Internet site is easy to copy. Often you can highlight whatever text or graphics that you want to copy, use the "copy" command, and then paste it into another document. Or you can print an entire page that is displayed on the monitor. The ease with which information can be copied, however, does not mean that users have a legal right to do so. Internet publications can claim the same legal protection as books, newspapers, CDs, movies, and other forms that are protected by copyright rules.

Most sites have copyright information. *Copyright* is the exclusive right, granted by law for a certain number of years, to make and dispose of literary, musical, or artistic work. Even if the copyright notice is not displayed prominently on the page, someone is responsible for the creation of whatever appears on a page. This means that you cannot use the information as your own. You must give credit to the person who created the work.

If Internet content, such as a music file, is copyrighted, it cannot be copied without the copyright holder's permission. To do so is a violation of copyright laws. It can lead to criminal charges for theft as well as civil lawsuits for monetary damages.

A company's logo or other graphic information on a Web site may be protected as a *trademark*, which means much the same thing as copyright but relates specifically to visual or commercial images rather than text or intellectual property. In addition, processes and business methods may be protected by *patents*, which guarantee the inventor exclusive copyright to the process or method for a certain time period.

Copyright law does provide certain exceptions to the general prohibition against copying. If copyright protection has lapsed on certain material, then it is deemed to be in the *public domain* and is available for anyone to copy. Also, the law allows for the fair use of properly identified copyrighted material that is merely a small part of a larger research project, for instance, or cited as part of a critique or review. For example, many governmental Web sites, such as the National Park Service (*http://www.nps.gov/*), U.S. Fish and Wildlife Service (*http://www.fws.gov/ pictures/*), NASA (*http://images.jsc.nasa.gov/*), and the National Oceanic and Atmospheric Administration (*http://www.photolib.noaa.gov/*), provide images that can be downloaded and used in Web pages and other documents. The NOAA site is shown in Figure 15-4.

FIGURE 15-4
National Oceanic and Atmospheric Administration Web page

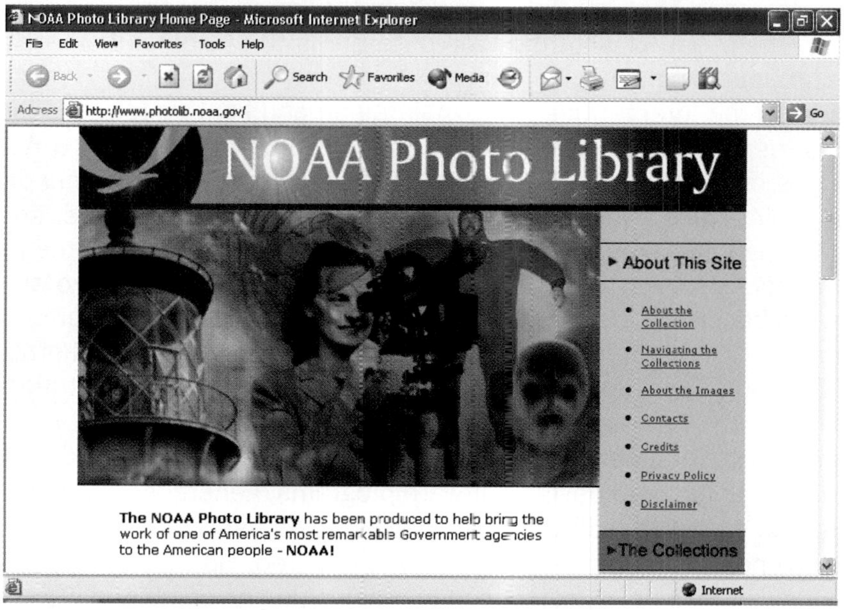

Software Piracy

Software piracy is the unauthorized copying of software. When you purchase a software program, you are not purchasing the software—you are purchasing a *software license* to use the program. Many companies, government organizations, and educational institutions purchase volume licenses. This gives these organizations the right to install a program on a specific number of computers. Most commercially marketed software is copyrighted. Copyrighted software cannot be duplicated legally for distribution to others.

Originally, many software companies attempted to stop the piracy by copy-protecting their software. They soon discovered, however, that this strategy was not foolproof and that software piracy is almost impossible to stop. Many software companies now require some sort of registration. This strategy works somewhat, but is not infallible and does not stop software piracy. *Shareware* is an alternative used by some companies. This software—usually downloadable from the Internet—is distributed on an honor system. Most shareware is free for an evaluation period but requires payment if you continue to use it beyond the evaluation period.

Technology Careers

INTERNET WEB DESIGNER/WEBMASTER

Every page on the Internet was designed by someone. Today, that someone is called a Web designer. The way a page looks on the Internet is the responsibility of the Web designer. The overall goal of the Web designer is to design and create a page that is efficient and appealing.

Each page on the Internet has to be maintained and kept up-to-date. The Webmaster is responsible for this task. A typical Webmaster manages a Web site. That usually includes creating content, adapting existing content in a user-friendly format, creating and maintaining a logical structure, and running the Web server software.

Not so long ago, both the design and maintenance functions were the responsibility of the Webmaster. However, with today's growing technology in hardware and software, these tasks are becoming more and more specialized and therefore performed by more than one person. Webmasters and Web designers can work in any organization that has a Web site. Some example organizations include educational institutions, museums, libraries, government agencies, and of course, businesses.

A person working in either of these two capacities needs to have skills in graphic design, HTML language, Web design software programs, general programming, and the ability to adapt to new Web technology as it evolves. An associate or bachelor's degree in computer science or graphic design usually is required. However, many employers will accept persons with extensive experience in graphic design combined with good computer skills. The starting salary for a Webmaster or Web designer will vary depending on location and experience. The average salary can range from $20,000 to $36,000.

Citing Internet Resources

Internet resources used in reports must be cited. In other words, you must give proper credit to any information you include in a report that is not your original thought. This also will provide the reader of the document with choices for additional research. In addition, it will allow the information to be retrieved again. You can find general guidelines for citing electronic sources in the *MLA Handbook for Writers of Research Papers*, published by the Modern Language Association. *The Chicago Manual of Style* is another source for this information.

Here are some samples of citing Internet resources as suggested in the *MLA Handbook for Writers of Research Papers*:

- *Online journal article*: Author's last name, first initial. (date of publication or "NO DATE" if unavailable). Title of article or section used [Number of paragraphs]. Title of complete work. [Form, such as HTTP, CD-ROM, E-MAIL]. Available: complete URL [date of access].

- *Online magazine article*: Author's last name, first initial. (date of publication). Title of article. [Number of paragraphs]. Title of work. [Form, such as HTTP, CD-ROM, E-MAIL] Available: complete URL [date of access].

- *Web sites*: Name of site [date]. Title of document. [Form, such as HTTP, CD-ROM, E-MAIL] Available: complete URL [date of access].

- *E-mail*: Author's last name, first name (author's e-mail address) (date). Subject. Receiver of e-mail (receiver's e-mail address).

Remember, anyone can put information on the Internet. Carefully evaluate any resources that you choose to use to ensure you have a high-quality resource that could really be of value to you.

Internet

For information concerning using MLA style for citing sources, visit *www.mla.org*.

Hoaxes, Urban Legends, and other False Information

A *hoax* is an attempt to deceive an audience into believing that something false is real. Sometimes this is perpetrated as a practical joke with a humorous intent; other times, it is an attempt to defraud and mislead.

Perhaps one of the most well-known media hoaxes—one that many consider the single greatest of all time—occurred on Halloween eve in 1938. Orson Welles shocked the nation with his Mercury Theater radio broadcast titled "The War of the Worlds." Despite repeated announcements before and during the program, many listeners believed that invaders from Mars were attacking the world.

In the 21st century, hoaxes, along with urban legends, myths, and chain letters, grow and flourish through the Internet. **Urban legends** are stories which might at one time have been partially true, but have grown from constant retelling into a mythical yarn. Much of this false information is harmless; however, some of these, such as chain letters, can have viruses attached to the message. It is not always easy to spot an e-mail or chain letter containing a virus, but looking for some of the following will help detect possible harmful files. Lesson 17 discusses viruses in detail.

- The e-mail is a warning message about a virus.

- The message might be very wordy, be in all capital letters, or include dozens of exclamation marks.

- The message urges you to share this information with everyone you know.

- The message appears credible because it describes the virus in technical terms.

- The message comes with an attachment, and you do not know who it is from.

If you identify any of the above, it is wise to delete the e-mail immediately. Also, use antivirus software and keep it updated.

One of the more popular Web sites displaying information about myths and hoaxes is the Vmyths Web site. You will visit this site in Step-by-step 15.1. (Internet access is required for this exercise.)

S TEP-BY-STEP 15.1

1. Start your browser and then type **http://www.vmyths.com** in the Address text box. Click the **Go** button or press **Enter** to display the Vmyths.com Web site, similar to that shown in Figure 15-5.

FIGURE 15-5
Vmyths Web site

2. Click the beginner's tour link (identified in Figure 15-5) and read the information. Follow your instructor's directions to either print a copy of the online page or write a paragraph summarizing what you read.

3. Click one of the **Hot News** links. Most likely the links on your monitor will be different from those shown in Figure 15-6. Follow your instructor's directions to either print a copy or write a paragraph summarizing what you read. Keep your browser open for Step-by-step 15.2.

FIGURE 15-6
Hot News story

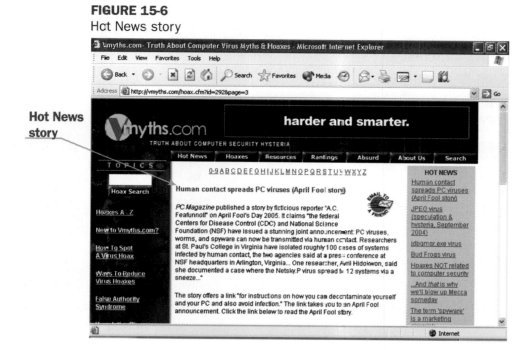

Hot News story

Other Legal and Ethical Issues

The ease of obtaining information from the Internet and of publishing information on it can contribute to other legal problems as well. Just because information is obtained from an Internet site does not mean that someone can copy it and claim it as his or her own, even noncopyrighted information. That's plagiarism. The Internet does not relieve an author of responsibility for acknowledging and identifying the source of borrowed material.

Likewise, the Internet does not relieve anyone of the burden of ensuring that information they publish is true. If someone publishes information about another person or organization and it is not true, they can be sued for libel and forced to pay compensation for any damage they caused. The Internet makes widespread publication of information easy. It also creates the potential for huge damages if the information turns out to be false.

The free flow of information via the Internet also creates opportunities for criminals to gather personal information, acquire credit, and conduct transactions using false identities. Identity theft, as it is called, is a growing problem that can cause big headaches for unsuspecting victims. Other criminal problems that the Internet has been fueling include sexual advances made to minors, anonymous threats, and rumors to manipulate stock prices. All are made easier by the Internet, but they are just as illegal and just as wrong.

And not all improper activities that make use of the Internet are necessarily illegal. Pranks, hoaxes, and making unfair use of free-trial "shareware" software may not be against the law, but they can still cause harm to innocent people—often more harm than their perpetrators might realize. The Internet is a powerful tool, for good and ill, and needs to be handled with care.

Evaluation Survey

You can use the information discussed in this lesson to construct a survey to evaluate electronic resources. Figure 15-7 shows a sample survey.

FIGURE 15-7
Survey form

CRITERIA FOR EVALUATING ELECTRONIC RESOURCES		
1. Can you identify the author of the page?	Yes ☐	No ☐
2. Is an e-mail address listed?	Yes ☐	No ☐
3. Can you access the site in a reasonable time?	Yes ☐	No ☐
4. Is the text on the screen legible?	Yes ☐	No ☐
5. Are the commands and directions easy to follow?	Yes ☐	No ☐
6. Is the information current?	Yes ☐	No ☐
7. When you perform a search, do you get what you expect?	Yes ☐	No ☐
8. Are instructions clearly visible?	Yes ☐	No ☐
9. Is the information updated regularly?	Yes ☐	No ☐
10. Make any comment you would like concerning the site.		

STEP-BY-STEP 15.2

1. Use your word-processing program and open **Step15-2** from the data files supplied for this course. This file contains the survey information presented in Figure 15-7.

2. Identify a site on the Internet and use the survey to evaluate the site. You may select a site containing a magazine article of interest to you, or any topic on which you might want to gather information.

3. Find a site that contains noncopyrighted images. Copy one or two of the images and paste them into your criteria evaluation page. Save the survey file using your first and last name.

4. Close your browser and your word-processing program. Submit your survey to your instructor.

SUMMARY

In this lesson, you learned:

- The criteria for evaluating Internet resources include authorship, content, copyright information, navigation, and quality.

- The Internet contains various types of resources, including electronic journals, magazines, newspapers, Web sites, and e-mail messages.

- Internet publications and Web site content can claim the same legal protection as books, newspapers, CDs, movies, and other forms that are protected by copyright law.

- It is very important to cite any information that you use from the Internet. The MLA style is widely used for citing electronic resources.

- Internet hoaxes, urban legends, and false information continue to increase because of the Internet.

VOCABULARY *Review*

Define the following terms:

Copyright	Public domain	Sponsored site
Currency	Shareware	Trademark
Hoax	Software license	Urban legends
Navigation	Software piracy	
Patent		

REVIEW *Questions*

MULTIPLE CHOICE

Select the best response for the following statements.

1. _____ is the illegal copying or use of software.
   A. Piracy
   B. Webmastering
   C. Counterfeiting
   D. Surfing

2. _____ refers to the age of information contained on a Web site.
   A. Date
   B. Infancy
   C. Currency
   D. Dead link

3. A company's logo or other graphic information might be protected as a _____.
   A. trademark
   B. patent
   C. public domain
   D. copyright

4. _____ is the exclusive right, granted by law for a certain number of years, to make and dispose of literary, musical, or artistic work.
   A. Copyright
   B. Security
   C. Privacy
   D. Resource

5. _____ is the ability to move through a Web site.
   A. Linking
   B. Grouping
   C. Citing
   D. Navigation

TRUE/FALSE

Circle T if the statement is true or F if the statement is false.

T   F   1. It can be assumed that all information found on the Internet is accurate.

T   F   2. The age of an article might affect its usefulness to a user.

T   F   3. Items contained in public domain are considered to be copyrighted.

T   F   4. A sponsored site is a site on the Web that has been approved by the Federal government.

T   F   5. Spelling and grammatical errors on a Web page might affect a user's opinion of a site.

FILL IN THE BLANK

Complete the following sentences by writing the correct word or words in the blanks provided.

1. _____ software cannot be duplicated legally for distribution to others.

2. All sites should have the _____ address of the author so the user can make contact.

3. When purchasing software, you are purchasing a software _____.

4. A(n) _____ is an attempt to deceive an audience into believing that something false is real.

5. A(n) _____ is responsible for managing and maintaining a Web site.

PROJECTS

CROSS-CURRICULAR—MATHEMATICS

Search the Internet for Web sites containing information on Olympic gold medalists. In the results list, pick at least two sites that you think might contain information relating to the number of medals won. Using the survey form shown in Figure 15-7, evaluate each site. Write a 100-word report on your evaluation of the sites. Be sure to include the URL of the site and elaborate on what you found in your answer to each of the survey questions.

CROSS-CURRICULAR—SCIENCE

Go to the Web site *http://www.csun.edu/search/navguide.html*. Review the section in the lesson on navigation, and then evaluate the navigation system and tools at this Web site. You will want to click links on various pages. Write a 100-word report that explains the site's system for navigating. Be sure to mention any problems you had in getting around the site.

CROSS-CURRICULAR—SOCIAL STUDIES

Use Google or another search engine and do a search on urban legends. Find one or two urban legends of particular interest, and write a report on why you think so many people believed the story to be true. Include the Web site addresses of sites that you accessed for this information.

CROSS-CURRICULAR—LANGUAGE ARTS

This lesson shows how to cite four Internet resources—online journal articles, online magazine articles, Web sites, and e-mail. Use the Internet and other resources to find examples of each. Copy and paste the original content into a word-processing document. Then, using the samples in your lesson, properly cite each example.

 ### WEB PROJECT

Start your browser, then access the *http://lib.nmsu.edu/instruction/evalcrit.html* Web site. Review the Web site evaluation criteria contained on this page. Click the **Examples** and **Suggestions** links and review the information on both of these pages. Use your word-processing program to prepare a report on your findings, including an overview of at least three things you learned about Web site evaluation. The report should be a minimum of two pages.

 ### TEAMWORK PROJECT

The Web site located at *http://gateway.lib.ohio-state.edu/tutor/les1/index.html* contains a tutorial on Web site evaluation. Six key ideas are discussed—purpose, author, content, coverage, currency, and recognition. Launch your browser and access this site. Each team member selects one or more of the six key ideas. Each member then completes the entire tutorial, and together the team prepares a one- or two-page report on the content of this site.

CRITICAL*Thinking*

"WYSIWYG" is a Web site project located at *http://www.saskschools.ca/~ischool/tisdale/ integrated/wysiwyg/students.htm*. Access this Web site and complete the activities to create a set of reliability rules. Share your set of rules with the other students or submit a written report to your instructor.

CREATING A WEB PAGE

OBJECTIVES

Upon completion of this lesson, you should be able to:

- Understand how a Web page works.
- Create a planning document.
- Understand and explain basic HTML syntax.
- Insert headings.
- Apply bold and italics.
- Insert and work with lists.
- Add links.
- Add graphics.
- Publish a Web page.

Estimated Time: 1.5 hours

VOCABULARY

Absolute link

Attribute

Background

Body

Cascading Style Sheet

Character entities

E-mail link

Head

Headings

Home page

Images

Lists

Relative link

Title

Web site

Web page authoring programs, such as Macromedia Dreamweaver and Microsoft FrontPage, are used to create Web pages and to develop Web sites. A **Web site** is a group of related Web pages. These Web page authoring programs create the underlying code for the Web page. However, the process of creating a Web page independently of these programs is not difficult. To comprehend and fully understand Web page creation and to better use an authoring program, it is important to have an understanding of the hypertext markup language (HTML) that makes up much of the code. The basic HTML tags are covered in this lesson.

How a Web Page Works

Have you ever wondered how a Web page works? When you consider the billions of Web pages on the Internet, you might make the assumption that creating a Web page is easier said than done. In fact, not only is it incredibly easy to create a Web page, it also is a lot of fun.

Before beginning the process of creating a Web page, you need an understanding of some basic terminology:

- *Web page*: This is a plain text document on a server connected to the World Wide Web. Every Web page is identified by a uniform resource locator (URL), or unique Web address.

- *HTML:* This is the basic language of the Web. HTML is a series of tags that are integrated into a text document. These tags describe how the text should be formatted when a Web browser displays it on the screen.

- *Web browser:* A Web browser is an application program that interprets the HTML tags within the page and then displays the text on the computer screen. Some of the most popular Web browsers are Microsoft Internet Explorer, FireFox, and Netscape Navigator.

- *Web server:* A Web server displays Web pages and renders them into final form so they can be viewed by anyone with an Internet connection and a Web browser. Every Web server has a unique Web address or URL.

You might infer from these basic terminology definitions that you need a Web server before you can create your Web page. This is not true. The only tools you need are your Web browser and a text-editing program such as WordPad or Notepad. A Web browser easily can display your Web page from a personal computer. Once you create a Web page and have it in final format, most likely you will want to publish it to a Web server. Publishing a Web page is covered later in the lesson.

> **Net Tip**
>
> You can view the HTML code for most Web pages on the Web. Access the Internet with your browser and find a Web page that you like. On your browser's menu bar, click **View** and then click **Source** to display the HTML code.

Planning a Document

Many times when people start a project, they have a tendency to jump right in without any planning. Sometimes this works, but more often than not, they find themselves having to back up and redo some of the work. Planning might take some extra time in the beginning, but it will save considerable time in the long run. Before you start creating your personal Web page, consider some of the elements you might want to include. Figure 16-1 shows a suggested list of items.

FIGURE 16-1
Sample Web page outline

Sample Web Page Outline

Title:
A title for your Web page

Page Content:
Hobbies
School favorites
Family
Favorite vacation destination
Favorite sport(s)

Hyperlinks:
Sony PlayStation
Favorite sports team
Favorite movie(s)
Professional organization

Closing
E-mail address
Favorite quote

- *Title*: The ***title*** can be anything you choose, but should be relevant to the content of the page. An example title is "David Edwards' Personal Web Page." (You would substitute your name for David Edwards.) When someone accesses your Web page on the Internet, the title is displayed on the browser's title bar; it is not displayed in the Web page content.

- *Page content*: Determine what you want to include in your Web page. Do you want to share information about your family, your hobbies, your school, or sports? Make a list of what features you would like to include. Limit the content to one topic per Web page.

- *Links*: A link is a graphic, line of text, or both on a Web page that connects to another page on the same Web site or to one on a Web server located anywhere in the world. To what other Web sites would you like to link? Make a note of these. You will need the URL, or Web site address, for each link.

- *Closing comments*: Do you want to include any closing comments? Perhaps you want to add your e-mail address so that someone accessing your Web page can contact you. Do not include any personal information such as your address and/or telephone number.

A Basic Page

An HTML page has two components—page content and HTML tags. The page content is that part of the document that is displayed in the browser. This could be, for example, a list of your hobbies or other information about yourself, your place of employment, and so on. The main page or index page of most Web sites is referred to as the ***home page***.

HTML tags are easily identifiable because they are enclosed in brackets: <HTML>. The tags are not displayed in the browser. The HTML tags define the structure and layout of the Web page.

- Many tags come in pairs with a start tag and an end tag. For instance, <TITLE> is a start tag and </TITLE> is an end tag. You identify an end tag by including the slash (</>) character before the name of the tag. The start and end tag identify the content between them as being HTML formatted. These sometimes are called *container tags*.

- Some tags can be a single entity—that is, they do not have to have an end tag. An example is the <BR> tag, which indicates a line break. However, adding an end tag will not affect how the content is displayed.

- Tags are not case sensitive, but it is best to select a format and stay with it. In this lesson, uppercase letters are used for all HTML tags.

- Some tags can contain ***attributes***, which is an identifier for the tag. For example, the <BODY> tag is required for all HTML documents. But if you wanted the background color of your Web page to be blue, you can add an attribute so your <BODY> tag would look like this: <BODY bgcolor = "Blue">.

Every new page you create requires a standard set of tags structured in a particular sequence. This sequence is shown in Figure 16-2. When creating this structure, you can type the tags on individual lines, like that shown in Figure 16-2. The lines can be single-spaced or double-spaced. Or, you can type the tags on one continuous line, such as the following: <HTML><HEAD><TITLE></TITLE></HEAD><BODY></BODY></HTML>. Generally, for readability purposes, it is better to use individual lines for tags.

FIGURE 16-2
Required HTML tags

Required HTML Tags
<HTML>
<HEAD>
<TITLE>Insert Page Title</TITLE>
</HEAD>
<BODY>
Type page content here
</BODY>
</HTML>

In addition, inserting spaces or tabs between the tags in a line does not affect how the content appears in the browser. In other words, it does not make any difference if you press the Spacebar 20 times or press the Tab key 50 times! The only content that appears is that which is contained between the two <TITLE> tags and that contained between the two <BODY> tags.

Following is an explanation of the tags.

■ *HTML*: As shown in Figure 16-2, the first line in the document is <HTML>, which is a start tag; the last line is </HTML>, which is an end tag. All other tags and page content are contained within these two tags.

■ *HEAD*: The *HEAD* tag can contain information about the document. This information does not appear as part of the Web page content. The <TITLE> tag is one of the more commonly used tags that is contained within the start and end <HEAD> tags. Keywords also are often contained within the HEAD. Keywords describe the Web page document and are used by some search engines.

■ *TITLE*: The *title* tag (<TITLE>) defines the page's official title. The content entered between the start and end title tags is displayed on the browser's title bar.

■ *BODY*: All Web page content, or the *body* of the page, is contained between the start and end <BODY> tags.

In the examples in this book, Windows Notepad is used as the text editor to create the HTML documents and Internet Explorer is used as the browser to display the Web page. As mentioned previously, however, you can use any browser to display your Web page and any text-editing program to create a Web page. You can use a word-processing program for text editing, for instance, but you must save your document in text format with an .htm extension.

In Step-by-step 16.1, you create a template containing the tags shown in Figure 16-2.

S TEP-BY-STEP 16.1

1. Start your text-editing program. If you are using Notepad, click **Start**, point to **All Programs** (or **Programs** for Windows 2000 users), point to **Accessories**, and then click **Notepad**.

2. Type the tags shown below. Press the spacebar between the <TITLE> tags to create the space.

<HTML>

<HEAD>

<TITLE>   </TITLE>

</HEAD>

<BODY>

</BODY>

</HTML>

3. Compare your screen to Figure 16-3A. Each tag should be on its own line. Do not worry if the spacing between tags differs from that shown in the figure.

4. Click **File** on the menu bar and then click **Save**. In the Save As dialog box, enter **template.htm** in the File name box. Click the **drop-down arrow** on the Save as type box and click **All Files**, as shown in Figure 16-3B. Then, click **Save**.

FIGURE 16-3
(A) HTML template
(B) Notepad Save As dialog box

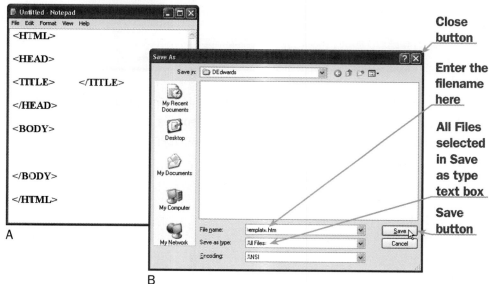

5. Close your text-editing program.

When you create HTML documents in the future, you can open this template file, save it with a different filename, and add your page content. Your next task is to open the template, add a Web page title and a line of page content, and then view your Web page in your browser. Note that most programs save with a particular file type or extension. To display this document name and to open the document, you might have to change the Files of type option to All files to view the list of documents.

Did You Know?

To insert a blank space into an HTML document, you type ** **. This is a nonbreaking space entity used to create horizontal white space.

STEP-BY-STEP 16.2

1. Start your text-editing program. Click **File** on the menu bar, and then navigate to the location where you saved your template. If you do not see the template file, click the **drop-down arrow** on the Files of type box, click **All Files**, and then click **template**, as shown in Figure 16-4. Then, click **Open**.

FIGURE 16-4
Notepad Open dialog box

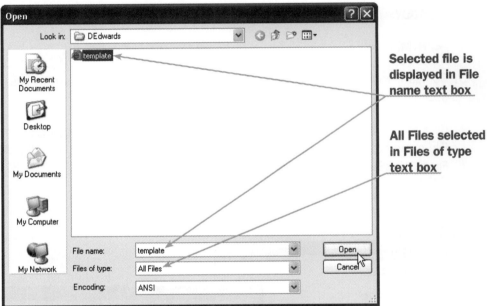

Selected file is displayed in File name text box

All Files selected in Files of type text box

2. Click between the start and end <TITLE> tags, and type **[Your first and last name]'s Web page**. When the browser displays the page, any extra spaces between the two title tags will be ignored. Therefore, it is OK, but not necessary, to delete the spaces.

3. Between the two <BODY> tags, type **Welcome to my Web page!**

STEP-BY-STEP 16.2 Continued

4. Click **File** on the menu bar and then click **Save As**. Save the document using your first and last name and the .htm extension. Use an underscore (_) between your first and last name (Example: *David_Edwards.htm*). Your Web page will look similar to that shown in Figure 16-5, except it will display your name instead of *David Edwards*.

FIGURE 16-5
HTML source page

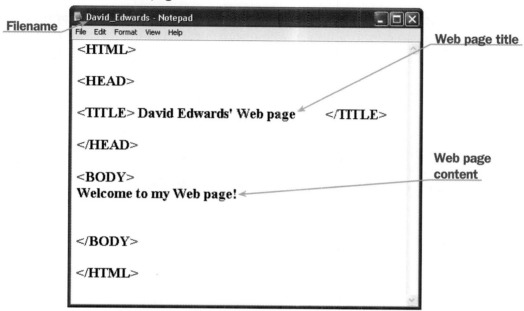

5. Start your browser.

6. Click **File** on the browser's menu bar and then click **Open** to display the Open dialog box.

7. Click **Browse**, locate your .htm file, click **Open**, and then click **OK**. The Web page is displayed in your browser, and is similar to that shown in Figure 16-6.

8. Close your browser. Keep your text-editing program open for Step-by-step 16.3.

FIGURE 16-6
Web page displayed in Internet Explorer

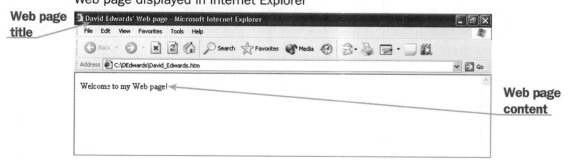

Congratulations! You have just created and displayed your first Web page.

Review your Web page as it appears in the browser and compare it to your HTML document. Notice that none of the HTML tags appear. The text you typed between the start and end <TITLE> tags is displayed in the browser's title bar. This text is not displayed as part of the document itself. The only text that is displayed as part of the document content is the text you typed between the start and end <BODY> tags: *Welcome to my Web page!*

Page Formatting

One of the first things you will discover when creating a Web page is that pressing the keyboard's Enter key has no effect on how a Web page appears in a browser. You can press Enter a dozen times or more, but it will not make a difference when the page is displayed. The browser ignores any blank lines you attempt to enter from the keyboard. Instead, you use HTML tags to start a new line and/or to leave spaces between lines.

Line Breaks

If you want to start a new line but not leave a space between lines, you use the break tag: <BR>. The break tag is a single entity. That is, you do not need a start and end tag. You can use the break tag to start a new line or you can use two break tags, one after the other, to insert a blank line.

Paragraph Breaks

A second way to insert a blank line is with the paragraph tag: <P>. An end tag </P> is not required, but many Web programmers include it as a matter of style. When the Web page is displayed in a browser, a paragraph tag shows a blank line between two paragraphs—basically the same thing as two line break tags <BR> entered consecutively.

In Step-by-step 16.3, you add content to your Web page, using break and paragraph tags to format the page.

 Technology Careers

CONSULTANT

Consultants provide professional advice or services. They have specialized knowledge that they can sell to their clients. Many consultants work on short-term projects for companies that might not have employees with the required skills for a particular job. Many consultants telecommute or work from home.

You can find successful consultants in just about every field imaginable. For instance, garage-sale consultants help you organize your garage and other consultants will help you arrange your closets. However, the information technology field has created an entire new field of consultants. Some examples are programming consultants, database consultants, and even Web designer and Web development consultants. If you enjoy working with computers and, in particular, developing Web pages, consulting might be a job field that you would want to investigate.

STEP-BY-STEP 16.3

1. At the end of the *Welcome to my Web page* line, type **
**.

2. Press **Enter**. (Remember that pressing Enter does not affect the way in which the Web page is displayed in a browser. You press Enter for readability purposes within your HTML document. Starting a new line or adding blank lines when creating your Web page makes it easier to read and edit your document.)

3. Type **I enjoy watching old movies.** Press **Enter** two times.

4. Type **<P>** and press **Enter**. Type **My favorite topic is mathematics.</P>**. Press **Enter**.

5. Type **<P>** and press **Enter**. Type **Football is my favorite sport.</P>**.

6. Click **File** on the menu bar and then click **Save**. The document should look similar to that shown in Figure 16-7. (Do not worry if the line spacing between tags on your page is different from that shown in the figure.)

FIGURE 16-7
HTML page

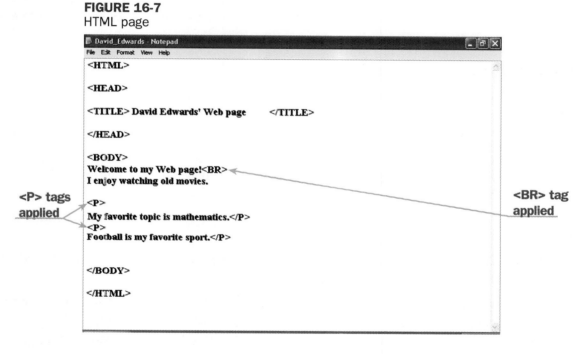

7. Start your browser.

8. Click **File** on the browser's menu bar and then click **Open**.

STEP-BY-STEP 16.3 Continued

9. Click **Browse**, locate your .htm Web page file, click **Open**, and then click **OK**. Your page opens in the browser, as shown in Figure 16-8.

FIGURE 16-8
Web page displayed in browser

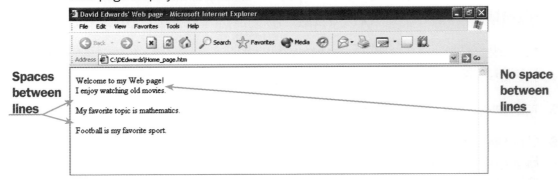

10. Compare your Web page to your HTML document. Note there is no blank line between the first two lines where you typed the <BR> tag, and there are blank lines between the two sentences where you typed the <P> tags.

11. Close your browser. Leave your text-editing program open for Step-by-step 16.4.

Lists

Organization of content on your Web page makes it more attractive and easier to read. Statistics indicate that people rarely read Web pages word by word; instead, they scan the page, picking out individual words and sentences. *Lists* are a popular way to arrange and organize text on a Web page. Within HTML, three types of lists are available:

- *Ordered list*: This generally is a numbered list and requires a start <OL> and an end </OL> tag. Each item in the list begins with <LI>.

- *Unordered list*: This generally is a bulleted list and requires a start <UL> and an end </UL> tag. Each item in the list begins with <LI>.

- *Definition list*: This is a list of terms with indented definitions, generally used for glossary items or other definitions. This list requires a start tag <DL> and an end tag </DL>. In addition, the tag <DT> is required for the term and <DD> is required for the definition.

In Step-by-step 16.4, you create the three types of lists.

STEP-BY-STEP 16.4

1. Click **File** on the menu bar and click **Open**. In the Open dialog box, click the **drop-down arrow** on the Files of type box and click **All Files**. Select the **template.htm** file and then click **Open**.

2. Click **File** on the menu bar and then click **Save As**. Click the **drop-down arrow** on the Save as type box and click **All Files**. Click in the **File name** box, type **HTML_examples.htm**, and then click **Save**.

STEP-BY-STEP 16.4 Continued

3. Type **HTML_examples** between the two Title tags.

4. Click below the <BODY> tag and type **Ordered List**. Press **Enter**.

5. Type **<OL>** to begin your ordered list. Press **Enter**.

6. Type **<LI>** to begin the first item in the list.

7. Type **bananas**. Press **Enter**. Type **<LI>** and then type **apples**. Press **Enter**. Type **<LI>** and then type **peaches**. Press **Enter**. Type **</OL>**. Press **Enter**.

8. Type **<P></P>**. Press **Enter**. Type **<P></P>**. Press **Enter** two times.

9. Type **Unordered List**. Press **Enter**.

10. Type the following. Press **Enter** after each line.
<UL>
<LI>beans
<LI>corn
<LI>okra
</UL>
<P></P>
<P></P>

11. Press **Enter** two times. Type the following. Press **Enter** after each line.
Definition List
<DL>
<DT>Apple
<DD>a fruit
<DT>Tomato
<DD>a fruit
<DT>Corn
<DD>a vegetable
</DL>
<P></P>
<P></P>

STEP-BY-STEP 16.4 Continued

12. Compare your document to Figure 16-9, make corrections if necessary, and then save your file. Note that the entire HTML document is not displayed in Figure 16-9—just the text and HTML tags you entered in this exercise.

FIGURE 16-9
HTML tags for list types

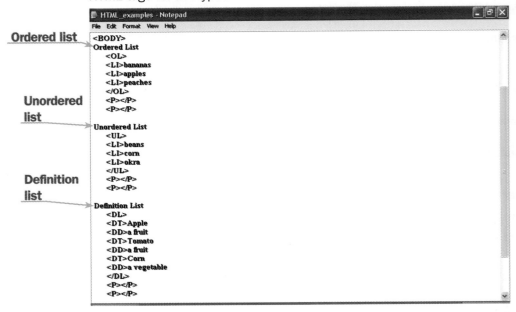

13. Display the file in your browser. It should look like that shown in Figure 16-10. Close the browser. Keep your text-editing program open for Step-by-step 16.5.

FIGURE 16-10
List types displayed in browser

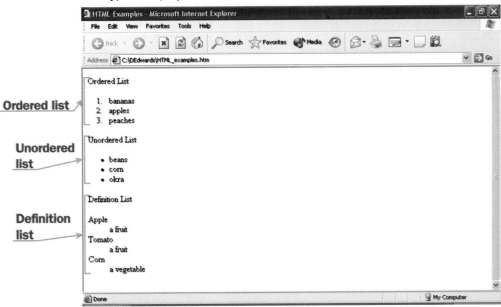

Text Formatting

Now that you have learned some ways you can control the placement of text in the browser, it is time to learn how to format the text. Just like formatting text within a word-processing program, you also can apply formatting to text that is displayed in a Web browser. Some of the text formatting tags you can apply are as follows:

- *Bold*: To bold text requires start <B> and end </B> tags. Text that is surrounded by these tags appears as bold in your browser.

- *Italics*: To display italicized text, use the start <I> and end </I> tags.

- *Underline*: To underline text, use the start <U> and end </U> tags.

You can apply one tag such as bold to a word, sentence, or paragraph, or you can apply two or all three tags at one time.

Center

Another way to organize text on the page is to use the <CENTER> tag. This tag requires both a start and end tag. Simply enclose the text between the start tag and the end tag and the text will be centered when displayed in a browser. You can center a single word, a sentence, a paragraph, a series of paragraphs, a table, or even an image.

Figures 16-11A and 16-11B shows how to enter the HTML formatting and centering tags and illustrates what they look like in a browser.

FIGURE 16-11

(A) HTML for bold, italics, underline, and center

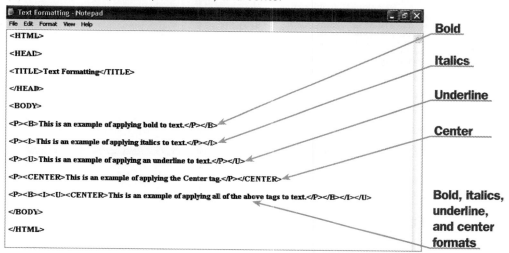

(B) Text formatting displayed in browser

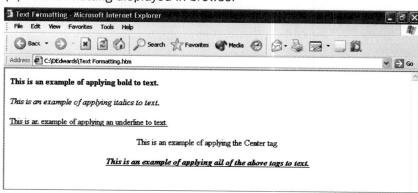

Headings

Styles are covered briefly in Lesson 10 of this course. A style is a set of formatting characteristics that you can apply to text in your document to quickly change its appearance. HTML does support styles, but only through style sheets. *Style sheets*, also known as *Cascading Style Sheets (CSS)*, are a collection of formatting rules that control the appearance of content in a Web page. Style sheets are an advanced topic and are not covered in this book. The HTML heading tags, however, do provide some formatting options. The characteristics of *headings* include the typeface, size, and the extra space above or below the heading. The browser you use, however, determines the final appearance.

Six levels of HTML headings are available. The start tag for the first level is <H1> and the end tag is </H1>. For the other five levels, just substitute the desired number within the start and end tags. Level 1 is the largest and level 6 is the smallest. In Figure 16-12A, notice that no break <BR> or paragraph <P> tags are added following each line because they are not needed. In Figure 16-12B in which the Web page is displayed in the browser, space appears between each of the headings. This is a characteristic of the heading tag. In Step-by-step 16.5, you add and center a heading.

FIGURE 16-12
(A) HTML for heading tags

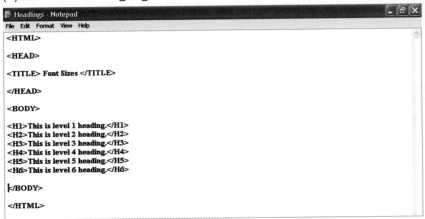

(B) Formatted headings displayed in browser

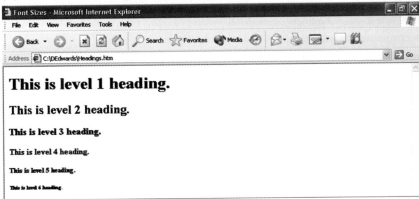

S TEP-BY-STEP 16.5

1. Your text editing program should still be open. Open your **template.htm** document and then save it as **Home_page.htm**. Type **[Your name's] Web page** between the start and end <TITLE> tags.

2. Click below the **<BODY>** tag. Type **<H1><CENTER>Welcome to the Web page of [your name]! </H1></CENTER>**. This applies the H1 heading format to the line of text and centers it on the page.

3. Press **ENTER** two times.

4. Type **My three favorite sports are:**. Then, use the **<B>** text formatting tag to apply bold to the text you just typed.

5. Create an unordered list **<UL>** listing your three favorite sports. Use the **<I>** text formatting tag to apply italics to each item in the list.

6. Save your file and then display it in your browser. Your Web page should look similar to that shown in Figure 16-13, but your data will be different.

7. Close your browser. Keep your Home_page.htm file open for Step-by-step 16.6.

FIGURE 16-13
Web page displayed in browser (your data will be different)

[Your Name]
Web page
title

Bold
applied

Italicized
unordered
list

Your name
appears
here

Heading 1
applied

Changing the Font, Font Size, and Font Color

When you browse the Internet, your browser displays the text based on a default font size, type, and color. Recall that a font is a design of type. The font, font size, and font color, however, can be changed. This is done through the start <FONT> and end </FONT> tags.

You probably know from experience that changing the font or text size in a word-processing program is easy; you can quickly make the text very small or very large. Your options within HTML are not as flexible as they are within a word-processing program. Most browsers support and display seven different font or text sizes. The sizes range from 1, which is the smallest, to 7, which is the largest. The default font size is 3. Recall that an attribute is an identifier for the tag. To change the font size, you add the SIZE attribute to the FONT tag, for example: <FONT SIZE = 5>. Figure 16-14A shows the HTML tags used to change font sizes, and Figure 16-14B shows how the various font sizes look in a browser.

FIGURE 16-14
(A) HTML tags for changing font sizes

(B) Font sizes displayed in browser

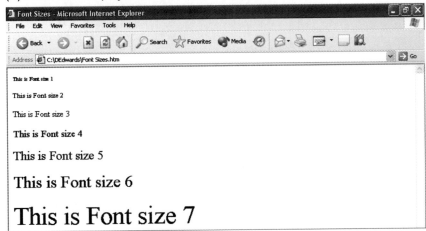

Changing the font color is just as easy as changing the font size. This is accomplished by using the COLOR attribute; for example: <FONT COLOR = RED>. Another option is to combine the font size and font color within one tag. Example: <FONT SIZE = 1 COLOR = RED>. Figure 16-15A shows the HTML tags used to change font color and size, and Figure 16-15B illustrates how the font color and size appear in a browser.

FIGURE 16-15

(A) HTML tags for changing font sizes and font color

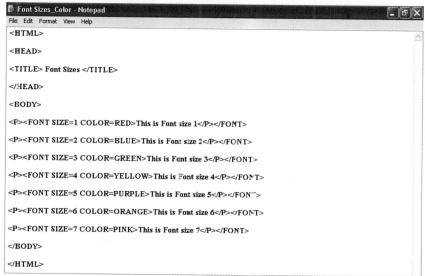

(B) Font sizes and colors displayed in browser

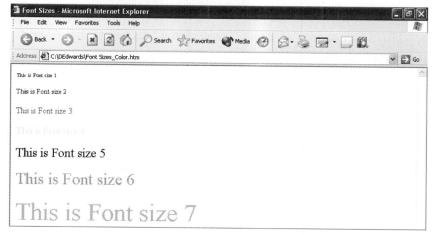

You also can change the font type. This is accomplished by using the FACE attribute; for example: <FONT FACE = ARIAL>. If desired, you can specify font color, size, and face all within one start and end tag. Figures 16-16A and 16-16B show examples of applying and displaying the face, color, and size attributes.

FIGURE 16-16
(A) Font tags specifying face, color, and size

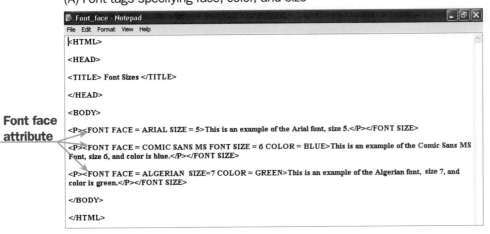

Font face attribute

(B) Font face, color, and size displayed in browser

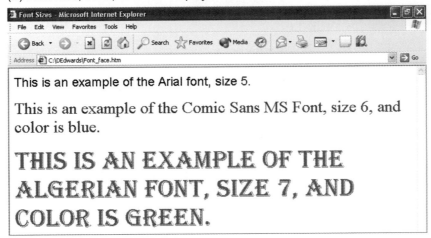

In Step-by-step 16.6, you apply the <FONT> tag and the FACE, SIZE, and COLOR attributes.

S TEP-BY-STEP 16.6

1. Your text-editing program should still be open. Click below the end unordered list </UL> tag, and then press **ENTER** two times.

2. Type **My favorite author is Charles Dickens.**

STEP-BY-STEP 16.6 Continued

3. Apply the **<FONT>** tag and the following attributes to the sentence you typed in Step 2: **<FONT FACE = ALGERIAN SIZE = 6 COLOR = RED>**. Do not forget to add the ending **</FONT>** tag. (If the Algerian font is not available on your computer, substitute another font such as Arial or Times New Roman.)

4. Save your file and display the Web page in your browser. It should look similar to that shown in Figure 16-17.

5. Close your browser. Keep your Home_page.htm file open for Step-by-step 16.7.

FIGURE 16-17
Web page displayed in browser

Font face, size, and color added to sentence

Links

A defining feature of any Web page is its links or hyperlinks, which are active references to other parts of the same document or to other documents. The other documents can be on the same computer in another folder or disk, on a local network server (intranet), or stored on a computer in another city, state, or country. When you click a link, the Web page associated with the link is displayed on the screen. Links within a document generally are absolute links, relative links, and e-mail links.

Absolute Links

Providing links between documents gives the user easy access to related information. Recall from Lesson 2 that every Web page on the Internet has its own unique address. If you know the address or URL of the document and the address of the computer on which it resides, you can link to it. *Absolute links* (also called external links) are links that give the full address to a Web page on the Internet. These links use a fixed file location or Web address. The fixed location identifies the destination by its full address. An example of an absolute link is *<A HREF = HTTP://WWW.ROCKCLIMBING.COM> Rock Climbing </A>*. The <A> within this tag represents *anchor* and the HREF represents *hyperlink reference*. Figure 16-18A shows how to create absolute links in an HTML document; Figure 16-18B shows how they appear in a browser.

FIGURE 16-18

(A) Font tags specifying absolute links

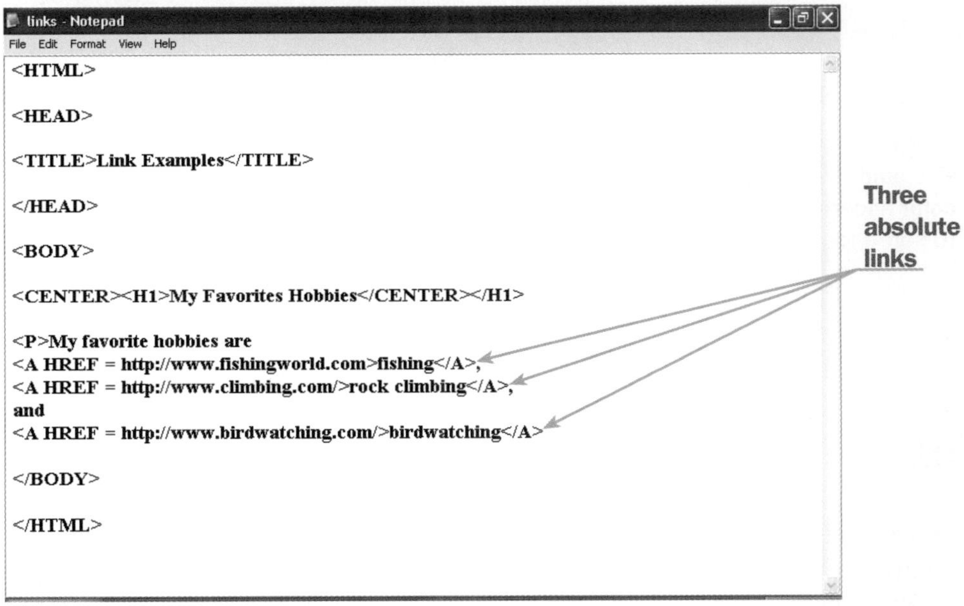

(B) Links displayed in browser

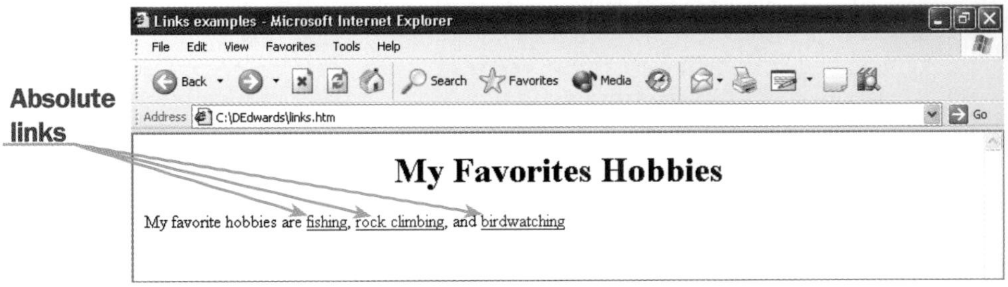

One of the greatest problems on the Web is that users do not know where they are going when they follow links. Most browsers, however, include the capability to pop open a short description of the link. When the user moves the mouse pointer over the link, the description is displayed at the bottom of the screen.

Relative Links

When all the files, including images and other related files, are saved in one folder or will be published on the same Web server, you can use relative links. A *relative link*, also called an *internal link*, gives the file location in relation to the current document. When you use relative links, you can move the folder and files that contain the hyperlink and maintain the destination of the link without breaking the path of the relative link.

The tags for a relative link are <A HREF = "FILE-NAME"> </A>. Assume that David Edwards' Web page is located in a folder named DEdwards. David has two pages in the DEdwards folder: Home_page and David_Edwards. He would like to link to his Home_page from his David_Edwards Web page. To do this, he creates a relative link. The link would look like the following: <A HREF = "Home_page">Home_page </A>.

Did You Know?

Some Web developers include *http://* as part of an absolute link; for example: *<A HREF = HTTP://WWW.ROCKCLIMBING.COM> Rock Climbing</A>*. However, it is not necessary to include the http protocol.

E-Mail Links

Another type of link is an e-mail link. An *e-mail link* displays a blank e-mail form containing the recipient's address. It is a good idea to include your e-mail address on every page of your site. When the user clicks the e-mail link, the browser starts a mail program, and the e-mail address automatically is inserted in the address line. You use the <A> tag to create the link; for example: *<A HREF="mailto:joesmith@hotmail.com">Joe Smith</A>*.

In Step-by-step 16.7, you add an absolute link to the name *Charles Dickens*, then add your name, and then an e-mail link. You will need to substitute your name and e-mail address for those used in Step 3 of the exercise. You must be online and have Internet access to display the Web site for the Charles Dickens Museum to which you link.

STEP-BY-STEP 16.7

1. Your *Home_page.htm* file should still be open. Click to the left of *Charles Dickens* and type: **<A HREF=http://www.dickensmuseum.com>**.

2. Click after the </FONT> tag at the end of *My favorite author is Charles Dickens* and type **</A>**. Press **Enter** two times.

3. Type **<P><A HREF="MAILTO:DAVIDEDWARDS@HOTMAIL.COM">David Edwards</A></P>**. (Substitute your name for *DAVIDEDWARDS* and your e-mail address for *HOTMAIL.COM*.)

4. Save your file and display the Web page in your browser.

5. Click the **Charles Dickens** link to display the Charles Dickens museum Web page. Click the browser's **Back** button to return to your Web page.

STEP-BY-STEP 16.7 Continued

6. Click your linked name to display the New Message dialog box. Your screen should look similar to that shown in Figure 16-19. If you are using Microsoft Office 2000, the dialog box may be different.

FIGURE 16-19
Links in the browser window

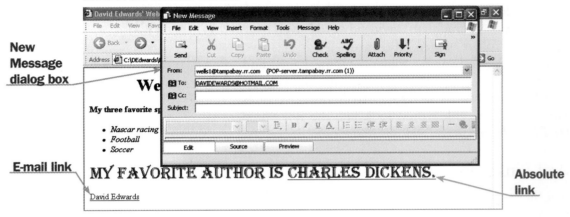

7. Send yourself an e-mail and then close the browser window. Close your text-editing program.

Ethics in Technology

UNDERSTANDING E-MAIL ENCRYPTION

When you send an e-mail message, you might not realize that it can literally bounce all over the world before it reaches its final destination. As your e-mail message travels from computer to computer, it might encounter "sniffers," or software programs that are waiting to alter or tamper with your e-mail. Most of the time, the e-mail that you send might not be that important. It could be a note to a friend or a request for information. On the other hand, it could contain your computer network login and password or maybe even a credit card number.

Several companies have made programs available to encrypt your e-mail. In fact, there are literally hundreds of e-mail encryption programs. If you are using recent versions of Netscape Communicator or Internet Explorer, you have encryption options. Internet Explorer, for example, has two different types of certificates to protect your privacy: a personal certificate and a Web site certificate.

Encryption programs work with cryptographic types. The user provides a password and the program turns the password into a cryptographic type. There is both a public type and a private type. The user retains the private type for decryption purposes.

Images

Images (also called *graphics*) add life to your Web site and make it exciting and fun. As much as they can add to a page, however, they also can slow the downloading of your Web page, especially for someone with slow access to the Internet. Many times when it takes too long to download a page, the person browsing the Web site clicks the browser's Stop button and moves on to another site. Keep this in mind when you are creating your pages.

Image Formats

Two popular image types (GIF and JPG) are supported by most browsers and are displayed on the Web

- *GIF*: This is the most commonly used file type. It stands for graphic interchange format and is pronounced "jif."

- *JPG* or *JPEG*: This is another commonly used file format that generally results in larger file sizes than GIF. This format is best used for photographs and other photo-quality images. JPEG stands for joint photographic experts group.

- *PNG*: This image type is native to Macromedia Fireworks and is not as widely used as GIF and JPEG. *PNG* stands for portable network graphics.

To add an image to your Web page, use the <IMG> tag. This is a single tag; that is, there is no end tag. However, many attributes are available that you can use within this tag. Table 16-1 on the next page contains a list of image attributes. Three of the most popular are as follows:

> **Net Tip**
>
> For information on broadband Internet connections (cable, fiber-optic, and DSL), access the *www.speedguide.net* Web site. This site has a little bit of everything dedicated to connection speed.

> **Internet**
>
> If you are looking for a Web site with free graphics and information on creating graphics, try Laurie McCanna, author of the "Creating Great Web Graphics" Web site located at *www.mccannas.com*.

- *SRC*: This stands for *source*, and is mandatory. An example is: *<IMG SRC = "David.gif">*.

- *ALT*: This stands for *alternate*. Use this attribute to provide alternative text. Some people with slow Internet access turn off automatic image loading. Using the ALT attribute provides them with an indication of the nature of the picture. For visually impaired users who use speech synthesizers with text-only browsers, the text in the ALT tag is spoken out loud. In some browsers, this text also appears when the pointer is over the image. An example is: *<IMG SRC = "David.gif" ALT = "David Edwards' picture">*.

- *ALIGN*: Use this attribute to align the image on the page—bottom, middle, right, left, or top. An example is: *<IMG SRC = "David.gif" ALT = "David Edwards' picture" ALIGN = left>*.

TABLE 16-1
Image attributes

ATTRIBUTE	FUNCTION
ALIGN	Controls alignment; options include bottom, middle, top, left, and right
ALT	Alternative text is displayed when the user moves the mouse pointer over the image
BORDER	Defines the border width
HEIGHT	Defines the height of the image
HSPACE	Defines the horizontal space that separates the text from the image
SRC	Defines the location or URL of the image
VSPACE	Defines the vertical space that separates the text from the image
WIDTH	Defines the width of the image

When you look at a Web page with images, the images appear to be part of the page. In reality, however, if the browser displays three images, you have four separate files—the HTML file and the three image files. When the browser encounters the <IMG> tag, it knows to look for the SRC or source. The image could be located in the same folder as your HTML document, or it could be located on a totally different computer on the other side of the world. If the image is in a folder on your computer and the folder also contains the HTML file in which the image will appear, an example link would be *<IMG SRC = "RACECAR.GIF">*. If it is an external link, you would specify the address of the image, just like you specify the address of an absolute link; for example: *<IMG SRC = "www.rockclimbing.com/David.gif">*.

You might wonder how the browser knows where to display the image on the page. The default is the left margin. You can, however, place images almost anywhere within the body of your Web page. They can be on a line by themselves, at the end of a paragraph, at the beginning of a line, in the middle of a line, and so on. Using the <ALIGN> tag and other attributes listed in Table 16-1, you can control to an extent where they are placed. Figure 16-20A shows how to enter image tags in an HTML document; Figure 16-20B shows how they appear in a browser.

FIGURE 16-20
(A) Image tags

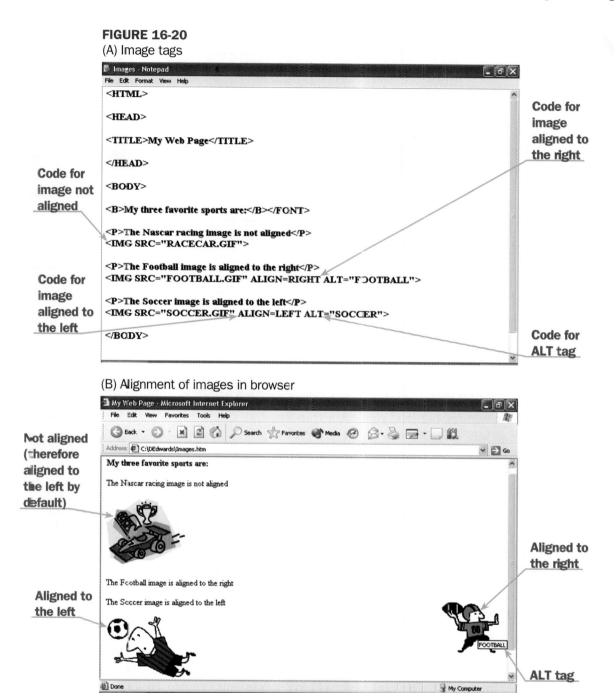

Code for
image not
aligned

Code for
image
aligned to
the left

Code for
image
aligned to
the right

Code for
ALT tag

(B) Alignment of images in browser

Not aligned
(therefore
aligned to
the left by
default)

Aligned to
the left

Aligned to
the right

ALT tag

Character Entities

Some characters have a special meaning in HTML, such as the less than sign (<) that defines the start of an HTML tag. In order for the browser to display these characters, you must insert *character entities* in the HTML document. A character entity has three parts: an ampersand (&), a # and an entity number, and a semicolon (;). The most common character entity in

---

Internet

Many places on the Web provide free images. Access the Hotbot search engine at *www.hotbot.com* and Ask Jeeves "Where can I find free graphics?"

HTML is the nonbreaking space. If you press the Spacebar five times in your HTML document, for example, the browser only recognizes one. However, for each nonbreaking space entity you type, a space is added to the content when it appears in the browser. Table 16-2 lists some of the more common character entities.

TABLE 16-2
Character entities

CHARACTER	DESCRIPTION	ENTITY
&	ampersand	&amp;
'	apostrophe	&#39;
>	greater than	&gt;
<	less than	&lt;
	nonbreaking space	
"	quotation mark	&quot;

Horizontal Rules and Bulleted Lists

Many Web designers use horizontal rules (also called lines) to separate blocks of text. The horizontal rule <HR> is a single-entry tag that renders a thin line that extends across the width of the browser window. Simply enter the tag and the line is displayed. It does not require an ending tag.

Another option for separating blocks of text is to use some type of graphical divider. Many graphical dividers are available for download on the Web, or you can create your own with a paint or draw program such as Jasc Paint Shop Pro or Adobe PhotoShop. To add a graphical horizontal line to your Web page, simply go to the location within the document where you would like it to appear. Then use the <IMG SRC> tag to insert it; for example: *<IMG SRC = "graphical_line.gif">*.

> **Internet**
>
> If you are looking for backgrounds for your Web site, then one of the first places you should visit is Yahoo!'s Background for Web Pages. Here you will find an extensive list of links to many Web sites. Just go to *www.yahoo.com*, click the **Images** link, and search for Web page backgrounds.

Earlier in this lesson, you learned how to create and display bulleted lists. Suppose you prefer graphical bullets instead of the standard bullets. This also is accomplished easily with the <IMG SRC> tag. Simply place the tag and the image name before the line of text. Figure 16-21A shows how to enter rule, line, and bullet tags in an HTML document; Figure 16-21B shows how they are displayed in a browser.

Backgrounds

As you surf the Web, you might notice the background color of many Web pages is either white or gray. Generally, the browser you are using determines the background color. You also might have noticed that many Web pages have color or an image for the *background*. You, too, can add color or images to the background of your Web pages. To add a background color, include the BGCOLOR attribute in the <BODY> tag; for example: *<BODY BGCOLOR = "PINK">*.

To add a background image to your Web page, specify the image name within the <BODY> tag; for example: *<BODY BACKGROUND = "IMAGE.GIF">*. Refer to Figure 16-21. Figure 16-21A shows how to enter a background color, a nonbreaking space, a horizontal rule, and graphical lines and bullet tags in an HTML document; Figure 16-21B shows how they appear in a browser.

FIGURE 16-21

(A) Background color, nonbreaking space, rule line, and bullet tags

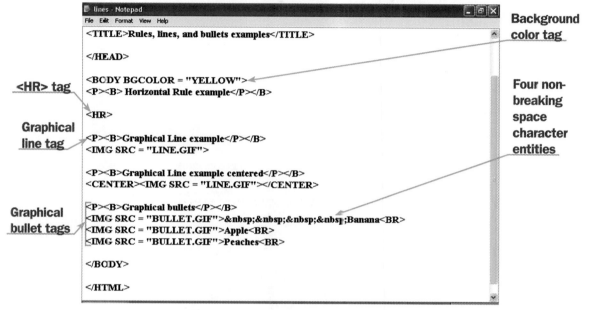

(B) Background color, nonbreaking space, rule, line, and bullet graphics in the browser

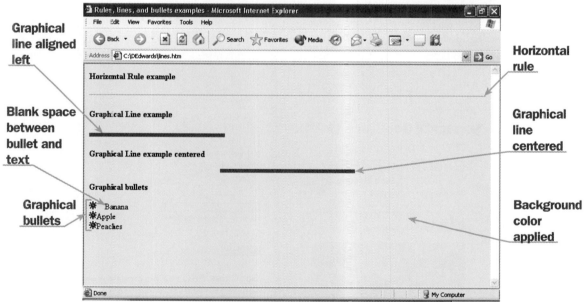

Publishing Your Web Page

Your school might have its own Web server that you can use to publish your Web page creations. If not, do not be dismayed. Several Web sites on the Internet offer free space. Two of the more popular of these are Tripod, located at *http://www.tripod.lycos.com/,* and Yahoo! GeoCities, located at *geocities.yahoo.com/home/.* See Figures 16-22A and 16-22B.

FIGURE 16-22

(A) Tripod free Web space

(B) Yahoo! Geocities free Web space

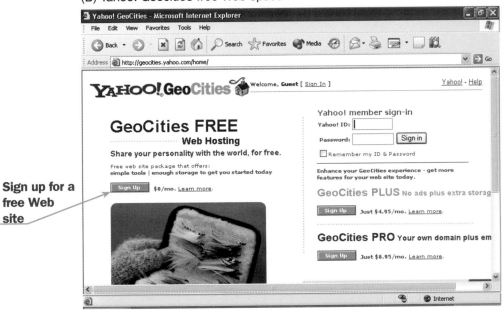

Most of the sites that provide free space also provide step-by-step instructions on how to upload your page. Just locate and click the "sign up" link or the link indicating a free home page or free space on their server. If you wonder how an organization can offer free space for you to save your Web pages, check out the advertising on the Web site. These companies generate their income by selling banners and other advertising space.

SUMMARY

In this lesson, you learned:

- A Web page is a document on the World Wide Web and is defined by a unique URL.

- HTML is the language of the Web.

- A Web browser is an application program that interprets the HTML tags within the page and then displays the text on the computer screen.

- A basic Web page has both page content and HTML tags.

- Some tags come in pairs, and others are single entities.

- Every Web page requires a particular set of tags structured in a particular format.

- Pressing the keyboard Enter key when creating a Web page has no effect on how the page is displayed.

- To start a new line in a Web page, use the break <BR> tag.

- To insert a blank line in a Web page, use the paragraph <P> tag.

- HTML supports three types of lists that you can use to organize text on a Web page.

- The <CENTER> tag is used to center text or graphics.

- HTML supports bold, italics, and underline text formatting.

- HTML supports changing of font size and font color.

- Seven different font sizes are supported by most browsers.

- Six levels of HTML headings are supported by most browsers.

- A link is an active reference to another part of the same document or to another document.

- A relative link gives the file location in relation to the current document.

- Absolute links are hyperlinks to other Web sites.

- One of the most common types of non-Web links is e-mail.

- Three different image types are supported by browsers—GIF, JPEG, and PNG.

- HTML supports the use of horizontal lines to separate blocks of text.

- HTML supports adding a background color or image to a Web page.

- Many Web sites provide free space online for publishing your Web page.

VOCABULARY *Review*

Define the following terms:

Absolute link	Character entities	Images
Attribute	E-mail link	Lists
Background	Head	Relative link
Body	Headings	Title
Cascading Style Sheets	Home page	

REVIEW *Questions*

MULTIPLE CHOICE

Select the best response for the following statements.

1. _____ is the language of the Web.
   A. Image
   B. BGCOLOR
   C. HTML
   D. HTTP

2. The _____ of your Web page is what appears on the browser title bar.
   A. body
   B. heading
   C. title
   D. closing

3. All Web page content is contained between the start and end _____ tags.
   A. Title
   B. Head
   C. IMG
   D. Body

4. To leave a blank line on a Web page document, use the _____ tag.
   A.
   B. <P>
   C. <END>
   D. <START>

5. Most browsers support _____ different font sizes.
   A. one
   B. three
   C. seven
   D. twelve

TRUE/FALSE

Circle T if the statement is true or F if the statement is false.

T   F   1. The only way you can view your Web page is to log on to a Web server.

T   F   2. Within a Web page, you can change the color of text.

T   F   3. All Web page backgrounds are either white or gray.

T   F   4. A relative link would link to another Web site.

T   F   5. Use the ALT attribute to display a text description of an image.

FILL IN THE BLANK

Complete the following sentences by writing the correct word or words in the blanks provided.

1. A(n) _____ is a thin line that extends across the width of the browser.

2. Use the _____ attribute to display a background color.

3. Use the _____ tag to create bold text.

4. A(n) _____ list generally is a numbered list.

5. To center text or an image on a Web page, use the _____ tag.

PROJECTS

CROSS-CURRICULAR—MATHEMATICS

Create a Web page document for your mathematics class. Include within this document a heading, a numbered list, a background color, and absolute links to two mathematics-related Web sites.

CROSS-CURRICULAR—SCIENCE

Select a special science project on which you might be working or an area of science in which you are interested. Create two Web pages for this project. Include somewhere within these two pages an H1 heading, a definition list, a background color, relative links from one of the Web pages to the other, and absolute links to at least one other Web site on your selected topic. Include at least two images in one of your Web pages.

CROSS-CURRICULAR—SOCIAL STUDIES

Ask your social studies instructor for a list of topics that you will study in the next month, or select a social studies-related topic in which you have an interest. Create a Web page on your selected topic. Include a heading and a background color. Use *"Links to (name of topic)"* for the heading. Search the Web for Web sites related to the topics. Create a list of absolute links to the Web sites. List at least 10 Web sites and include a short description of what can be found at each Web site.

CROSS-CURRICULAR—LANGUAGE ARTS

Your instructor has asked you to write an article about your last vacation. After you write the article, convert it to a Web page document. Illustrate the page with images and graphical dividers.

 ### WEB PROJECT

You are a member of a group learning about HTML and how to create and publish Web pages. Your instructor has asked you to put together a presentation on HTML commands not covered in this lesson. You are to research, report, and present an example of at least two linked Web pages and display the HTML code used to create the Web pages.

 ### TEAMWORK PROJECT

Now that you have the basic skills necessary to create a Web page, you want to create at least three pages identifying your favorite hobby. Create the hobby Web pages. Use as many tags as possible that were introduced in this lesson. To extend your HTML knowledge, use *www.ask.com* for HTML tutorial links. Include any additional HTML tags that you might find in one of these tutorials. Create a link from each page to the other page.

CRITICAL *Thinking*

Investigate the possibility of publishing one of the Web pages you created in the preceding end-of-lesson projects. Review the information presented at the end of this lesson on the Lycos and Yahoo! Web sites, which provide free Web site hosting. Then, use a search engine such as Google and search for and locate at least one other Web site that provides free Web site space. Compare the three Web sites and determine which one you would select to host your Web page. Explain why you selected the particular Web site to host your site.

Technology, the Workplace, and Society

As the age of innovation blazes its way into the world of technology, changes are taking place in every aspect of life—from home to school to the workplace. And the changes are swift and dramatic. Just as soon as we settle in and become comfortable with a new technological change, along comes something more innovative and different. As things look now, the world is in for a lot more of this type of change. Some of these changes have, unfortunately, also brought about concerns over things such as computer crimes, computer health-related issues, and even the need for laws to protect those injured by computer crimes and offenses.

Education

Many similarities exist between today's schools and those of 40 or 50 years ago. In many classrooms, the students still sit in rows and the teacher stands at the front of the class, lecturing and using a chalkboard. However, in other classrooms, a technological revolution is taking place.

Many people predict that technology will change the entire structure of education. Others believe the way in which most students receive education today—students and teacher in a traditional classroom—will remain for many years. Regardless of who is right, one thing is certain: Technology is having a tremendous impact on education in general and in more and more classrooms around the world.

Internet

The Internet and the World Wide Web are the biggest factors affecting education today. For instance, not so long ago, if a science teacher gave the class a project to find out how a television works, the students would go to the library and do the research. In many of today's classrooms, the students most likely go to the Internet, and maybe to the HowStuffWorks Web site to find this information. See Figure 17-1. Using the Internet is a fast and easy way to find the information you need.

FIGURE 17-1
HowStuffWorks Web site

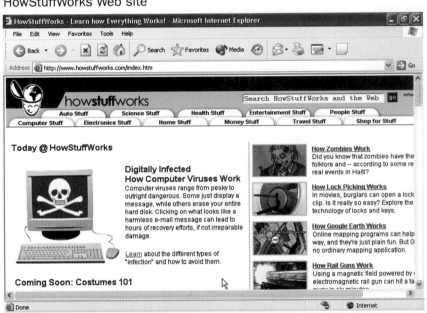

Perhaps you are having a geography test next week, and you would like to "pretest" your geography knowledge. You can use the Internet as your resource. One site you might visit is the National Geographic Bee (*http://www.nationalgeographic.com/geographybee/index.html*), which is shown in Figure 17-2, or the CIA Geography Trivia Game page (*http://www.cia.gov/cia/ciakids/games/geography/2003/index.shtml*).

FIGURE 17-2
National Geographic Web page

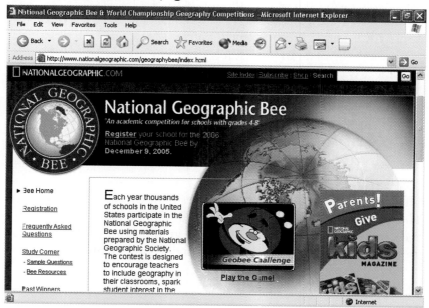

You might have had an opportunity to participate in or work with a *WebQuest*. Bernie Dodge developed the WebQuest Model at San Diego State University. This type of activity uses the Internet for investigation and problem solving. Hundreds of WebQuests have been developed by teachers and professors. Example WebQuests include countries around the world, politics, learning about money, and so on. You can find a list and a link to some of these at *http://webquest.sdsu.edu/*. An example of one interesting WebQuest is titled Decisions! Decisions! (*http://drb.lifestreamcenter.net/Lessons/decisions/index.htm*). See Figure 17-3.

FIGURE 17-3
Decisions! Decisions! WebQuest

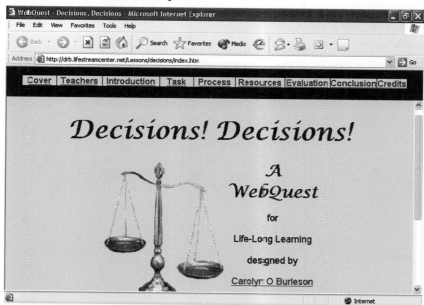

Online Learning

For some time, people have been able to obtain their education via distance learning methods. Traditional methods include television and correspondence courses that are completed through the mail. In the last few years, the Internet has become a way to deliver *online learning*. At the elementary and secondary school levels, the Department of Education supports an initiative called the Star Schools Program. This program provides online education learning to millions of learners annually.

Imagine, if you will, being able to complete high school from home. This is possible in some states. For instance, any high school student who is a Florida resident can attend the Florida Virtual School online for free. This is a certified diploma-granting school, open any time—night or day. Students enroll, log on, and complete their work through the guidance of a certified Florida high school teacher. See Figure 17-4. Several other states also provide similar programs.

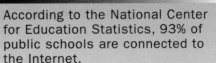

Did You Know?

According to the National Center for Education Statistics, 93% of public schools are connected to the Internet.

You might be given an assignment to read a book or an article in a journal. Instead of having to check out a book or journal from the library, you might be able to access and read it on the computer.

FIGURE 17-4
Florida Virtual School Web site

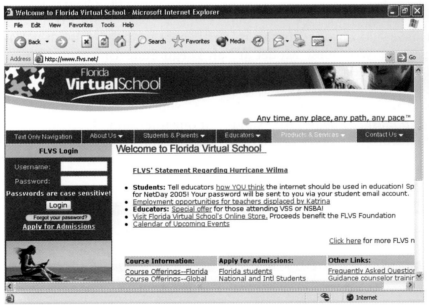

New types of programs are on the market that help teachers deliver online courses. These programs are an integrated set of Web-based teaching tools that provide guidance and testing for the student. Two of the more popular of these are Blackboard and WebCT. See Figure 17-5.

FIGURE 17-5
WebCT example

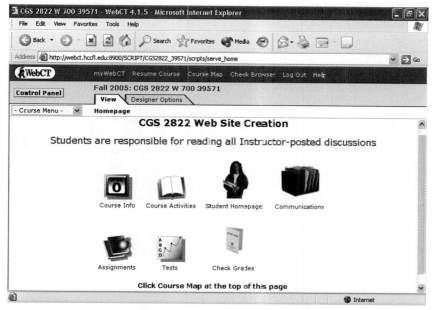

Computer-Based Learning

Most likely, 20 or 30 students are in your class. And all of these students (plus yourself) learn in different ways and at different rates. Likewise, information can be presented in many formats and at different levels. This could be through lectures, homework, group projects, movies, and so on. The more ways in which information can be presented, the more opportunities everyone has to use their own learning styles so they can master the particular topic.

You might have heard the terms *computer-based learning* or computer-assisted instruction (CAI). These are examples of instructional methods by which the teacher uses the computer to deliver the instruction. Basically, this type of instruction uses a computer as a tutor. For many students this is one of the most effective ways to learn. For example, you might have difficulty understanding a specific mathematics concept, such as how to calculate percentages. Your teacher might suggest a special computer program to help reinforce that difficult concept. Using such a program provides you with the opportunity to master the idea by reviewing the concept as many times as necessary. See Figure 17-6. Or you might be taking a biology class and instead of using live specimens for experiments, you may complete all of your lab assignments using computer software. These types of labs are called dry labs.

FIGURE 17-6
Students at work in computer lab

Simulations

Learning can be fun for everyone, especially if it is done through computer simulation. *Simulations* are models of real-world activities, designed to allow the user to experiment and explore environments that might be dangerous, unavailable, or inaccessible. Using simulations, you can explore other worlds and settings without leaving your classroom. Simulations are fun and engaging and allow learners to apply new skills in a risk-free environment. With this type of model, you learn by doing. You can find simulations on the Internet, or the simulations might come on a CD-ROM that you run from a local computer.

Some example simulations are as follows:

The Stock Market

Many of you probably have heard about fortunes being made and lost in the stock market. If you would like to see how good your investing skills are, you might want to try The Stock Market Game located at *www.smgww.org*. This simulation is for students of all ages—from middle school to adults. By playing this game, you learn about finance and the American economic system. To participate in this game, you invest a hypothetical $100,000 in the stock market and follow your investments over a 10-week time period. See Figure 17-7.

FIGURE 17-7
Stock Market simulation game

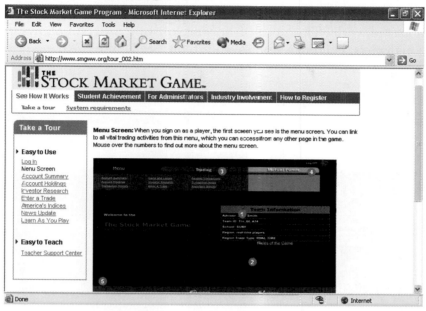

The Renaissance

Maybe you are interested in the Renaissance era and would like to explore and learn more about this historical period. You can do this through simulation. Try the Renaissance Connection located at *http://www.renaissanceconnection.org/*. See Figure 17-8. You also will find links to several other simulations and resources from this site.

FIGURE 17-8
Renaissance Connection

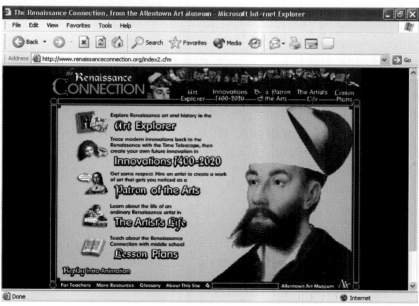

SimCity

One of the earliest and still most popular simulations is SimCity. Several versions of this program have been released, including one that runs on handheld computers. It is used extensively in schools throughout the world. This problem-solving software program allows the user to create a city, including highways, buildings, homes, and so on. See Figure 17-9.

FIGURE 17-9
SimCity simulation

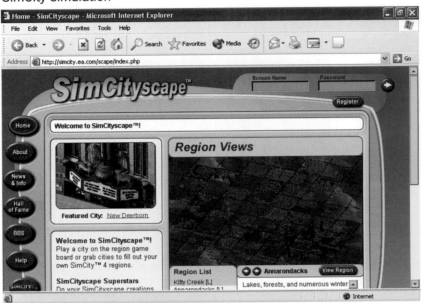

Scientific Discovery and Technological Innovations

Our world is changing at an ever-increasing pace. Currently, people around the world are able to communicate with each other almost instantaneously. The amount of available information is increasing each and every day. In fact, it is continuing to increase faster than we can process it. On the positive side, the information and discoveries are contributing to a better lifestyle for many people. Predictions are that we will learn to cure many diseases and continue to increase our life span.

But there is another aspect to all of this. Within all of this change, other predictions are that an antitechnology backlash is possible. Many people feel technology is creating a world that is out of control. Moral and cultural dilemmas are becoming more and more common, and many people want to return to a simpler, slower way of life.

Whether society could and would return to something simpler is highly debatable. Even today, there are very few places in the world that are not affected by technology. And many scientists say we're "only at the Model-T stage" of what is to come. Let's take a brief look at some of the predicted and possible scientific changes on the horizon.

Artificial Intelligence

Some of you who enjoy science fiction might have read the book or seen the movie *2001: A Space Odyssey*. In this movie, originally released in the late 1960s and re-released in 2000, a computer referred to as HAL controls a spaceship on its way to Mars. This computer has artificial intelligence, so it never makes a mistake. No computer such as HAL yet exists, but artificial intelligence is still a branch of computer science. Computer scientists have made much advancement in this area.

The concept of *artificial intelligence* (AI) has been around for many years. In fact, the term was coined in 1956 by John McCarthy at the Massachusetts Institute of Technology. The goal for this software is to process information on its own without human intervention. There are many ways in which artificial intelligence applications are being developed and are being used today. Some examples are as follows:

- *Game playing*: The most advances have been made in this area.

- *Natural language*: This offers the greatest potential rewards by allowing people to interact easily with computers by talking to them.

- *Expert systems*: These are computer programs that help us make decisions. For instance, an expert system might help your parents determine the best type of insurance for their particular needs.

- *Robotics*: When we think of robotics, we might think of humanoid robots like those in *Star Wars*. In real life, however, we do not see this type of robot in our society. Robots, mostly used in assembly plants, are capable only of limited tasks. One of the newest types of robots is called a *bot*, commonly used by search engines.

Many universities throughout the world, such as Iowa State University, have artificial intelligence research labs. See Figure 17-10.

FIGURE 17-10
Web site for Iowa State University's artificial intelligence research lab

Genetic Engineering

The human life span has more than doubled in the last 200 years. We now can expect to live almost 80 years. Implications are that the average life span in the 21st century will continue to increase, possibly dramatically. One of the major factors contributing to this increase is *genetic engineering*, which refers to changing the DNA in a living organism. See Figure 17-11. Many groups of people argue against this technology. The supporters, however, point out many benefits. Here are some examples:

- Increasing resistance to disease

- Enabling a plant or animal to do something it would not typically do

- Enabling a fruit to ripen without getting too mushy

FIGURE 17-11
Changing a plant's DNA

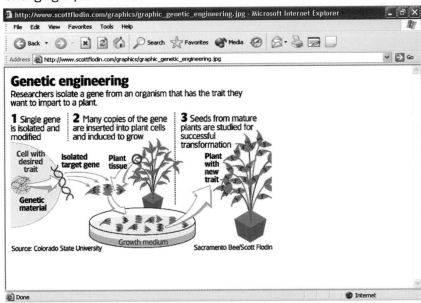

One of the most widely known projects ever developed within this area was the Human Genome Project. Its goal was to identify all of the approximately 100,000 genes in human DNA, store and analyze this data, and address the ethical, legal, and social issues surrounding the project. The project was coordinated by the Department of Energy and the National Institute of

Health. Because of the data and resources resulting from this project, some observers such as Bill Gates and former President Bill Clinton predict the 21st century will be the "biology century."

Virtual Reality

The term *virtual reality (VR)* means different things to different people. A general definition is an artificial environment that feels like a real environment. This environment is created with computer hardware and software. Virtual reality and simulation share some common characteristics. Simulation is sometimes referred to as desktop VR. However, virtual reality provides more of a feeling of being in the actual environment—of using all or almost all of the five senses. The user is immersed completely inside the virtual world, generally through some head-mounted display. This helmet contains the virtual and auditory displays. Virtual reality is used in many different ways and areas. Some examples are as follows:

- *Education*: Virtual environments can help students have a better understanding of history. Imagine experiencing World War II as though you were really there. Or maybe you would like to experience what it would be like to live during the age of dinosaurs. With a virtual world, you feel as though you are part of the environment.

- *Training*: You may have had an opportunity to play a virtual game. If so, you might have felt you were part of the action. You could control much of the environment and make choices as to what your next move would be. A variation of this type of virtual reality is being used to train pilots, navigators, and even astronauts. These individuals are put into virtual life and death situations where they must make decisions. This helps prepare them in the event a similar situation occurs in real life.

 Ethics in Technology

WHO IS RESPONSIBLE?

Increasingly, computers participate in decisions that affect human lives. Consider medical safety, for instance, and consider that just about everything in a hospital is tied to a computer. So what happens if these machines do not produce the expected results? What happens if they have been incorrectly programmed?

When programmers write a program, they check for as many conditions as possible. But there always is the chance they might miss one. So what happens if a computer malfunctions and applies a high dosage of radiation? Or what happens if two medications are prescribed to an individual and the computer does not indicate that the medications are incompatible? Or what happens when someone calls for an ambulance and the system does not work and there is no backup?

Then the question becomes: Who is responsible for these mishaps? Is it the programmer? Is it the company? Is it the person who administered the radiation treatment?

The incidents described here actually happened. These are ethical issues that are being decided in court.

■ *Medicine*: The Virtual Reality Medical Center in San Diego, California, is using virtual reality in combination with physiological monitoring and feedback to treat anxiety disorders, such as fear of flying, fear of heights, fear of public speaking, claustrophobia, panic disorders, and so on. See Figure 17-12.

FIGURE 17-12
Using VR for relaxation during medical procedure

Computing Trends

Nanotechnology and quantum and optical computing are predicted to be technologies of the future. *Nanotechnology* relates to creating computer components that are fewer than 100 nanometers in size. To put the concept of nanotechnology into perspective, consider the following: The width of a single grain of sand is about 900,000 nanometers! Many scientists predict that nanotechnology will make possible the production of ever-smaller computers that can process data considerably faster than today's computers and can store vastly greater amounts of information.

Optical computing uses light beams for the internal circuits instead of electricity. Thus, it has the advantage of small size and high speed. This type of computing has definite advantages—light beams are much faster than electricity and they can cross each other, providing for even faster speeds. Enormous hurdles must still be overcome before a true optical computer exists.

Quantum computing uses the laws of quantum mechanics and the way that atoms can be in more than one state at once to do computational tasks. Quantum computing is still in the pioneer stage, but shows great promise. Its strong point is in the areas of encryption and code-breaking.

> **Did You Know?**
>
> Nanoparticles are expected to be so inexpensive that they can be integrated into fabrics and other materials, creating military uniforms that defend against bullets and germ warfare.

These are just a few examples of activities taking place today. As in the past, it is certain that scientific discovery and technological innovation will greatly affect our economic and military developments in the future. Predictions are that science and technology will continue to advance and become more widely available and utilized around the world. Some people forecast, however, that the benefits derived from these advancements will not be evenly distributed.

Work and Play

How will technology affect us as individuals in our work and social life? Although no one knows what the future will bring, predictions are numerous. Many people predict that with high-skilled work more in demand, semi-skilled work will start to disappear. We have discussed already some of the changes taking place in education and how genetic engineering is helping increase life expectancy. As a result of these advances, what types of changes can we expect in the economy and in our personal lives?

Global Economy

One thing is certain about the new economy: Knowledge is the greatest asset. However, knowledge will be limited by time—it can be incredibly valuable one moment and worthless the next. The spread and sharing of knowledge, the development of new technologies, and an increased recognition of common world problems present unlimited opportunities for economic growth.

Consider banking, finance, and commerce. Electronic technology is having a dramatic effect on these industries. Think about currency. Will it become obsolete? Most likely it will. Already, huge amounts of money zip around the globe at the speed of light. Technology is affecting the way information and money are transmitted. You no longer have to go to the bank to do your banking; you can do it in the comfort of your home using online banking. Online banking allows you to transfer money electronically, which makes it possible for you to pay your bills online and check your account balances. This can all be done from anywhere in the world!

> ### Did You Know?
>
> The economy created by the Internet is generating enormous environmental benefits by reducing the amount of energy and materials consumed by businesses. It is predicted that the Internet will revolutionize the relationship between growth and the environment.

Electronic Commerce

You probably have read about the Industrial Revolution and how it affected our world. The Internet economy is being compared to the Industrial Revolution. *Electronic commerce*, or e-commerce, which means having an online business, is changing the way our world does business.

We find e-commerce in every corner of the modern business world. Statistics indicate that over a billion people are connected to the Internet. Internet speed will increase as more people add fiber-optics, cable modems, or digital subscriber lines (DSL). All of this activity and high-speed connections indicate more online businesses. Some analysts predict that within the next 10 years, Internet-based business will account for up to 10% of the world's consumer sales. And the Center for Research in Electronic Commerce at the University of Texas indicates that out of the thousands of online companies most are not the big Fortune 500 companies—they are smaller companies.

Within this electronic business, one can buy and sell products through the Internet. When it comes to buying online, many people hesitate because they fear someone will steal their credit card numbers. However, *digital cash* is a technology that might ease some of those fears. The digital cash system allows someone to pay by transmitting a number from one computer to another. The digital cash numbers are issued by a bank and represent a specified sum of real money; each number is unique. When one uses digital cash, there is no way to obtain information about the user. Also, some credit card companies have a virtual account option.

As you read about electronic commerce, you might wonder about the effects it will have on you personally. You or someone in your family might have already made a purchase online. Buying online will become much more common in the future, and you might find it becomes a way of life. You also could see an increase in spam—junk mail sent to your e-mail address. Several states are already looking at ways to legislate against this new junk mail.

Internet

Want to find out more about the Internet and electronic commerce or create your own e-commerce store? The Yahoo! Small Business Web site provides e-commerce hosting (*http://smallbusiness. yahoo.com/merchant/*).

The introduction of electronic commerce has also generated a number of new jobs and new categories of jobs. This might be something you want to consider as you look toward a future career. Some examples include Webmasters, programmers, network managers, graphic designers, Web developers, and so on. You also might think about going into an online business for yourself. Individuals with imagination and ambition will discover that the greatest source of wealth is their ideas.

The Workplace

The computer has caused many changes in the workplace. The way information is managed has changed. Instead of file cabinets and paper file folders, electronic copies of documents can be created and stored.

Computers also can be used to improve communication in a business. A computer network can be a vital tool for helping work run more smoothly. One category of software that assists in communicating over a network is called groupware. *Groupware* refers to programs and software that help people work together even if they are located far from each other. One of the more common types of groupware is e-mail. E-mail is an easy and cost-effective way for users to communicate across short or long distances. E-mail allows users to keep documentation of correspondence about a particular topic, something that is lacking with telephone communication.

Groupware also includes electronic calendars and daily/monthly planners. With this software, users enter their own individual appointments that are then available across the network. All meetings are scheduled in the electronic calendar system, which then checks to see that everyone invited can attend. This software can also check the electronic room scheduling system and find a conference room for the meeting.

Collaborative writing software is another form of groupware. This software allows different users to add their own parts, comments, and changes to a single common document, such as a report. The software keeps track of the additions from each user. The changes can be accepted or rejected in the final document. Database software can also be used collaboratively, with different departments providing their own data, such as product specifications or due dates, in the database for the whole company to see and use.

A related type of groupware is project management software. This software allows users to track time lines and processes for complicated projects that involve many workers and departments. Every department can contribute to the information and track its own parts of the project, ensuring that everything is accomplished correctly and on time.

Another type of groupware is video conferencing. This allows users at different locations to hold a virtual meeting without traveling to a central location. Cameras and microphones connected to each person's computer allow users to see and talk to each other.

Many employers allow their employees to work from home. This arrangement is called telecommuting. It involves using communications technology to keep the employee connected to the office. Telecommuting has many advantages for both the employer and the employee. It saves traveling time and expense, and it allows the employee to work at a time that is convenient.

Personal Lives

Computers play such an important part in our lives. Sometimes we take for granted the role they play because they work "behind the scenes." When you order a pizza, the order is transmitted through a computer. When you get money out of an ATM, the transaction is completed by a computer. And let us not forget the latest-model cars. Many have features such as wipers that turn on automatically and directions available at a moment's notice, and some will even slow down the car if it gets too close to an object in front of it!

Will our personal lives become almost like *Star Trek*? Many people predict they will. Just as technology is affecting our work environment, it also is affecting our personal lives.

In the 20th Century, society witnessed all types of changes in the places people lived. They moved from the farms to the cities and then to the suburbs. The 21st Century also will witness changes as the home becomes the center for work, entertainment, learning, and possibly even health care. More and more people will telecommute or run businesses from their homes. As a result, they will have to manage their own lives in a world of uncertainty. This will be a great change for many people. They will have to make decisions about how to separate their business and personal lives.

Some examples of potential technological advances that could affect our personal lives are as follows:

- *Clothes that fight odor and bacteria*: Some clothing companies are manufacturing clothes that keep you comfortable and smelling good. For example, jackets that grow warmer as the temperature drops, and sweat socks that resist bacteria and odors. Or, how about clothing that kills mosquitoes on contact?

- *The flying car*: This has long been a fantasy of the American public, but the question is: How long will it be before we all have flying cars? It probably will be a few more years before we are flying around like the Jetsons, but there are possibilities on the horizon. Moller International has developed a personal vertical takeoff and landing vehicle (VTOL).

The Skycar is able to operate in a much less restrictive area than a helicopter or airplane and is less expensive and safer. These factors allow this type of future transportation to be addressed and investigated for the first time. See Figure 17-13.

FIGURE 17-13
Moller Web site–Skycar

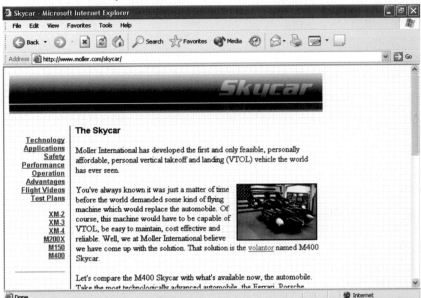

■ *Nonlethal weapons*: A company in San Diego is working on a nonlethal weapon that uses two ultraviolet laser beams. These two beams of UV radiation ionize paths in the air to create "wires" in the atmosphere. This device is harmless, but it can immobilize people and animals at a distance.

■ *Smart shoes and smart seats*: When we think of technology, not too many of us consider our shoes. No matter how expensive our shoes are, they can still become uncomfortable after wearing them for long hours. A technology called expansive polymer gel uses a micro voltage to expand or contract the gel. Weight can be evenly distributed and heat dissipated. This technology also is being applied to car seats.

Technological Issues

It is true that computers have made a positive impact in our lives. They have made our daily lives much easier, our work more efficient, learning more interesting and convenient, and even our game playing more exciting. However, problems exist, such as misuse of information, computer crimes, risks of using hardware and software, health issues, privacy, and security.

Misuse of Information

Use of the Internet has grown at an astounding rate. Users are able to access a multitude of information in a very short amount of time. Putting together a report is a snap with the ability to access information on almost any topic with just a few clicks. This is causing a rise in plagiarism and violation of copyright laws. *Plagiarism* is presenting someone else's ideas or work as your own, without authorization. *Copyright* is the legal protection for authors of creative works. It guards against the unlawful copying or using of someone else's original work. Some specific examples of plagiarism include:

- Buying a report from a "free term paper" Web site

- Paraphrasing information from a source, but not indicating that the information is taken directly from that source

- Having someone else write a report for you

Types of Computer Crimes

What is *computer crime*? It is a criminal act committed through the use of a computer; for example, getting into someone else's system and changing information or creating a computer virus and causing damage to information on others' computers. Computer crime is a bigger problem than most people realize. Billions of dollars every year are lost to corporations because of this often undetected, and therefore unpunished, crime. Computer crimes have increased since data communications and computer networks have become popular. Many computer crimes consist of stealing and damaging information and stealing actual computer equipment. Other types of computer crimes include:

- Unauthorized use of a computer

- Infection of a computer by a malicious program (a virus)

- Harassment and stalking on the computer

- Theft of computer equipment

- Copyright violations of software

- Copyright violations of information found on the Internet

Computer Fraud

Computer fraud is conduct that involves the manipulation of a computer or computer data in order to obtain money, property, or value dishonestly or to cause loss. Examples of computer fraud include stealing money from bank accounts or stealing information from other people's computers for gain.

Computer Hacking

Computer hacking involves invading someone else's computer, usually for personal gain or just the satisfaction of doing it. Hackers usually are computer experts who enjoy having the power to invade someone else's privacy. They can steal money or they can change or damage data stored on a computer.

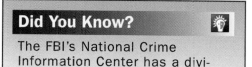

Did You Know?

The FBI's National Crime Information Center has a division for computer crime.

Computer Viruses

A *virus* is a program that has been written, usually by a hacker, to cause the corruption of data on a computer. The virus generally is attached to an executable file (like a program file) and spreads from one file to another once the program is executed. A virus might cause major damage to a computer's data, or it might do something as minor as display messages on your screen. There are different variations of viruses:

- A *worm* makes many copies of itself, resulting in the consumption of system resources that slows down or actually halts tasks. Worms do not have to attach themselves to other files.

- A *time bomb* is a virus that does not cause its damage until a certain date or until the system has been booted a certain number of times.

- A Trojan horse is a virus that does something different from what it is expected to do. It might look like it is doing one thing while in actuality it is doing something quite different (usually something disastrous).

In order to protect your computer against virus damage:

- Use antivirus software. This software should always run on your computer and should be updated regularly.

- Be careful in opening e-mail attachments. It is a good idea to save them to disk before reading them so that you can scan them. It is also a good idea to open messages only from people you know.

- Do not access files copied from disks or downloaded from the Internet without scanning them first. Figure 17-14 shows online security check and virus scan options.

FIGURE 17-14
Virus Scan

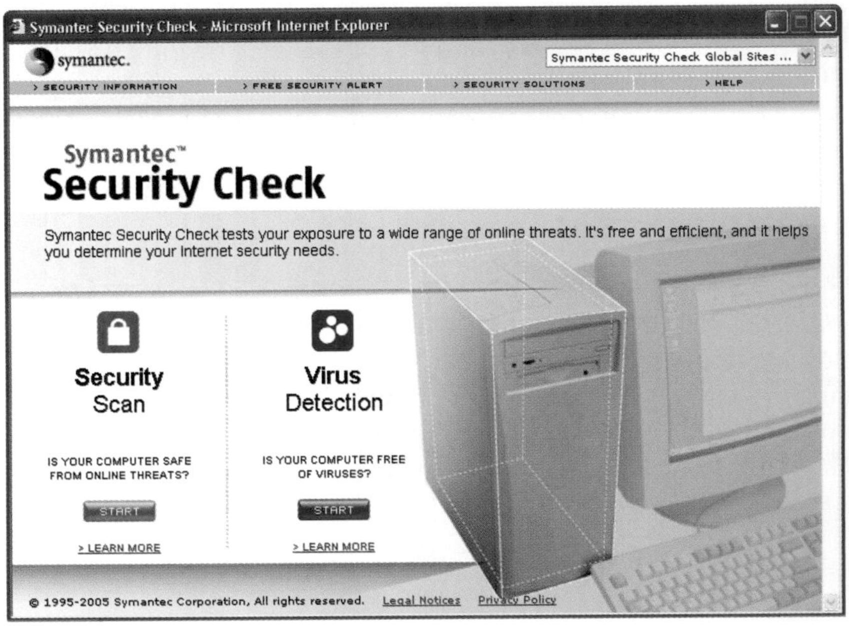

Other Computer Crimes

Theft of computer time also is a crime committed regularly in the workplace. This crime is committed when an employee uses a company's computer for personal use, such as running a small side business, keeping records of an outside organization, or keeping personal records. When you are engaged in these types of activities on the job, you are not being as productive as you could be for your employer.

Using the information you see on someone else's computer screen or on a printout to profit unfairly is theft of output.

Changing data before it is entered into the computer or after it has been entered into the computer is called *data diddling*. Anyone who is involved with creating, recording, encoding, and checking data can change data.

Risks of Using Computer Hardware and Software

Computer equipment as well as data stored on computers are subject to various types of hazards. These include damage caused by improper use by employees, damage caused by improper configurations, fire, flood, and even electrical outages or storms. Many of these conditions can be prevented by proper planning, such as providing employees with appropriate training to use and safeguard the equipment. Computers should be equipped with surge protectors and other types of protection to prevent outages. When flooding is a possibility, it is a good idea to locate computers above the first floor of a building.

Illegally copying and using software is called software piracy. It has become a big problem because it is so easy to copy software. Software piracy costs software companies millions of dollars in sales each year. Many persons are misusing shareware as well. Shareware is software you can use for free for a specified period of time to try it out. If you decide you like the software and it meets your needs, you are supposed to pay for it.

> ### Did You Know?
> The first computer crime, electronic embezzlement, was committed in 1958.

> ### Did You Know?
> The penalty for copying software can be up to $250,000, five years in prison, or both.

Health Issues

Working on computers for long periods of time can cause various types of health problems and concerns. These are referred to as ergonomic-related concerns and are usually caused by repetitive motions that result in wear and tear on the body, such as rapid hand and wrist movement. A very common disorder caused by using a keyboard on a consistent basis is carpal tunnel syndrome. One remedy to reduce this condition is to replace a regular keyboard with an ergonomic keyboard. This type of keyboard will take the stress off the wrists and reduce injury. Problems can also occur because of poor lighting or inappropriate furniture and equipment such as the type of monitor used. It is the responsibility of the employer to provide a safe working environment for employees, which will result in a healthy and productive workforce. Figure 17-15 shows an example of an ergonomically designed workstation.

FIGURE 17-15
Workstation ergonomics

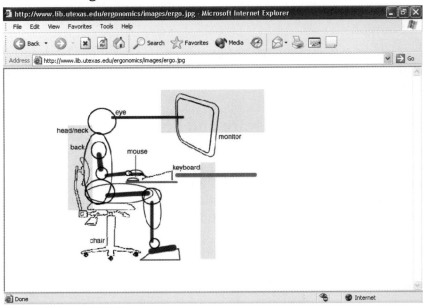

Privacy

The amount of personal information electronically available on each of us is astonishing. You probably would be surprised to know the extent to which this information is available and to whom it is available. Many companies gather information to create databases and sell or trade this information to others.

Any time you submit information on the Internet, it is possible for this information to be used for various situations. Information also can be gathered from online data regarding school, banking, hospitals, insurance companies, and any other information supplied for such everyday activities.

Much of the information gathered and sold can result in your name being added to mailing lists. Companies use these lists for marketing purposes. Information regarding one's credit history also is available for purchase. Using credit cards to purchase merchandise on the Internet can be risky. Some sites are advertised as being secure. If the sites are not secure, your credit card number can be released and used.

Security

Computer security is necessary to keep hardware, software, and data safe from harm or destruction. Some risks to computers are natural causes, some are accidents, and some are intentional. It is not always evident that some type of computer crime or intrusion has occurred. Therefore, it is necessary that safeguards for each type of risk be put into place. It is the responsibility of companies or individuals to protect their data.

The best way to protect data is to control access to the data. The most common form of restricting access to data is the use of passwords. Passwords are used to protect against unauthorized use. Users must have a password in order to log into a system. Companies sometimes restrict access to certain computers. Passwords usually are changed periodically.

Other security measures include the following:

■ Making security a priority—maintaining and enforcing security measures

■ Using electronic identification cards to gain access to certain areas within a building or department

■ Protecting individual companies' networks from external networks by using firewalls— special hardware and software that allow users inside the organization to access computers outside the organization while keeping outside users from accessing their computers

■ Using antivirus software to protect data

■ Instituting a selective hiring process that includes careful screening of potential employees, and dismissal of employees who refuse to follow security rules

■ Regularly backing up data and storing it off site

■ Employing *biometric security measures*, which examine a fingerprint, a voice pattern, or the iris or retina of the eye and compare them against employee records; this method of security is usually used when high-level security is required (see Figure 17-16)

FIGURE 17-16
Biometric security measures

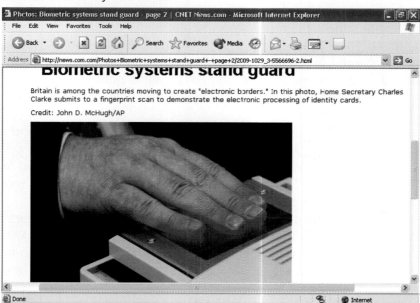

Protection for Technology Injuries

Many laws have been passed in an effort to assist those injured by computer crimes and other technology issues. However, many of the offenses are difficult to prove. A list of some of the laws that protect users follows:

■ Copyright Act of 1976—protects the developers of software

■ Software Piracy and Counterfeiting Amendment of 1983—protects software development companies from the copying and use of their software programs

■ Electronic Communication Privacy Act of 1986—prohibits the interception of data communications

■ Computer Fraud and Abuse Act of 1986—prohibits individuals without authorization from knowingly accessing a company computer to obtain records from financial communications

In addition, many states have individual laws governing computer crimes that happen within their states.

 Technology Careers

SIMULATION ANALYST

Simulation analysts and consultants work with all types of companies of any size. Their primary job is to investigate different options to determine which would be the best for a particular situation. For instance, health care company administrators might want to implement a new system for filing and processing insurance claims. Before spending a huge amount of money, they might hire a simulation analyst to determine which system would best meet their needs. Or a bank is going to bring in a new system to process checks. It hires an analyst to do simulation modeling of what the system might and might not do.

Some necessary skills include the ability to see detail in a system and to be a good technical writer. The person should be a logical thinker and have good analytical skills. A good memory is an additional asset. Opportunities and the need for simulation analysts are increasing. One of the reasons for the increase is that more and more companies are applying simulation to a larger variety of problems.

As a consultant, you would probably do some traveling. Consulting fees are usually quite generous, with some simulation analysts making as much as $75,000 or more per year. You might find some analysts with only a two-year degree, but generally you need at least a bachelor's degree in computer information systems or computer engineering.

SUMMARY

In this lesson, you learned:

- Technology is having a tremendous impact on education. Many people predict that technology will change the entire structure of education.

- The Internet and the World Wide Web are the biggest factors affecting education today.

- Some people predict an antitechnology backlash.

- Electronic commerce is the buying and selling of goods and services using the Internet.

- Digital cash allows someone to pay online by transmitting a number from one computer to another.

- New jobs and new job categories are being developed because of the Internet and electronic commerce.

- Some technological advances are voice recognition, nonlethal weapons, space travel, flying cars, smart shoes and smart seats, clothes that fight odors, and electronic shopping.

- Computer crime has become a major problem, costing companies billions of dollars annually.

- Computer fraud is conduct that involves the manipulation of a computer or computer data for dishonest profit.

- Computer hacking involves invading someone else's computer. Sometimes it is done for financial gain and sometimes just as a prank.

- A computer virus is a program that has been written to cause corruption of data on a computer.

- To protect against viruses, install and keep an antivirus program running on your computer. Be sure to update regularly.

- Computer security is necessary to keep hardware, software, and data safe from harm or destruction.

- The most common way to control access to data is to use passwords.

- Illegally copying and using software is called software piracy. It has cost companies millions of dollars in lost sales.

- Laws have been passed in an effort to assist those who have been injured by computer crimes and offenses. Many computer crimes are difficult to prove and prosecute.

VOCABULARY *Review*

Define the following terms:

Artificial intelligence (AI)	Electronic commerce	Simulation
Biometric security measures	Genetic engineering	Time bomb
Computer-based learning	Groupware	Virtual reality (VR)
Computer crime	Nanotechnology	Virus
Computer fraud	Online learning	WebQuest
Computer hacking	Optical computing	Worm
Data diddling	Plagiarism	
Digital cash	Quantum computing	

REVIEW *Questions*

MULTIPLE CHOICE

Select the best response for the following statements.

1. _____ invade other people's computers.
   A. Hackers
   B. Programmers
   C. Trojan horses
   D. System analysts

2. Software that users may use on a trial basis is called _____.
   A. freeware
   B. shareware
   C. antivirus software
   D. Microsoft Office

3. _____ is the delivery of education over the Internet.
   A. Simulation
   B. Online learning
   C. Virtual reality
   D. None of the above

4. _____ is a criminal act that is committed through the use of a computer.
   A. Hacking
   B. Piracy
   C. Shareware
   D. Nanotechnology

5. The buying and selling of goods on the Internet is called _____.
   A. economic commerce
   B. electronic commerce
   C. on-hand business
   D. local commerce

TRUE/FALSE

Circle T if the statement is true or F if the statement is false.

T   F   1. With digital cash, you can pay someone by transmitting a number from one computer to another.

T   F   2. Worms, time bombs, and Trojan horses are variations of viruses.

T   F   3. Hackers only invade other people's computers for fun.

T   F   4. Submitting a report to your teacher that you obtained from a "free term paper" Web site is an example of plagiarism.

T   F   5. Simulations are models of real-world activities.

FILL IN THE BLANK

Complete the following sentences by writing the correct word or words in the blanks provided.

1. Computer _____ is necessary to keep hardware, software, and data safe from harm or destruction.

2. Using _____, which are models of real-world activities, you learn by doing.

3. _____ systems are a type of artificial intelligence.

4. _____ security measures involve examining a fingerprint, a voice pattern, or the iris or retina of the eye.

5. The _____ project was developed to identify all of the genes in human DNA and explore ethical, legal, and social issues surrounding genetic engineering.

PROJECTS

CROSS-CURRICULAR—MATHEMATICS

Computer crimes have been responsible for the loss of millions of dollars. Some crimes result in more loss than others. Use the Internet and other resources to locate information on lost revenue due to computer crimes. If you have access to spreadsheet software, prepare this information in a spreadsheet and create formulas that will not only add the totals, but also display the percentage of each crime's portion of the total. Some keywords that might be helpful in your search are *computer crime, computer crime costs, hackers, viruses,* and *software piracy.* Use various search engines to research each term.

CROSS-CURRICULAR—SCIENCE

Use the Internet and other resources to identify early security measures that were used to protect computers and computer data. Describe how these measures counteracted the intrusions which were made. Write a report on your findings to share with your classmates. You might find helpful information at *www.looksmart.com*.

CROSS-CURRICULAR—SOCIAL STUDIES

Viruses have been around for quite a while. Use the Internet and other resources to research the history of early computer viruses. Prepare a report to share with your classmates on the types of viruses and the damage they caused. Also, include any information you might find on the person who programmed the virus, if possible. Use a search engine and the keywords *computer viruses* or *early computer viruses*.

CROSS-CURRICULAR—LANGUAGE ARTS

The year is 2070. You were born in 2055. Use your word-processing program to write a letter to someone who was born at the beginning of the century and tell him or her about your life and your community.

 WEB PROJECT

It is probably impossible to go through an entire day without being involved in some way with computer technology. Prepare a poster indicating each computer technology you encounter/use during an entire day. Describe the computer technology activity. Include information as to how you use it.

 TEAMWORK PROJECT

Your instructor has assigned to you and a team member a project relating to the global economy and electronic commerce. You and your partner are to prepare a report on what information you would need to know before setting up an e-commerce Web site. Create a PowerPoint presentation and present it to your class.

CRITICAL *Thinking*

Congratulations on your new job at Bank International. Assume that your supervisor has asked you to research and prepare a report on biometric security measures. After you thoroughly research this project, create a report listing each item you selected and explain why you selected that particular item. Submit your report to your instructor.

COMPUTERS AND SOCIETY

REVIEW *Questions*

FILL IN THE BLANK

Complete the following sentences by writing the correct word or words in the blanks provided.

1. The _____ portion of a URL gives you information concerning the appropriateness of the site for your area of study, for example, .edu and .gov.

2. The main page or index page of most Web sites is referred to as the _____.

3. _____ is the ability to use links to move through a site.

4. _____ are a popular way to arrange and organize text on a Web page; examples are ordered and unordered.

5. _____ is the exclusive right, granted by law for a certain number of years, to make and dispose of literary, musical, or artistic work.

6. _____ refers to the age of information, the length of time it has been posted on the Internet, and how often it is updated.

7. _____ is the buying and selling of goods and services using the Internet.

8. _____ links give the full address to a Web page on the Internet.

9. _____ is the language of the Web.

10. _____ is conduct that involves the manipulation of a computer or computer data for dishonest profit.

MULTIPLE CHOICE

Select the best response for the following statements.

1. _____ is the ability to move through a Web site.
   A. Surfing
   B. Navigation
   C. Citing
   D. Sharing

2. A Web page is a document on the World Wide Web and is defined by a unique _____.
   A. CPU
   B. URL
   C. HTML
   D. JPEG

3. AltaVista, Excite, Yahoo!, and Google are examples of _____.
   A. domains
   B. search engines
   C. electronic resources
   D. shareware

4. _____ is the unauthorized use of software.
   A. Software piracy
   B. Stemming
   C. Copyright violation
   D. Data diddling

5. Game playing, expert systems, and robotics are examples of _____.
   A. simulations
   B. artificial intelligence
   C. e-commerce
   D. distance learning

6. The _____ system allows someone to pay by transmitting a number from one computer to another.
   A. checking account
   B. credit card
   C. electronic commerce
   D. digital cash

7. All of the following are examples of groupware *except* _____ .
   A. project management software
   B. collaborative writing software
   C. video conferencing
   D. desktop publishing

8. A _____ is a program that has been written to cause corruption of data on a computer.
   A. Web quest
   B. computer virus
   C. hacker
   D. simulation

9. _____ is the language of the Web.
   A. TCP/IP
   B. MAN
   C. DSL
   D. HTML

10. All of the following are examples of lists you can use to organize information or data in a Web page *except* _____.
    A. numeric
    B. ordered
    C. unordered
    D. definition

TRUE/FALSE

Circle T if the statement is true or F if the statement is false.

T   F   1. Many Web sites provide free space online for publishing Web pages.

T   F   2. A relative link on a Web page gives the file location in relation to the current document.

T   F   3. Passwords are useless in controlling access to data.

T   F   4. HTML is a protocol that controls how Web pages are formatted and displayed.

T   F   5. Clicking an e-mail link on a Web page displays a blank e-mail form containing the recipient's address.

T   F   6. Information is only as good as the source.

T   F   7. Computer crimes are considered minor crimes.

T   F   8. The translation of *caveat lector* is "Let the reader beware."

T   F   9. Domains are programs written to query and retrieve information stored in a database.

T   F   10. The criteria for evaluating resources include authorship, content, copyright information, navigation, and quality control.

PROJECTS

CROSS-CURRICULAR—MATHEMATICS

Computer crimes have been responsible for the loss of millions of dollars. Some crimes result in more loss than others. Use the Internet and other resources to locate information on lost revenue due to the top five computer crimes. If you have access to spreadsheet software, prepare this information in a spreadsheet and write formulas that will add the totals for each crime and the percentage of each crime's portion of the overall total. Some keywords that might be helpful are *computer crimes*, *computer crime costs*, *hackers*, and *software piracy*. Use various search engines.

CROSS-CURRICULAR—SCIENCE

There have been many, many technological advances that have made our lives and work much easier. New advances are being developed daily. Use the Internet and other resources to identify future advances and prepare a report that identifies at least five of these advances and explain how they might impact our lives.

CROSS-CURRICULAR—SOCIAL STUDIES

The typewriter was probably the first "technology" device used in the workplace. Use the Internet and other resources to research other technology devices used in the workplace in the "early" days of technology. Use word-processing software to present your findings in a table.

Include the name of the device, a brief description of the device, and an explanation of how it impacted the workplace.

CROSS-CURRICULAR—LANGUAGE ARTS

Prepare a handout that identifies electronic sources and how to cite these sources when using them in a report or other research. Include samples in your handout. Use your desktop publishing skills to format the handout attractively.

 ### WEB PROJECT

Technology has changed considerably the way instruction is delivered in recent years. Use the Internet and other resources to research how technology will continue to change education. Prepare a report identifying and describing at least two new educational technologies that will affect education in the future.

 ### TEAMWORK PROJECT

It is time to elect a new mayor in your hometown and there are two candidates running for the position. You are one candidate. Select a partner to be your "opponent" for the mayor's position. Each of you is to create three to four Web pages for your campaign that will provide information for potential voters. Use as many of the tags as possible to make your Web pages useful and attractive. Remember, you want to be mayor!

CRITICAL*Thinking*

Many companies are allowing their employees to work from home. This is another example of how technology has changed the workplace. The trend will increase over the next 10 years or so. There are many advantages and disadvantages for both the employee and the employer. After conducting research, prepare a report that discusses both. Include at the end of your report whether or not you would consider working from home. Explain your choice.

SIMULATION

JOB 3-1

You and your partner have decided that a Web page would be very beneficial for advertising your Computer Help OnCall business. Recall from the Unit 2 Review that Computer Help OnCall offers the following services: computer setup, network support, virus detection and removal, software installation, laptop computer repair, printer services, data backup and restore, and wireless network setup. Design two to three Web pages advertising your business. Include elements that will make the pages appealing and user friendly. You might refer to the flyer you prepared for Job 2-2 in the Unit 2 Review as you design and develop your Web pages.

JOB 3-2

You have noticed that many students in your computer classes are having difficulty selecting appropriate electronic resources for their term papers and citing the selected sources. They are spending hours surfing the Internet to locate legitimate information. As a result, you have asked your instructor if you could develop and give a presentation on the criteria for evaluating electronic resources. Use the information in this unit and other sources to develop a five- to six-slide presentation.

PORTFOLIO *Checklist*

Include the following activities from this unit in your portfolio:

_____ Lesson 15 Mathematics Cross-Curricular Report

_____ Lesson 16 Language Arts Cross-Curricular Web Page

_____ Lesson 17 Science Cross-Curricular Report

_____ Unit 3 Review Mathematics Cross-Curricular Spreadsheet

_____ Unit 3 Review Social Studies Cross-Curricular Report

_____ Unit 3 Review Job 3-1 Business Web Page

_____ Unit 3 Review Job 3-2 Electronic Resources Presentation

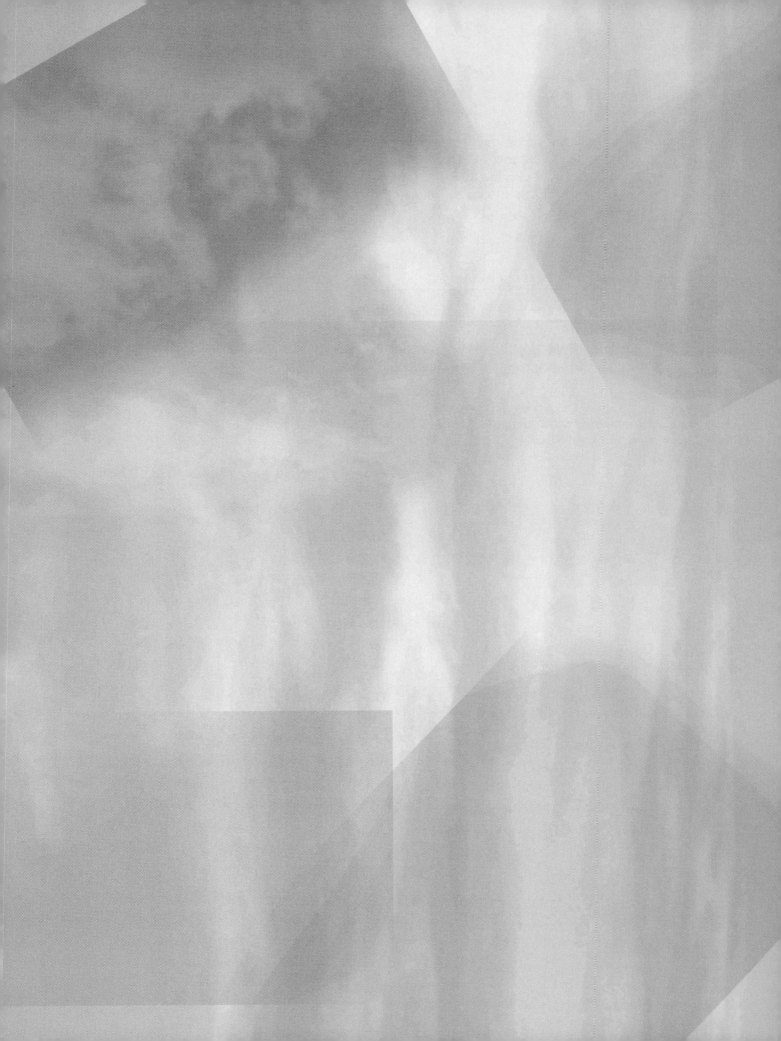

802.11 A family of standards governing wireless transmissions.

A

Absolute cell reference In a worksheet, cell contents that will not change when copied or moved to another cell.

Active cell Currently selected cell in a worksheet.

Adapter card A circuit board that enhances the functions of a system component and/or provides connections to peripheral devices.

Address bar The space in a window that displays the name of the open folder or object.

Alignment The placement of text between the left and right margins; text can be aligned at the left, at the right, or in the center.

American Standard Code for Information Interchange (ASCII) A coding scheme used to represent data.

Animation Adds movement to text, graphics, and other objects on a Powerpoint slide or a Web page.

Application software Software that helps you perform a specific task, such as word processing, desktop publishing, and so on; also called productivity software.

Arithmetic/logic unit (ALU) A component of the microprocessor; performs arithmetic, comparison, and logical operations.

Arrange in Groups Allows you to group files by any detail of the file, such as name, size, type, or date modified.

Artificial intelligence (AI) Software that can process information on its own without human intervention.

Attachments Documents, images, figures, and other files that you can attach to an e-mail message.

Audio input The process of inputting sound into the computer.

AutoFormats Customized preset styles that come with Excel.

AutoSearch An Internet Explorer feature; used to view a list of likely matches in the Search bar, and display the most likely Web page in the main window

B

Bandwidth The transmission capacity of a communications channel.

Baseband Low bandwidth.

Basic input/output system (BIOS) Contains the code that controls the most common devices connected to a computer.

Binary Machine language, which is ones and zeros.

Biometric security measures Security measures that examine a fingerprint, a voice pattern, or the iris or retina of the eye.

Biometrics An authentication technique using automated methods of recognizing a person based on a physiological or behavioral characteristic.

BIOS ROM A chip that contains nonvolatile memory.

Bit A zero or one in computer code.

Blog A short form for weblog, a personal journal published on the Web.

Bluetooth Uses radio waves to connect mobile devices such as cell phones, PDAs, and notebook computers.

Boolean logic Boolean logic used to search Web site databases; consists of three logical operators: AND, OR, and NOT.

Booting The process of starting a computer.

Broadband High bandwidth.

Browser Software program used to retrieve documents from the Internet.

Bump keys Keys with a small dot in the center or a dash at the bottom to assist in correct finger position.

Bus topology In a network, all devices are connected to and share a master cable.

Byte Made up of eight bits; a byte represents a single character, such as the letter A.

C

Cable modem Uses coaxial cable to send and receive data.

Cache memory High-speed RAM that is used to increase the speed of the processing cycle.

Campus Area Network (CAN) A collection of local area network within a limited geographical space, such as a university campus or a military base.

Cathode ray tube Used for computer monitor; large sealed glass tube; screen is coated with dots of red, green, and blue phosphor material.

Cell reference The name or address of a spreadsheet cell.

Cell Point at which a column and row meet in a spreadsheet.

Central processing unit (CPU) Also called the microprocessor, the processor, or central processor, it is the brains of the computer.

Channel The media that carries or transports the message; this could be telephone wire, coaxial cable, microwave signal, or fiber optic.

Chart Graphical representation of worksheet or table data.

Chat room An area online where you can chat with other members in real-time.

Circuit board A thin plate or board that contains electronic components.

Client/server network A type of architecture in which one or more computers on the network acts as a server.

Clients Computers on a network that are not acting as a server.

Coaxial cable The primary type of cabling used by the cable television industry; also widely used for computer networks.

Collapse The minus sign button in the Folders pane of Windows Explorer, which hides additional levels of folders within the selected folder.

Communication devices Facilitate the transmitting and receiving of data, instructions, and information.

Communications channel The link through which data is transmitted.

Computer crime A criminal act committed through the use of a computer.

Computer fraud Conduct that involves the manipulation of a computer or computer data in order to obtain money, property, or value dishonestly or to cause loss.

Computer hacking Invading someone else's computer, usually for personal gain or just the satisfaction of doing it.

Computer system Input, output, and processing devices grouped together.

Computer Electronic device that receives data, processes data, stores data, and produces information.

Computer-based learning Instructional methods where the teacher uses the computer to deliver the instruction.

Concept searching Used for Web site searching; the search engine tries to determine what you mean and displays links to Web sites that relate to the keywords.

Contacts Information on friends, family, and other individuals with whom you work or communicate with on a regular basis; stored in an address book.

Content Advisor A filtering program developed by Microsoft and is part of the Internet Explorer Web browser.

Contents pane In Windows Explorer, the right pane that displays the folders and files that are contained in the folder or disk selected in the Folders pane.

Control unit Coordinates all of the CPU's activities.

Controller A device that controls the transfer of data from the computer to a peripheral device and vice versa.

Copyright The exclusive right, granted by law for a certain number of years, to make and dispose of literary, musical, or artistic work.

Currency Refers to the age of the information, how long it has been posted, and how often it is updated.

D

Data communications The transmission of data from one location to another.

Data diddling Changing data before it is entered in the computer or after it has been entered in the computer.

Data projector Output device that projects the image from a computer screen onto a larger screen; primarily used for presentations.

Data Information entered into the computer to be processed. Consists of text, numbers, sounds, video, and images.

Database management system (DBMS) A software program that is used to create, maintain, and provide controlled accesses to data.

Database window The command center for working with Access objects.

Database A collection of related information organized in a manner that provides for rapid search and retrieval.

Datasheet In a database, a row-and-column table view of the data in tables, forms, and queries.

Datasheet view In a database, it is a row-and-column view of data in a table, form, or query.

Decoding Part of the machine cycle; the process of translating the instruction into signals the computer can execute.

Decryption Using a key to unscramble information and return it to the original text.

Deep Web See *Invisible Web*.

Design templates Predesigned formats containing color schemes, styled fonts, background graphics, and so on, that can be applied to a presentation.

Design view In a database, it is used to create a table, form, query, and report.

Desktop computer Computer that fits on a desktop.

Destination Location where a copied file or folder will reside.

Details view Displays the name of the file or folder, along with information on the file size, the file type, and the date the file was created or last modified.

Dial-up modem Enables a computer to transmit data over analog telephone lines.

Digital camera A camera using digital technology.

Digital cash Allows someone to pay by transmitting a number from one computer to another; the digital cash numbers are issued by a bank and represent a specified sum of real money; each number is unique.

Digital pen Pen-like writing instrument that allow the user to input information by writing on a PDA or other mobile device or to use the pen as a pointer.

Disk cache A portion of RAM set aside for temporarily holding information read from a disk.

Domain name The unique name that identifies an Internet site.

Dot matrix printer An impact printer; prints by transferring ink to the paper by striking a ribbon with pins.

Download To transfer (data or programs) from a server or host computer to one's own computer or device.

DSL Uses a digital subscriber line (DSL) to connect a computer to the Interent.

E

Editing Changing the text in an existing document.

Electronic commerce Conducting business and business transactions online.

Electronic communication Communication using computers.

Electronic mail (E-mail) The transmission of files and data using a computer network.

E-mail address Consists of three parts—user name of the individual, the "@" symbol, and the user's domain name.

Embedded operating system System that includes technologies and tools that enable developers to create a broad range of devices. This operating system, which resides on a ROM chip, is used on small handheld computers and wireless communication devices.

Encrypting Scrambling a message so that it can only be read by someone with the key.

Ergonomic keyboard A keyboard designed to relieve stress on the hands and wrists that can result from repeated and/or longtime keying.

Ethernet Was the first approved industry standard protocol; one of the more popular LAN protocols.

Executing Part of the machine cycle; the process of carrying out the processor commands.

Execution cycle (E-cycle) Amount of time it takes the central processing unit to execute an instruction and store the results in RAM; also called instruction cycle (I-cycle).

Expand The plus sign button in the Folders pane of Windows Explorer, which displays all folders and subfolders on a disk.

Expansion board Enhances functions of a component of the system unit and/or provides connections through a port to peripheral devices.

Expansion slot Openings on the motherboard where an expansion board, also called an adapter card, can be inserted.

Extended Binary Coded Decimal Interchange Code (EBCDIC) Standard computer code used mostly in very large computers.

Extranet Networks that allow outside organizations, such as suppliers and vendors, to access internal company Web sites.

F

Favorites A method of storing individual Web pages or Web locations on your computer.

Fax machine An input/output device; transmits and receives documents over a telephone line.

Fax modem An input/output device; transmits and receives documents through a computer.

Fetching Part of the machine cycle; the process of obtaining a program instruction or data item from RAM.

Fiber-optic cable Physical media; used to transfer data; made from thin, flexible glass tubing.

Fields A column in a database table. Each field contains a specific piece of information for a record.

File allocation table (FAT) A special log on the disk which keeps track of the data storage location.

File management The process of organizing and keeping track of files.

File Transfer Protocol (FTP) An Internet standard that allows users to download and upload files to and from other computers on the Internet.

File The instructions the computer needs to operate (called program files or executable files); it may contain a text document you can read (often referred to as a document file); or a file may contain an image or other media.

Filmstrip view Available in Windows Explorer picture folders; displays pictures in a single row of thumbnail images.

FireWire A type of external bus; also known as IEEE 1394 and IEEE 1394b.

Flag Status column Column in the Outlook window to which you can assign a flag that can be used to identify a message. Flags can be used as reminder notices or to identify the importance of a message.

Floppy disk A storage device; flat circles of iron oxide-coated plastic enclosed in a hard plastic case.

Folder Used to organize files into manageable groups.

Folders pane Left pane in Windows Explorer that displays a hierarchy of disks, folders, and files on the computer.

Font style Attributes, such as bold, italics, and underlining, that are applied to a font.

Font The design of a typeface.

Footer Information that appears at the bottom of every page in a document in Office documents.

Format Painter Formatting tool that allows you to copy the formatting on selected text and apply it to other text.

Formatting a) The process of preparing a disk so you can write data to and read data from the disk; b) applying certain attributes to text, specifying margins, spacing, and so on; enhancing the text in a document.

Forms In a database, the object used to enter data in a table.

Formula prefix The equal sign (=) that is entered before a formula in a worksheet cell.

Formula A statement that performs a calculation in a spreadsheet.

Function A built-in formula that is a shortcut for common calculations, such as summing and finding the average.

G

Gateway A combination of software and hardware that links two different types of networks that use different protocols.

Genetic engineering Refers to changing the DNA in a living organism.

Graphical user interface (GUI) An interface that displays a symbolic desktop.

Graphics tablet A flat drawing surface on which the user can draw figures or write something freehand.

Groupware Refers to programs and software that help people work together even if they are located in different physical locations.

H

Hard copy A printout; printed information.

Hard disk Primarily used to store data inside of the computer, although removable hard disks also are available.

Hard return Moves the insertion point to the next line of type; pressing the ENTER key.

Hardware The tangible, physical computer equipment that can be seen and touched.

Header Information that appears at the top of every page in a document or at the top of every page in a worksheet.

Hits The number of returns or hyperlinked Web sites addresses displayed based on your keyword Web search; also called results.

Hoax An attempt to deceive an audience into believing that something false is real.

Home Area Network (HAN) A network contained within a user's home.

Home page The main page or index page of a Web site.

Home row keys Keys on the keyboard from which all keystrokes are made. These keys are a, s, d, f, j, k, l, and ;.

Host computer A computer to which other computers are connected so that the host can manage time-intensive computing tasks.

Host node A node where a host processor is located.

Hot plugging The ability to add and remove devices to a computer while the computer is running and have the operating system automatically recognize the change.

Hyperlinks Objects on a Web page that, when clicked take you to another location on the same Web page or to other Web page

Hypertext markup language (HTML) A text-based program used to create documents to display in a browser; a series of tags that are integrated into a text document and describe how the text should be formatted.

Hypertext transfer protocol (HTTP) Communication protocol used to connect to servers on the World Wide Web. The primary function of HTTP is to establish a connection with a Web server and transmit HTML pages to the user's browser.

I

IBM AIX An IBM variation of UNIX.

Icon Small image that represents a file, command, or another computer function.

Icons view Displays a small icon identifying the type of file with the filename or folder name beneath. These are typically arranged in horizontal rows in Windows Explorer.

IEEE 1394 See *FireWire*.

Impact printer Uses a mechanism that actually strikes the paper to form letters and images.

Index The third part of a search engine; when the spider finds a page, it feeds the data to the index; also called the Indexer.

Indexer See *Index*

Information processing cycle Series of input, process, output, and storage activities performed using a computer.

Information Data that has been organized and processed so that it is meaningful and useful.

Inkjet printer Output device where the color is sprayed onto the paper.

Input Data entered in a computer to be processed.

Input devices Devices used to input data into the computer.

Insertion point A blinking vertical line that shows your current position in a document.

Instant messaging E-mail feature that allows you to send and receive messages while you and the contact are both logged on to the Internet.

Instruction cycle (I-cycle) See *Execution cycle*.

Internet service provider (ISP) A company that provides an Internet connection.

Internet The largest network, used as a communication tool.

Interoperability The ability of software and hardware on multiple machines from multiple vendors to communicate meaningfully.

Intranet A network used exclusively by the members of an organization for distributing company information.

Invisible Web Searchable databases; not available through traditional search engines; also called Deep Web.

IrDA The sending of signals using infrared light waves.

ISDN (Integrated Services Digital Network) Modems that connect your computer to the Internet.

Item A particular piece of information stored in an Outlook folder.

J

Joystick A type of input device primarily used for games; a plastic or metal rod mounted on a base.

K

Keyboard The most commonly-used input device for entering numeric and alphabetic data into a computer.

Keyboarding The ability to key text by using the correct fingers without looking at the keys.

Keyword A descriptive word within a Web document.

L

Label printer Output device; prints labels.

Label Alphabetic text or data that will not be used in a formula in a spreadsheet.

Language translators Convert English-like software programs into machine language that the computer can understand.

Large format printer Output device; used for drawings and drafting output.

Laser printer Output device; produces images using the same technology as copier machines.

Leaders Characters that fill in blank spaces between columns of text and/or numbers.

Line printer A high speed impact printer.

Line spacing Controls the amount of space between lines of text in a document.

Linux An open-source operating system program that is free and one that programmers and developers can use or modify as they wish.

List view Provides a list of file and folder names with small icons identifying the type beside each name. These typically are arranged vertically.

LISTSERVs A mailing list software program that automatically distributes mailing lists on a particular subject.

Local Area Network (LAN) Connects personal computers, workstations, and other devices such as printers, scanners, or other devices.

M

Mac OS Operating system designed for Apple's Macintosh computers and Macintosh clones.

Machine cycle A combination of the instruction cycle and one or more execution cycles.

Magnetic tape Storage media; mostly used for making backup copies of large volumes of data.

Mailing list A group of e-mail addresses that are used for easy and fast distribution of information to multiple e-mail addresses simultaneously.

Main memory See *Random access memory*.

Mainframe computer Large and powerful computers used for centralized storage, processing, and management of large amounts of data.

Margins White space around the edge of a page that frames a document.

Math symbols Used with search engine math.

Memory On the computer's motherboard; where the data is stored.

Menu bar Displays a list of commands.

Metropolitan Area Network (MAN) A network that interconnects users with computer resources in a designated geographic area.

Microwave A signal that is sent through space in the form of electromagnetic waves.

Mid-range server A computer on a network that manages network resources.

Mobile computers Personal computers such as notebook computers and tablet PCs.

Mobile devices Electronic devices that fit into the palm of your hand, such as PDAs and smart phones.

Mobile printer A small, battery-power printer; primarily used to print from a notebook computer.

Modem An acronym for modulate-demodulate; a communications hardware device that facilitates the transmission of data by converting analog signals to digital and vice versa.

Modifier keys Keyboard keys that are used in conjunction with other keys; Ctrl, Alt, and Shift.

Modulate-demodulate Converts analog signals to digital and vice versa.

Monitor Output device; produces soft copy.

Motherboard Circuit board that contains components such as the central processing unit, memory, controllers, and expansion ports and slots.

Mouse The most commonly-used pointing device for personal computers.

MP3 A file format that allows audio compression at near-CD quality.

MS-DOS A command-line interface for microcomputers.

Multifunctional device Output device that provides the functionality of a printer, a scanner, a copier, and a fax machine.

Multimedia The use of text, graphics, audio, and video in some combination to create an effective means of communication and interaction.

Multitasking Allows a single user to work on two or more applications that reside in computer memory at the same time.

N

Nanotechnology Technology that relates to creating computer components that are less than 100 nanometers in size.

Navigation The ability to use links to move through a Web site.

Neighborhood Area Network (NAN) Generally consists of access points, in which networking services are shared among neighboring businesses and residences.

Network interface card (NIC) Enables and controls the sending and receiving of data between the computers in a network.

Network operating system Resides on a network server and is designed specifically to support a network.

Network A group of two or more computers linked together; connects one computer to other computers and to peripheral devices such as printers.

Newsgroup An online discussion group where participants exchange messages on a specific topic.

Nodes Computers and other peripheral devices on a network.

Nonimpact printer Forms characters without striking the paper; examples are ink jet and laser printers.

Normal view In PowerPoint, the default view that contains the Outline and Slides tabs, the Slide pane, the Notes pane, and the View buttons.

Notes pane Used to enter information that the presenter may refer to as the presentation is being delivered.

O

Objects The components in a database; objects include tables, forms, queries, and reports.

Online conferencing Also called Web conferencing; is used to hold group meetings or live presentations over the internet.

Online learning Education delivered online.

Online service provider (OSP) An online service provider is an entity which provides a service online.

Operating system Provides an interface between the user or application program and the computer hardware.

Optical computing Uses light beams for the computer's internal circuits instead of electricity.

Optical storage Uses laser technology to read and write data on silver platters.

Order of evaluation The sequence by which mathematical operations in a formula are performed.

Outline tab Organizes the content of the presentation.

Outlook Express An abbreviated version of Microsoft Outlook.

Output devices Devices that display processed data or information.

Output Data processed by a computer.

P

Packets The small chunks of data that an e-mail message is broken into when it is sent; automatically reassembled into their original format when they reach their destination.

Palm OS A competing operating system with Windows Mobile; runs on Palm handhelds and other third-party devices.

Parallel port Computer port that can that transfer data eight bits at a time.

Patent Guarantees the inventor exclusive rights to the process or method for a certain period of time.

PC-DOS IBM's version of MS-DOS.

Peer-to-peer network A network configuration where all of the computers on a network are equal.

Peripheral devices Devices such as keyboards, monitors, printers, and the mouse.

Personal Area Network (PAN) The interconnection of personal digital devices within the range of about 30 feet.

Personal computers Computers designed for use by an individual.

Personal information management (PIM) A program that you can use to organize your schedule, keep track of your contacts, and manage e-mail.

Plagiarism Presenting someone else's ideas or work as your own, without authorization.

Plotter An output device generally used by architects and engineers.

Plug and Play Refers to the ability of a computer system to automatically configure expansion boards and other devices.

Pointer The object on the screen that is controlled by an input device.

Pointing device An input device that allows a user to position the pointer on the screen.

Pointing stick A pressure-sensitive device that looks like a pencil eraser. It is located on some keyboards, generally between the G, H and B keys.

Points The standard measurement unit for fonts, approximately 1/72 of an inch; the higher the point size, the larger the font.

Port The point at which a peripheral device attaches to a system unit so it can send data or receive information from the computer.

Presentation software A computer program used to organized and present information in the form of a slide show.

Primary key Assigned to a field, it uniquely identifies each record in a database table.

Printhead The mechanism inside the printer that prints.

Protocol An agreed-upon format for transmitting data between two devices.

Public domain Material on which copyright protection has lapsed, thereby making it available for anyone to copy.

Q

Quantum computing Uses the laws of quantum mechanics and the way that atoms can be in more than one state at once to do computational tasks.

Query Database object that lets you specify criteria by which you search the data stored in a table.

QWERTY The arrangement of the alphanumeric keys on a standard keyboard; refers to the first six keys on the top row of letters.

R

Random access memory (RAM) A type of computer chip; short-term, volatile memory.

Range A contiguous group of cells.

Read-only memory (ROM) A type of computer chip that stores specific instructions to manage the computer's operations; non-volatile.

Receiver A computer receiving a message.

Records Rows in a database table that consist of a group of related fields.

Related search Preprogrammed queries or questions suggested by the search engine.

Relative cell reference In a worksheet, cell contents that change relative to the cell to which they are copied or moved.

Report Database object used for presenting data in an attractive format, and used primarily for printing.

Results See *Hits*.

Ring topology A type of architecture where the network devices are connected in a circle.

Router Directs network traffic.

Ruler The area on the screen that is used to change paragraph indentations and margin settings in Microsoft Word.

S

Sans serif Fonts that do not have lines at the ends of the strokes of each letter.

Satellite Wireless media; contains equipment that receives data transmission, amplifies it, and sends it back to earth.

Scanner Input device used to make digital copy of pictures or other documents.

Search engine math A method of searching the Internet using math symbols.

Search engine A software program that enables the user to search the Internet using keywords.

Selecting Identifying text by clicking and dragging the I-beam across the text to highlight it.

Sender A computer sending a message.

Serial port Computer port that can transfer data one bit at a time; generally used by the modem and mouse.

Serif Fonts that have lines at the ends of the strokes of each letter.

Server A computer on a network that manages the network resources.

Shareware Software that is free for an evaluation period but requires payment if you continue to use it beyond the evaluation period.

Signature Consists of text and/or pictures that you create that automatically is added to the end of outgoing e-mail messages.

Simulation Models of real-world activities, designed to allow the user to experiment and explore environments that may be dangerous, inaccessible, or unavailable.

Sizing handles The small squares surrounding a selected image or piece of art that you drag to resize the image or art.

Slide layout In Microsoft PowerPoint, refers to the way text and objects are arranged on a slide.

Slide pane In Microsoft PowerPoint, displays the currently selected slide, on which you can enter and edit text, insert graphics, images, or audio and video clips, apply formats, and so forth.

Slide Show view The current slide fills the computer screen; in this view, you can click to progress through your slides and see the a PowerPoint presentation as your audience will see it.

Slide Sorter view Displays thumbnails or miniature images of all slides in a PowerPoint presentation.

Slides tab Displays thumbnail images of each slide in a PowerPoint presentation. Click an image to display that slide in the Slide pane.

Soft copy Information displayed on a monitor.

Software license Agreement between a software developer and the buyer that gives the buyer the right to use the program.

Software piracy The unauthorized copying of software.

Software Intangible set of instructions that tells the computer what to do; program or instructions that give directions to the computer.

Solid-state storage A nonvolatile, removable medium that uses integrated circuits.

Source The file to be copied.

Spam Unsolicited e-mail.

Speakers Output device; produces sound.

Spider A search engine robot that searches the Internet for keywords.

Sponsored site A site that has paid a search engine a fee in exchange for being listed in the "sponsored sites" section.

Spreadsheet A row and column arrangement of data.

Star topology A type of architecture in which all devices are connected to a central hub or computer.

Status bar Area on the screen that displays information about the document including current page number, total pages in the document, location of the insertion point, and the status of some of the specialized keys.

Stemming Used with search engines, when you search for a word, the search engine also includes the "stem" of the word; also called truncation.

Storing Part of the machine cycle; means writing the processed result to memory.

Styles Pre-designed formatting options that have been saved.

Stylus Pen-like writing instrument that allows the user to input information by writing on a PDA or other mobile device or to use the pen as a pointer.

Subject directories A search tool where data is organized by subject categories.

Supercomputer Fastest type of computer; used for specialized applications requiring immense amounts of mathematical calculations.

Switch A device located at the telephone company's central office that establishes a link between a sender and receiver of data communications.

Systems software A group of programs that coordinate and control the resources and operations of a computer system.

T

Tab stop Location on the Microsoft Word horizontal ruler that tells the insertion point to stop when the Tab key is pressed.

Table An arrangement of information in rows and columns; primary object in a database that contains the raw data.

Telephony Technology associated with the electronic transmission of voice, fax, or other information between distant parties.

Text area The area on the screen that will contain the information that you type.

Thermal printer Output device; forms characters by heating paper.

Thumbnails view In Windows Explorer, displays the files and folders within a folder as small images, with the filename or folder name displayed beneath it.

Tiles view In Windows Explorer, displays a large icon identifying the type of file with the filename or folder name, the type of file, and the size of the file displayed beneath.

Time bomb A virus that does not cause its damage until a certain date or until the system has been booted a certain number of times.

Timed writings Keyboarding drills used to develop speed and accuracy.

Title bar Area of the window that displays the name of the document you are working on as well as the name of the software program you are using.

Token ring A LAN protocol where all of the computers are arranged in a circle.

Toolbar Row of buttons at the top of the browser or other software programs; area of the screen that displays icons (little pictures) of commonly used commands.

Topology The geometric arrangement of how a network is set up and connected.

Touch display Input device; a special screen with pictures or shapes.

Touch typing Entering text by using the correct fingers without look at the keys.

Touchpad An input device commonly used on laptop computers. To move the pointer, slide your fingertip across the surface of the pad.

Trackball A pointing device that works like a mechanical mouse turned upside down.

Tracks A circle on a magnetic media storage device; where data is stored.

Trademark   Legal protection for a company's logo or other graphic information.

Transitions   In PowerPoint, determine how slides move in and out of view in a presentation; you can attach special visual and sound effects to them.

Transmission Control Protocol and Internet Protocol (TCP/IP)   The protocol used by LANs and WANs that has been adopted as a standard to connect hosts on the Internet.

Transmission media   Physical or wireless media used to transmit data.

Truncation   See *Stemming*.

Twisted-pair cable   A type of inexpensive physical media used to transmit data.

U

Uniform Resource Locator (URL)   An address for a resource or site on the World Wide Web. Browsers use this address to located files and other remote services.

Universal Serial Bus (USB)   A port that that supports data transfer rates of up to 480 million bits per second (Mbps); replacing the standard serial and parallel ports on newer computers.

UNIX   An open-source operating system.

Urban legends   Stories which may at one time have been partially true and that have grown from constant retelling into a mythical yarn.

USB Flash drive   A small removable data storage device that uses flash memory.

Usenet   A collection of news or discussion groups.

User interface   The part of the operating system with which we interact when using our computer.

Users   The people who use computers.

Utility programs   Programs designed to complete specialized tasks related to managing the computer's resources, file management, and so forth.

V

Value   Numeric data, or data that will be used in a formula, in a spreadsheet.

Video input   The process of capturing full-motion images with a type of video camera.

Views   Format in which you can display and work with the various objects in a database.

Virtual reality (VR)   An artificial environment that feels like a real environment.

Virus   A program that has been written, usually by a hacker, to cause the corruption of data on a computer.

Voice input   The process of using a microphone to input voice; a category of audio input.

Voice recognition   The computer's capability of distinguishing spoken words.

W

Web page   A document written in HTML that can be accessed on the Internet. Every Web page has a unique address called a URL.

Web server   A computer that delivers (serves up) Web pages. Every Web server has an IP address and possibly a domain name.

WebQuest   Educational activity; uses the Internet for investigation and problem solving.

Wheel   A steering-wheel type of device used with games to simulate driving a vehicle.

Wide area network (WAN)   Covers a large geographical area.

Wi-Fi (wireless fidelity)   This technology identifies any network based on the 802.11 family of standards.

Wildcard character   The asterisk character, which can be used to search the Internet when you do not know the complete spelling of a word.

Windows CE   A scaled-down Windows operating system, designed for including or embedding in mobile and other devices with limited functionality.

Windows Mobile   An operating system that works on specific types of PDAs such as Pocket PC and Smartphones.

Windows   Microsoft's graphical user interface operating system.

Wireless access point   A mechanism that connects wireless communication devices together to create a wireless network.

Word wrap Word-processing feature that wraps text to the next line when it reaches the right margin.

WordArt Microsoft Office tool for adding special effects to text.

Workbook Excel file that contains individual worksheets.

Worksheet Sheet within an Excel workbook file that contains a row-and-column grid of cells.

World Wide Web A network of servers linked together by a common protocol, allowing access to millions of hypertext resources.

Worm A virus that makes copies of itself.

Z

Zoom Slider A device on a keyboard that makes it easy to zoom in for a closer look at documents, spreadsheets, pictures, maps, and Web pages.

INDEX

A

absolute cell references in spreadsheets, 270

absolute links on Web pages, 396–397

access, controlling Internet, 36

Access (Microsoft)
creating database files, 291–292
described, 289
tables in, 293–302
using forms, 302–306
using queries, 307–310
using reports, 310–314

access points (APs) described, 146

accessing
disk drives, 190–191
e-mail, 320
the Internet, 27–28, 36

accounts, e-mail, 322

active cells in spreadsheets, 264

adapter cards, 81, 112

adding
animation to slides, 254–255
charts to presentations, 250–252
clip art to presentations, 247–249
e-mail contacts, 342–345
fields to databases, 294–295
graphics and images to documents, 228–231
new records to database, 306–307
objects to spreadsheets, 278–279
RAM to your computer, 78
records to database tables, 296–299
text to slides, 245–246
transitions to slides, 252–254
WordArt to presentations, 249–250

addition (+) operator in spreadsheets, 266

address bar, Internet Explorer, 30–31

address books, managing e-mail, 342–345

addresses
e-mail, 322–323, 324
Web page, 26

administrative assistant career skills, 176

Adobe Photoshop, 402

Advanced Research Projects Agency (ARPA), 21

advertisements
banner ads, 50
e-mail, 341
spam, 63

aligning
data in spreadsheets, 272
text, 219, 222

AltaVista search engine, 59–61, 67

ALU (arithmetic/logic unit), 76

American Standard Code for Information Exchange (ASCII) data representation, 85

AND, Boolean logical operator, 59

Andreesen, Marc, 25

angle brackets (< >) around HTML tags, 379

animation, adding to slides, 254–255

antivirus programs, 331, 426

Apple Computer operating systems, 121

application software, 9

applications software, 118

arguments in Excel functions, 267

arithmetic computations performed by computers, 7

arithmetic/logic unit (ALU) 76

ARPANET, 12, 14, 21–22

art, clip. See clip art

artificial intelligence (AI), 417

ASCII (American Standard Code for Information Exchange) data representation, 85

asterisk (*) and search wildcards, 61

at (@) sign in e-mail addresses, 322–323

Atanasoff, Dr. John, 6

attachments, e-mail, 328, 331

attributes, HTML tag, 379, 399, 400

audio devices, Windows XP Control Panel, 99–101

audio input
described, 96–97
speech recognition software, 182

AutoContent wizard (PowerPoint), 243

AutoCorrect feature (Word), 213

AutoFormat tool (Excel), 274

automatic message responses, 335

AutoSearch (Internet Explorer), searching with, 33–34

AutoSum feature (Excel), 268

averaging in spreadsheets, 267

B

backgrounds, Web pages, 402–403

backing up files, folders, 199

bandwidth of communication channels, 146

banner ads, 50

bar code scanners, 97

baseband described, 146

basic input/output system. See BIOS

Bcc field, e-mail, 324, 335, 346

Berners-Lee, Dr. Tim, 24

Berry, Clifford, 6

binary numbers
and computer systems, 76
described, displaying, 76–77

biometrics
fingerprint reader (fig.), 93
identification techniques, 98–99
security measures, 429

BIOS (basic input/output system), 132

BIOS ROM, 80

bits, bytes, 81

Blackboard teaching tool, 412–413

blocking e-mail senders, 335

blogs (Web logs), 41

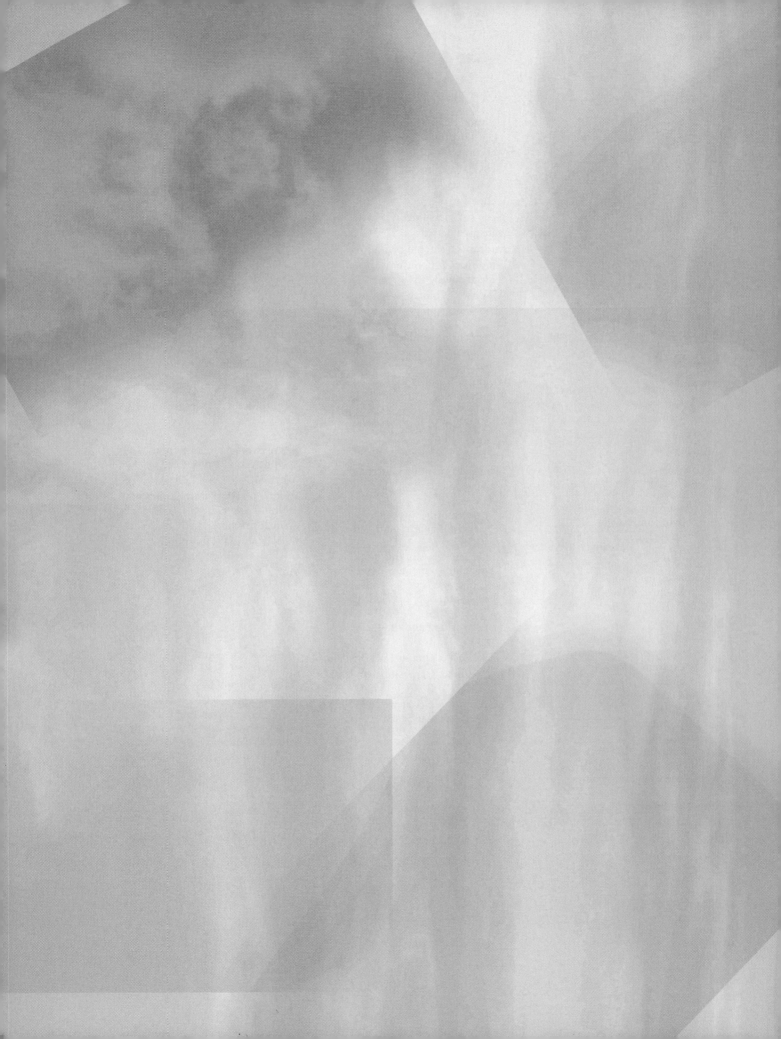

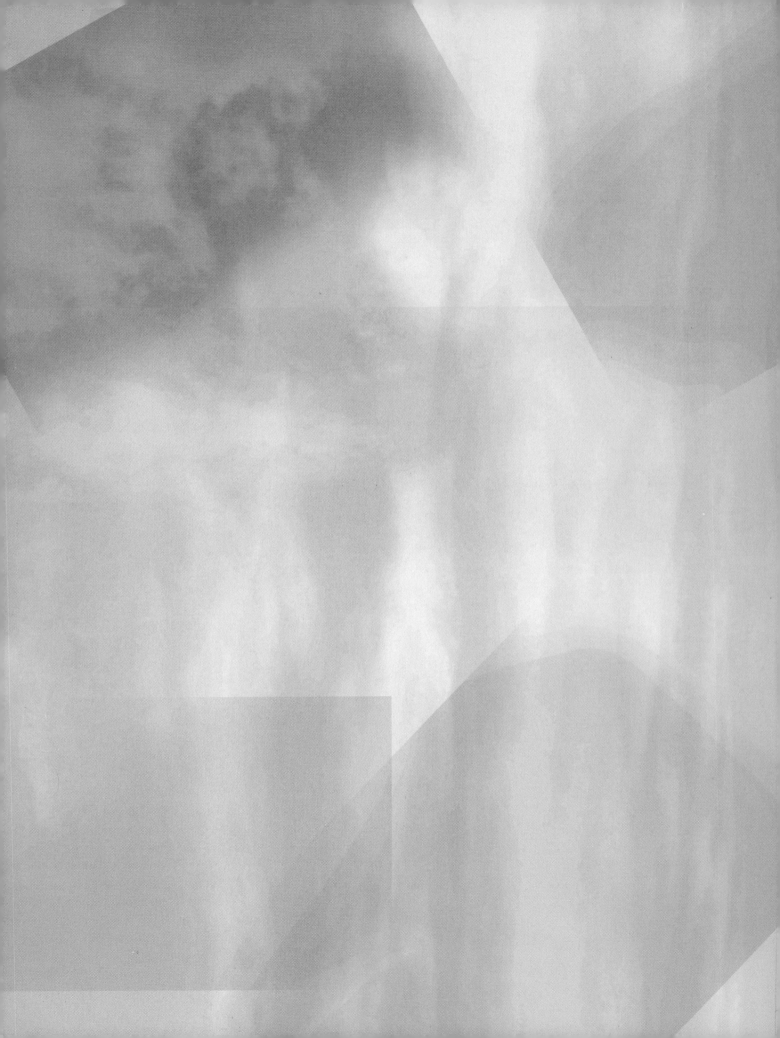